SEVEN SEAS ENTERTAINMENT PRESENTS

DICTATORIAL G

story and art by **AYUMI KANOU**

VOLUME 2: SNOW WHITE

TRANSLATION
Jocelyne Allen

ADAPTATION
Shanti Whitesides

LETTERING
Jennifer Skarupa

LOGO DESIGN
Courtney Williams

COVER DESIGN
Nicky Lim

PROOFREADER
Janet Houck

MANAGING EDITOR
Adam Arnold

PUBLISHER
Jason DeAngelis

DICTATORIAL GRIMOIRE VOL. 2
© Ayumi Kanou 2012
Edited by MEDIA FACTORY.
First published in Japan in 2012 by KADOKAWA CORPORATION.
English translation rights reserved by Seven Seas Entertainment, LLC.
Under the license from KADOKAWA CORPORATION, Tokyo.

Seven Seas books may be purchased in bulk for educational, business, or promotional use. For information on bulk purchases, please contact Macmillan Corporate & Premium Sales Department at 1-800-221-7945 (ext 5442) or write specialmarkets@macmillan.com.

Seven Seas and the Seven Seas logo are trademarks of Seven Seas Entertainment, LLC. All rights reserved.

ISBN: 978-1-937867-94-2

Printed in Canada

First Printing: January 2014

10 9 8 7 6 5 4 3 2 1

FOLLOW US ONLINE: www.gomanga.com

READING DIRECTIONS

This book reads from *right to left*, Japanese style. If this is your first time reading manga, you start reading from the top right panel on each page and take it from there. If you get lost, just follow the numbered diagram here. It may seem backwards at first, but you'll get the hang of it! Have fun!!

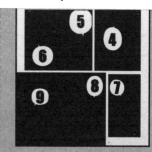

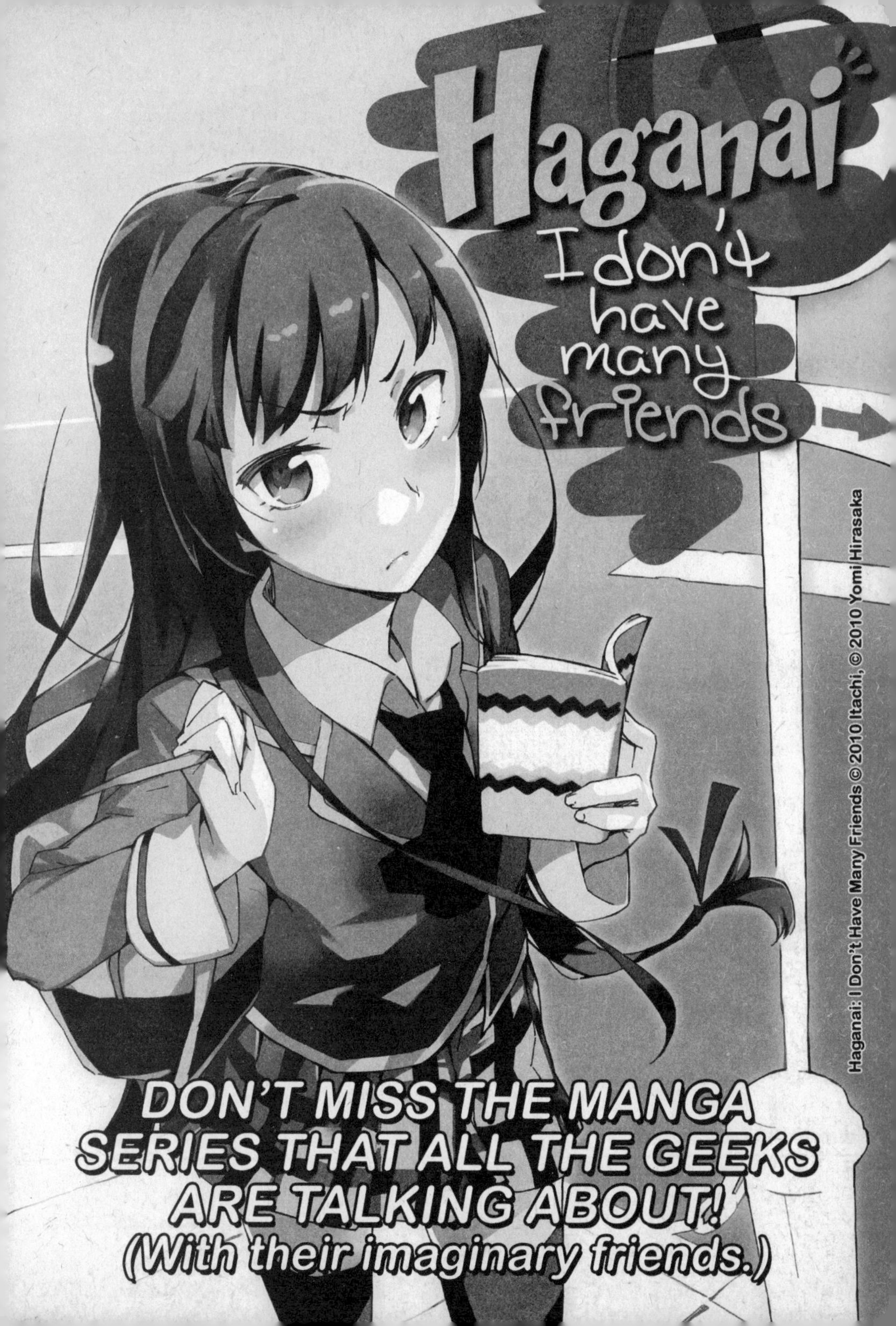
Haganai
I don't have many friends
DON'T MISS THE MANGA SERIES THAT ALL THE GEEKS ARE TALKING ABOUT!
(With their imaginary friends.)
Haganai: I Don't Have Many Friends © 2010 Itachi, © 2010 Yomi Hirasaka

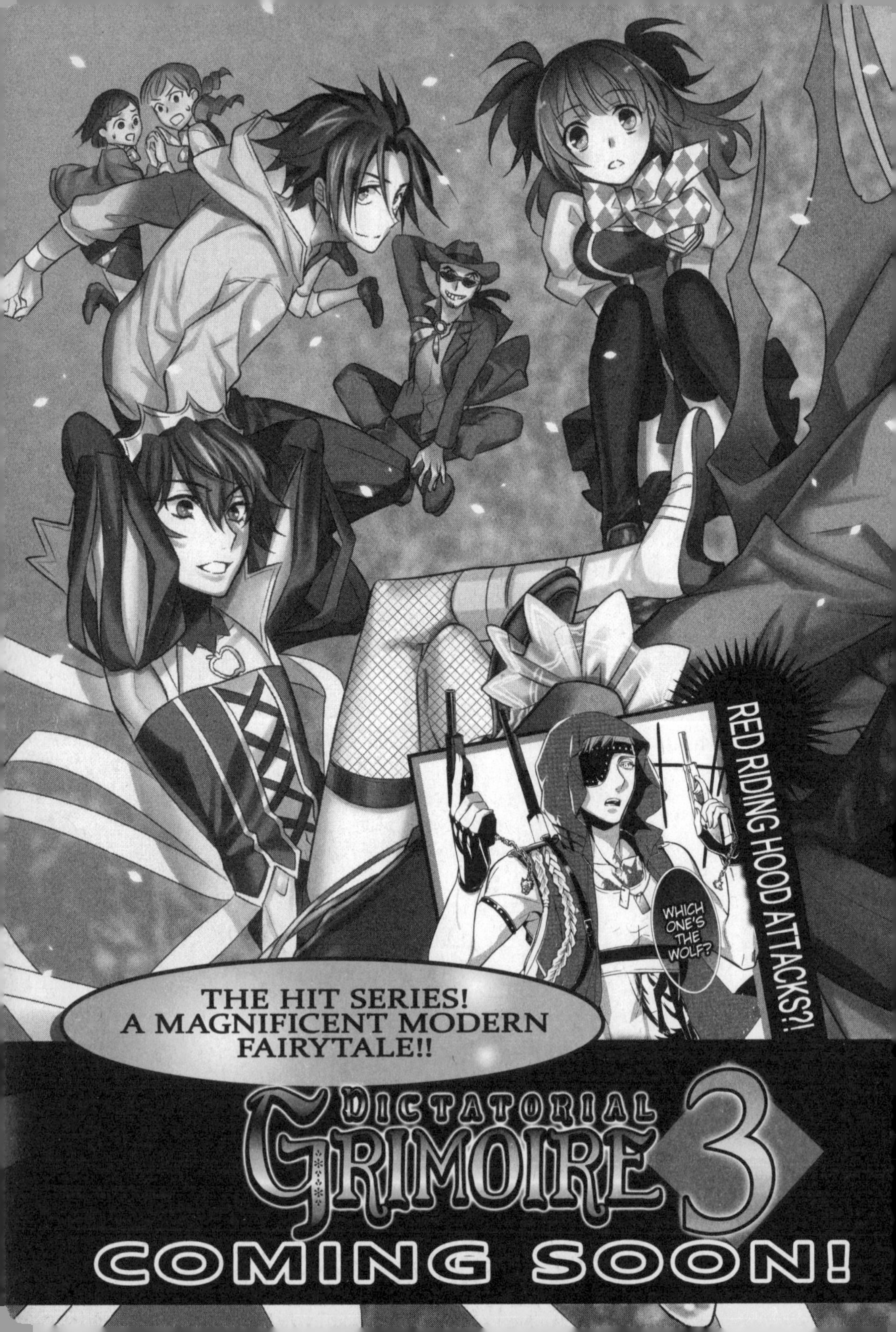
RED RIDING HOOD ATTACKS?!
WHICH ONE'S THE WOLF?
THE HIT SERIES!
A MAGNIFICENT MODERN FAIRYTALE!!
DICTATORIAL GRIMOIRE 3
COMING SOON!

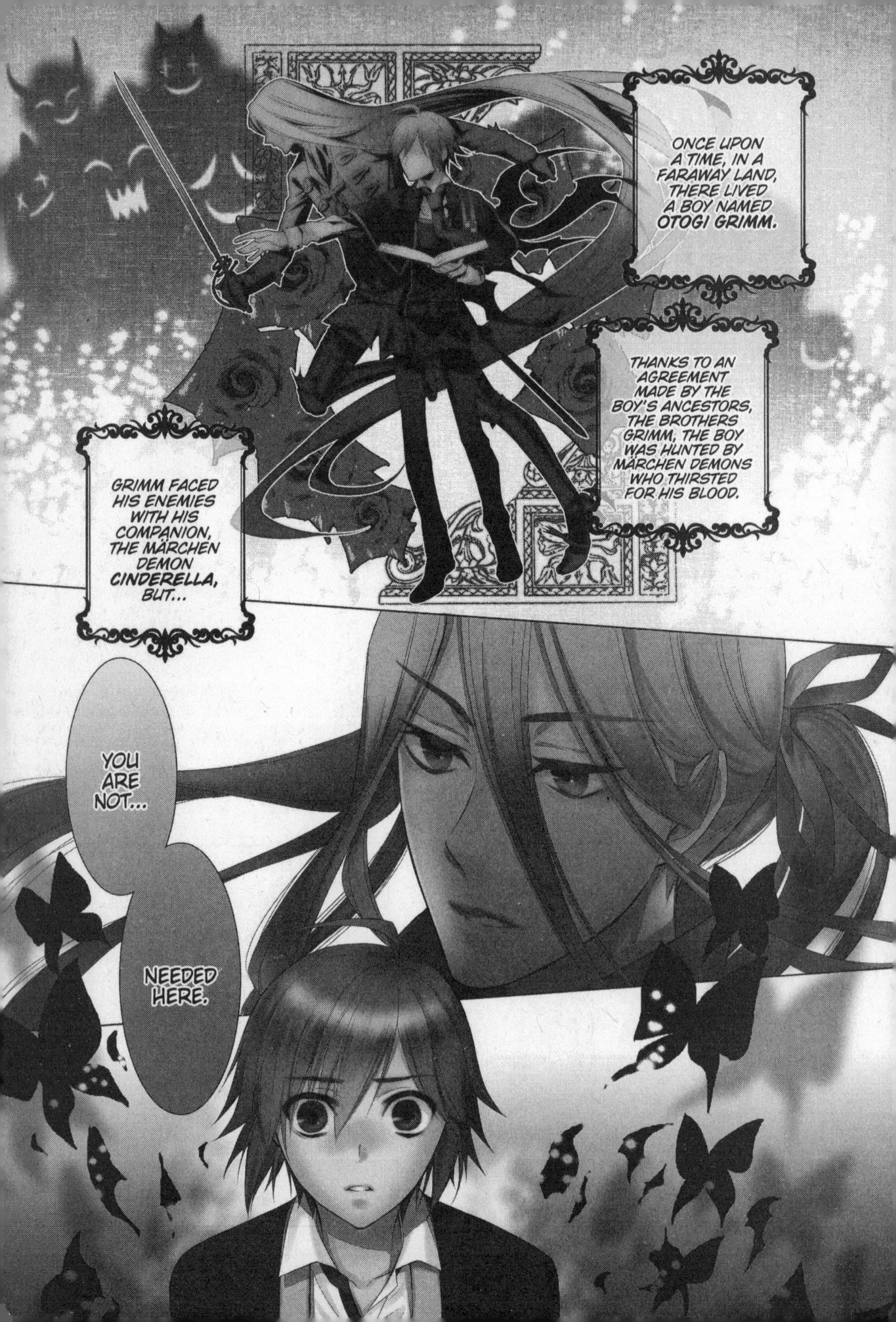
ONCE UPON A TIME, IN A FARAWAY LAND, THERE LIVED A BOY NAMED OTOGI GRIMM.
THANKS TO AN AGREEMENT MADE BY THE BOY'S ANCESTORS, THE BROTHERS GRIMM, THE BOY WAS HUNTED BY MÄRCHEN DEMONS WHO THIRSTED FOR HIS BLOOD.
GRIMM FACED HIS ENEMIES WITH HIS COMPANION, THE MÄRCHEN DEMON CINDERELLA, BUT...
YOU ARE NOT...
NEEDED HERE.

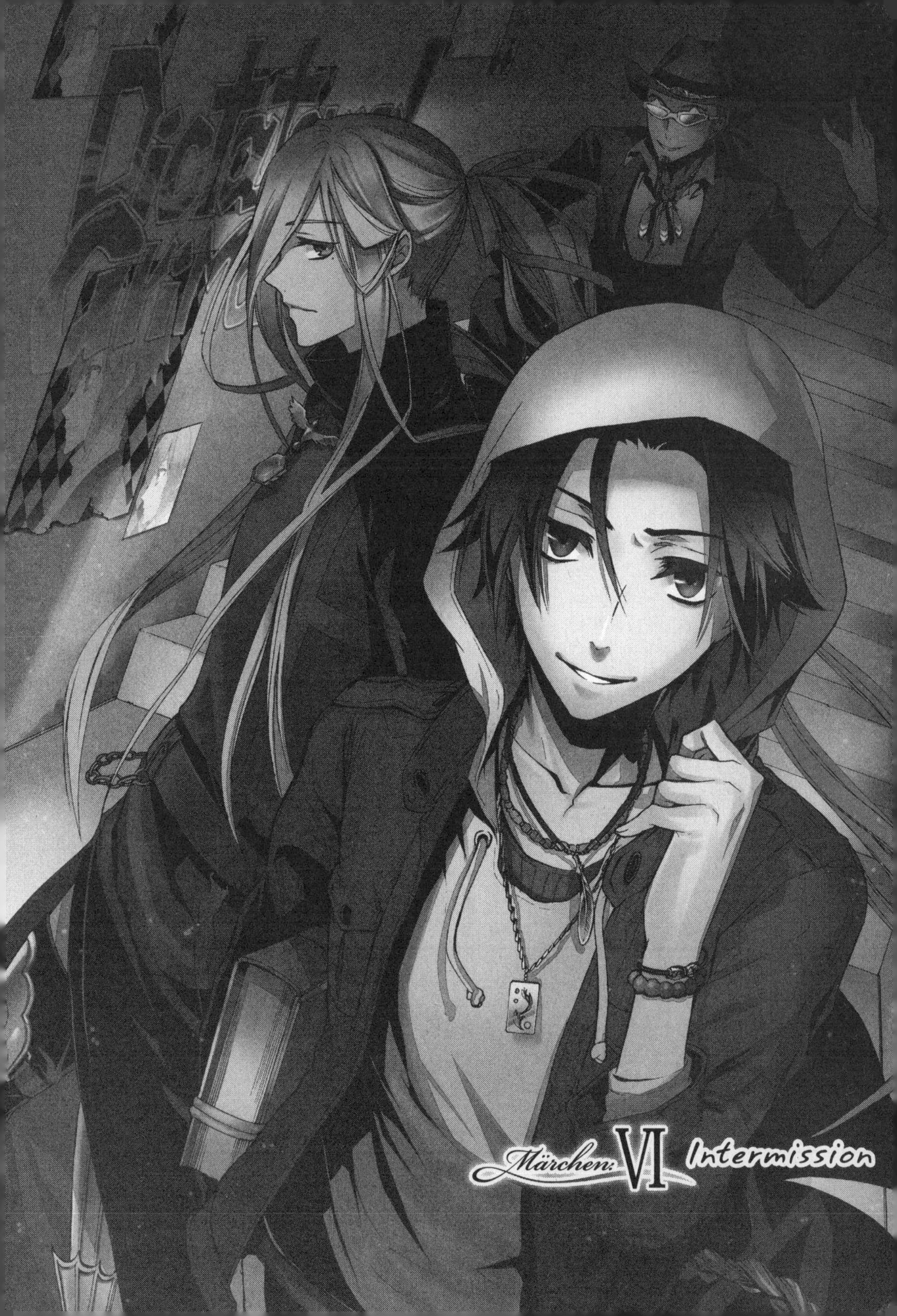
Märchen: VI Intermission

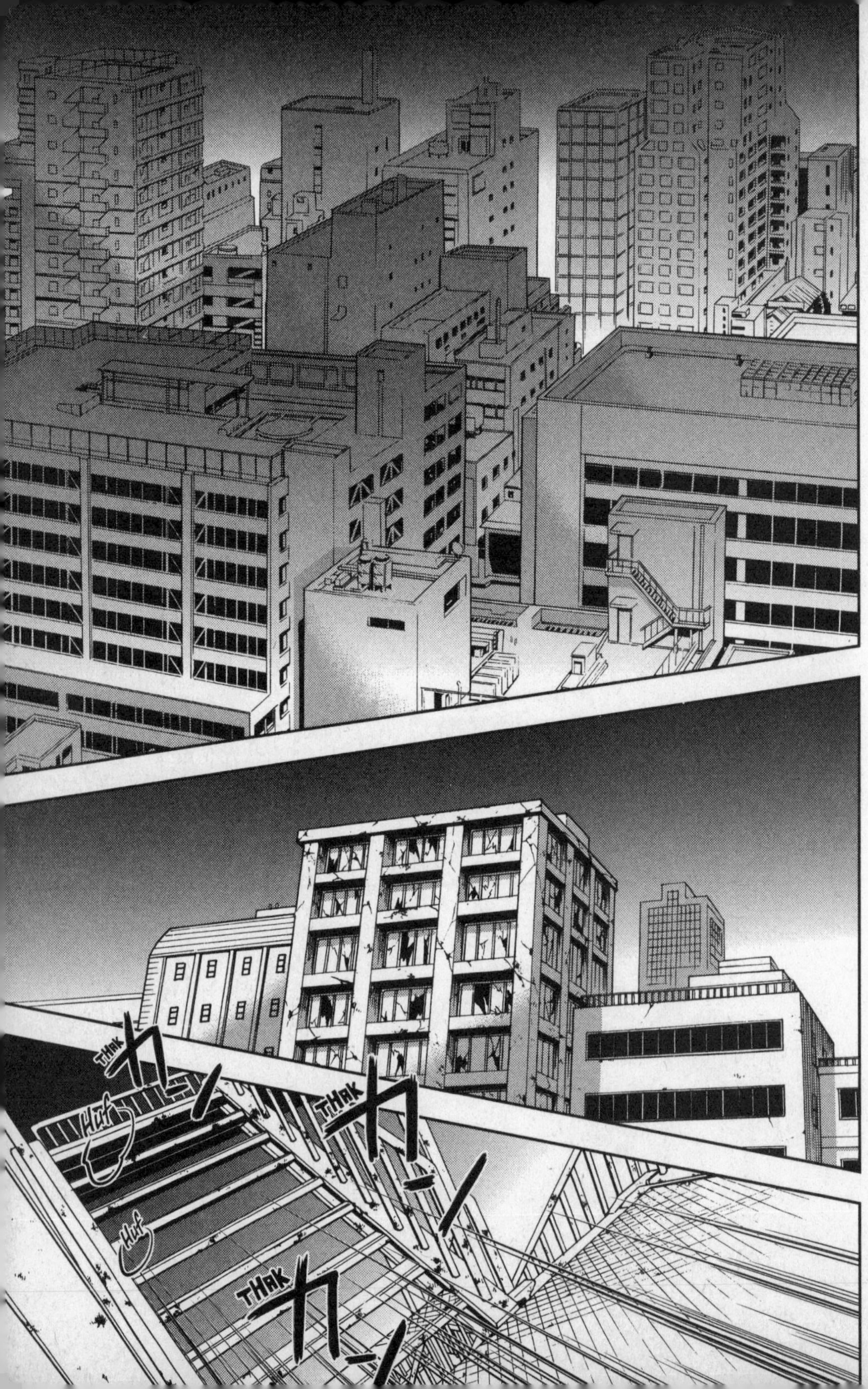
THAK
THAK
Huf
Huf
THAK

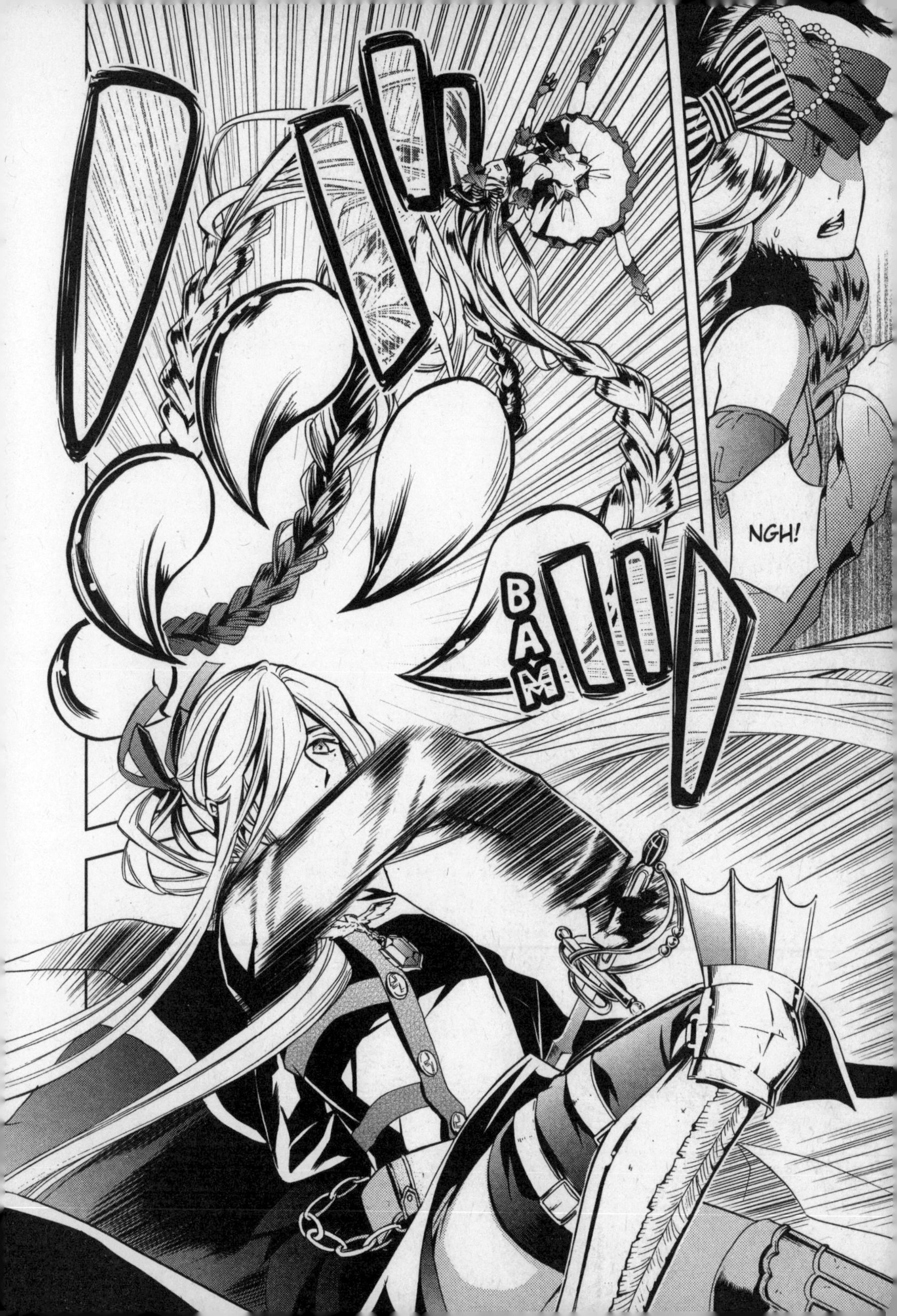
NGH!
BAM

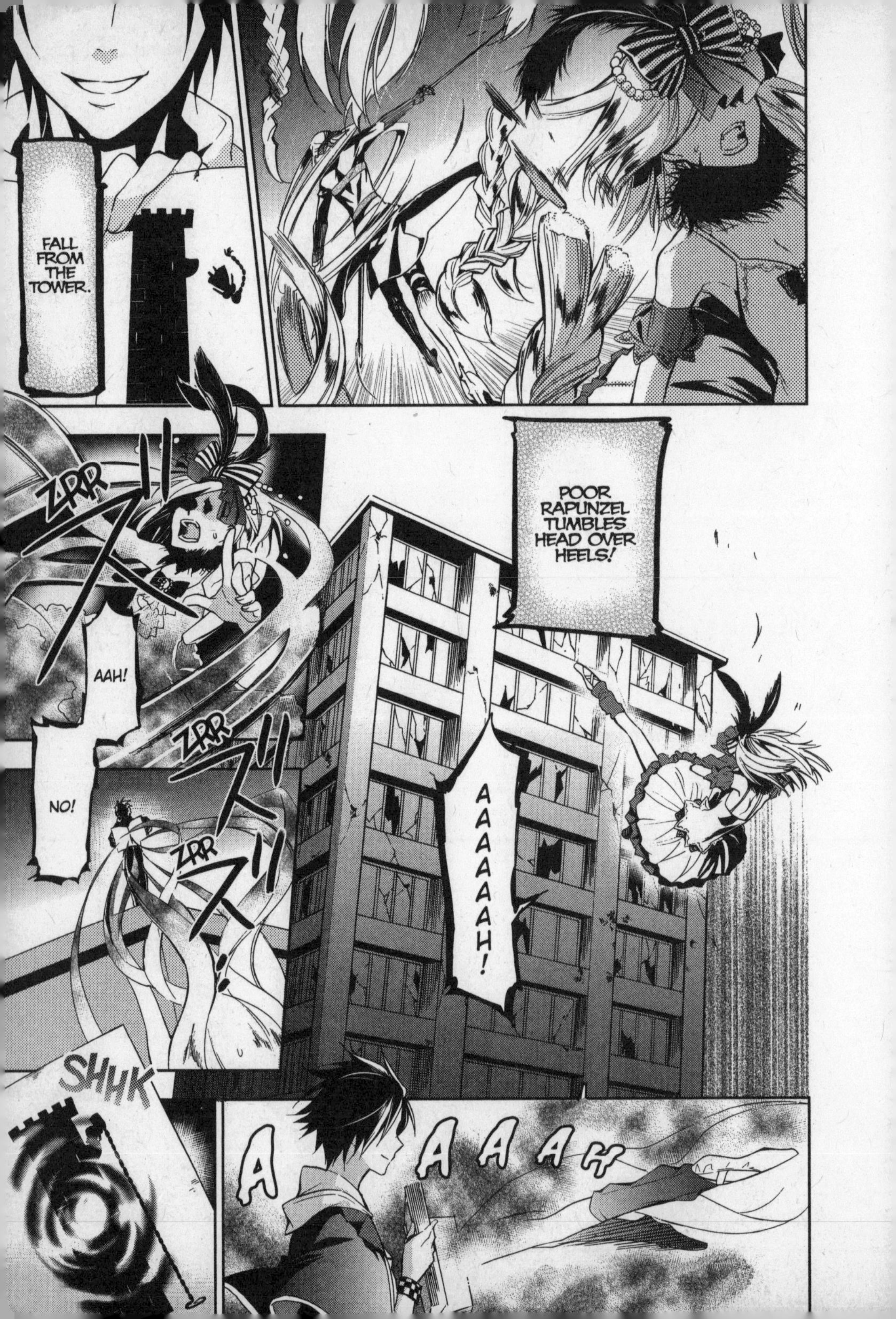
FALL FROM THE TOWER.
POOR RAPUNZEL TUMBLES HEAD OVER HEELS!
AAAAAAH!
ZRR
AAH!
ZRR
NO!
ZRR
A A A A H
SHHK

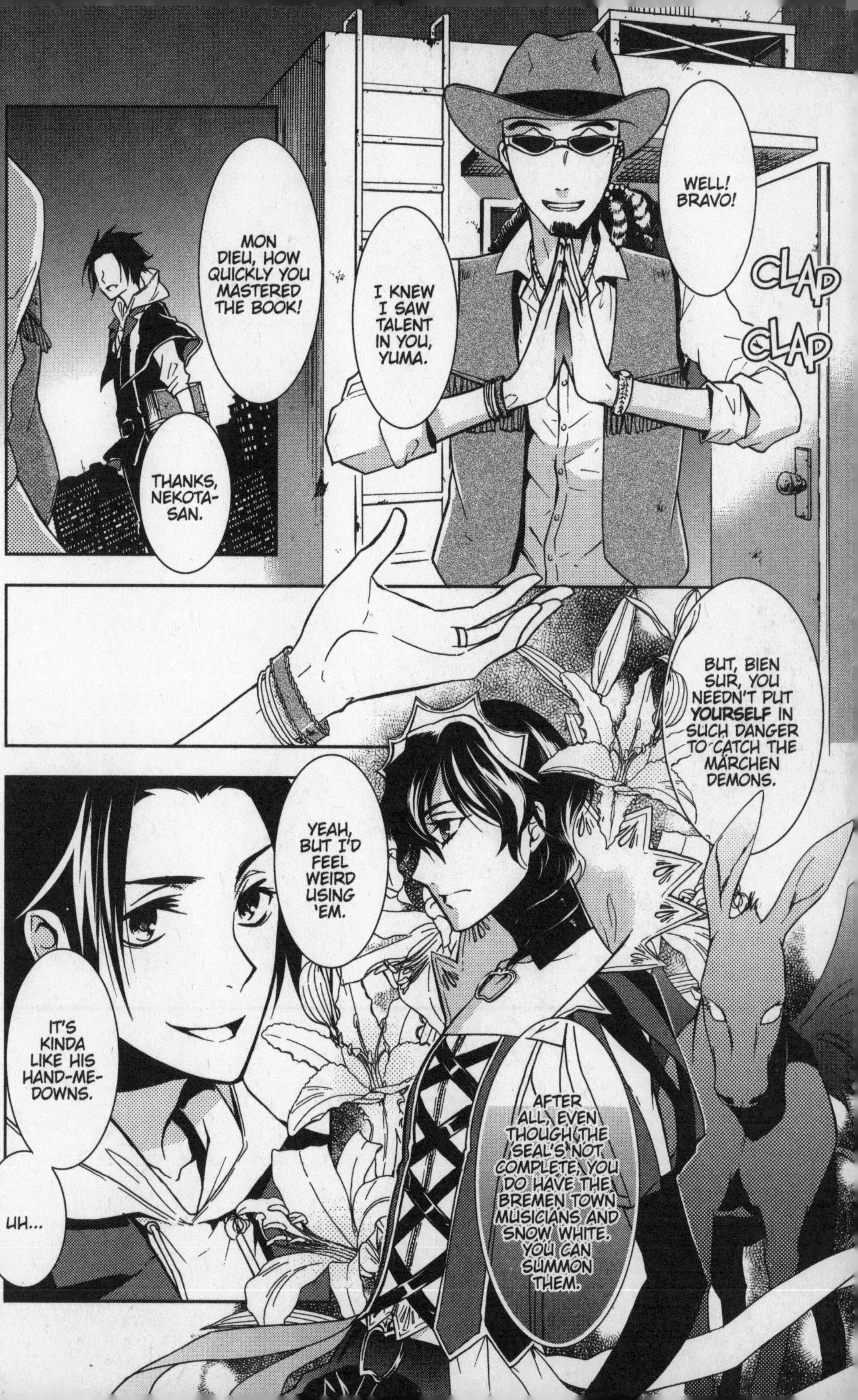
WELL! BRAVO!
CLAP
CLAP
I KNEW I SAW TALENT IN YOU, YUMA.
MON DIEU, HOW QUICKLY YOU MASTERED THE BOOK!
THANKS, NEKOTA-SAN.
BUT, BIEN SUR, YOU NEEDN'T PUT **YOURSELF** IN SUCH DANGER TO CATCH THE MÄRCHEN DEMONS.
AFTER ALL, EVEN THOUGH THE SEAL'S NOT COMPLETE, YOU DO HAVE THE BREMEN TOWN MUSICIANS AND SNOW WHITE. YOU CAN SUMMON THEM.
YEAH, BUT I'D FEEL WEIRD USING 'EM.
IT'S KINDA LIKE HIS HAND-ME-DOWNS.
UH...

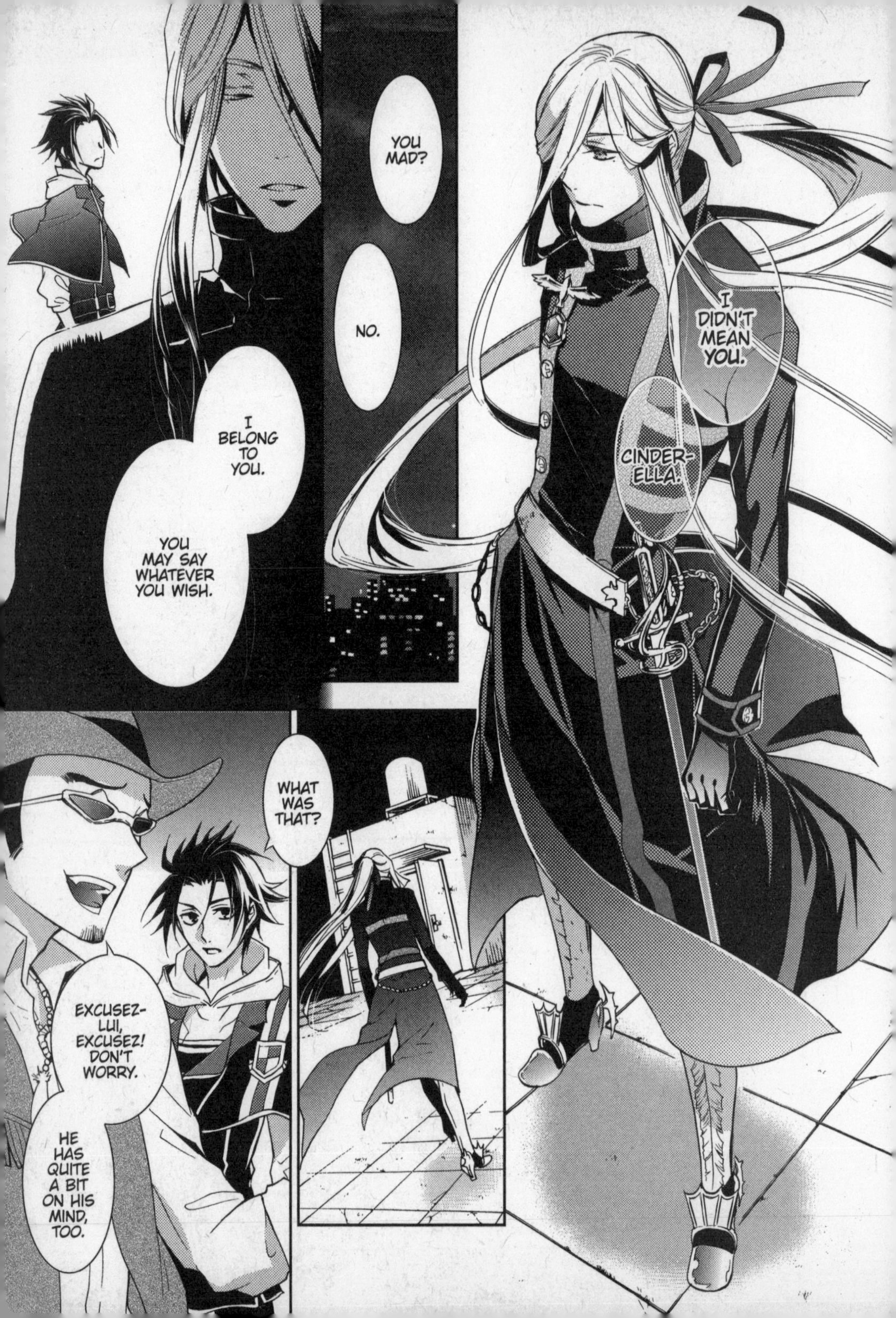
I DIDN'T MEAN YOU.
CINDER-ELLA.
YOU MAD?
NO.
I BELONG TO YOU.
YOU MAY SAY WHATEVER YOU WISH.
WHAT WAS THAT?
EXCUSEZ-LUI, EXCUSEZ! DON'T WORRY.
HE HAS QUITE A BIT ON HIS MIND, TOO.

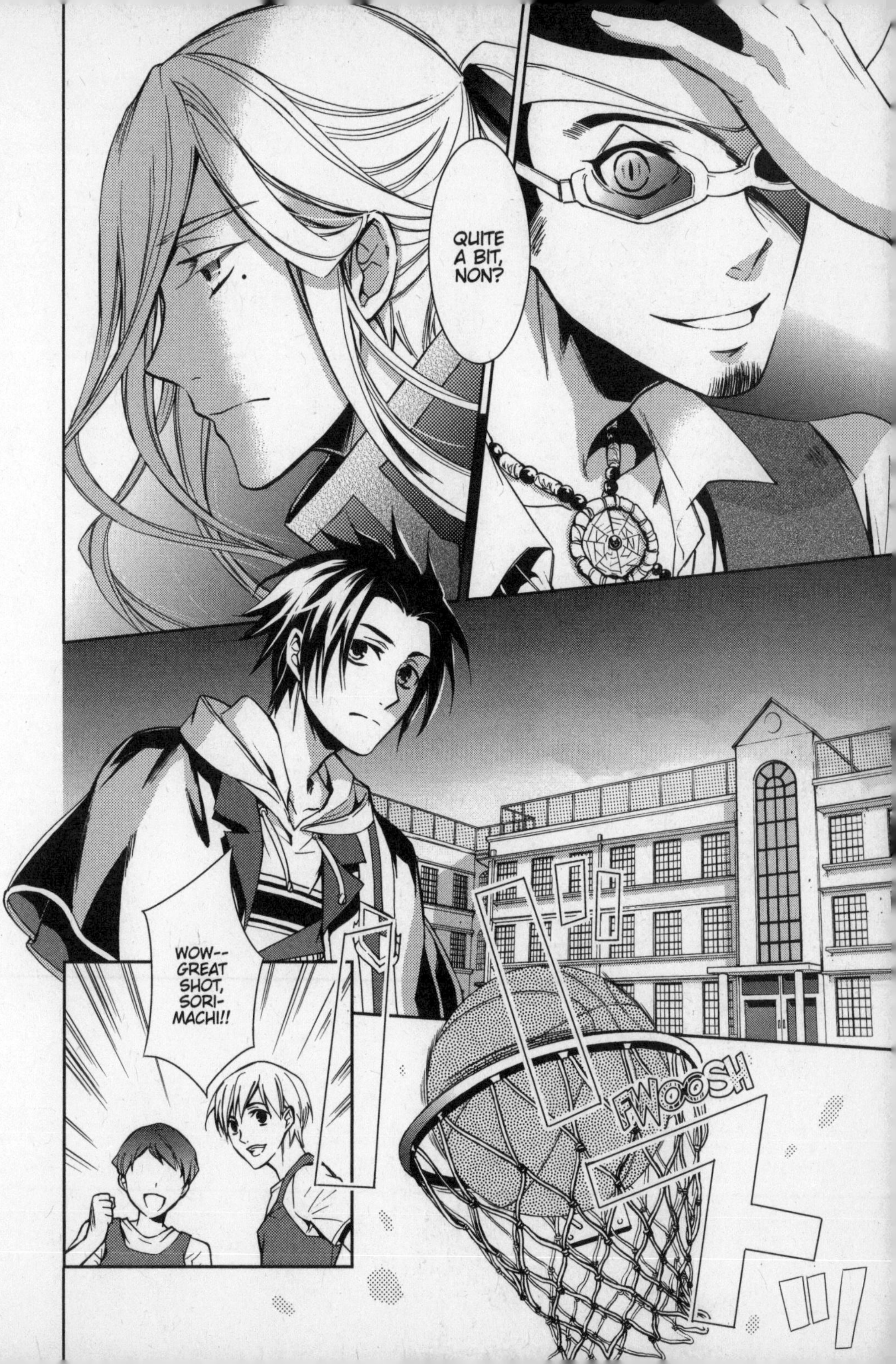
QUITE A BIT, NON?
WOW-- GREAT SHOT, SORI-MACHI!!
FWOOSH

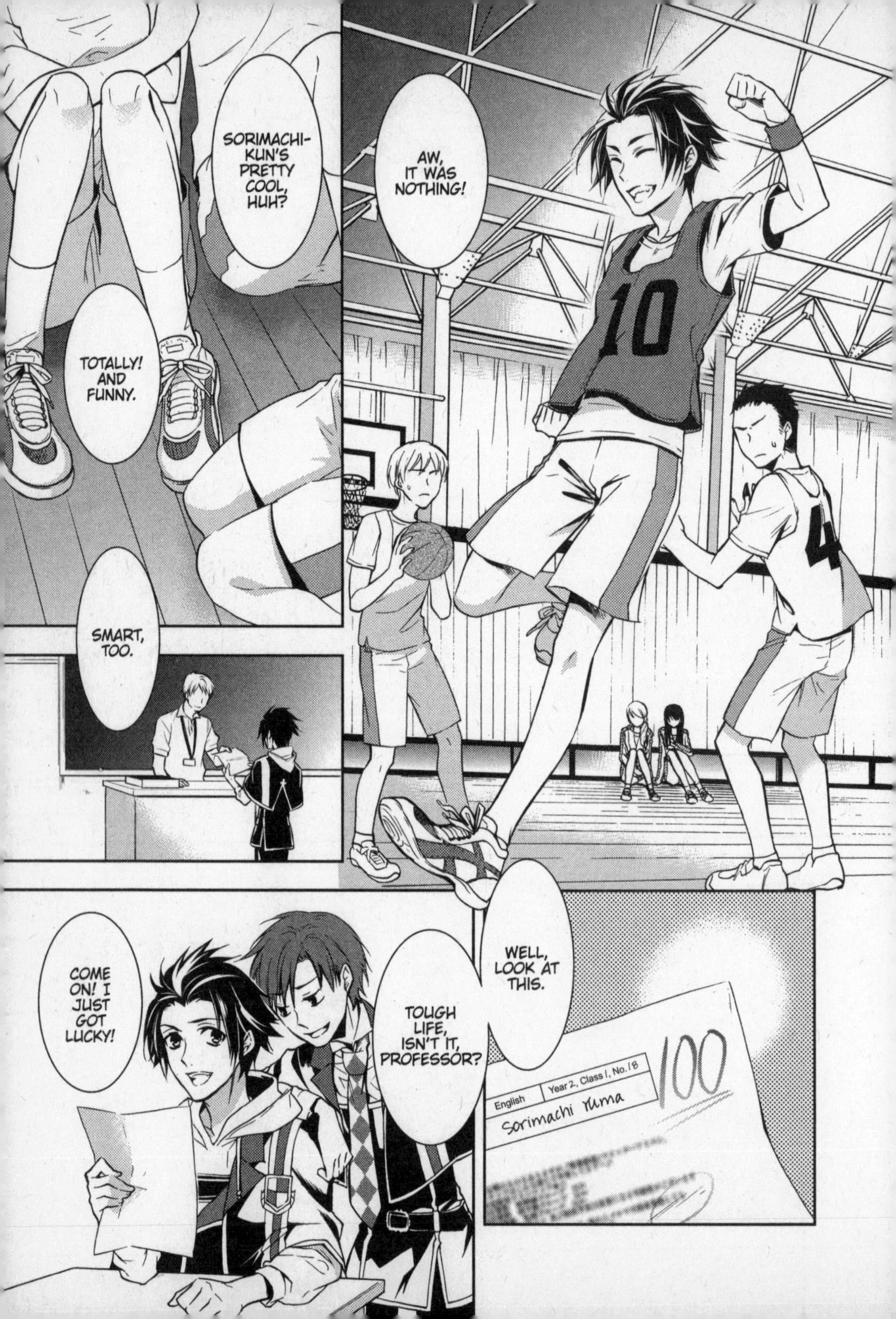
AW, IT WAS NOTHING!
SORIMACHI-KUN'S PRETTY COOL, HUH?
TOTALLY! AND FUNNY.
SMART, TOO.
WELL, LOOK AT THIS.
100
English
Year 2, Class 1, No. 18
Sorimachi Yuma
TOUGH LIFE, ISN'T IT, PROFESSOR?
COME ON! I JUST GOT LUCKY!

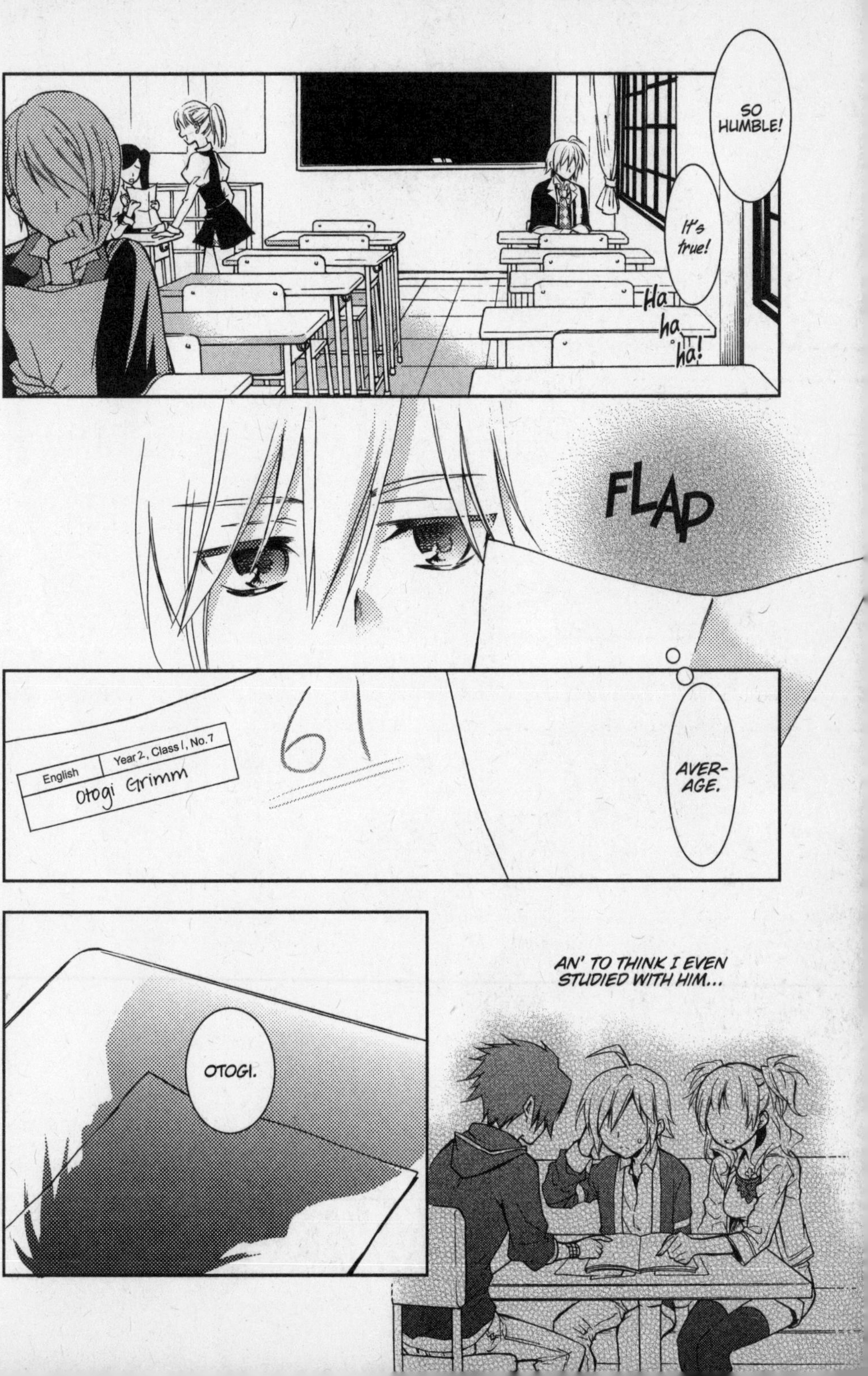
SO HUMBLE!
It's true!
Ha ha ha!
FLAP
AVER-AGE.
English
Year 2, Class I, No.7
Otogi Grimm
61
AN' TO THINK I EVEN STUDIED WITH HIM...
OTOGI.

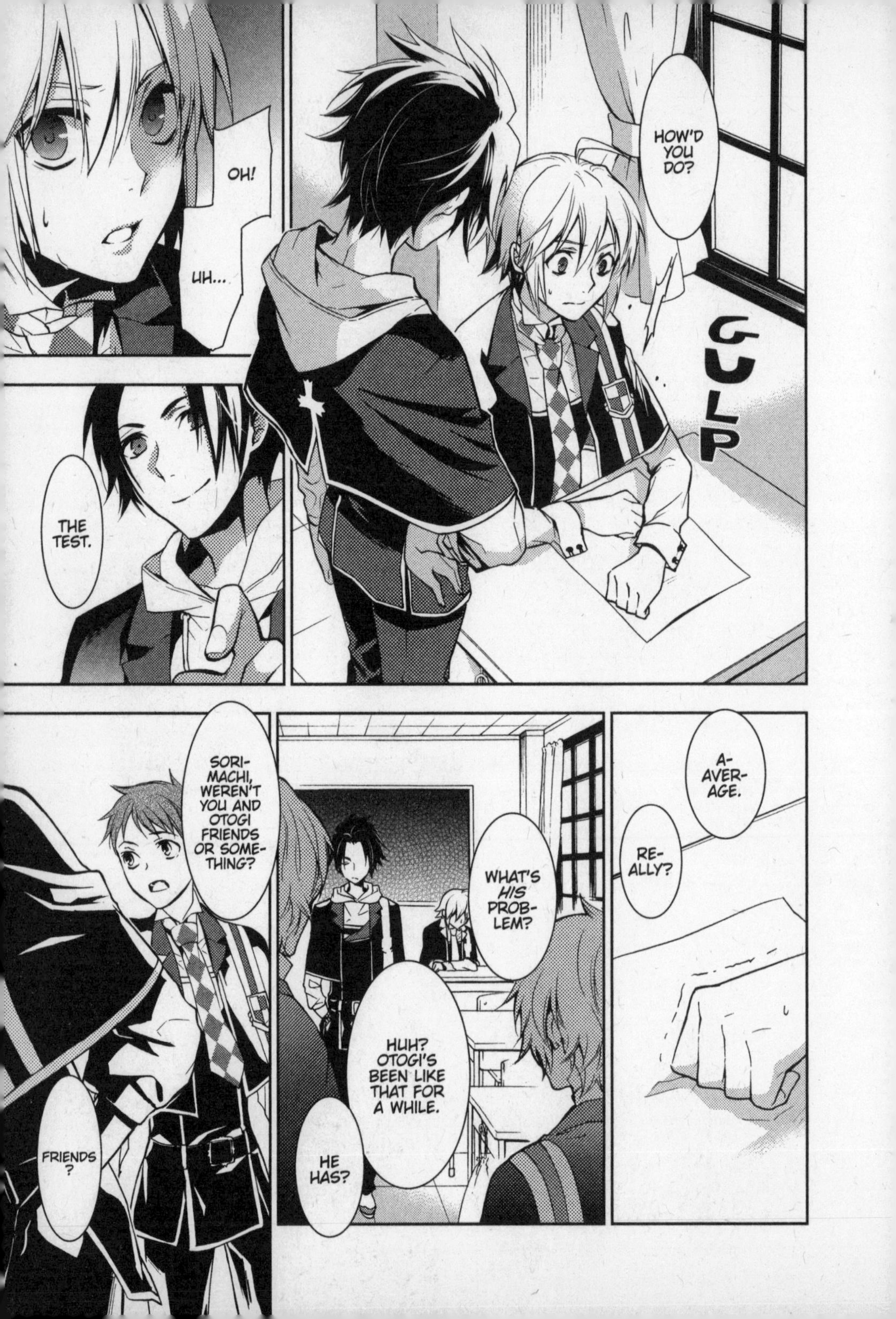
HOW'D YOU DO?
GULP
OH!
UH...
THE TEST.
A-AVER-AGE.
RE-ALLY?
WHAT'S *HIS* PROB-LEM?
HUH? OTOGI'S BEEN LIKE THAT FOR A WHILE.
HE HAS?
SORI-MACHI, WEREN'T YOU AND OTOGI FRIENDS OR SOME-THING?
FRIENDS?

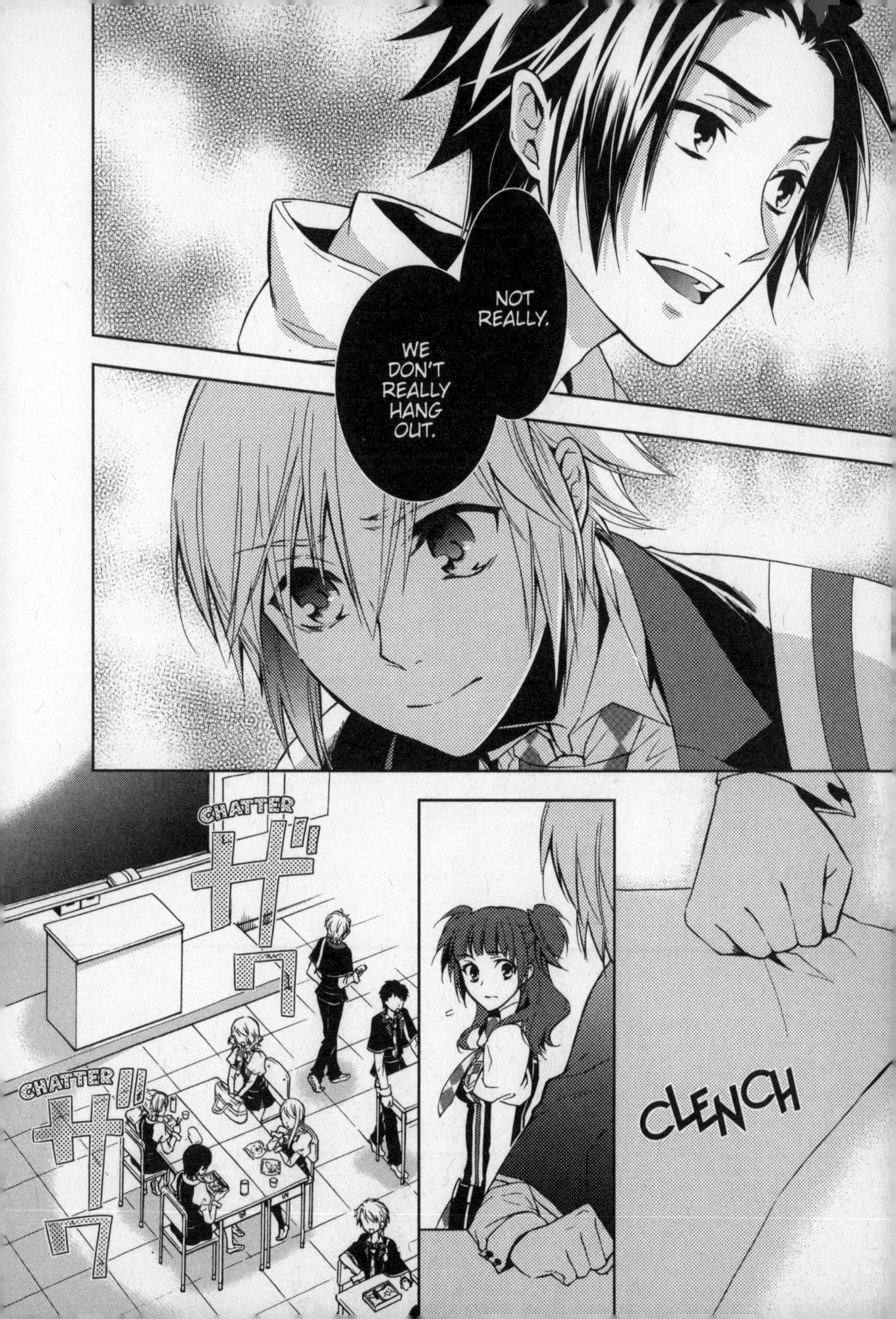
NOT REALLY.
WE DON'T REALLY HANG OUT.
CLENCH
CHATTER
CHATTER

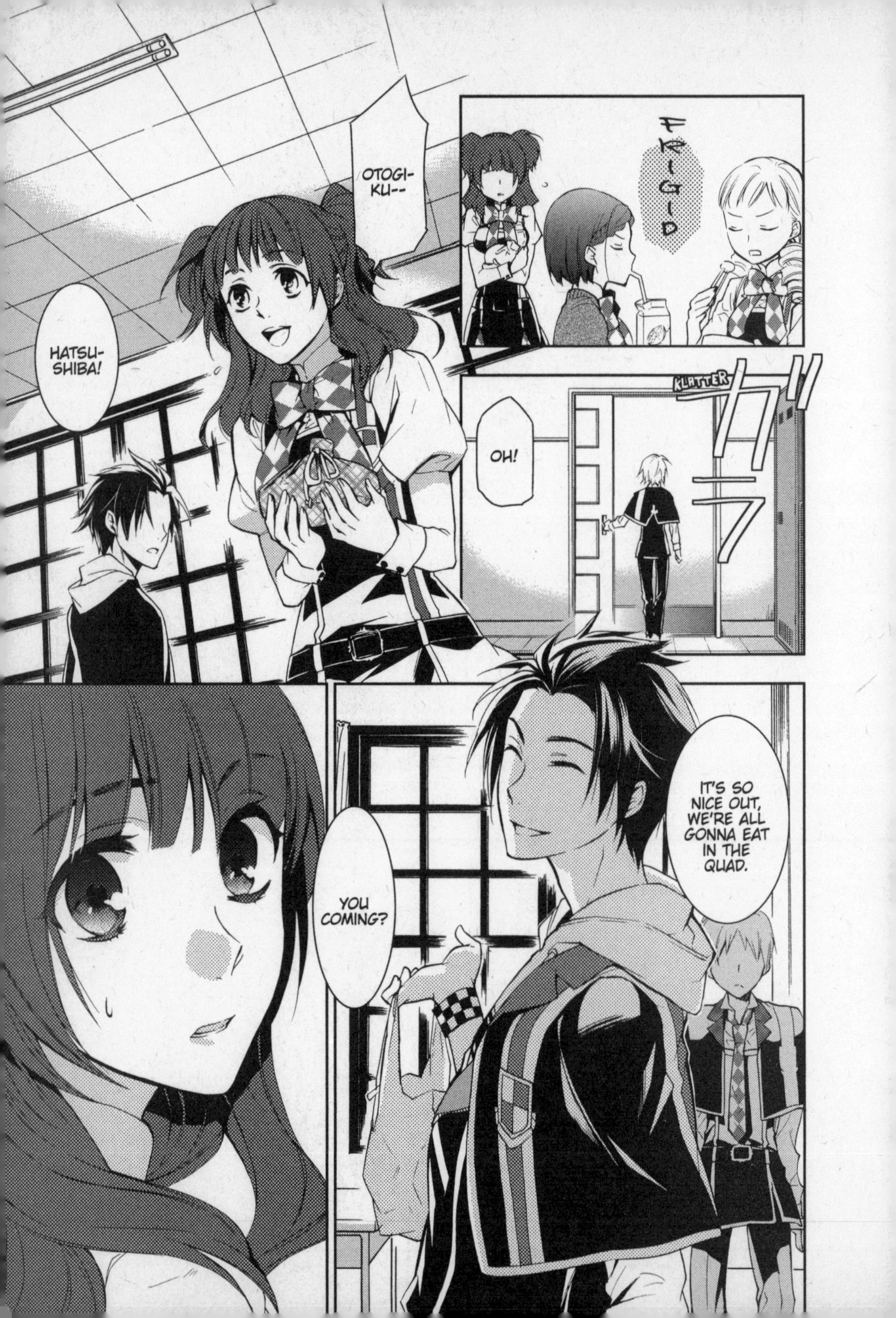
FRIGID
KLATTER
ガラ
OH!
OTOGI-KU--
HATSU-SHIBA!
IT'S SO NICE OUT, WE'RE ALL GONNA EAT IN THE QUAD.
YOU COMING?

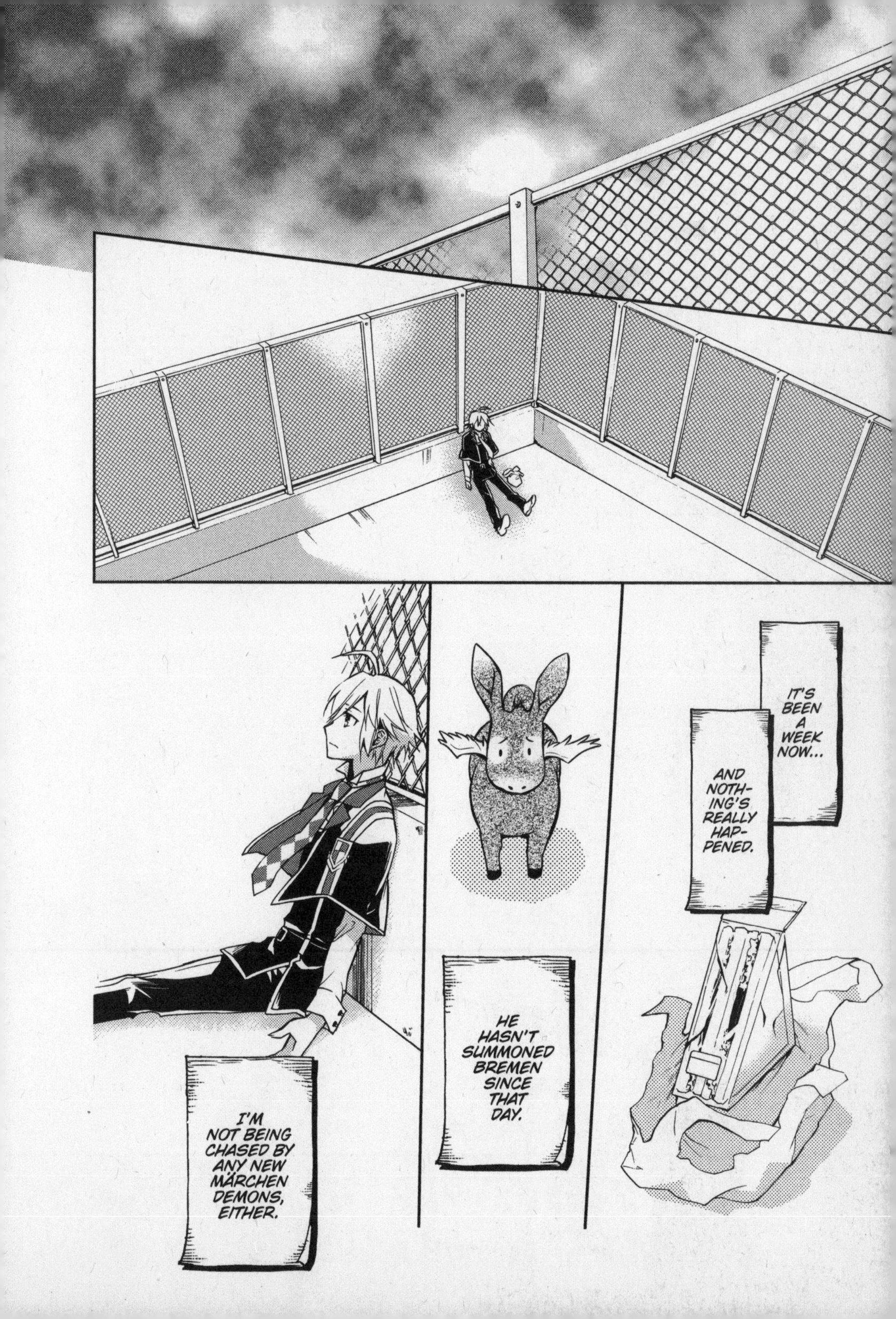
IT'S BEEN A WEEK NOW...
AND NOTHING'S REALLY HAPPENED.
HE HASN'T SUMMONED BREMEN SINCE THAT DAY.
I'M NOT BEING CHASED BY ANY NEW MÄRCHEN DEMONS, EITHER.

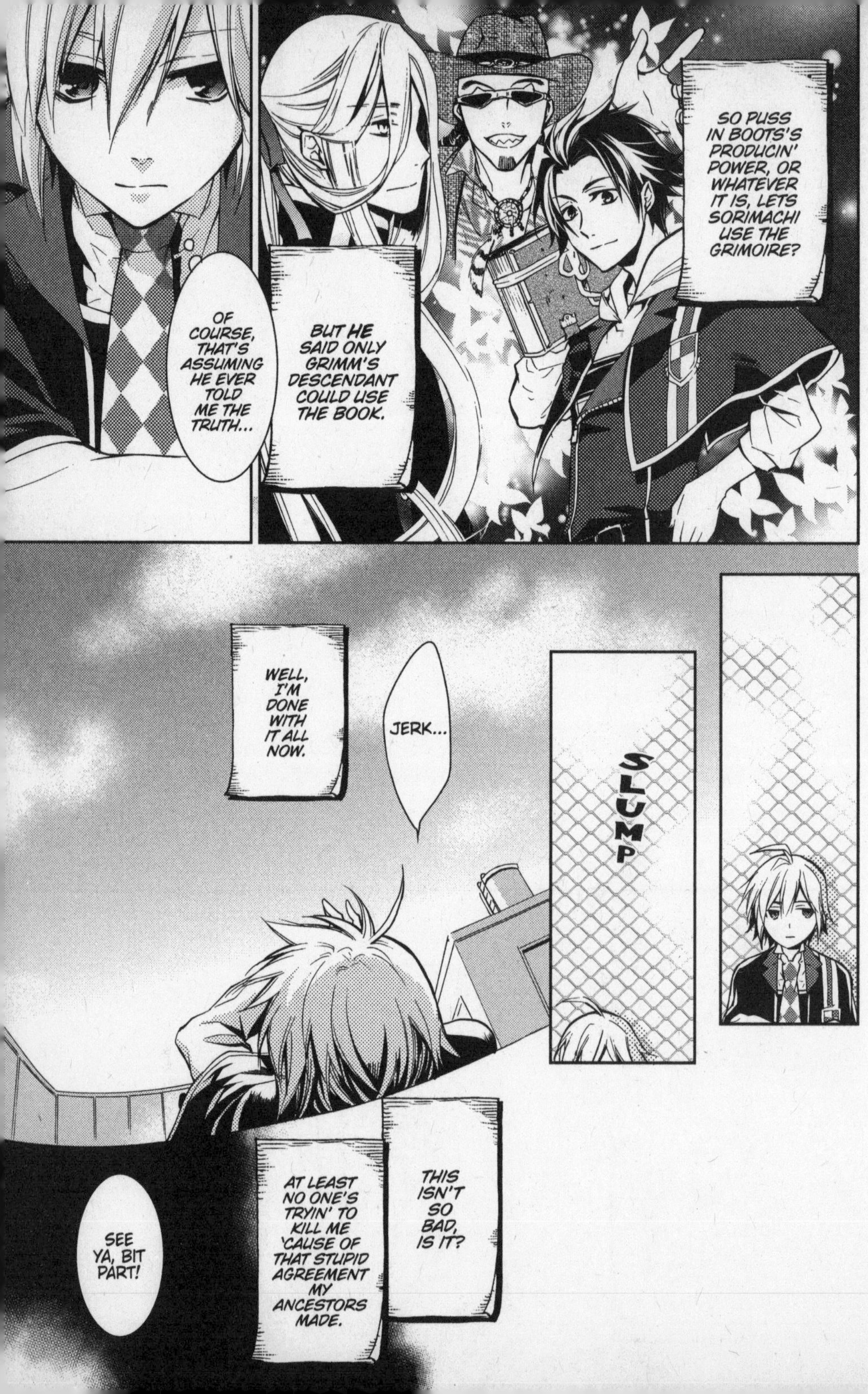
SO PUSS IN BOOTS'S PRODUCIN' POWER, OR WHATEVER IT IS, LETS SORIMACHI USE THE GRIMOIRE?
BUT HE SAID ONLY GRIMM'S DESCENDANT COULD USE THE BOOK.
OF COURSE, THAT'S ASSUMING HE EVER TOLD ME THE TRUTH...
SLUMP
WELL, I'M DONE WITH IT ALL NOW.
JERK...
THIS ISN'T SO BAD, IS IT?
AT LEAST NO ONE'S TRYIN' TO KILL ME 'CAUSE OF THAT STUPID AGREEMENT MY ANCESTORS MADE.
SEE YA, BIT PART!

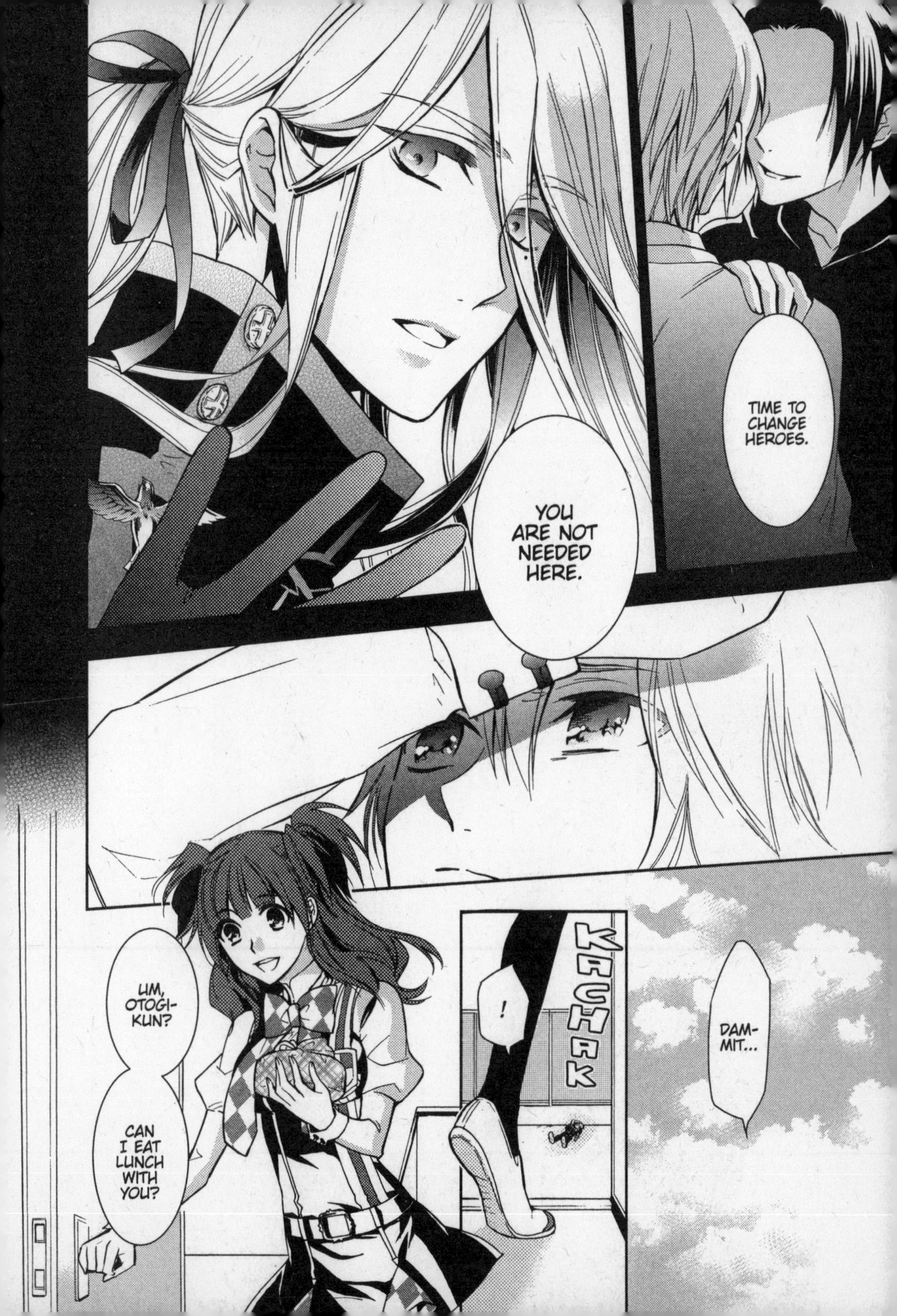
TIME TO CHANGE HEROES.
YOU ARE NOT NEEDED HERE.
DAM-MIT...
KACHAK
!
UM, OTOGI-KUN?
CAN I EAT LUNCH WITH YOU?

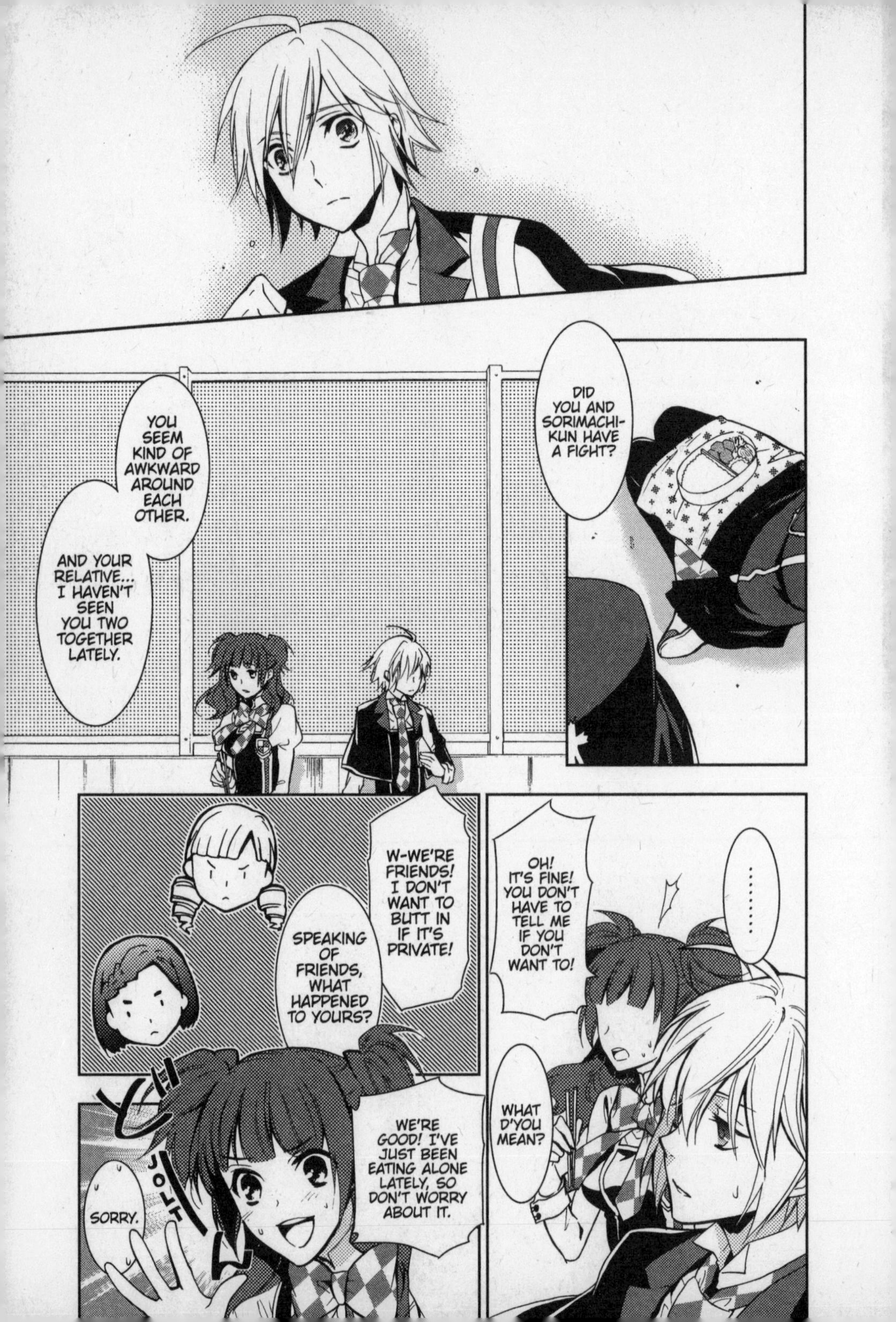
DID YOU AND SORIMACHI-KUN HAVE A FIGHT?
YOU SEEM KIND OF AWKWARD AROUND EACH OTHER.
AND YOUR RELATIVE... I HAVEN'T SEEN YOU TWO TOGETHER LATELY.
......
OH! IT'S FINE! YOU DON'T HAVE TO TELL ME IF YOU DON'T WANT TO!
WHAT D'YOU MEAN?
W-WE'RE FRIENDS! I DON'T WANT TO BUTT IN IF IT'S PRIVATE!
SPEAKING OF FRIENDS, WHAT HAPPENED TO YOURS?
WE'RE GOOD! I'VE JUST BEEN EATING ALONE LATELY, SO DON'T WORRY ABOUT IT.
JOLT
SORRY.

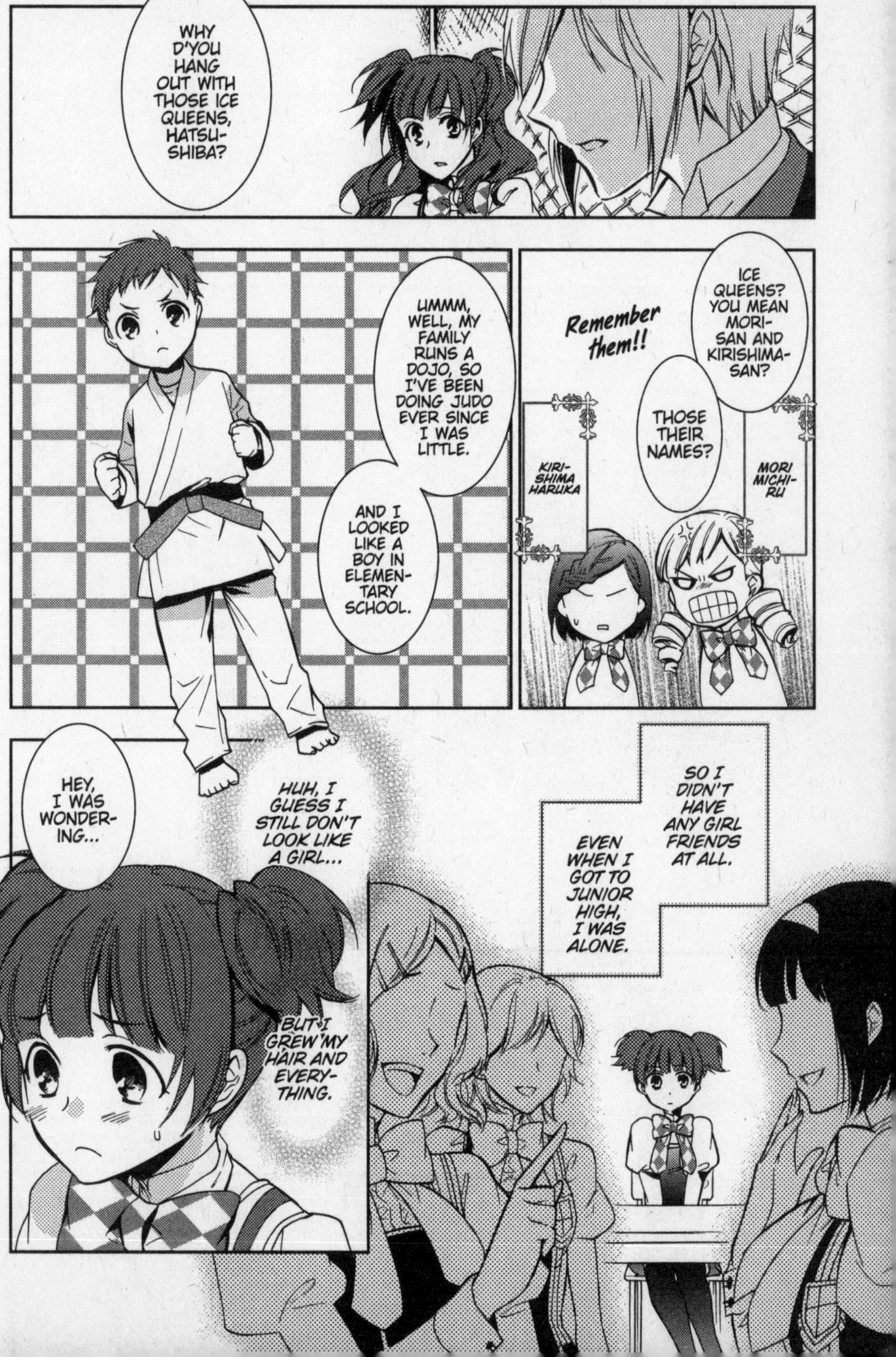
WHY D'YOU HANG OUT WITH THOSE ICE QUEENS, HATSU-SHIBA?
ICE QUEENS? YOU MEAN MORI-SAN AND KIRISHIMA-SAN?
Remember them!!
THOSE THEIR NAMES?
MORI MICHIRU
KIRISHIMA HARUKA
UMMM, WELL, MY FAMILY RUNS A DOJO, SO I'VE BEEN DOING JUDO EVER SINCE I WAS LITTLE.
AND I LOOKED LIKE A BOY IN ELEMENTARY SCHOOL.
SO I DIDN'T HAVE ANY GIRL FRIENDS AT ALL.
EVEN WHEN I GOT TO JUNIOR HIGH, I WAS ALONE.
HEY, I WAS WONDERING...
HUH, I GUESS I STILL DON'T LOOK LIKE A GIRL...
BUT I GREW MY HAIR AND EVERYTHING.

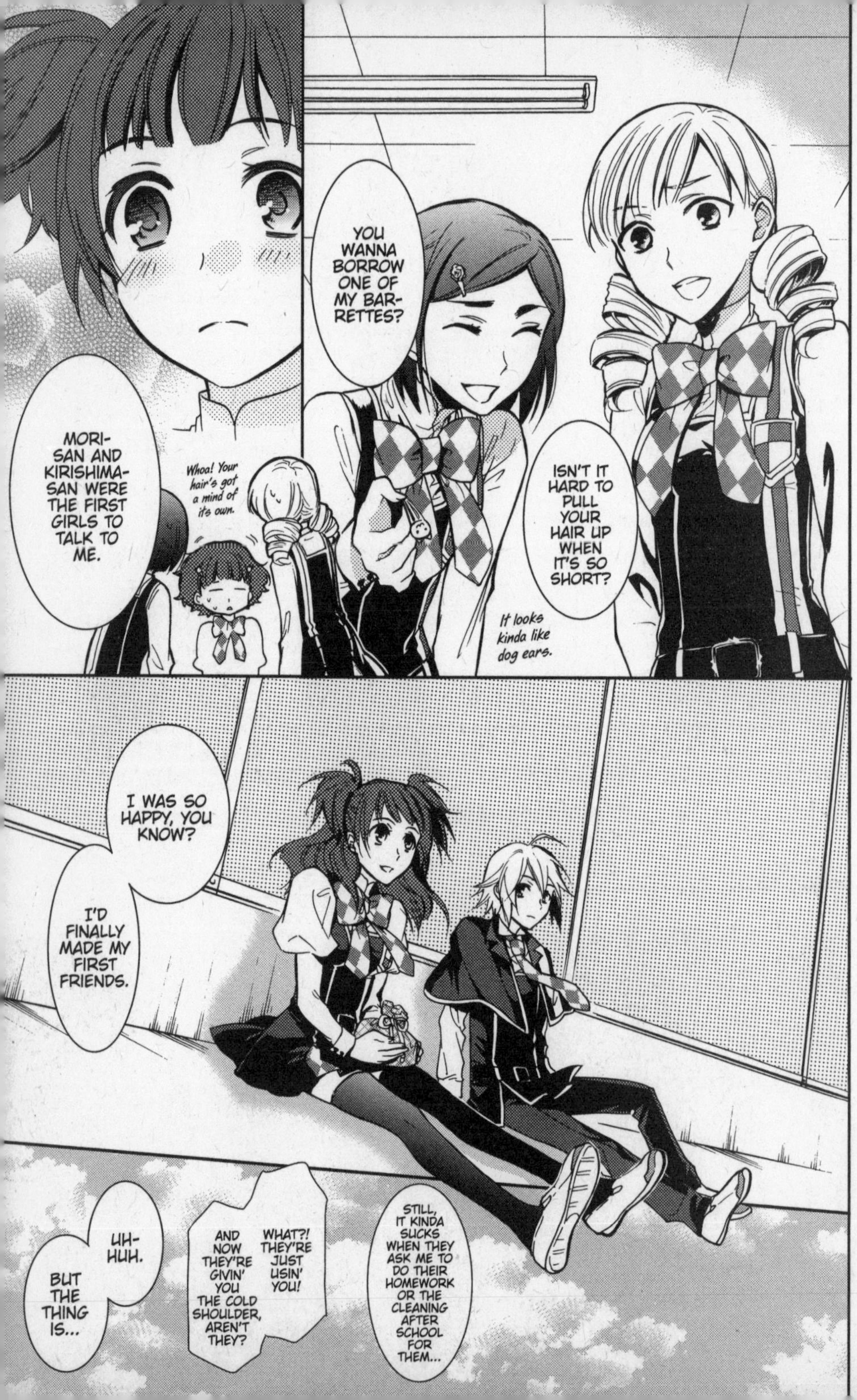
ISN'T IT HARD TO PULL YOUR HAIR UP WHEN IT'S SO SHORT?
It looks kinda like dog ears.
YOU WANNA BORROW ONE OF MY BAR-RETTES?
Whoa! Your hair's got a mind of its own.
MORI-SAN AND KIRISHIMA-SAN WERE THE FIRST GIRLS TO TALK TO ME.
I WAS SO HAPPY, YOU KNOW?
I'D FINALLY MADE MY FIRST FRIENDS.
STILL, IT KINDA SUCKS WHEN THEY ASK ME TO DO THEIR HOMEWORK OR THE CLEANING AFTER SCHOOL FOR THEM...
WHAT?! THEY'RE JUST USIN' YOU!
AND NOW THEY'RE GIVIN' YOU THE COLD SHOULDER, AREN'T THEY?
UH-HUH.
BUT THE THING IS...

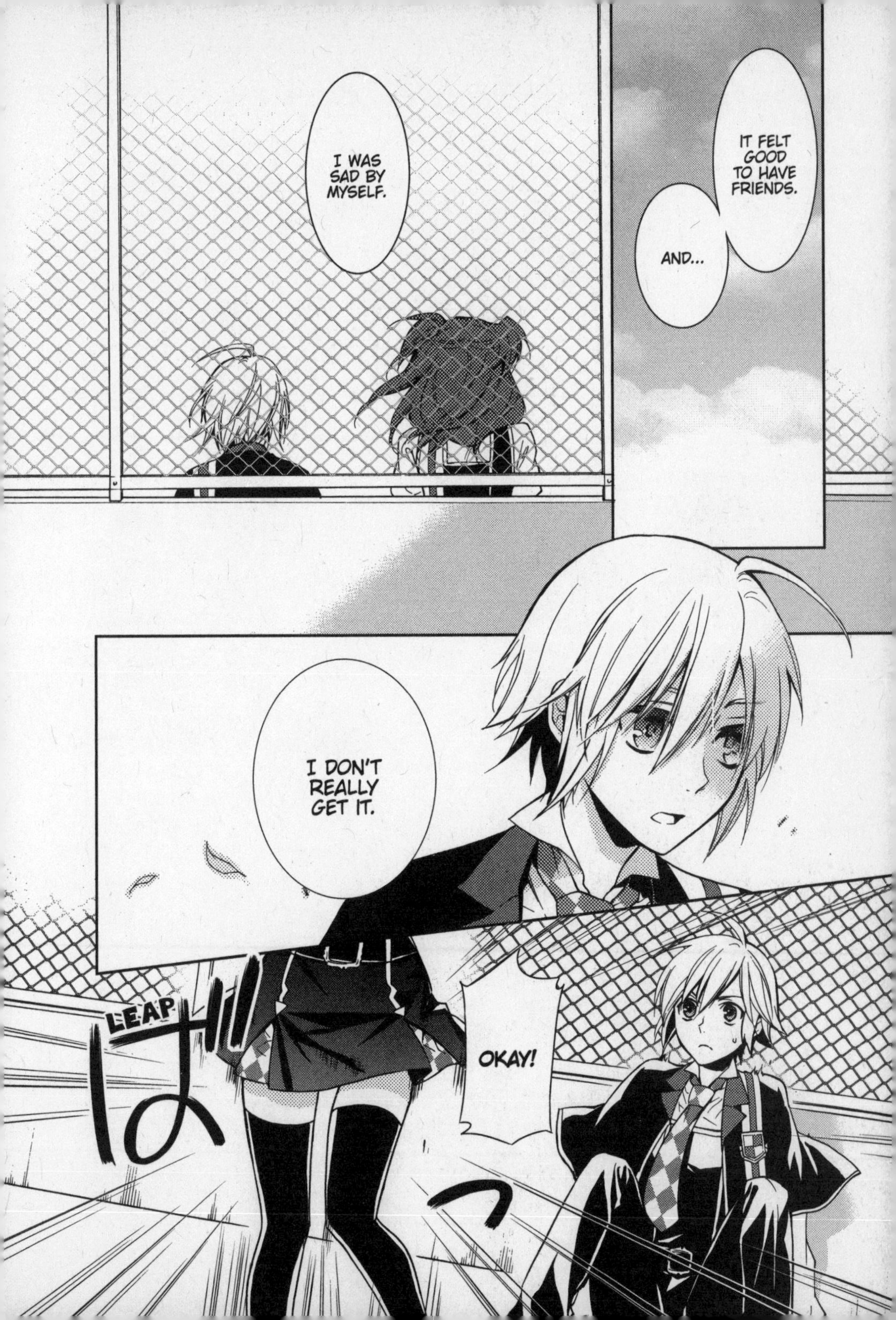
IT FELT GOOD TO HAVE FRIENDS.
AND...
I WAS SAD BY MYSELF.
I DON'T REALLY GET IT.
OKAY!
LEAP

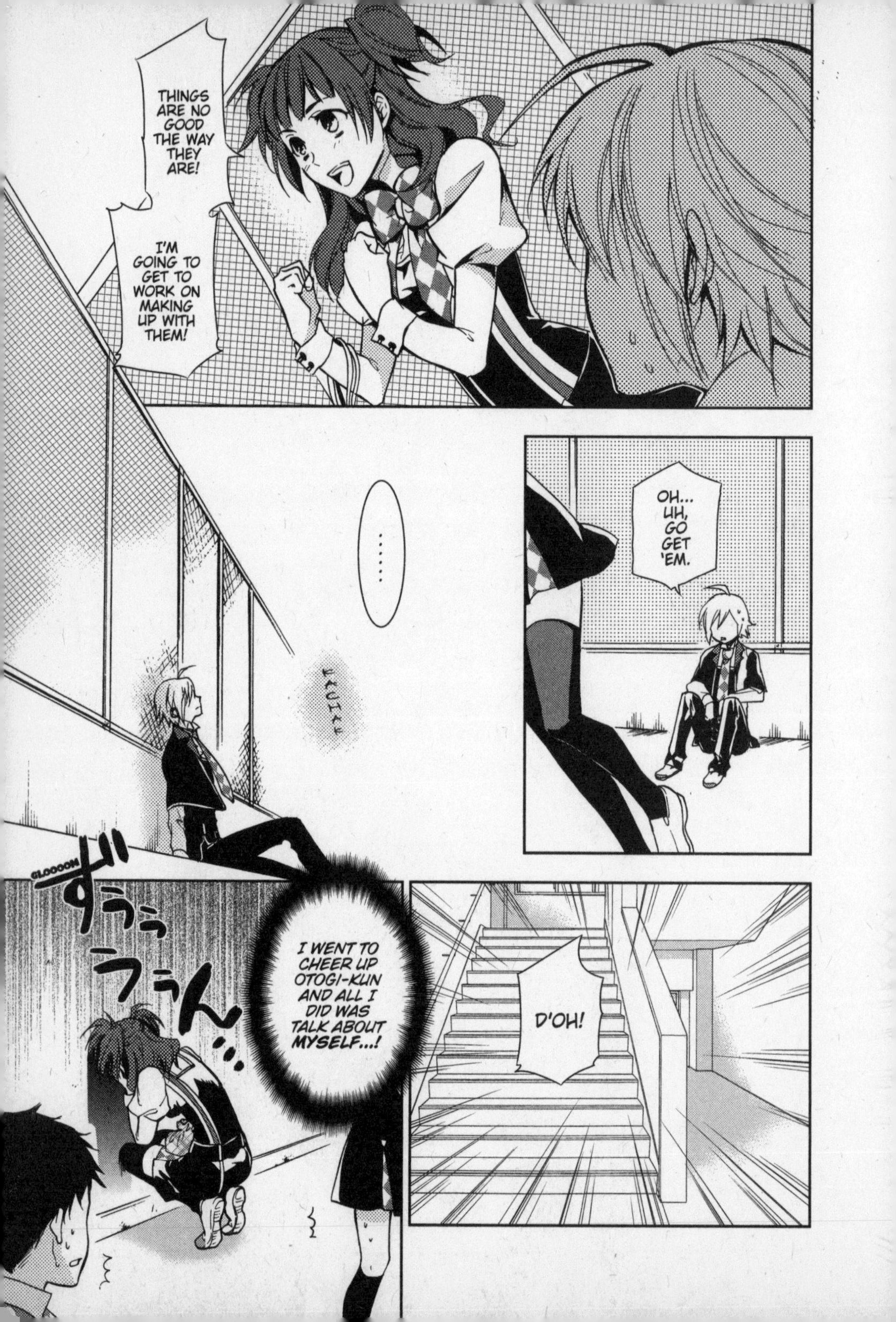
THINGS ARE NO GOOD THE WAY THEY ARE!
I'M GOING TO GET TO WORK ON MAKING UP WITH THEM!
OH... UH, GO GET 'EM.
......
D'OH!
GLOOOOH
I WENT TO CHEER UP OTOGI-KUN AND ALL I DID WAS TALK ABOUT MYSELF...!

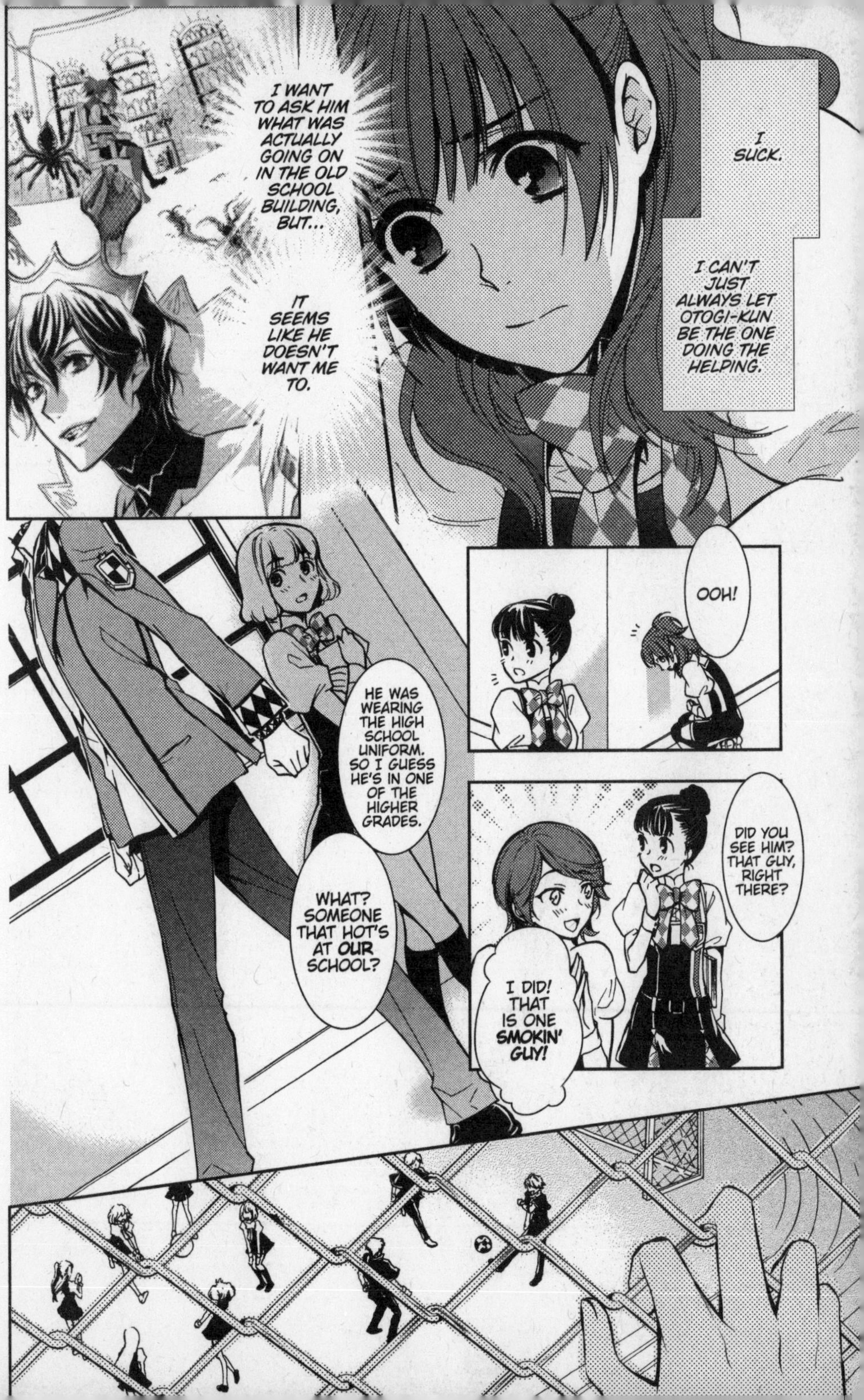
I SUCK.
I CAN'T JUST ALWAYS LET OTOGI-KUN BE THE ONE DOING THE HELPING.
I WANT TO ASK HIM WHAT WAS ACTUALLY GOING ON IN THE OLD SCHOOL BUILDING, BUT...
IT SEEMS LIKE HE DOESN'T WANT ME TO.
OOH!
DID YOU SEE HIM? THAT GUY, RIGHT THERE?
I DID! THAT IS ONE SMOKIN' GUY!
HE WAS WEARING THE HIGH SCHOOL UNIFORM. SO I GUESS HE'S IN ONE OF THE HIGHER GRADES.
WHAT? SOMEONE THAT HOT'S AT OUR SCHOOL?

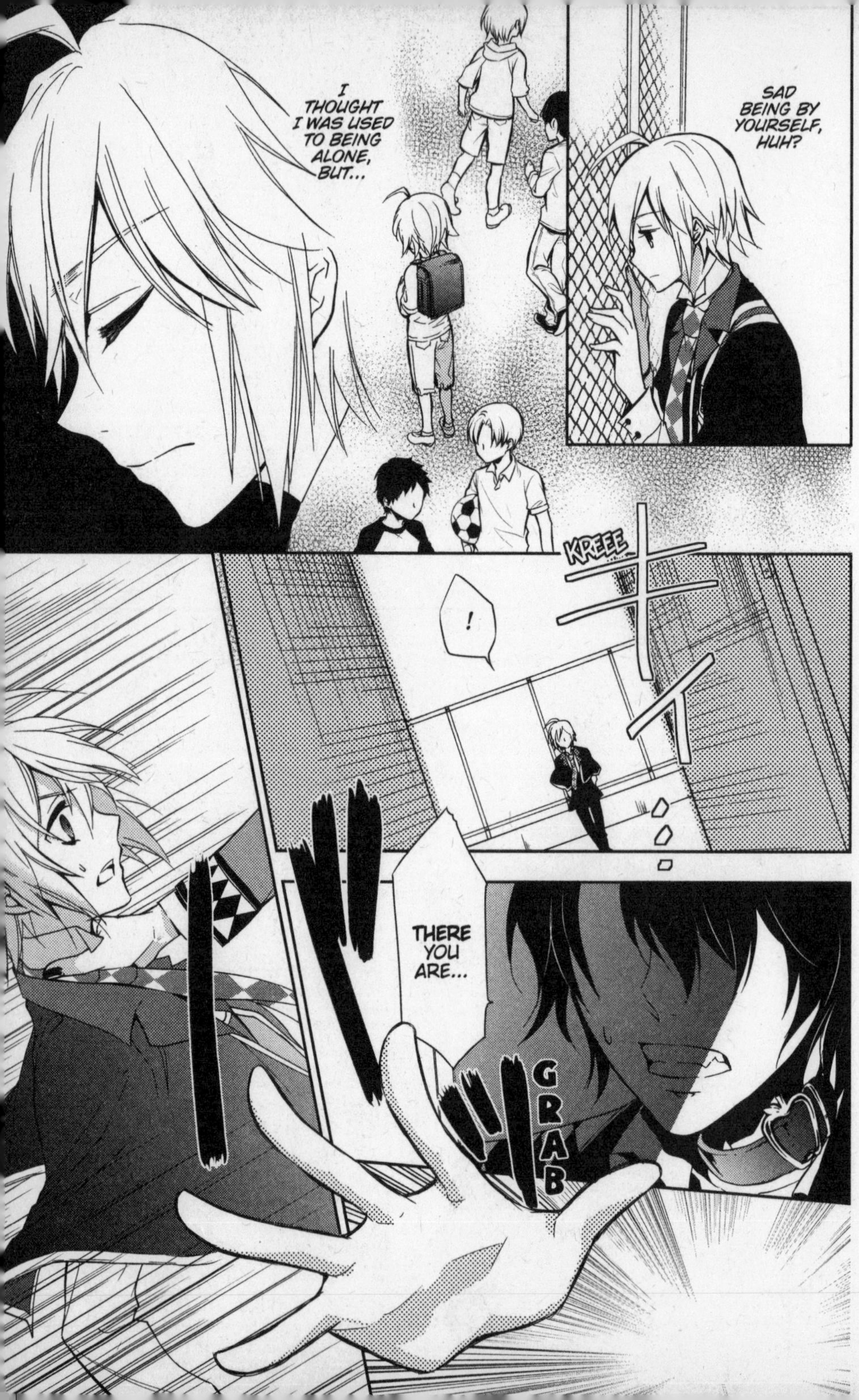
SAD BEING BY YOURSELF, HUH?
I THOUGHT I WAS USED TO BEING ALONE, BUT...
KREEE
!
THERE YOU ARE...
GRAB

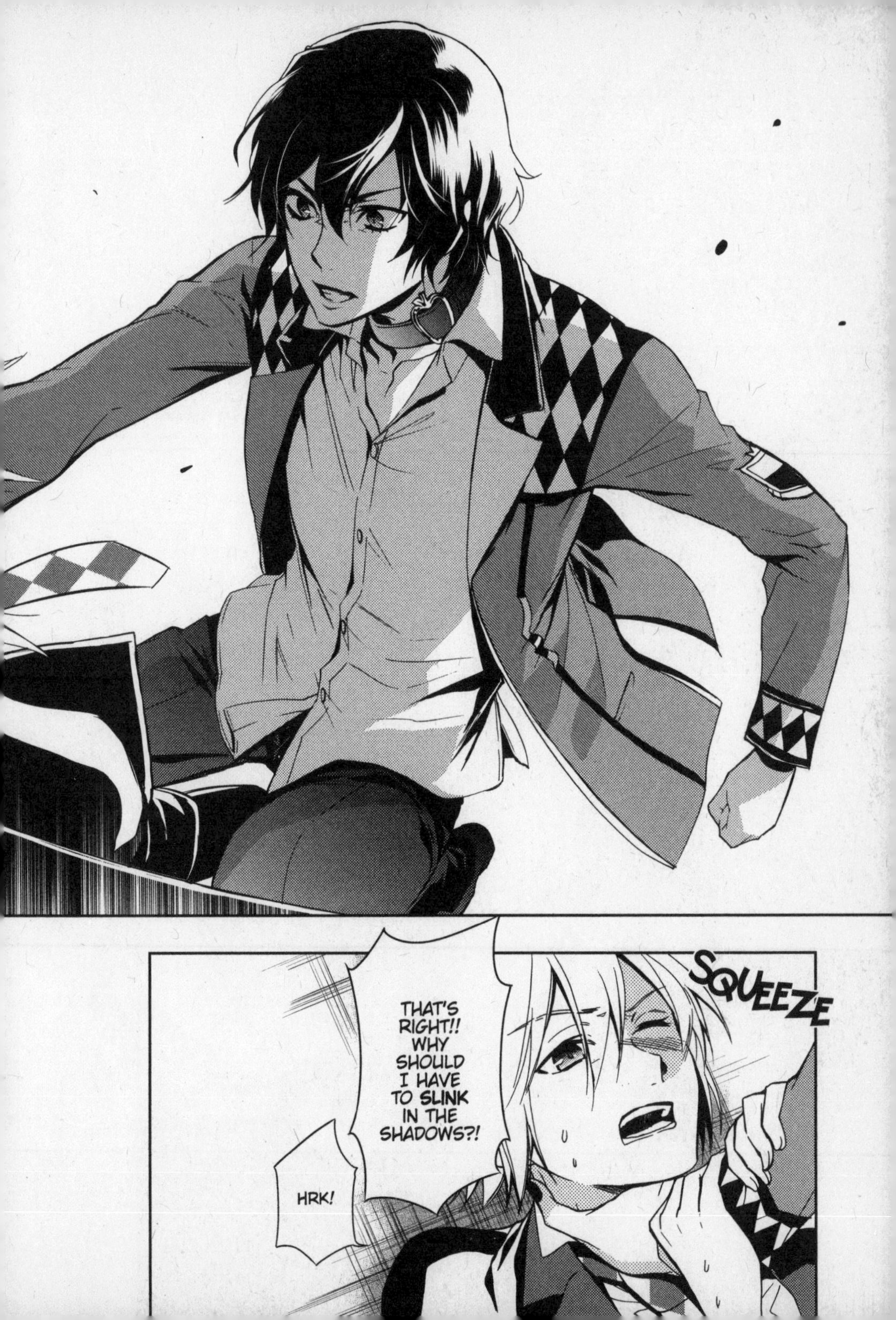
SQUEEZE
THAT'S RIGHT!! WHY SHOULD I HAVE TO SLINK IN THE SHADOWS?!
HRK!

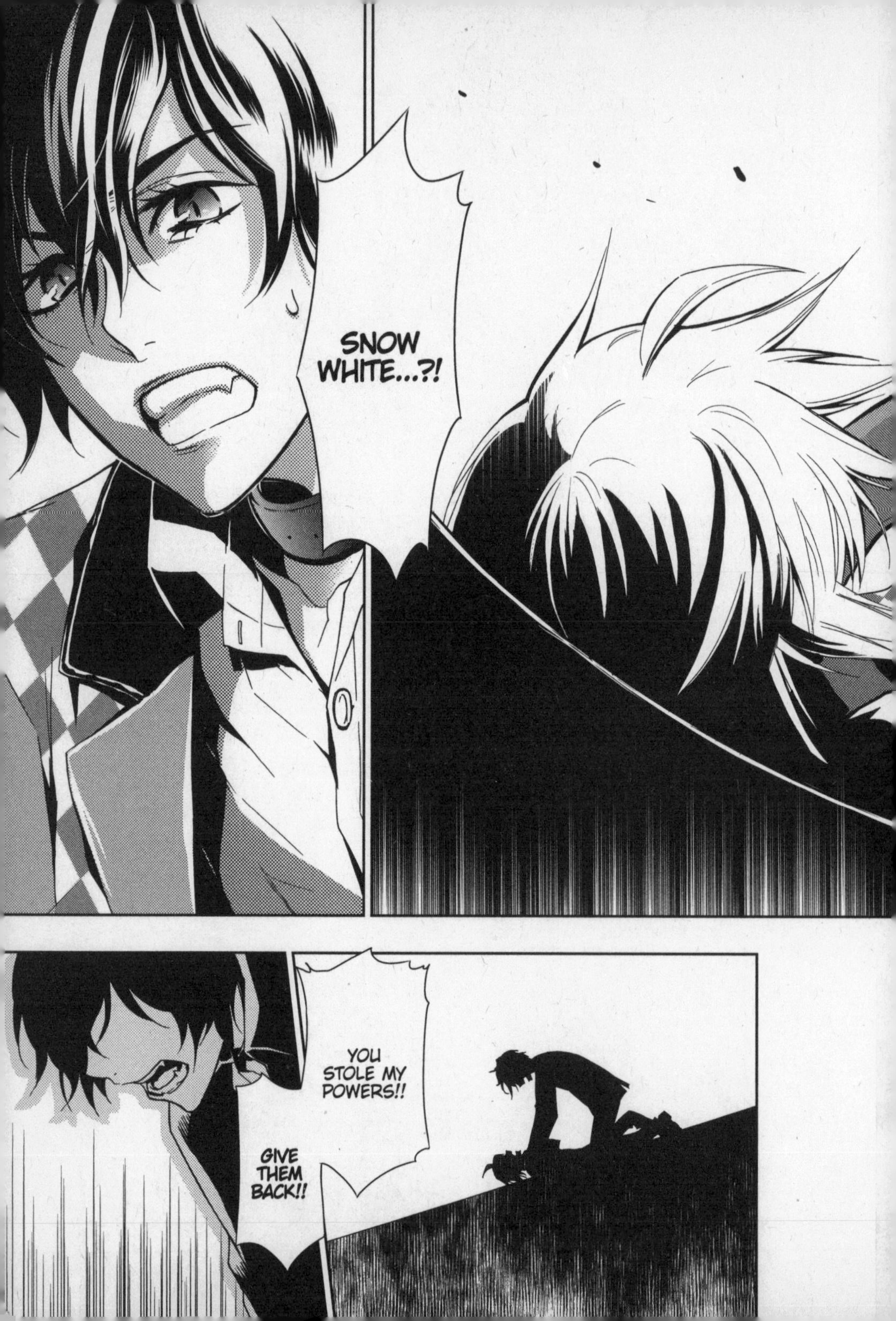
SNOW WHITE...?!
YOU STOLE MY POWERS!!
GIVE THEM BACK!!

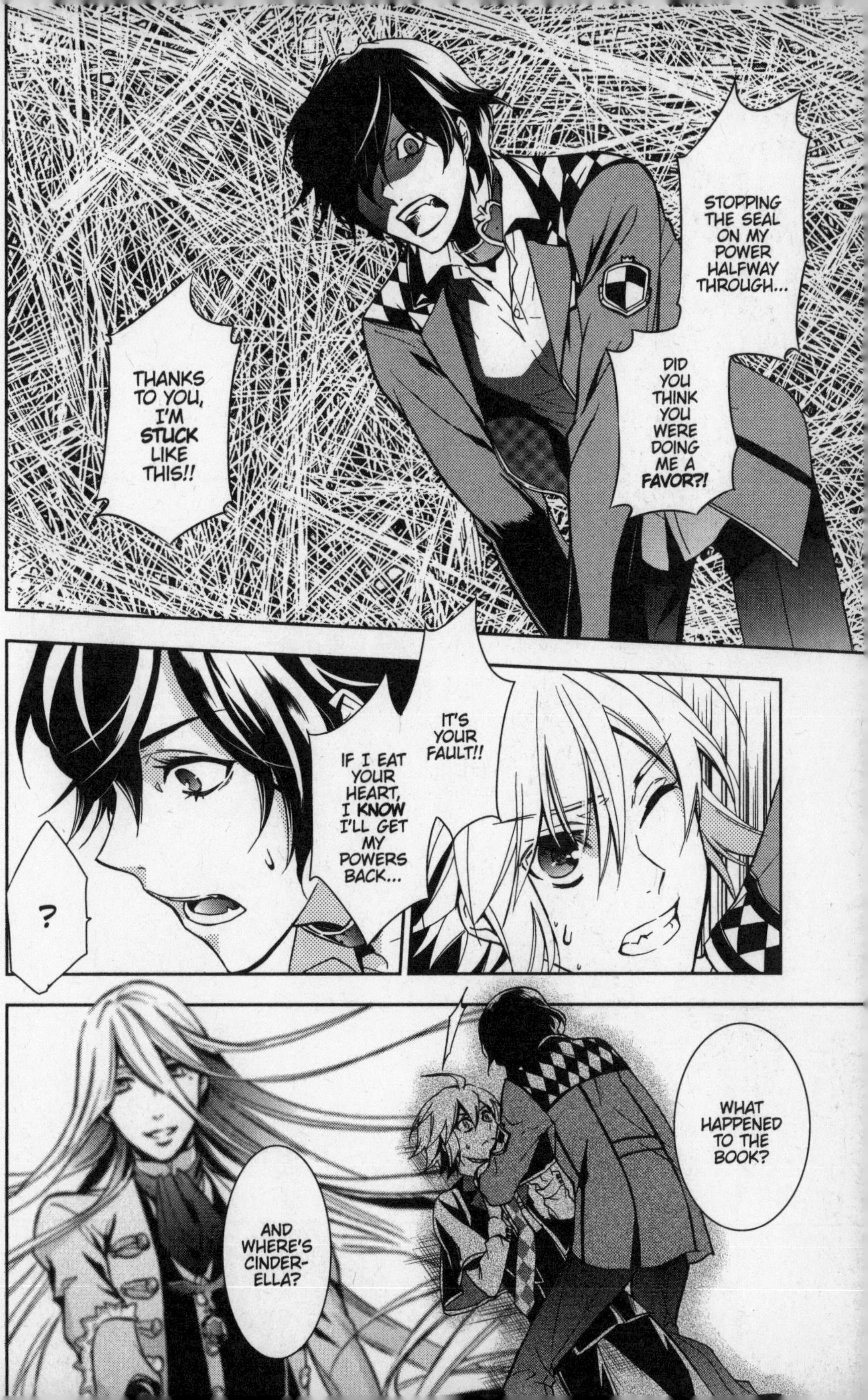
STOPPING THE SEAL ON MY POWER HALFWAY THROUGH...
DID YOU THINK YOU WERE DOING ME A FAVOR?!
THANKS TO YOU, I'M STUCK LIKE THIS!!
IT'S YOUR FAULT!!
IF I EAT YOUR HEART, I KNOW I'LL GET MY POWERS BACK...
?
WHAT HAPPENED TO THE BOOK?
AND WHERE'S CINDERELLA?

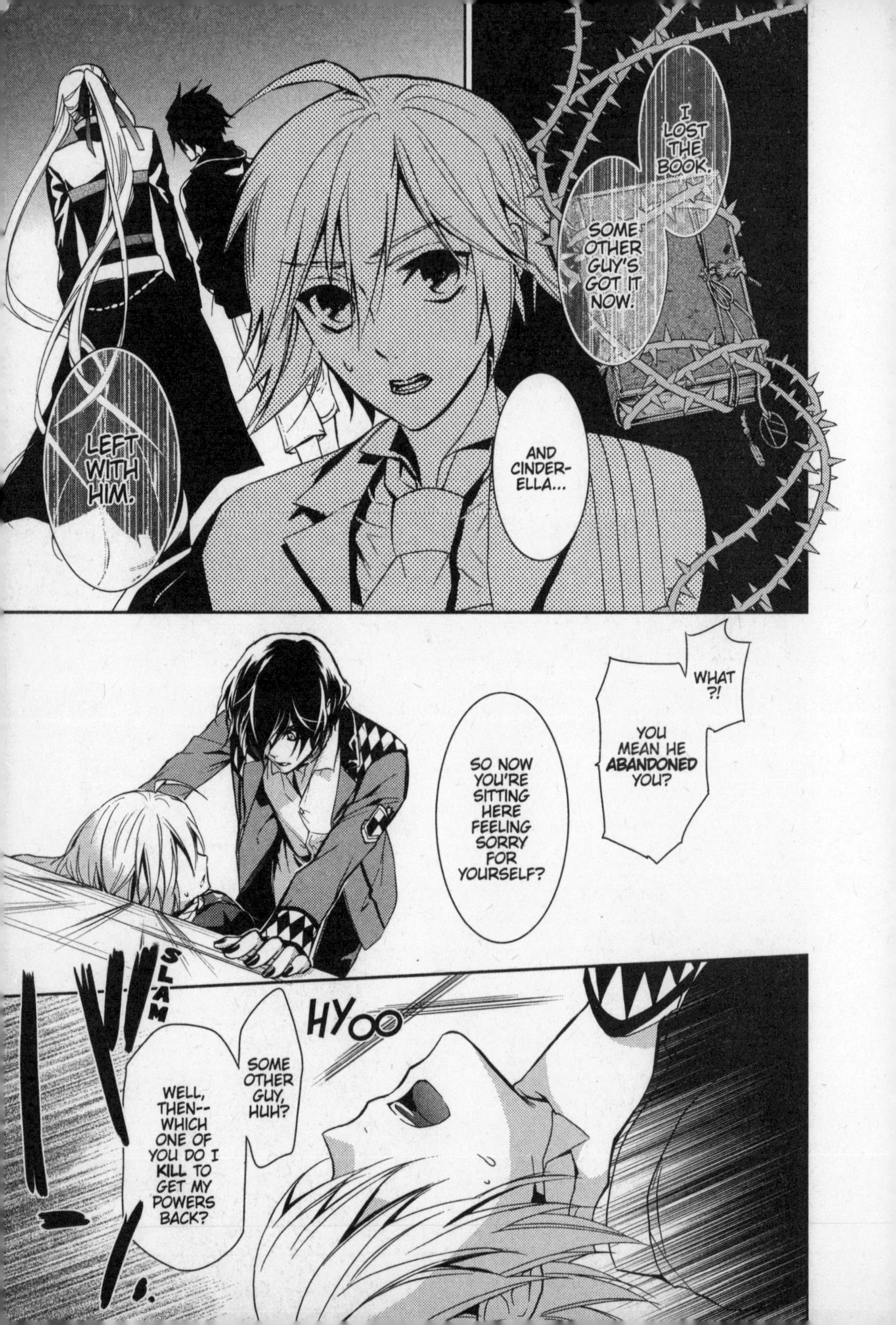
I LOST THE BOOK.
SOME OTHER GUY'S GOT IT NOW.
AND CINDER-ELLA...
LEFT WITH HIM.
WHAT?!
YOU MEAN HE **ABANDONED** YOU?
SO NOW YOU'RE SITTING HERE FEELING SORRY FOR YOURSELF?
SLAM
HYOO
SOME OTHER GUY, HUH?
WELL, THEN-- WHICH ONE OF YOU DO I **KILL** TO GET MY POWERS BACK?

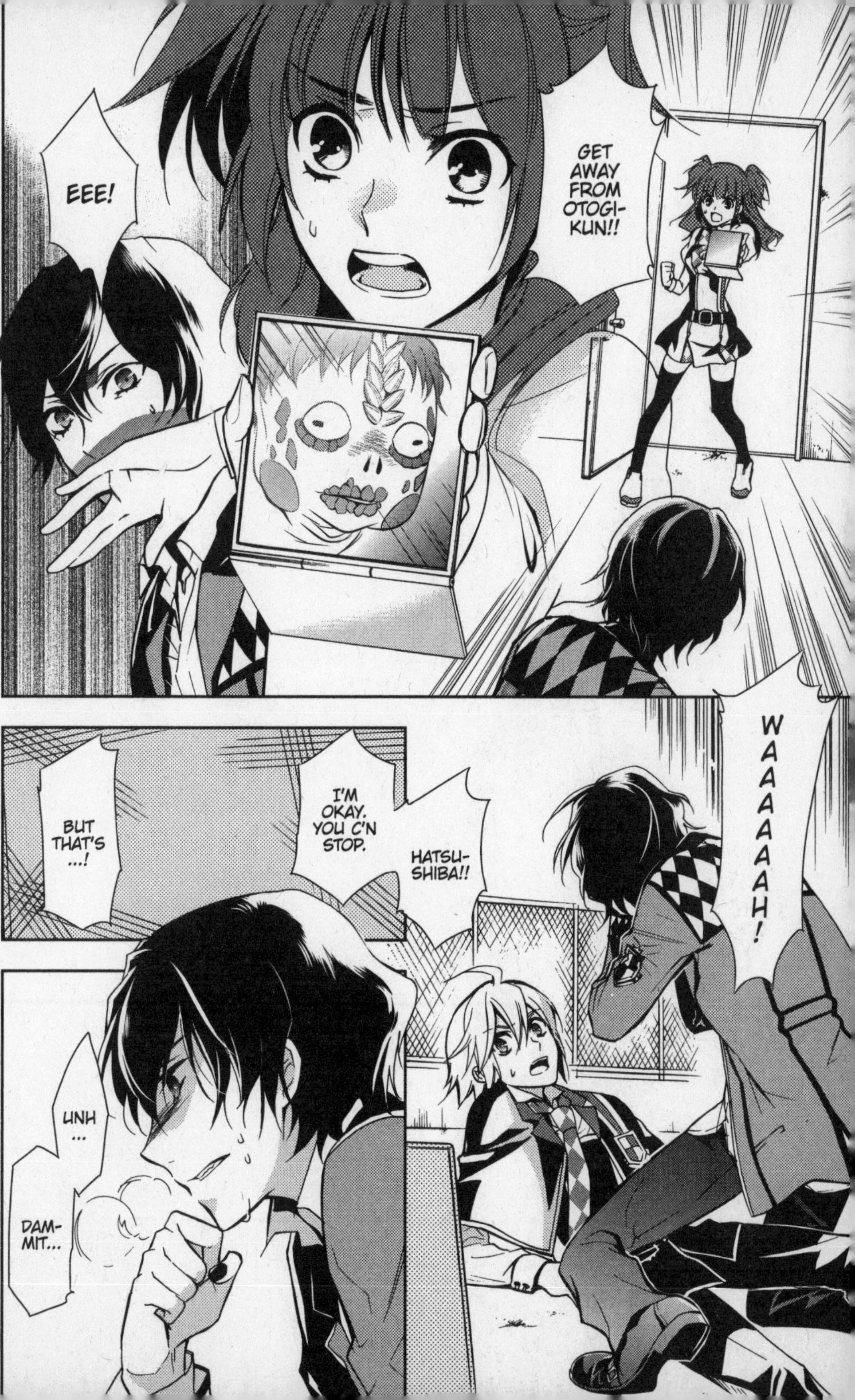
GET AWAY FROM OTOGI-KUN!!
EEE!
WAAAAAAAAH!
HATSU-SHIBA!!
I'M OKAY. YOU C'N STOP.
BUT THAT'S ...!
UNH ...
DAM-MIT...

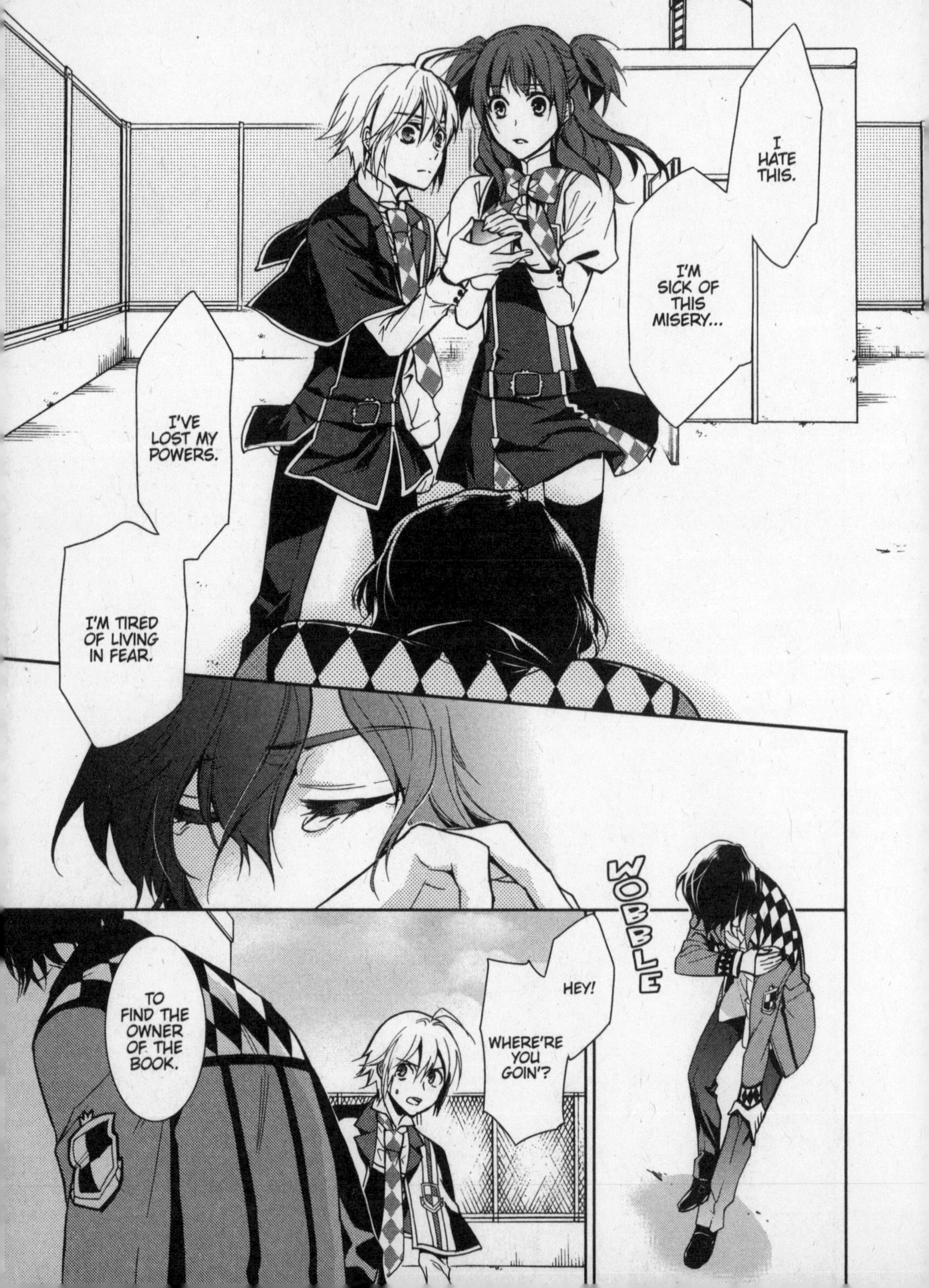
I HATE THIS.
I'M SICK OF THIS MISERY...
I'VE LOST MY POWERS.
I'M TIRED OF LIVING IN FEAR.
WOBBLE
HEY!
WHERE'RE YOU GOIN'?
TO FIND THE OWNER OF THE BOOK.

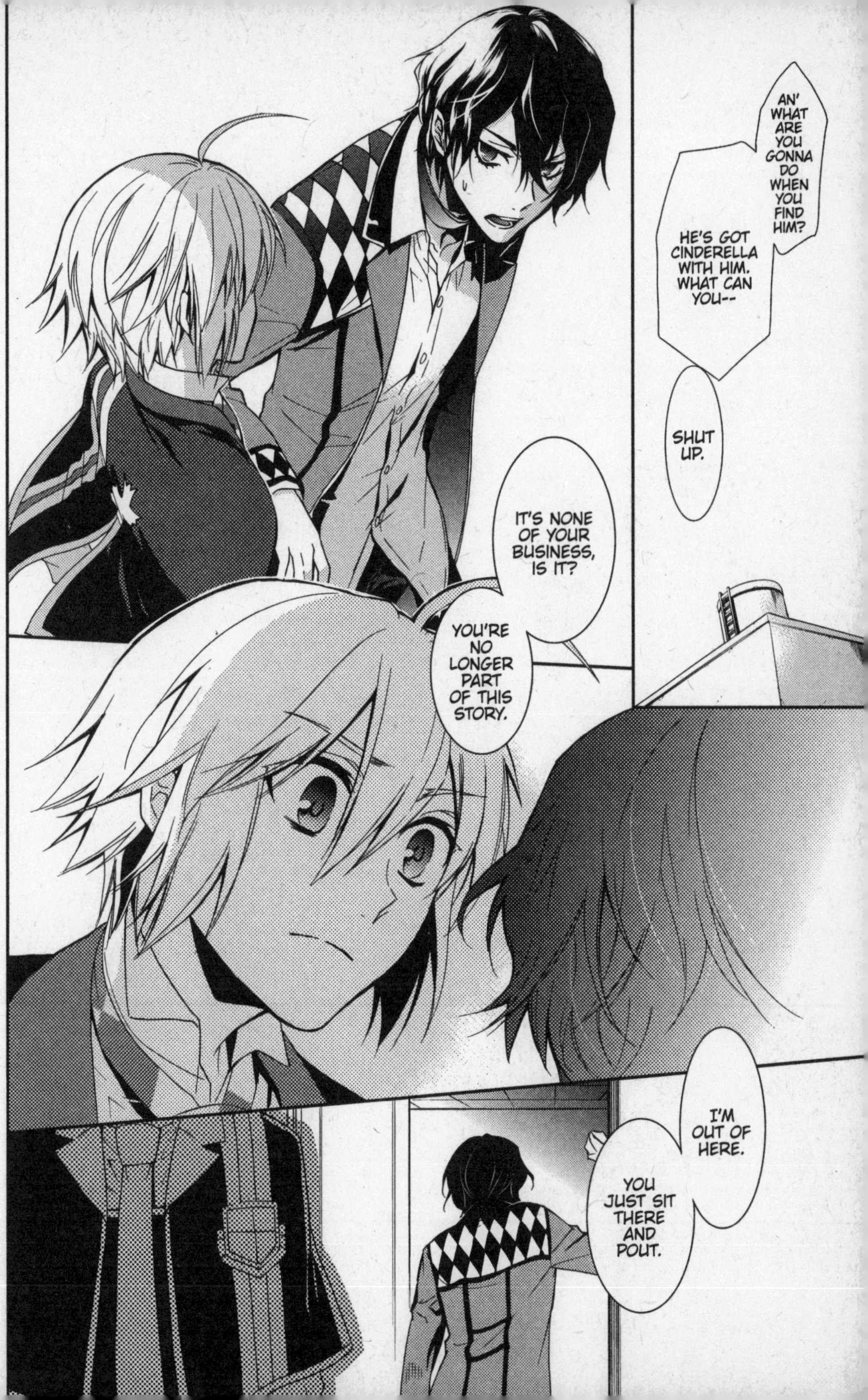
AN' WHAT ARE YOU GONNA DO WHEN YOU FIND HIM?
HE'S GOT CINDERELLA WITH HIM. WHAT CAN YOU--
SHUT UP.
IT'S NONE OF YOUR BUSINESS, IS IT?
YOU'RE NO LONGER PART OF THIS STORY.
I'M OUT OF HERE.
YOU JUST SIT THERE AND POUT.

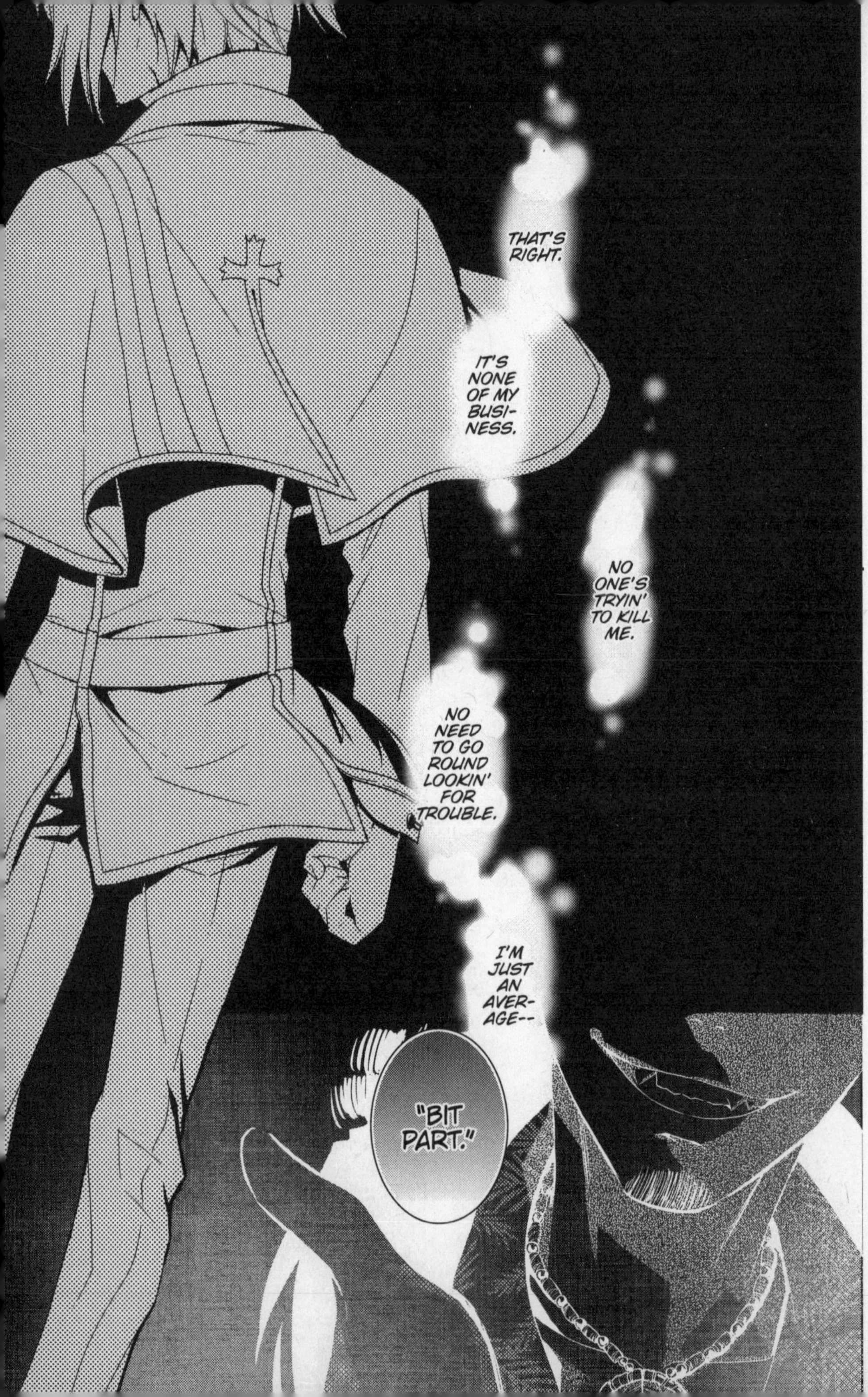
THAT'S RIGHT.
IT'S NONE OF MY BUSI-NESS.
NO ONE'S TRYIN' TO KILL ME.
NO NEED TO GO ROUND LOOKIN' FOR TROUBLE.
I'M JUST AN AVER-AGE--
"BIT PART."

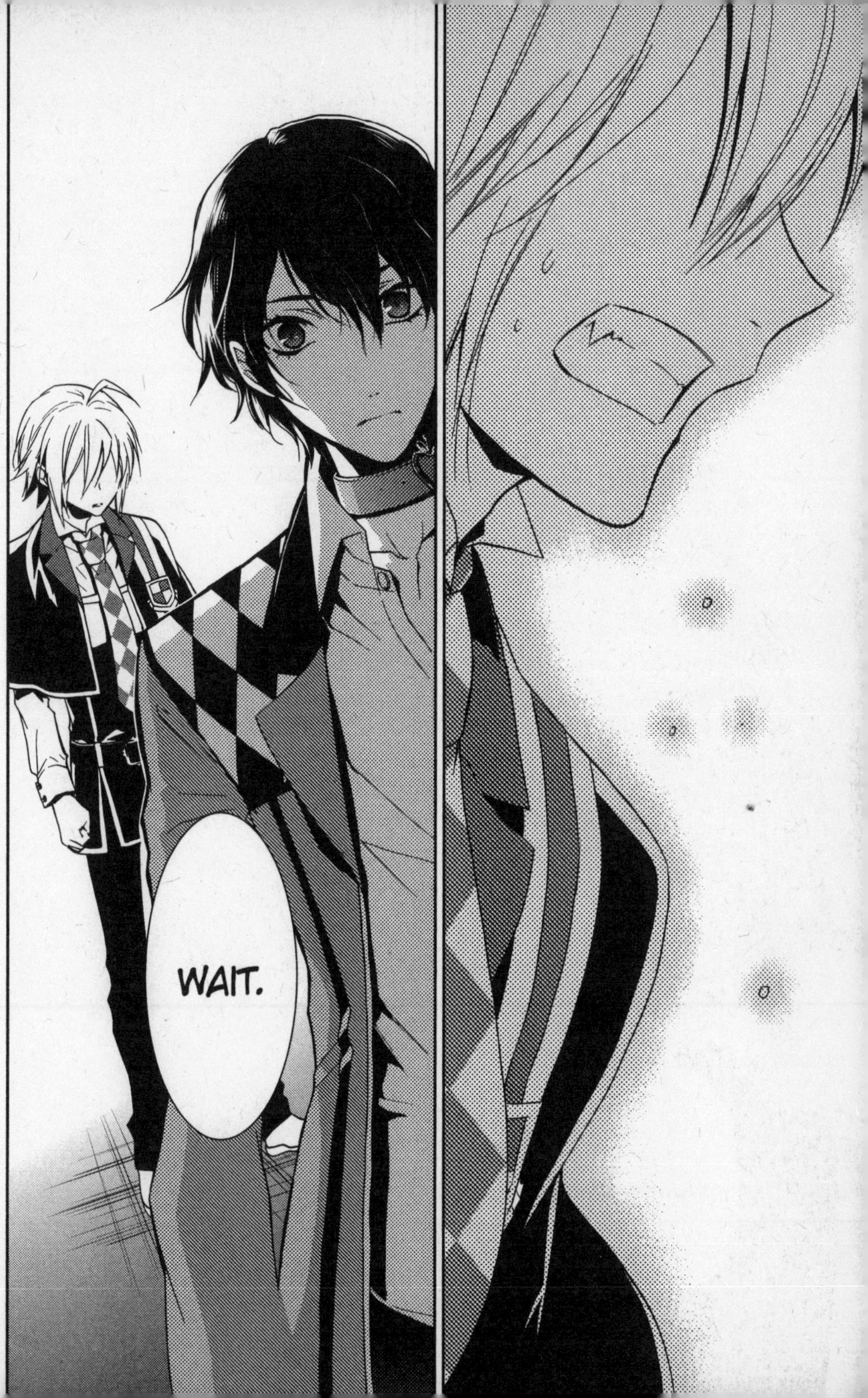
WAIT.

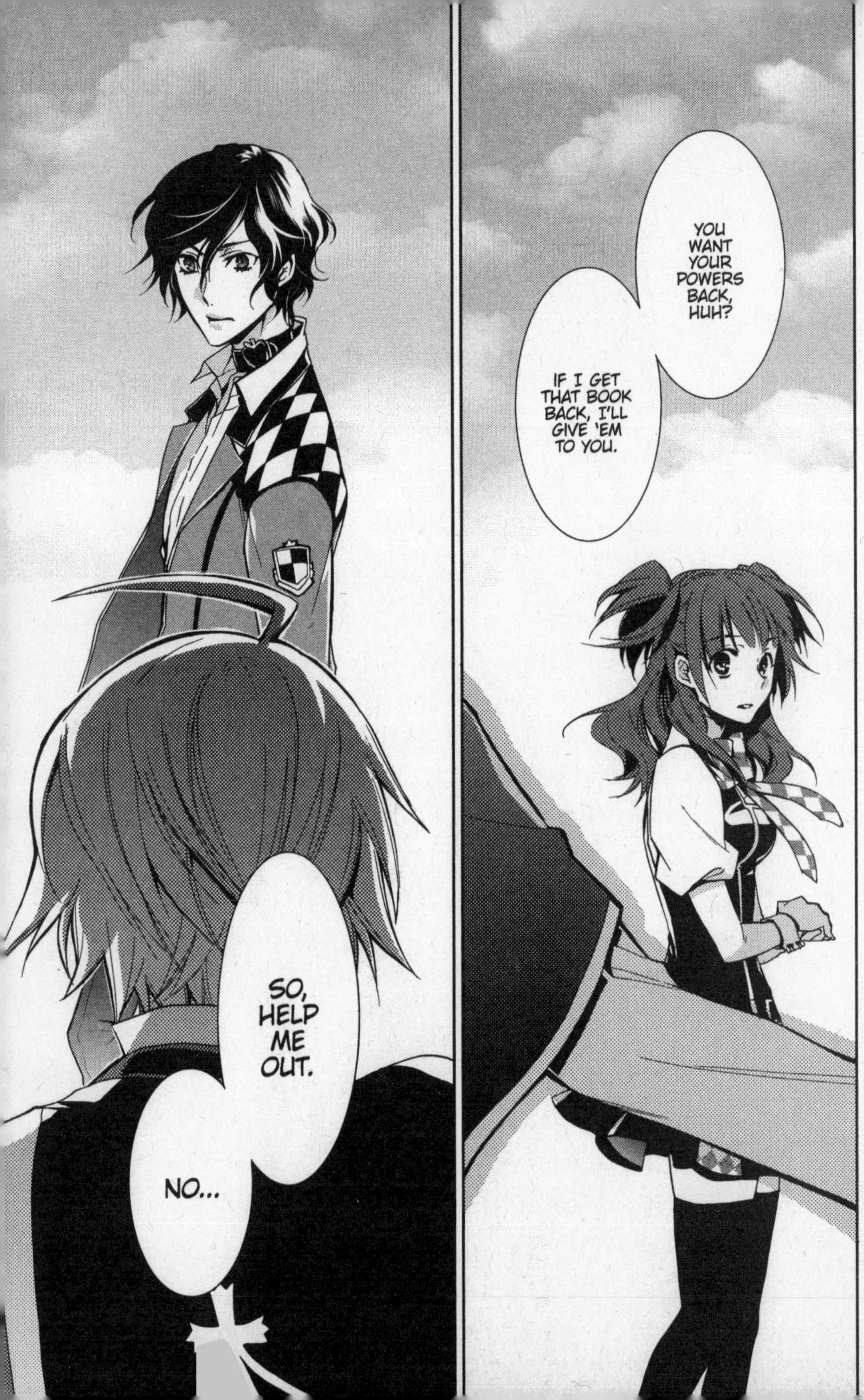
YOU WANT YOUR POWERS BACK, HUH?
IF I GET THAT BOOK BACK, I'LL GIVE 'EM TO YOU.
SO, HELP ME OUT.
NO...

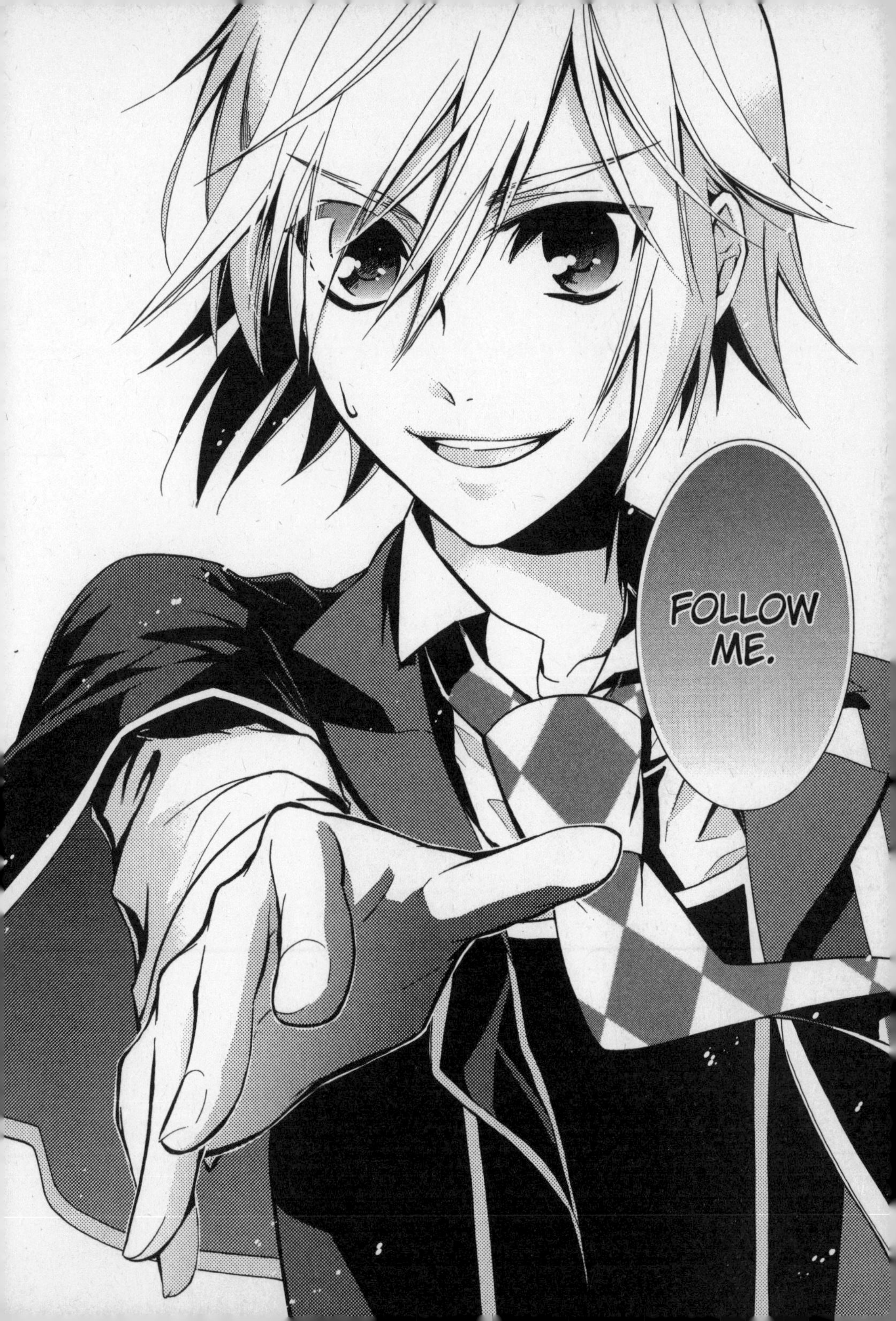
FOLLOW ME.

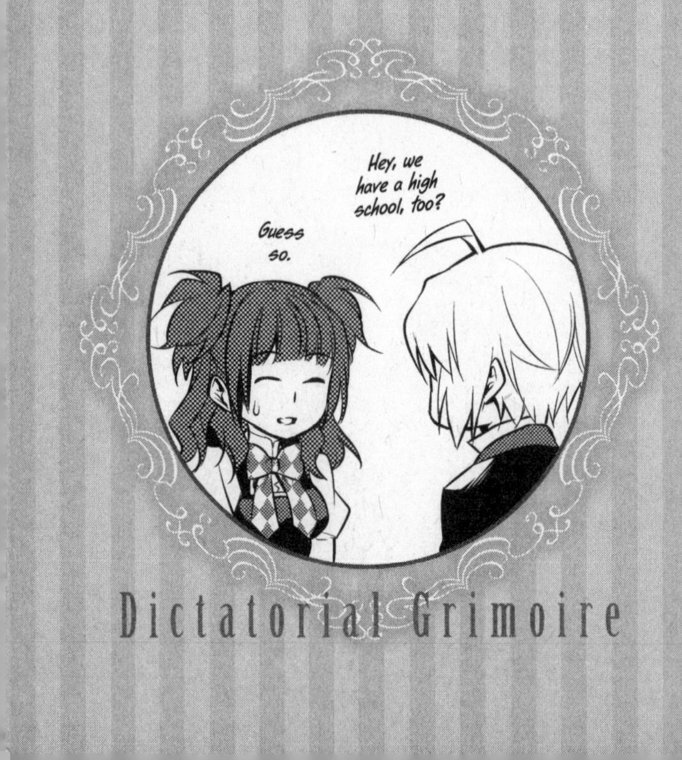
Hey, we have a high school, too?
Guess so.

Dictatorial Grimoire

独裁グリムワール
Dictatorial Grimoire

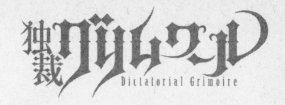

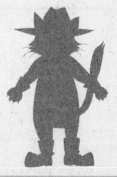

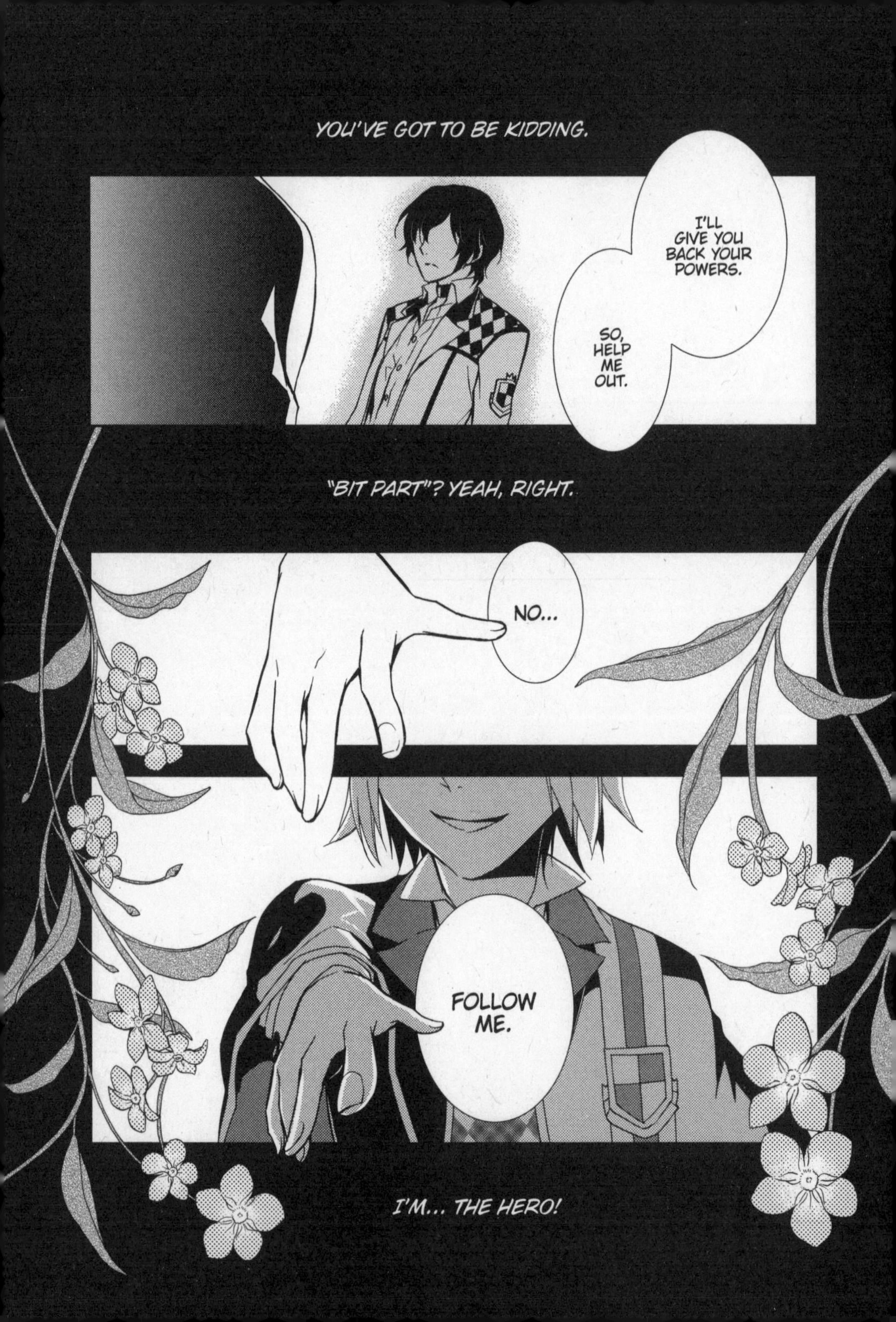
YOU'VE GOT TO BE KIDDING.
I'LL GIVE YOU BACK YOUR POWERS.
SO, HELP ME OUT.
"BIT PART"? YEAH, RIGHT.
NO...
FOLLOW ME.
I'M... THE HERO!

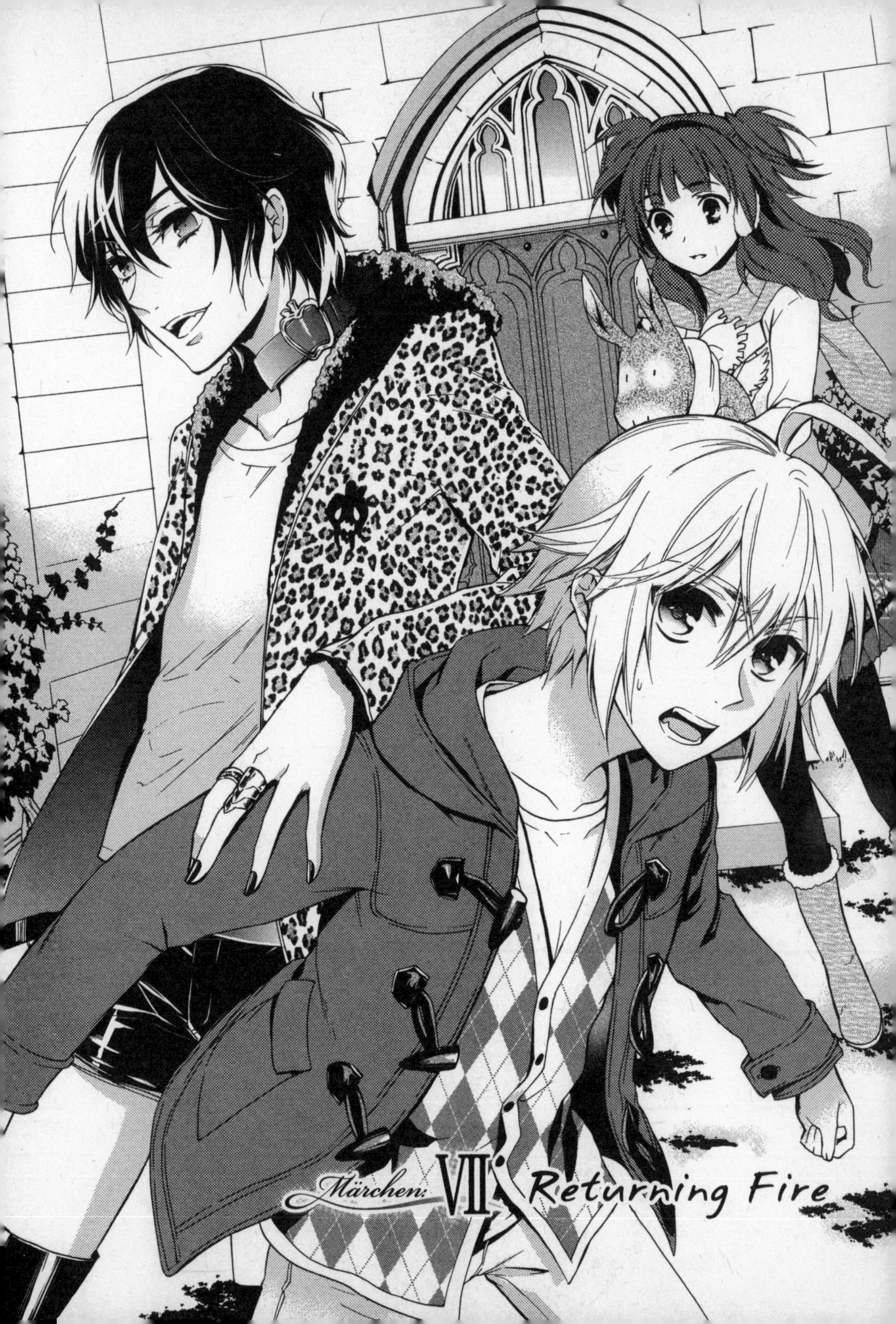
Märchen: VII Returning Fire

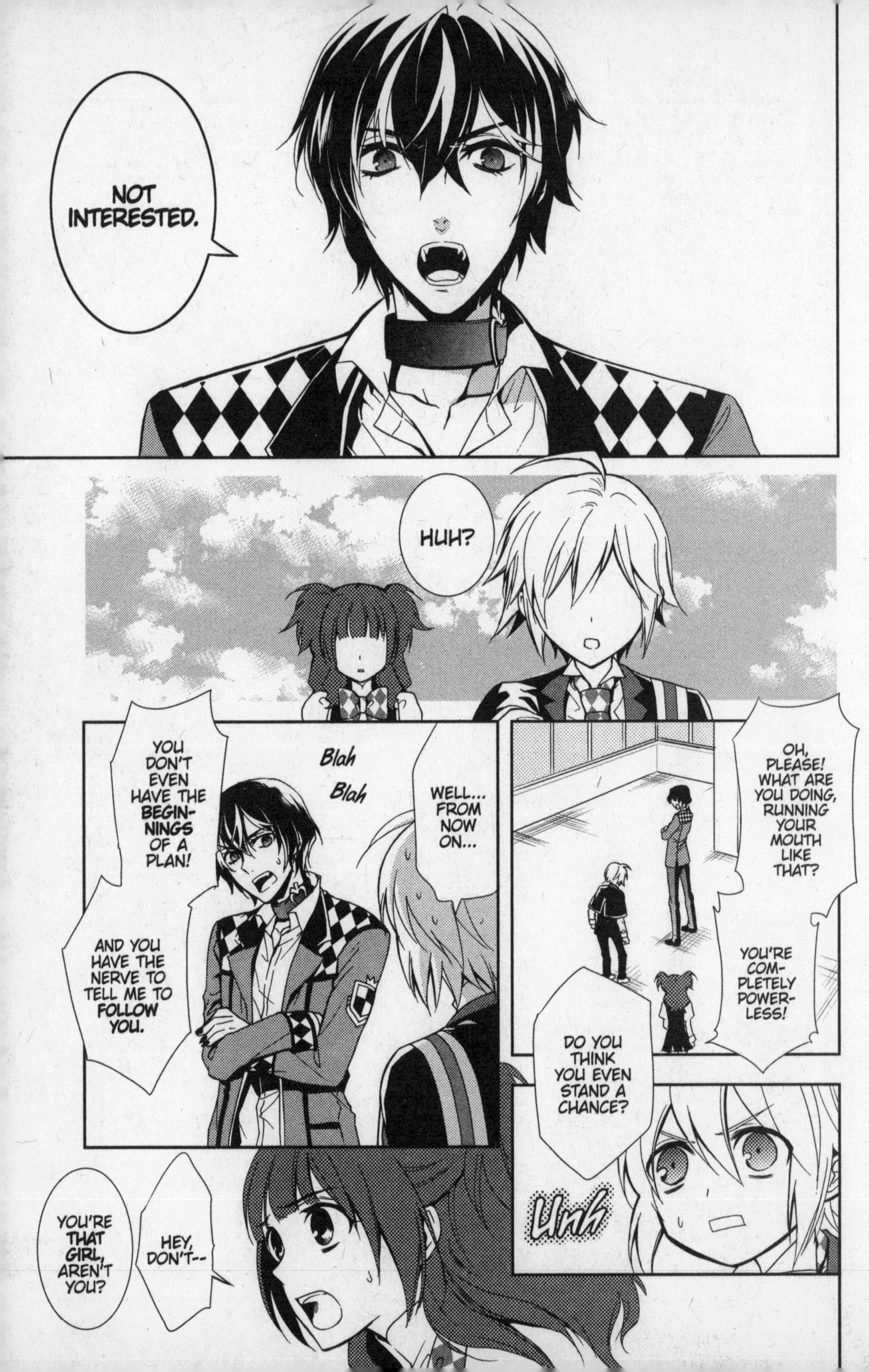
NOT INTERESTED.
HUH?
OH, PLEASE! WHAT ARE YOU DOING, RUNNING YOUR MOUTH LIKE THAT?
YOU'RE COMPLETELY POWERLESS!
DO YOU THINK YOU EVEN STAND A CHANCE?
WELL... FROM NOW ON...
Blah Blah
YOU DON'T EVEN HAVE THE BEGINNINGS OF A PLAN!
AND YOU HAVE THE NERVE TO TELL ME TO FOLLOW YOU.
Unh
HEY, DON'T--
YOU'RE THAT GIRL, AREN'T YOU?

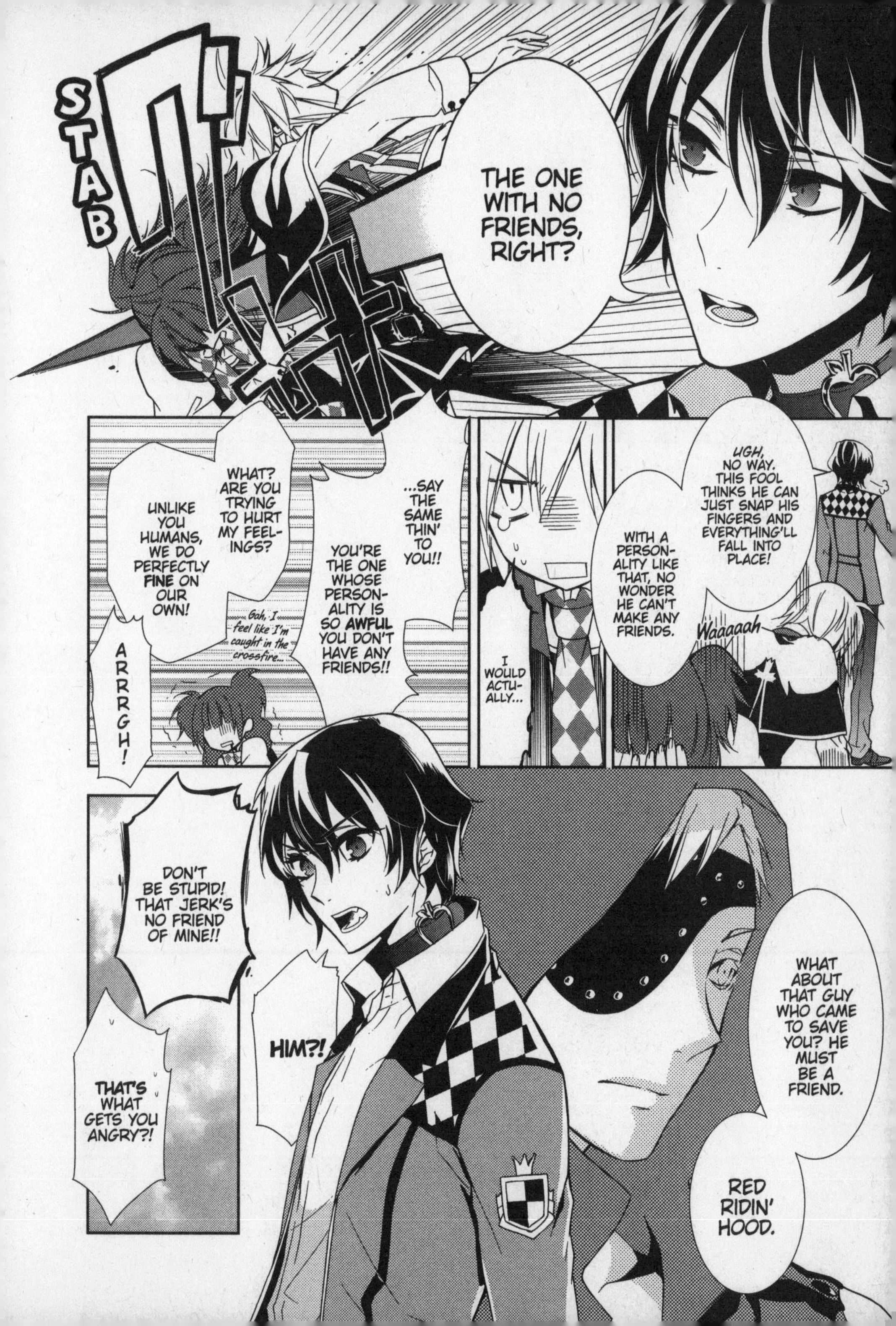
THE ONE WITH NO FRIENDS, RIGHT?
STAB
UGH, NO WAY. THIS FOOL THINKS HE CAN JUST SNAP HIS FINGERS AND EVERYTHING'LL FALL INTO PLACE!
Waaaaah
WITH A PERSONALITY LIKE THAT, NO WONDER HE CAN'T MAKE ANY FRIENDS.
I WOULD ACTUALLY...
...SAY THE SAME THIN' TO YOU!!
YOU'RE THE ONE WHOSE PERSONALITY IS SO AWFUL YOU DON'T HAVE ANY FRIENDS!!
WHAT? ARE YOU TRYING TO HURT MY FEELINGS?
UNLIKE YOU HUMANS, WE DO PERFECTLY FINE ON OUR OWN!
Gah, I feel like I'm caught in the crossfire...
ARRRGH!
WHAT ABOUT THAT GUY WHO CAME TO SAVE YOU? HE MUST BE A FRIEND.
RED RIDIN' HOOD.
HIM?!
DON'T BE STUPID! THAT JERK'S NO FRIEND OF MINE!!
THAT'S WHAT GETS YOU ANGRY?!

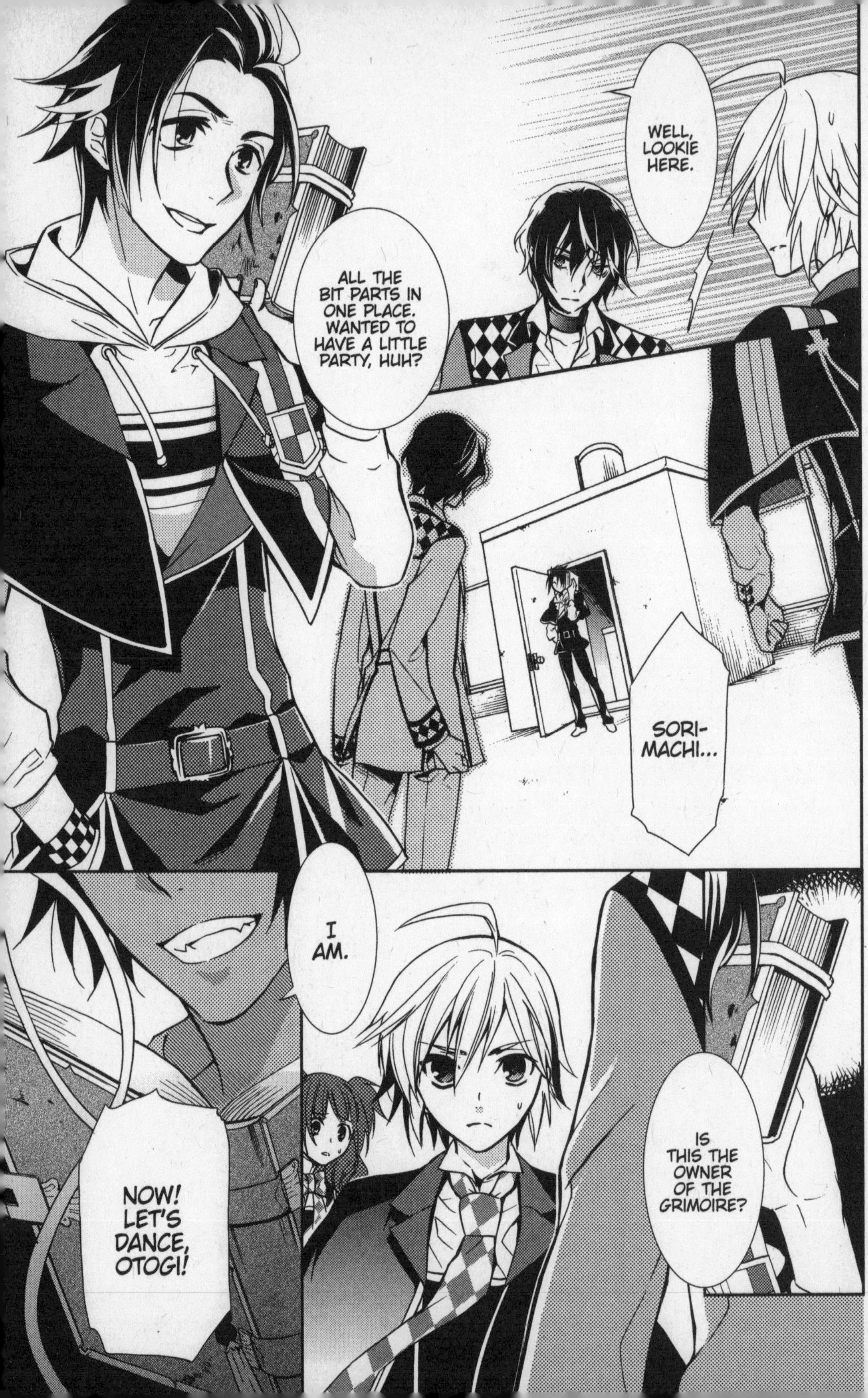
WELL, LOOKIE HERE.
SORI-MACHI...
ALL THE BIT PARTS IN ONE PLACE. WANTED TO HAVE A LITTLE PARTY, HUH?
IS THIS THE OWNER OF THE GRIMOIRE?
I AM.
NOW! LET'S DANCE, OTOGI!

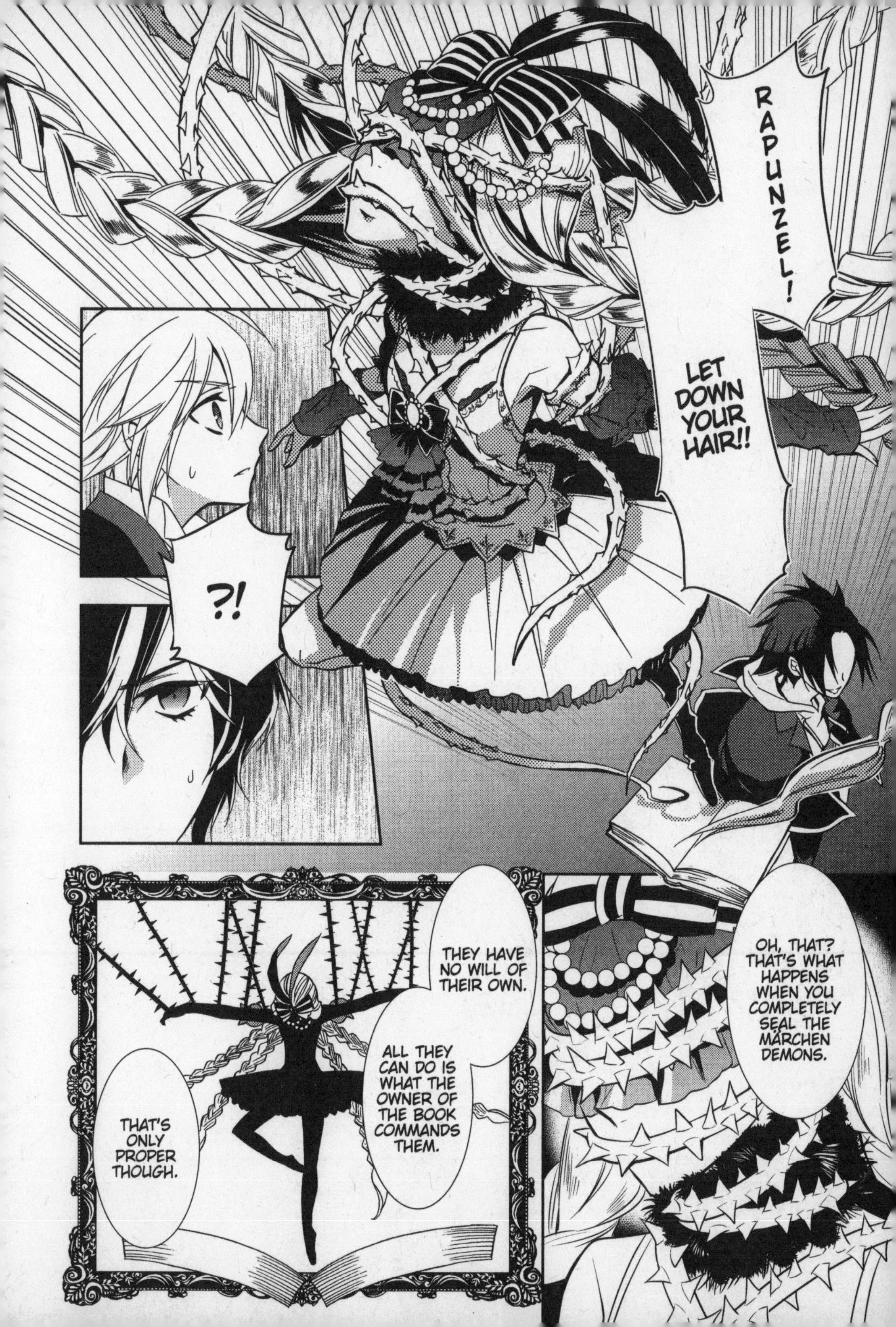
RAPUNZEL!
LET DOWN YOUR HAIR!!
?!
OH, THAT? THAT'S WHAT HAPPENS WHEN YOU COMPLETELY SEAL THE MÄRCHEN DEMONS.
THEY HAVE NO WILL OF THEIR OWN.
ALL THEY CAN DO IS WHAT THE OWNER OF THE BOOK COMMANDS THEM.
THAT'S ONLY PROPER THOUGH.

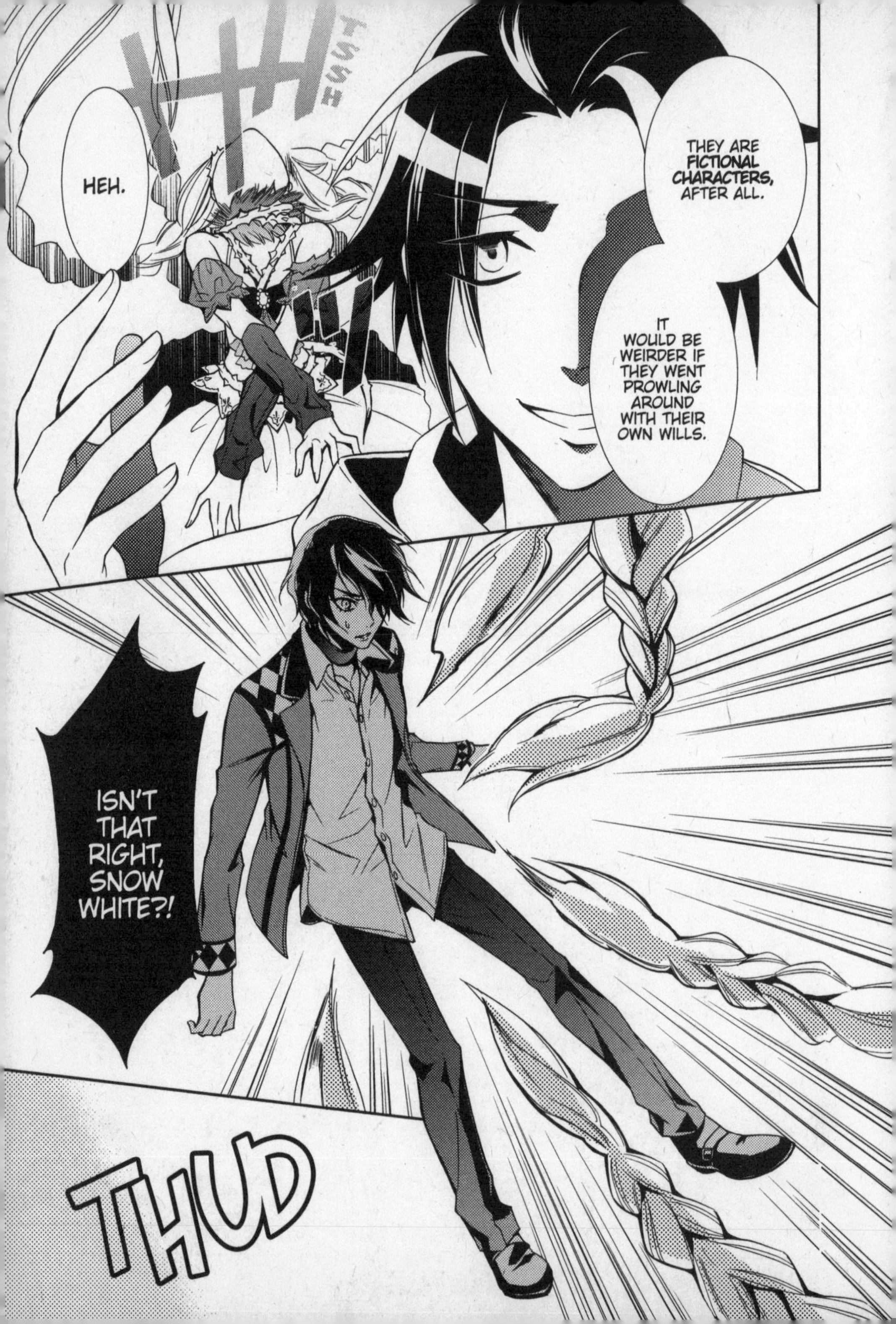
TSSH
HEH.
THEY ARE FICTIONAL CHARACTERS, AFTER ALL.
IT WOULD BE WEIRDER IF THEY WENT PROWLING AROUND WITH THEIR OWN WILLS.
ISN'T THAT RIGHT, SNOW WHITE?!
THUD

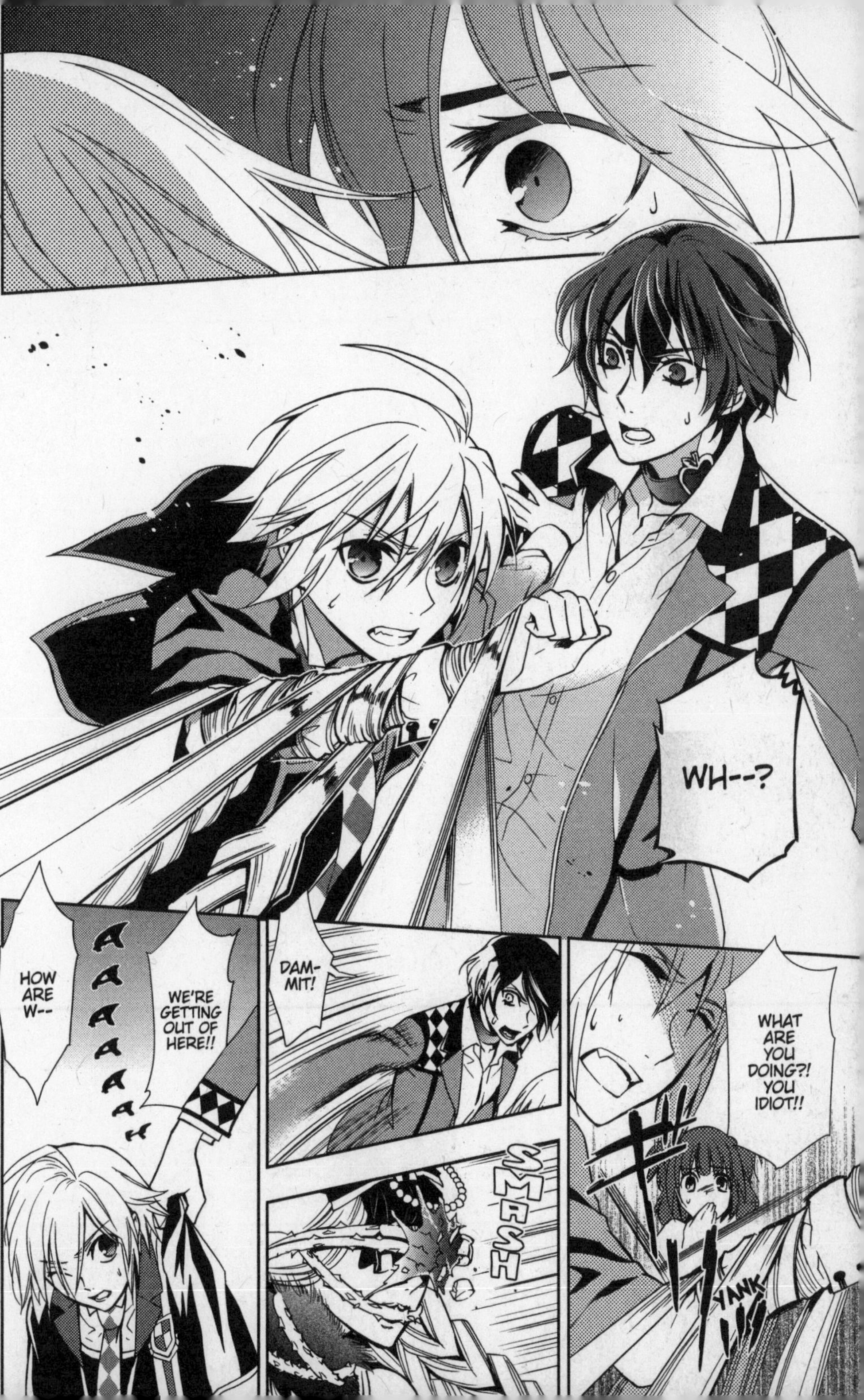
WH--?
WHAT ARE YOU DOING?! YOU IDIOT!!
YANK
DAM-MIT!
SMASH
WE'RE GETTING OUT OF HERE!!
HOW ARE W--
AAAAAAAAH

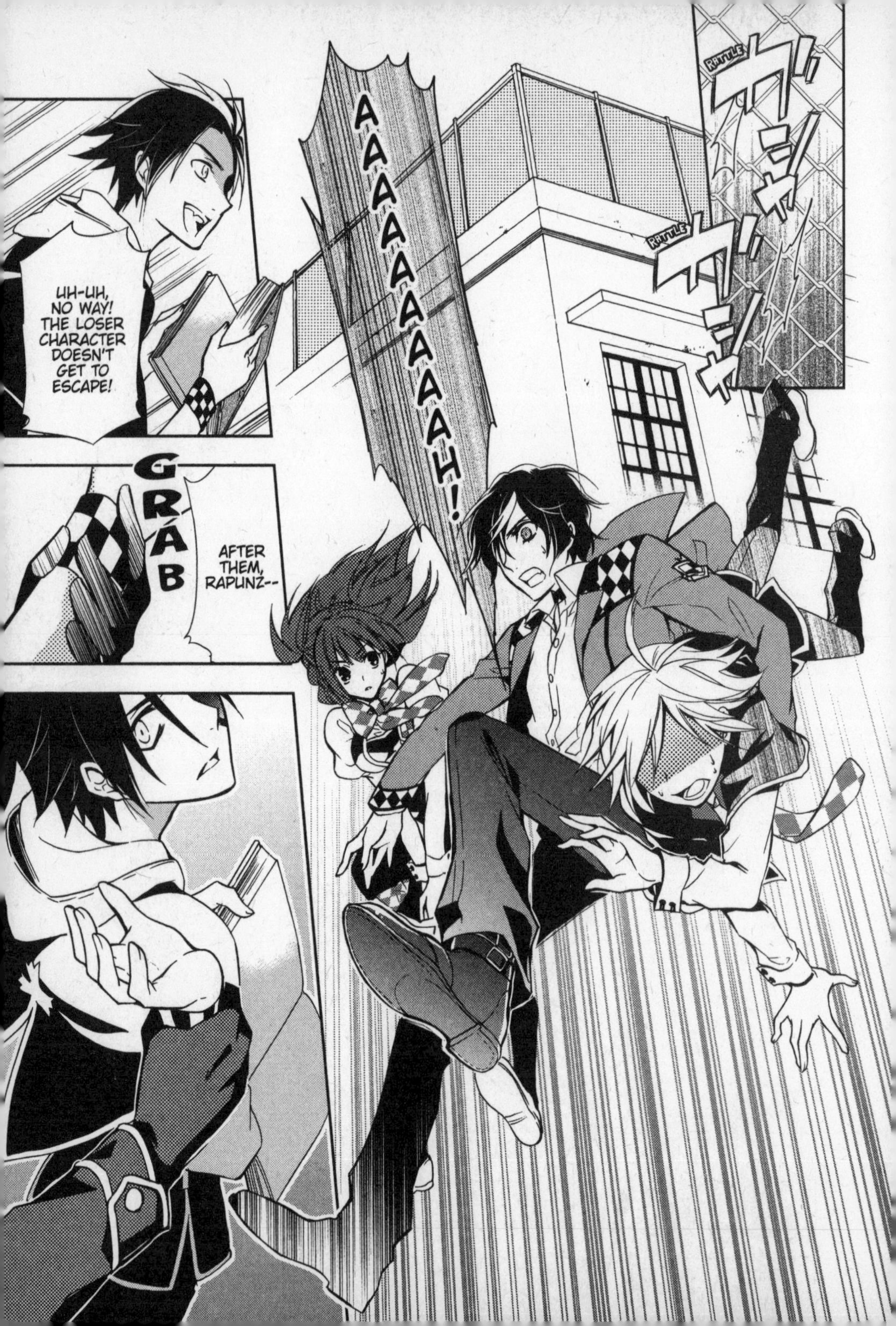
RATTLE
RATTLE
AAAAAAAAAH!
UH-UH, NO WAY! THE LOSER CHARACTER DOESN'T GET TO ESCAPE!
GRAB
AFTER THEM, RAPUNZ--

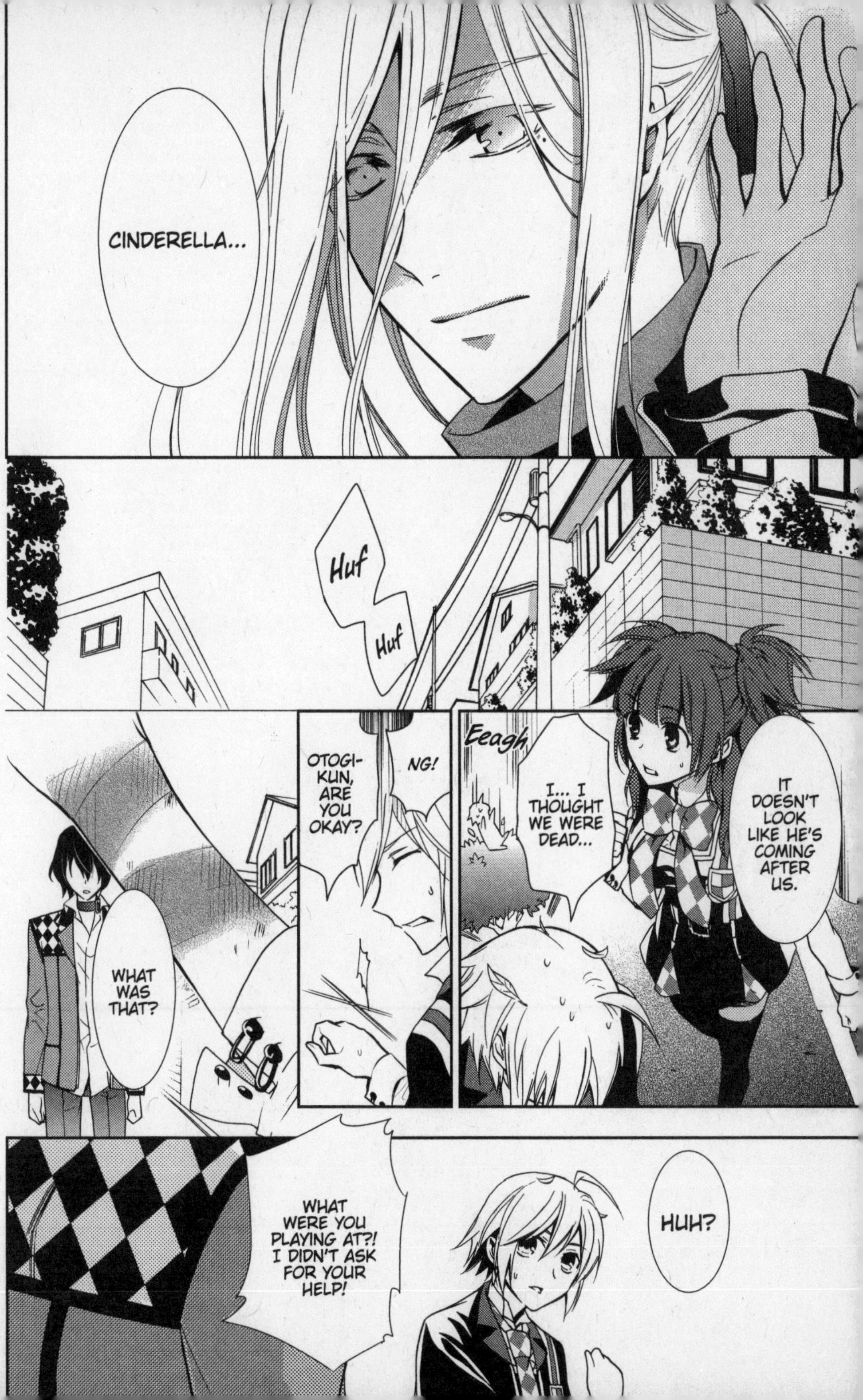
CINDERELLA...
Huf
Huf
IT DOESN'T LOOK LIKE HE'S COMING AFTER US.
Eeagh
I... I THOUGHT WE WERE DEAD...
NG!
OTOGI-KUN, ARE YOU OKAY?
WHAT WAS THAT?
HUH?
WHAT WERE YOU PLAYING AT?! I DIDN'T ASK FOR YOUR HELP!

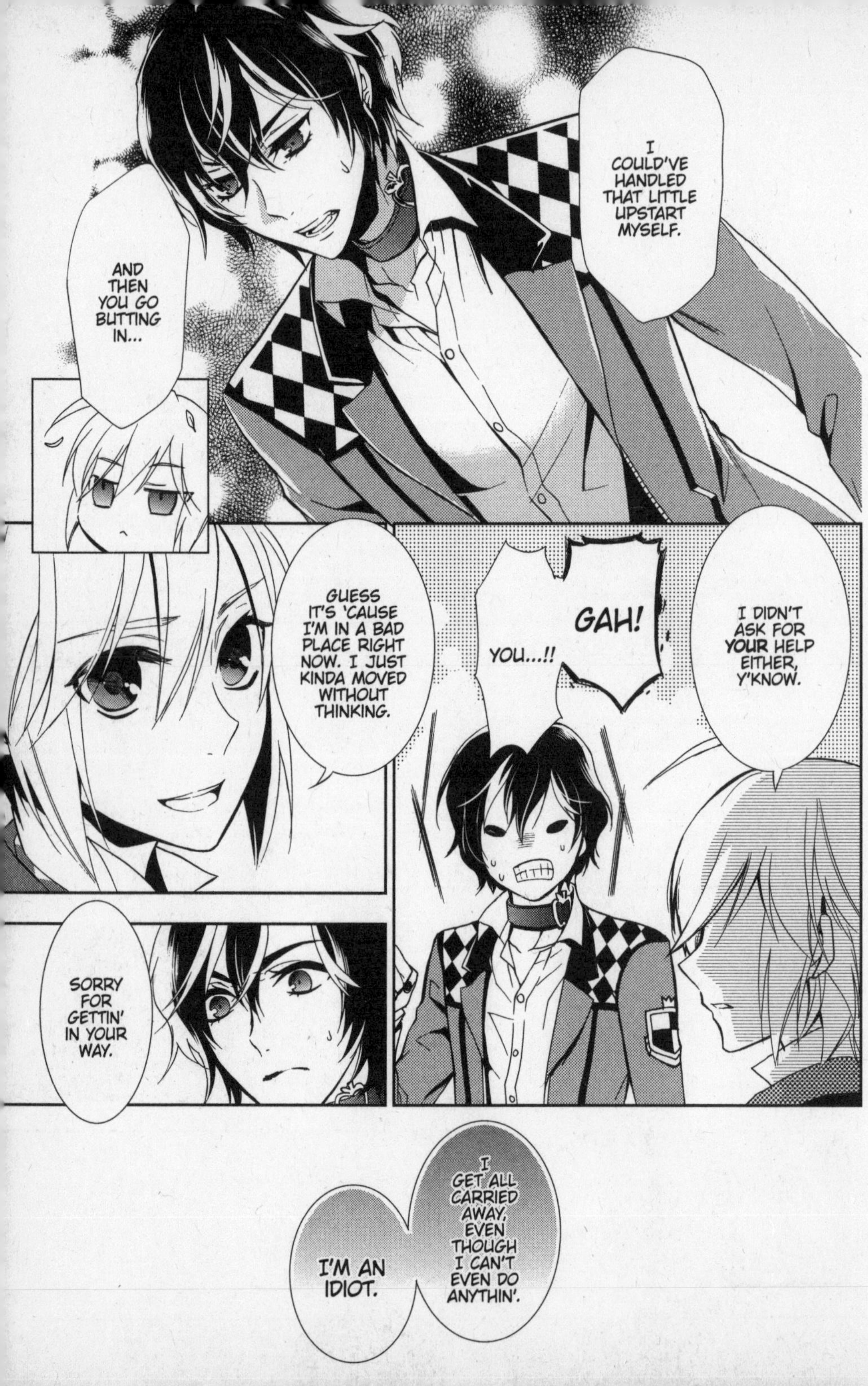
I COULD'VE HANDLED THAT LITTLE UPSTART MYSELF.
AND THEN YOU GO BUTTING IN...
I DIDN'T ASK FOR YOUR HELP EITHER, Y'KNOW.
GAH!
YOU...!!
GUESS IT'S 'CAUSE I'M IN A BAD PLACE RIGHT NOW. I JUST KINDA MOVED WITHOUT THINKING.
SORRY FOR GETTIN' IN YOUR WAY.
I GET ALL CARRIED AWAY, EVEN THOUGH I CAN'T EVEN DO ANYTHIN'.
I'M AN IDIOT.

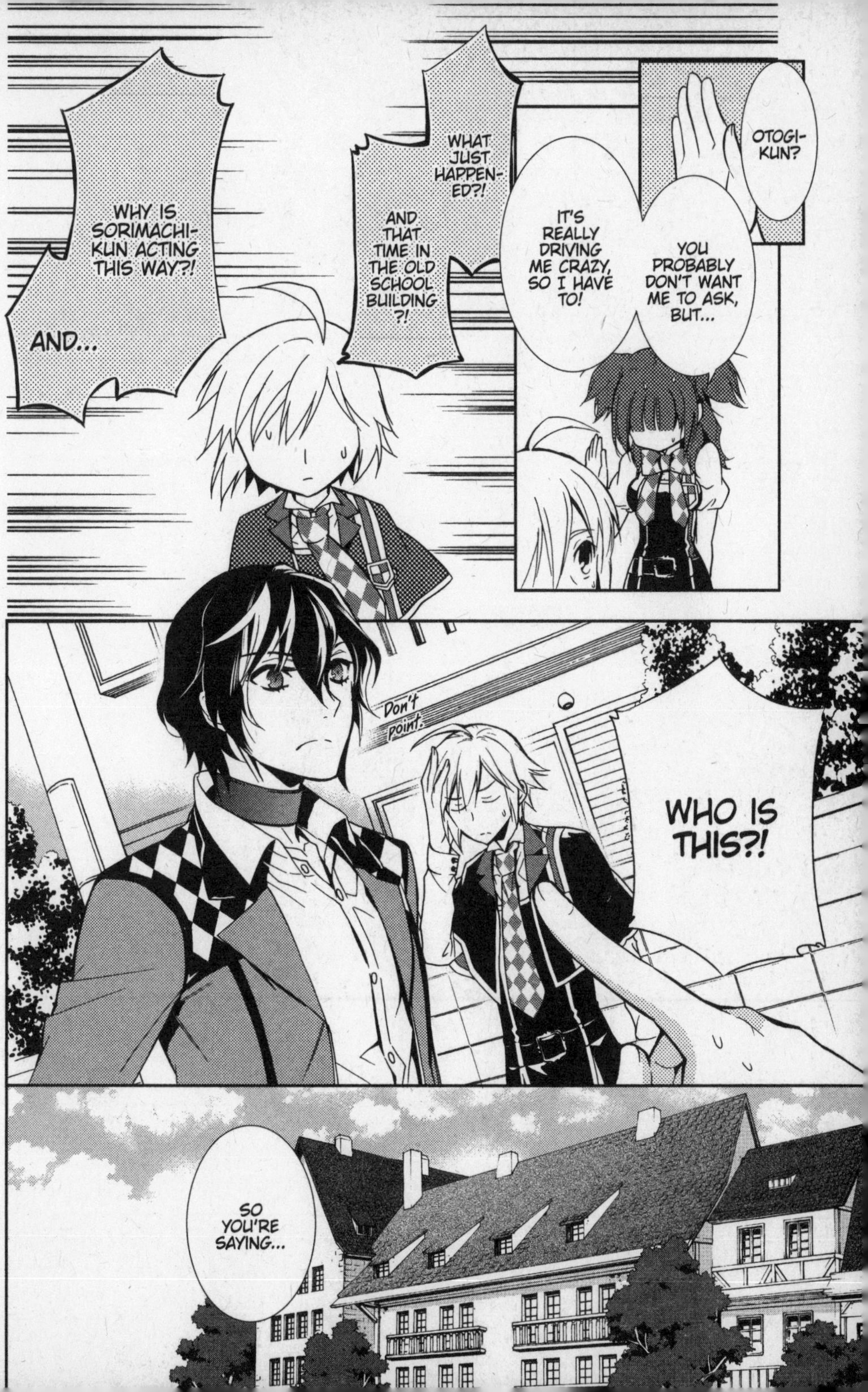
OTOGI-KUN?
YOU PROBABLY DON'T WANT ME TO ASK, BUT...
IT'S REALLY DRIVING ME CRAZY, SO I HAVE TO!
WHAT JUST HAPPENED?!
AND THAT TIME IN THE OLD SCHOOL BUILDING?!
WHY IS SORIMACHI-KUN ACTING THIS WAY?!
AND...
WHO IS THIS?!
Don't point.
SO YOU'RE SAYING...

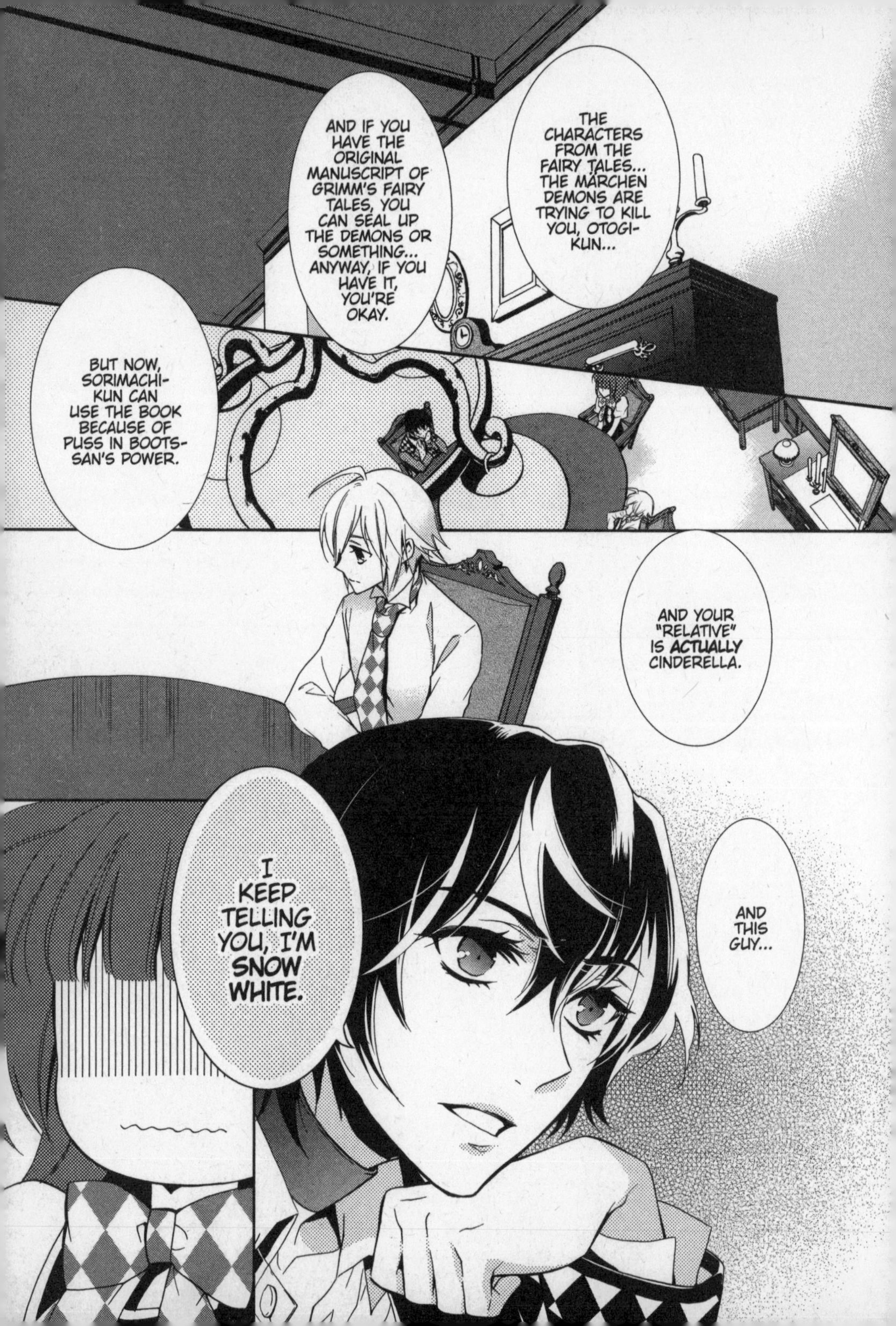
THE CHARACTERS FROM THE FAIRY TALES... THE MÄRCHEN DEMONS ARE TRYING TO KILL YOU, OTOGI-KUN...
AND IF YOU HAVE THE ORIGINAL MANUSCRIPT OF GRIMM'S FAIRY TALES, YOU CAN SEAL UP THE DEMONS OR SOMETHING... ANYWAY, IF YOU HAVE IT, YOU'RE OKAY.
BUT NOW, SORIMACHI-KUN CAN USE THE BOOK BECAUSE OF PUSS IN BOOTS-SAN'S POWER.
AND YOUR "RELATIVE" IS **ACTUALLY** CINDERELLA.
AND THIS GUY...
I KEEP TELLING YOU, I'M SNOW WHITE.

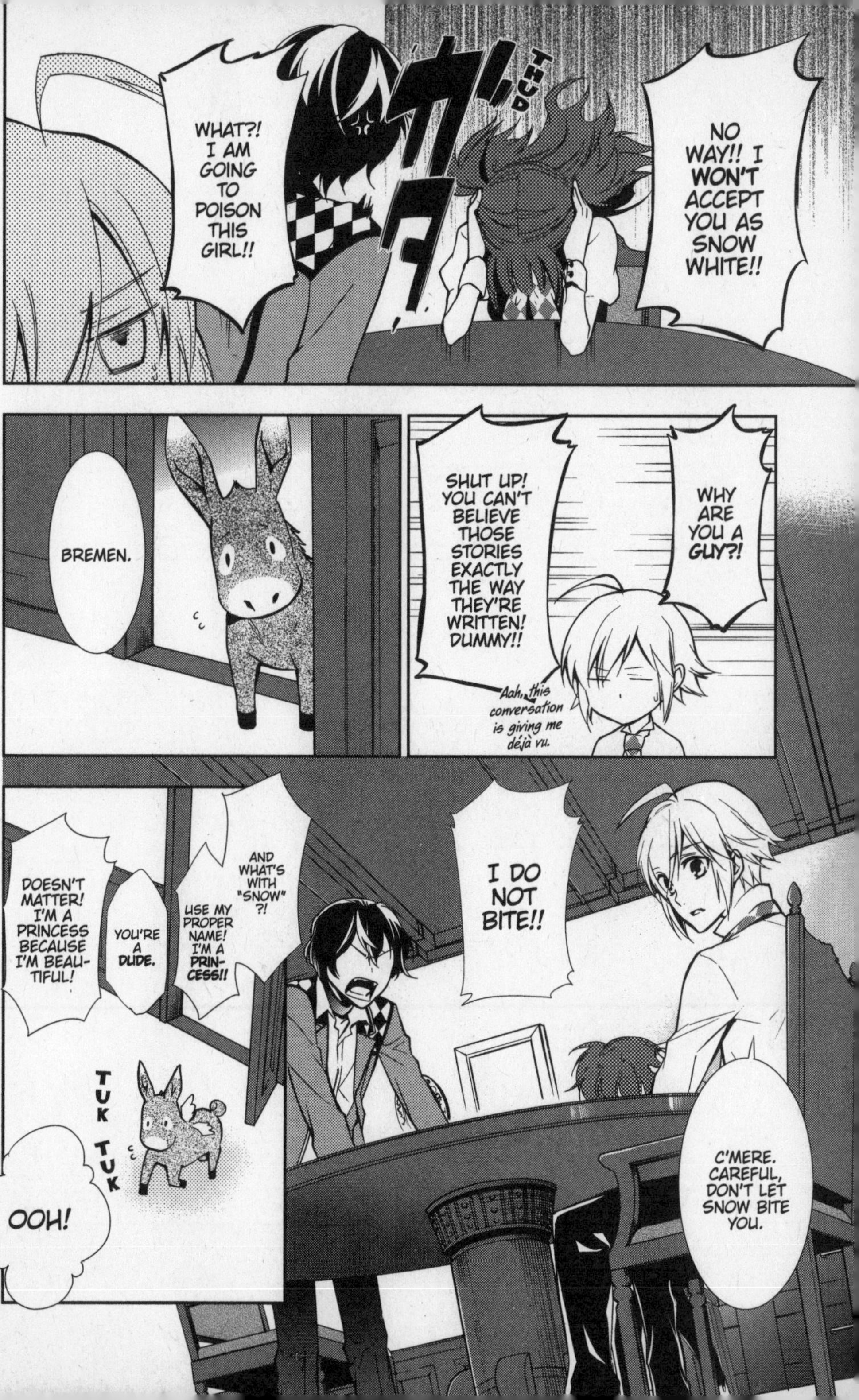
NO WAY!! I WON'T ACCEPT YOU AS SNOW WHITE!!
THUD
WHAT?! I AM GOING TO POISON THIS GIRL!!
WHY ARE YOU A GUY?!
SHUT UP! YOU CAN'T BELIEVE THOSE STORIES EXACTLY THE WAY THEY'RE WRITTEN! DUMMY!!
Aah, this conversation is giving me déjà vu.
BREMEN.
I DO NOT BITE!!
AND WHAT'S WITH "SNOW"?!
USE MY PROPER NAME! I'M A PRINCESS!!
YOU'RE A DUDE.
DOESN'T MATTER! I'M A PRINCESS BECAUSE I'M BEAUTIFUL!
C'MERE. CAREFUL, DON'T LET SNOW BITE YOU.
TUK TUK
OOH!

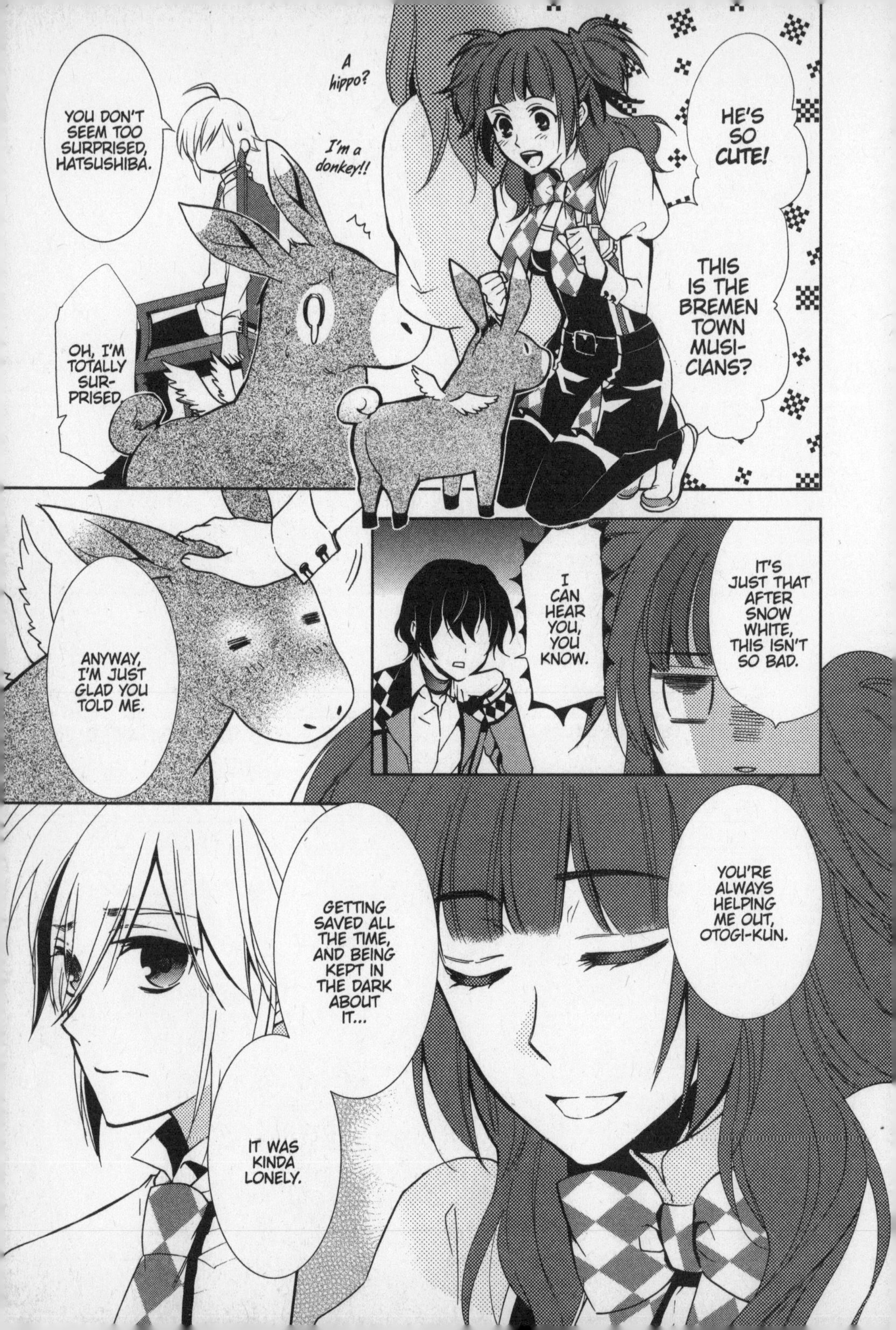
HE'S SO CUTE!
THIS IS THE BREMEN TOWN MUSICIANS?
A hippo?
I'm a donkey!!
YOU DON'T SEEM TOO SURPRISED, HATSUSHIBA.
OH, I'M TOTALLY SURPRISED
IT'S JUST THAT AFTER SNOW WHITE, THIS ISN'T SO BAD.
I CAN HEAR YOU, YOU KNOW.
ANYWAY, I'M JUST GLAD YOU TOLD ME.
YOU'RE ALWAYS HELPING ME OUT, OTOGI-KUN.
GETTING SAVED ALL THE TIME, AND BEING KEPT IN THE DARK ABOUT IT...
IT WAS KINDA LONELY.

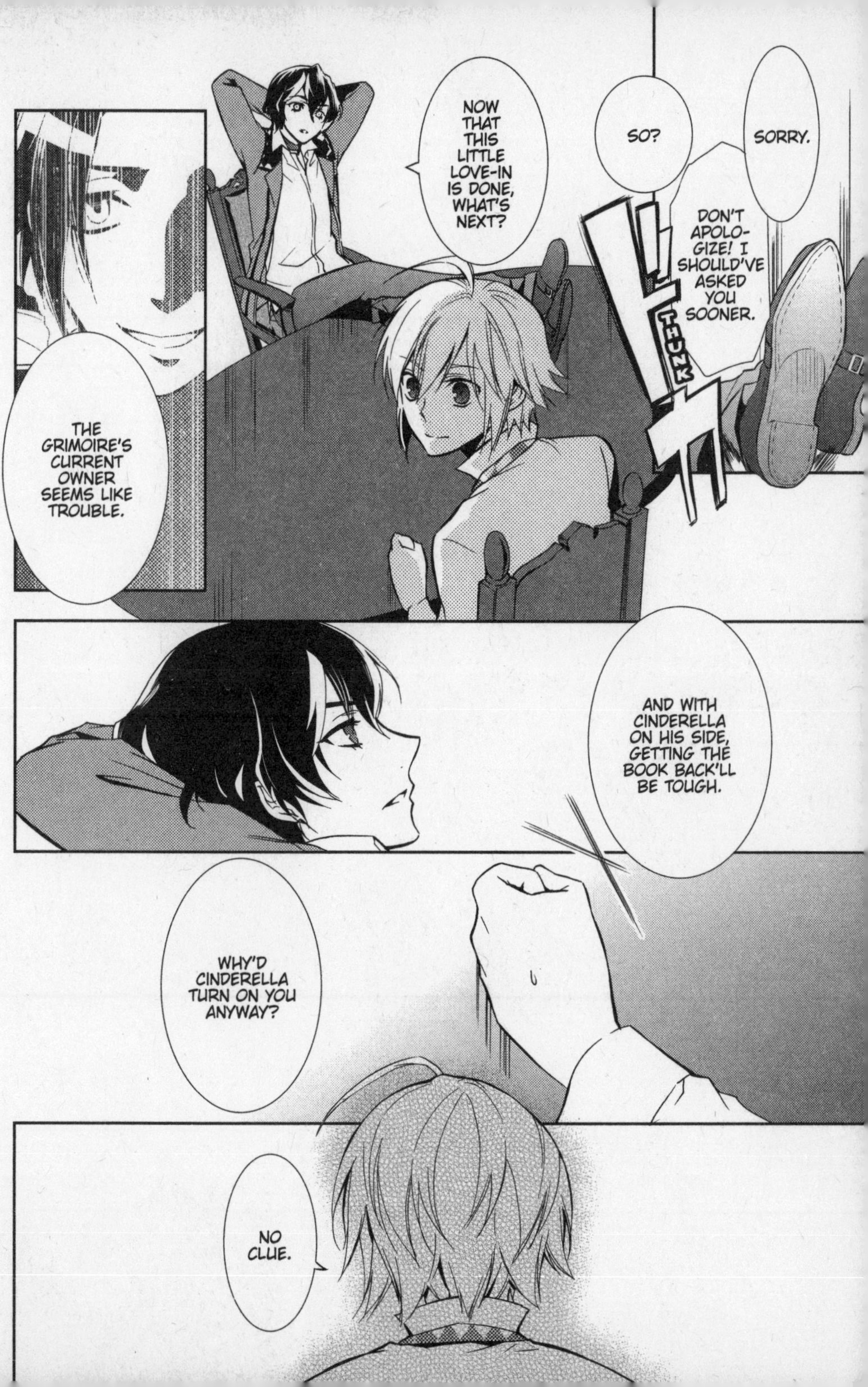
SORRY.
SO?
DON'T APOLOGIZE! I SHOULD'VE ASKED YOU SOONER.
THUNK
NOW THAT THIS LITTLE LOVE-IN IS DONE, WHAT'S NEXT?
THE GRIMOIRE'S CURRENT OWNER SEEMS LIKE TROUBLE.
AND WITH CINDERELLA ON HIS SIDE, GETTING THE BOOK BACK'LL BE TOUGH.
WHY'D CINDERELLA TURN ON YOU ANYWAY?
NO CLUE.

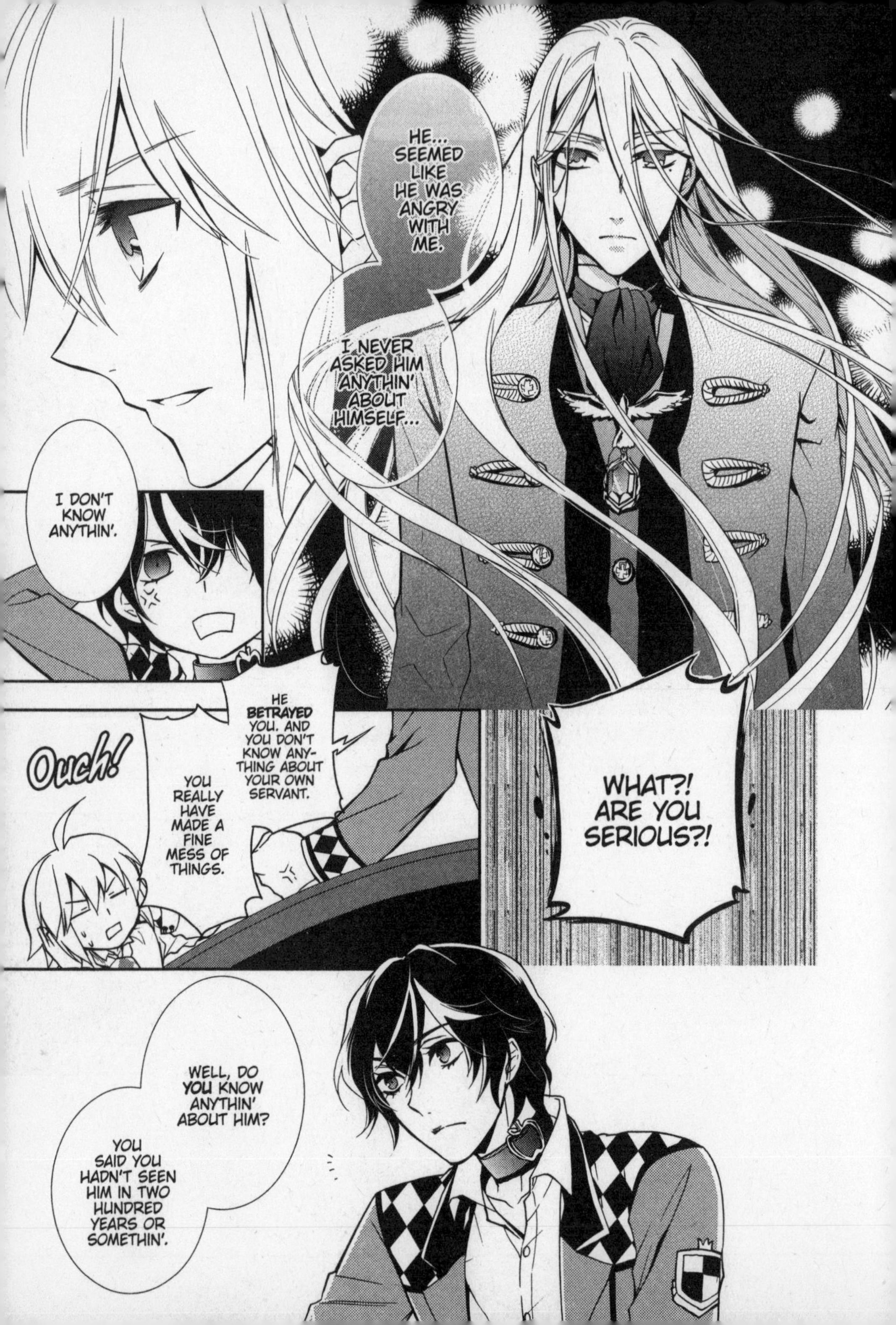
HE... SEEMED LIKE HE WAS ANGRY WITH ME.
I NEVER ASKED HIM ANYTHIN' ABOUT HIMSELF...
I DON'T KNOW ANYTHIN'.
WHAT?! ARE YOU SERIOUS?!
HE **BETRAYED** YOU. AND YOU DON'T KNOW ANYTHING ABOUT YOUR OWN SERVANT.
Ouch!
YOU REALLY HAVE MADE A FINE MESS OF THINGS.
WELL, DO **YOU** KNOW ANYTHIN' ABOUT HIM?
YOU SAID YOU HADN'T SEEN HIM IN TWO HUNDRED YEARS OR SOMETHIN'.

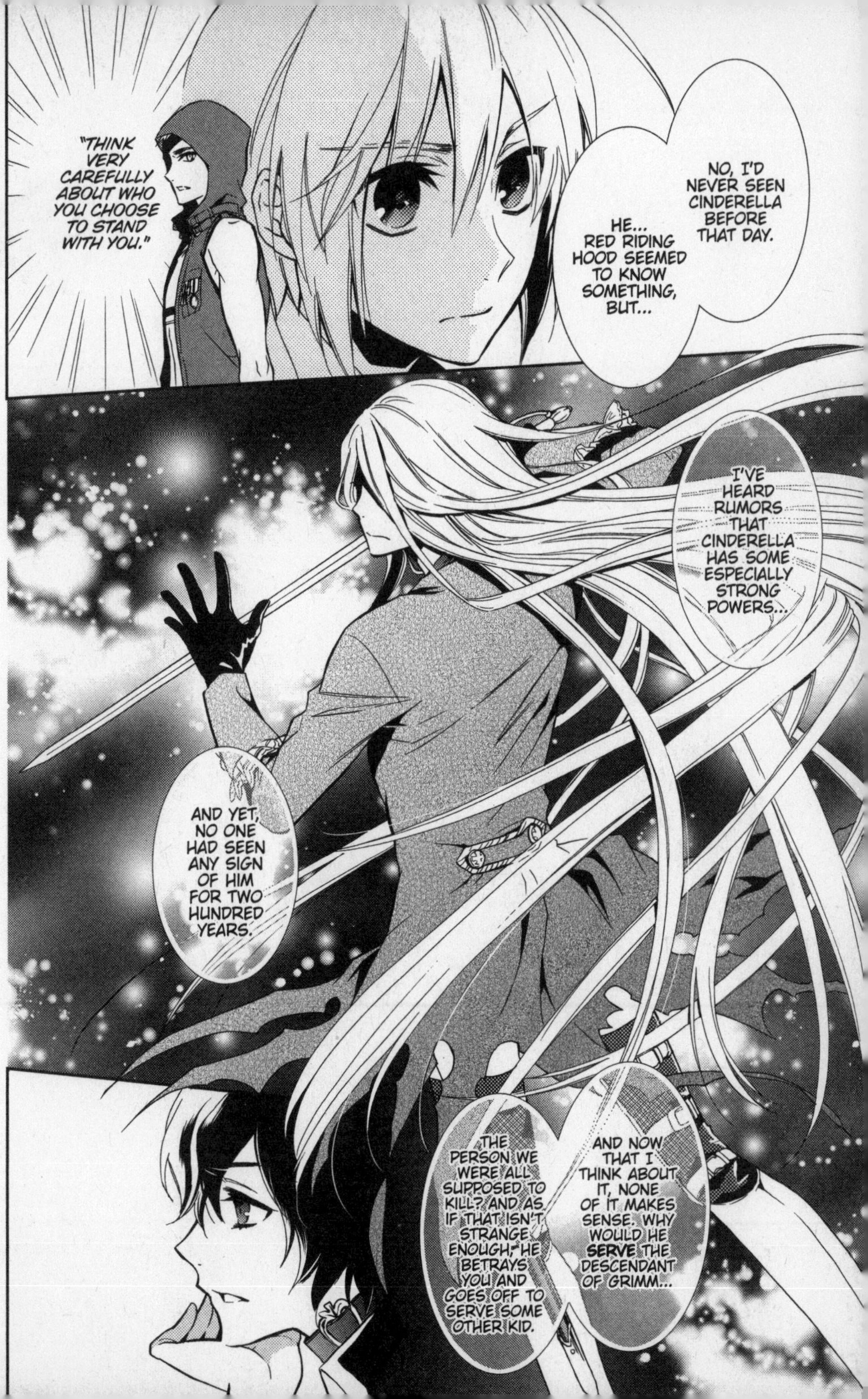
NO, I'D NEVER SEEN CINDERELLA BEFORE THAT DAY.
HE... RED RIDING HOOD SEEMED TO KNOW SOMETHING, BUT...
"THINK VERY CAREFULLY ABOUT WHO YOU CHOOSE TO STAND WITH YOU."
I'VE HEARD RUMORS THAT CINDERELLA HAS SOME ESPECIALLY STRONG POWERS...
AND YET, NO ONE HAD SEEN ANY SIGN OF HIM FOR TWO HUNDRED YEARS.
AND NOW THAT I THINK ABOUT IT, NONE OF IT MAKES SENSE. WHY WOULD HE SERVE THE DESCENDANT OF GRIMM...
THE PERSON WE WERE ALL SUPPOSED TO KILL? AND AS IF THAT ISN'T STRANGE ENOUGH, HE BETRAYS YOU AND GOES OFF TO SERVE SOME OTHER KID.

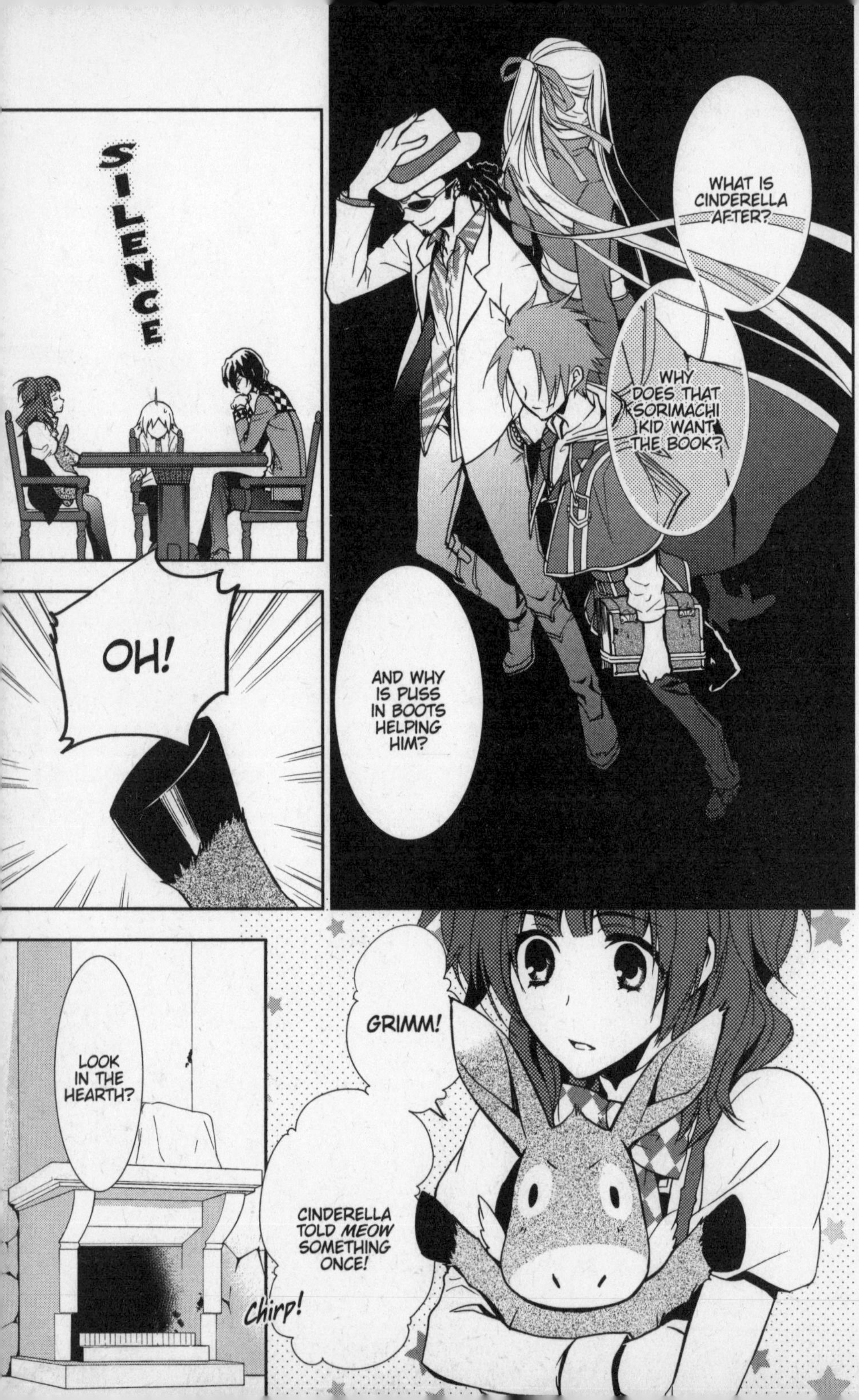
WHAT IS CINDERELLA AFTER?
WHY DOES THAT SORIMACHI KID WANT THE BOOK?
AND WHY IS PUSS IN BOOTS HELPING HIM?
SILENCE
OH!
GRIMM!
CINDERELLA TOLD *MEOW* SOMETHING ONCE!
Chirp!
LOOK IN THE HEARTH?

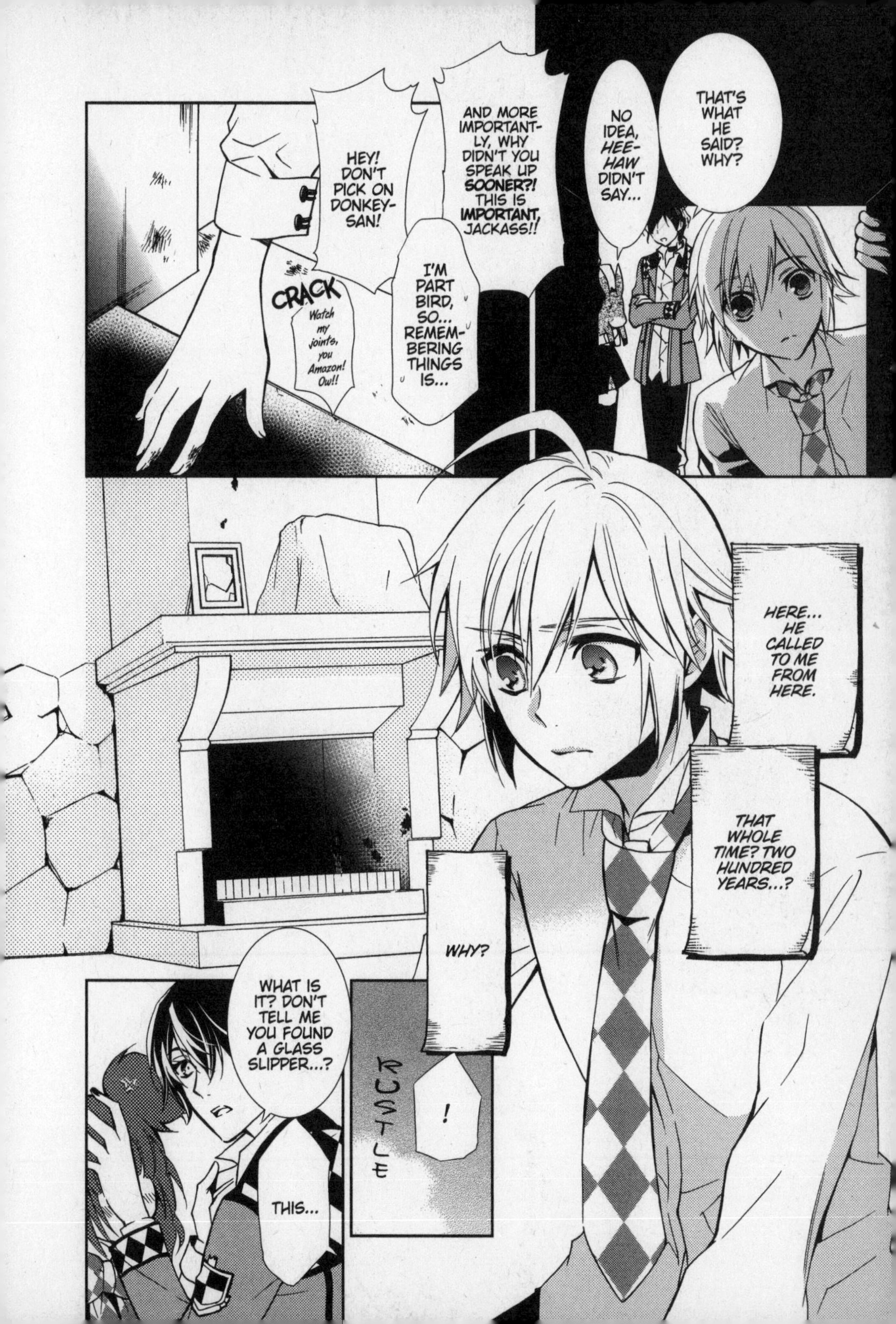
THAT'S WHAT HE SAID? WHY?
NO IDEA, HEE-HAW DIDN'T SAY...
AND MORE IMPORTANTLY, WHY DIDN'T YOU SPEAK UP SOONER?! THIS IS IMPORTANT, JACKASS!!
HEY! DON'T PICK ON DONKEY-SAN!
I'M PART BIRD, SO... REMEMBERING THINGS IS...
CRACK
Watch my joints, you Amazon! Ow!!
HERE... HE CALLED TO ME FROM HERE.
THAT WHOLE TIME? TWO HUNDRED YEARS...?
WHY?
!
RUSTLE
WHAT IS IT? DON'T TELL ME YOU FOUND A GLASS SLIPPER...?
THIS...

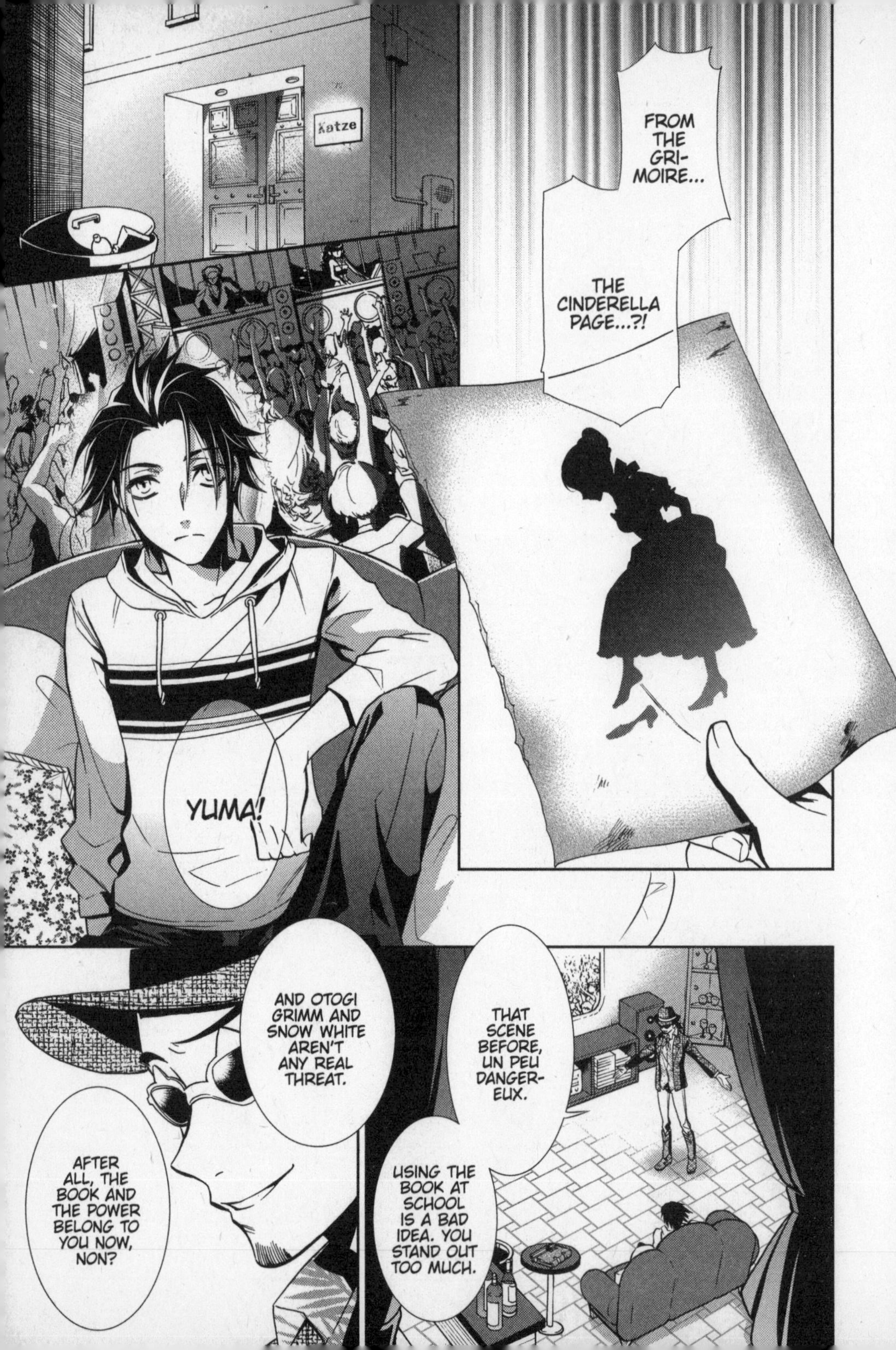
FROM THE GRI-MOIRE...
THE CINDERELLA PAGE...?!
Katze
YUMA!
THAT SCENE BEFORE, UN PEU DANGER-EUX.
USING THE BOOK AT SCHOOL IS A BAD IDEA. YOU STAND OUT TOO MUCH.
AND OTOGI GRIMM AND SNOW WHITE AREN'T ANY REAL THREAT.
AFTER ALL, THE BOOK AND THE POWER BELONG TO YOU NOW, NON?

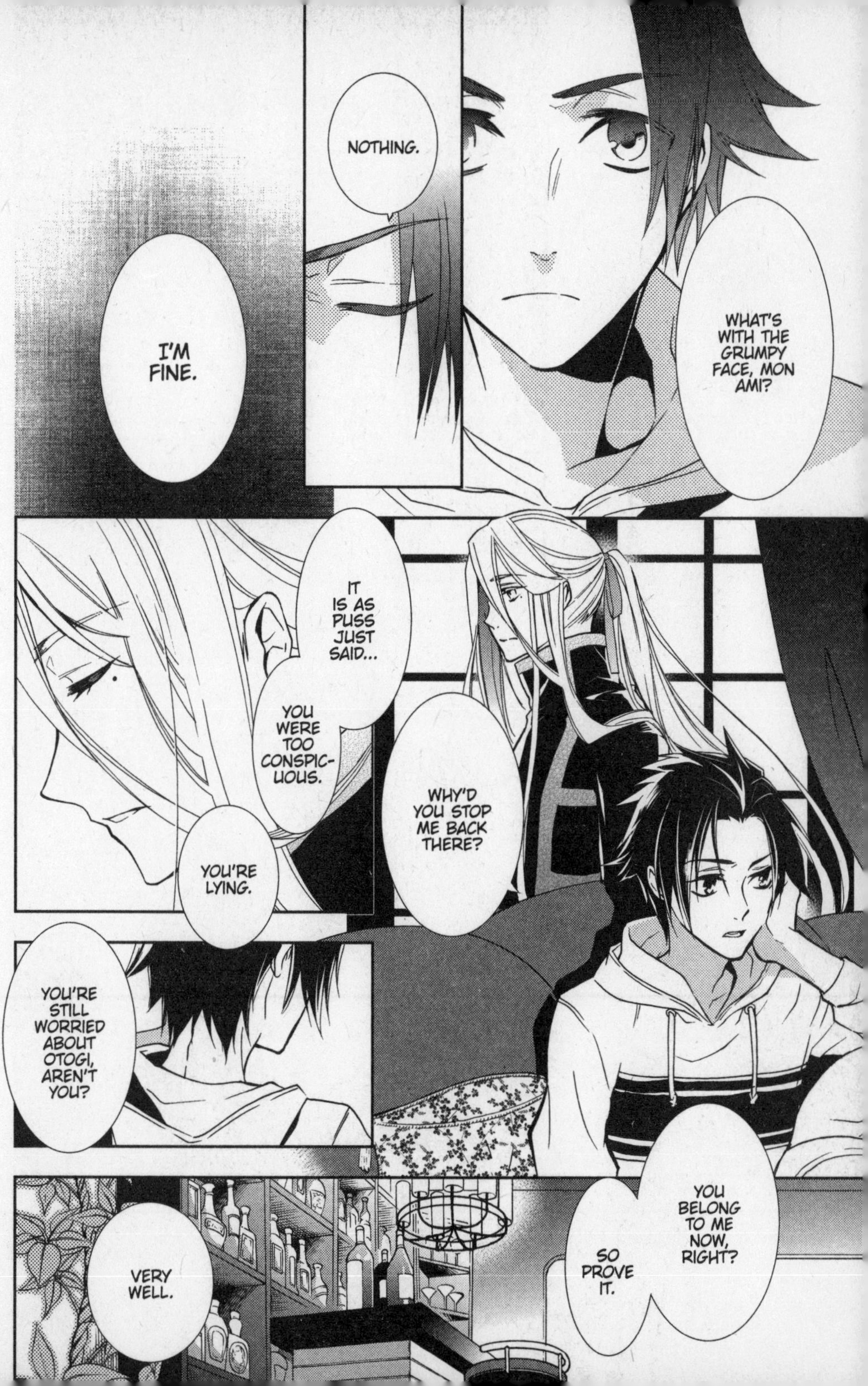
WHAT'S WITH THE GRUMPY FACE, MON AMI?
NOTHING.
I'M FINE.
WHY'D YOU STOP ME BACK THERE?
IT IS AS PUSS JUST SAID...
YOU WERE TOO CONSPICUOUS.
YOU'RE LYING.
YOU'RE STILL WORRIED ABOUT OTOGI, AREN'T YOU?
YOU BELONG TO ME NOW, RIGHT?
SO PROVE IT.
VERY WELL.

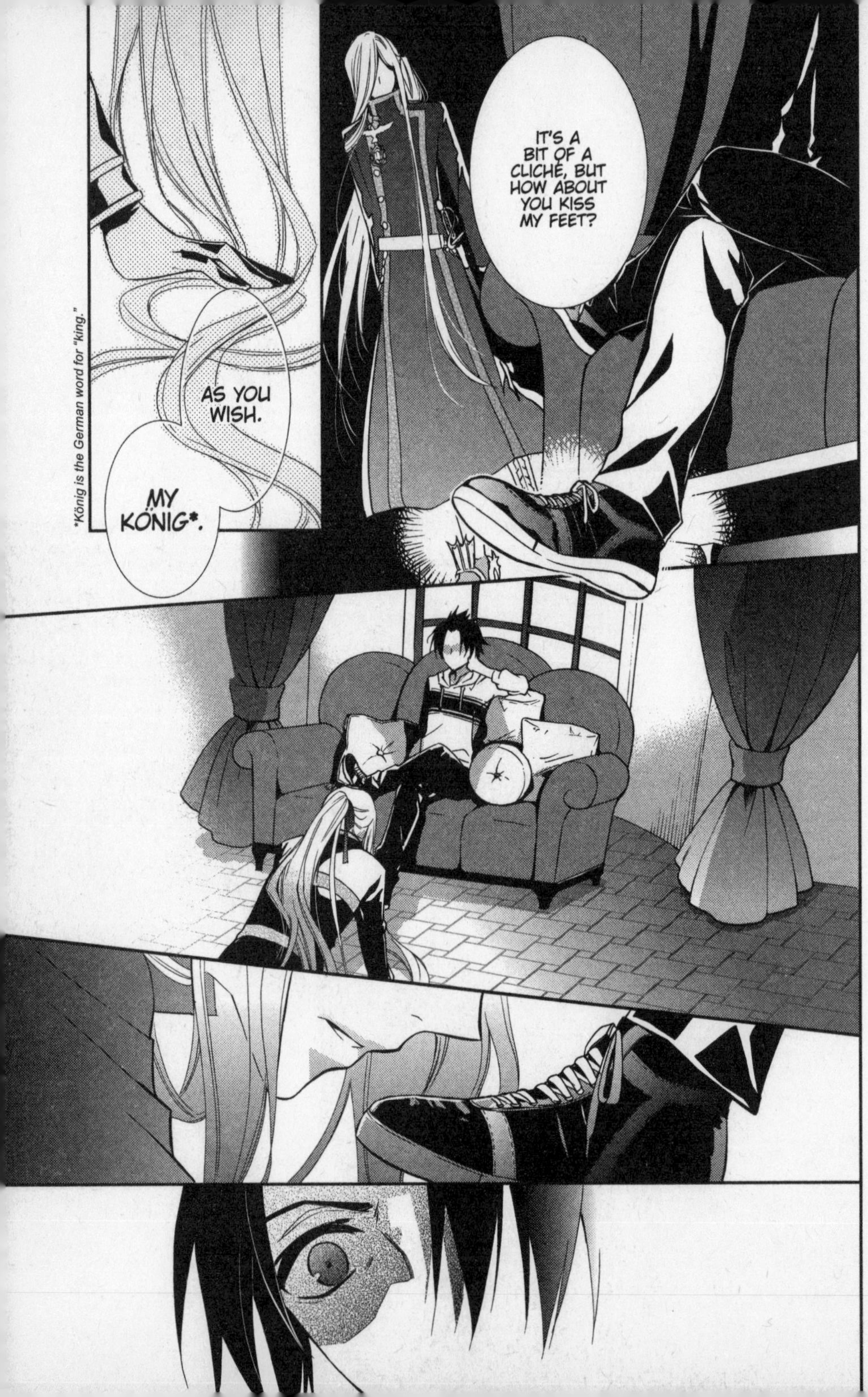
IT'S A BIT OF A CLICHÉ, BUT HOW ABOUT YOU KISS MY FEET?
AS YOU WISH.
MY KÖNIG*.

*König is the German word for "king."

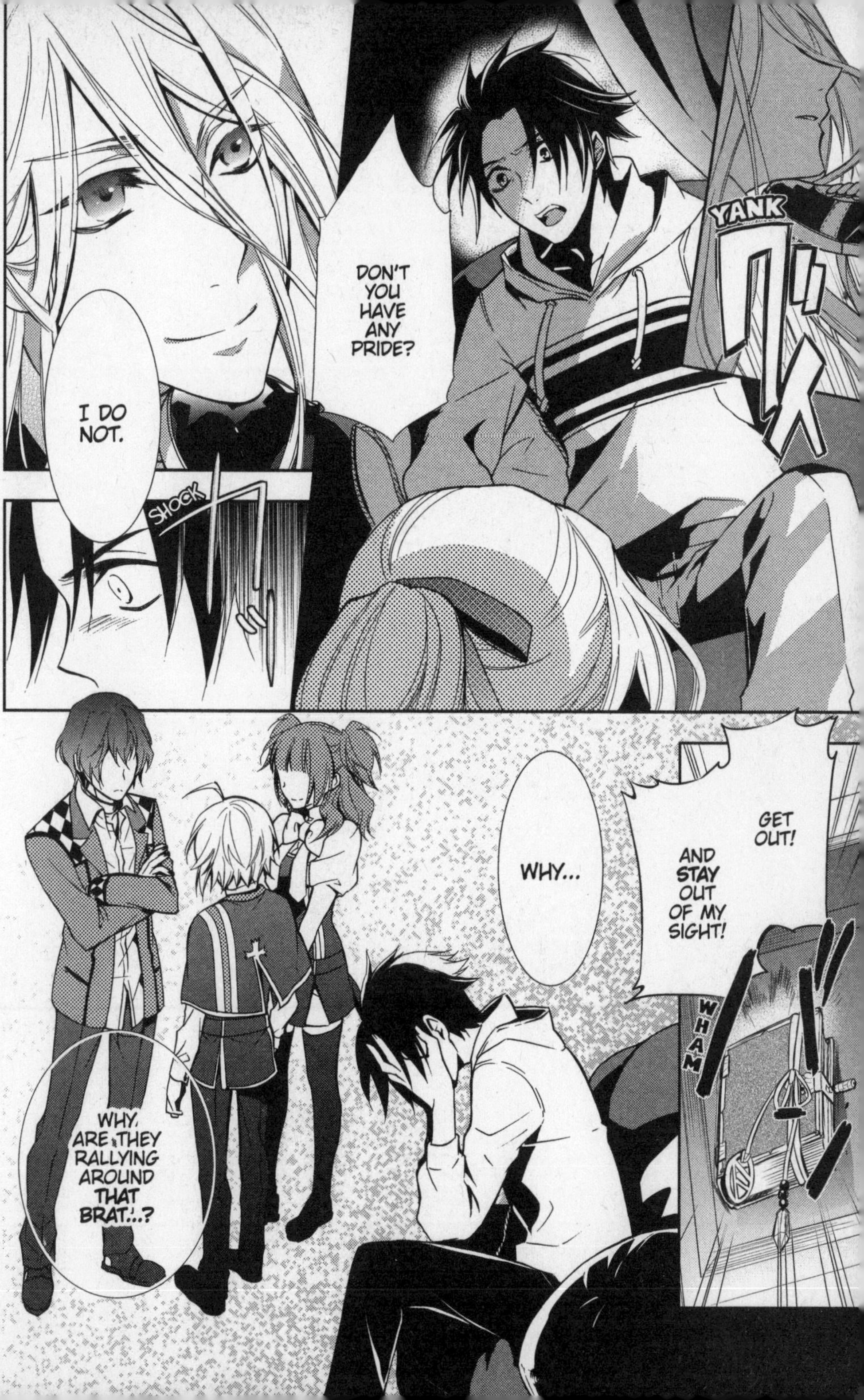
YANK
DON'T YOU HAVE ANY PRIDE?
I DO NOT.
SHOCK
GET OUT!
AND STAY OUT OF MY SIGHT!
WHAM
WHY...
WHY ARE THEY RALLYING AROUND THAT BRAT...?

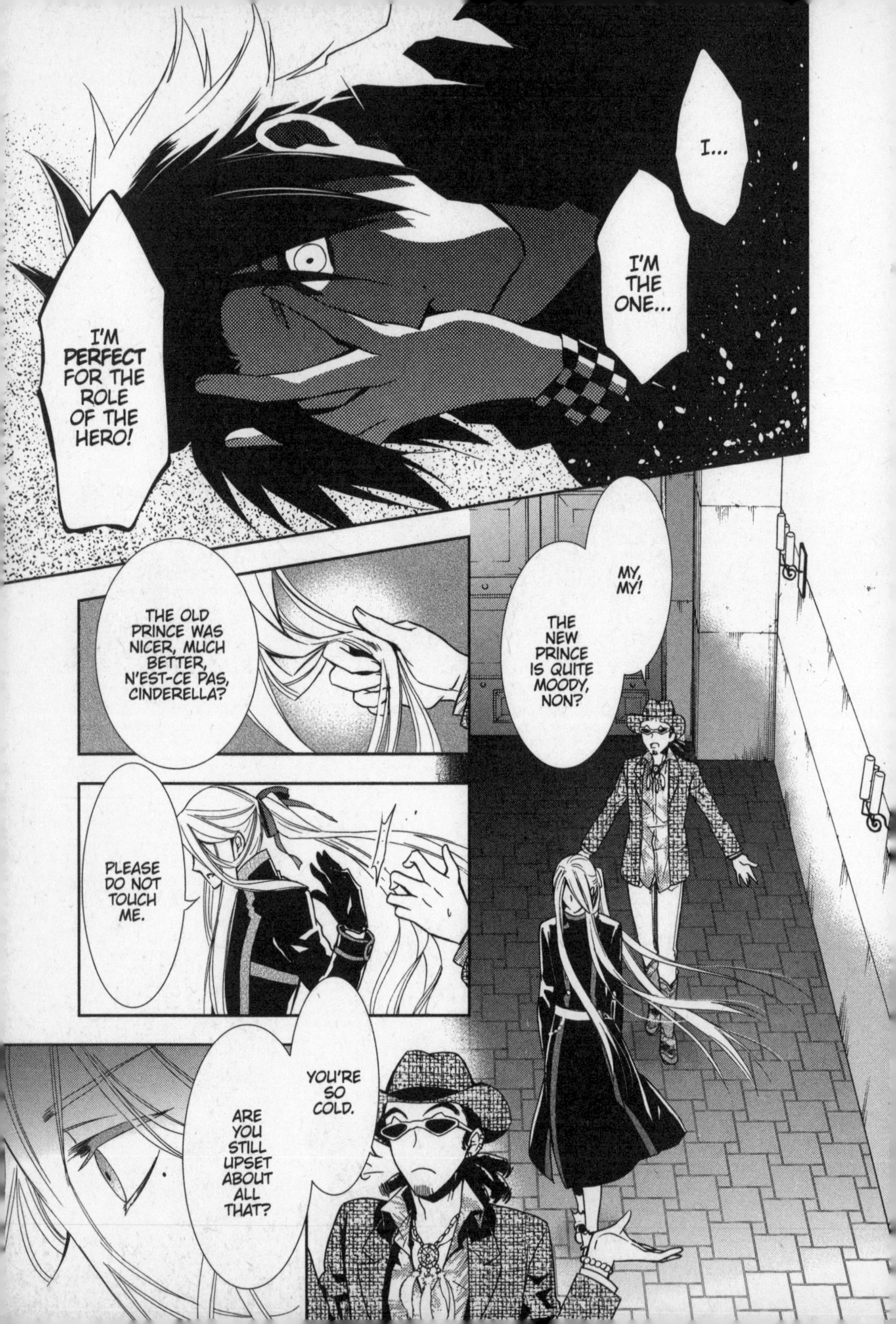
I...
I'M THE ONE...
I'M PERFECT FOR THE ROLE OF THE HERO!
MY, MY!
THE NEW PRINCE IS QUITE MOODY, NON?
THE OLD PRINCE WAS NICER, MUCH BETTER, N'EST-CE PAS, CINDERELLA?
PLEASE DO NOT TOUCH ME.
YOU'RE SO COLD.
ARE YOU STILL UPSET ABOUT ALL THAT?

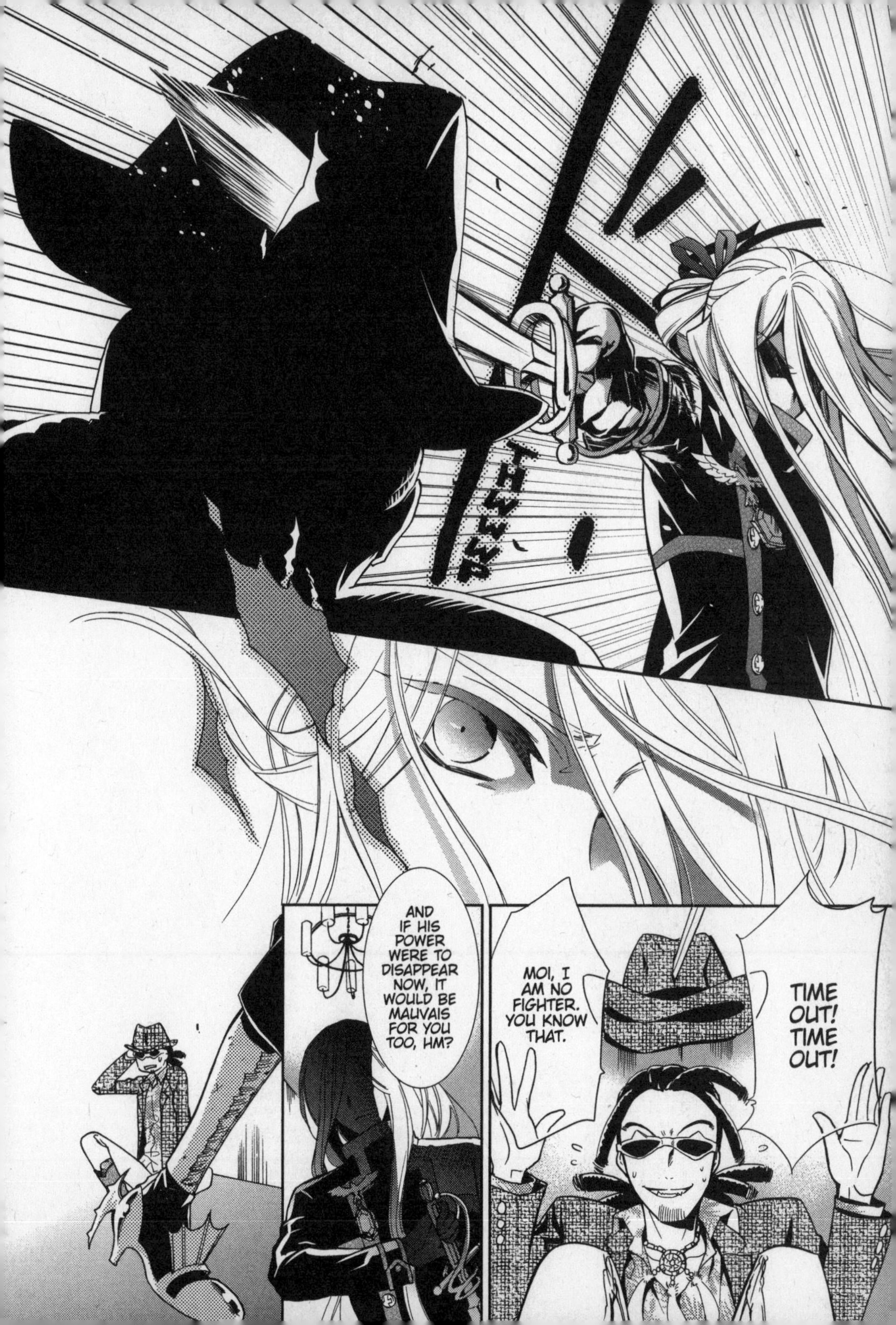
THWWWP
TIME OUT! TIME OUT!
MOI, I AM NO FIGHTER. YOU KNOW THAT.
AND IF HIS POWER WERE TO DISAPPEAR NOW, IT WOULD BE MAUVAIS FOR YOU TOO, HM?

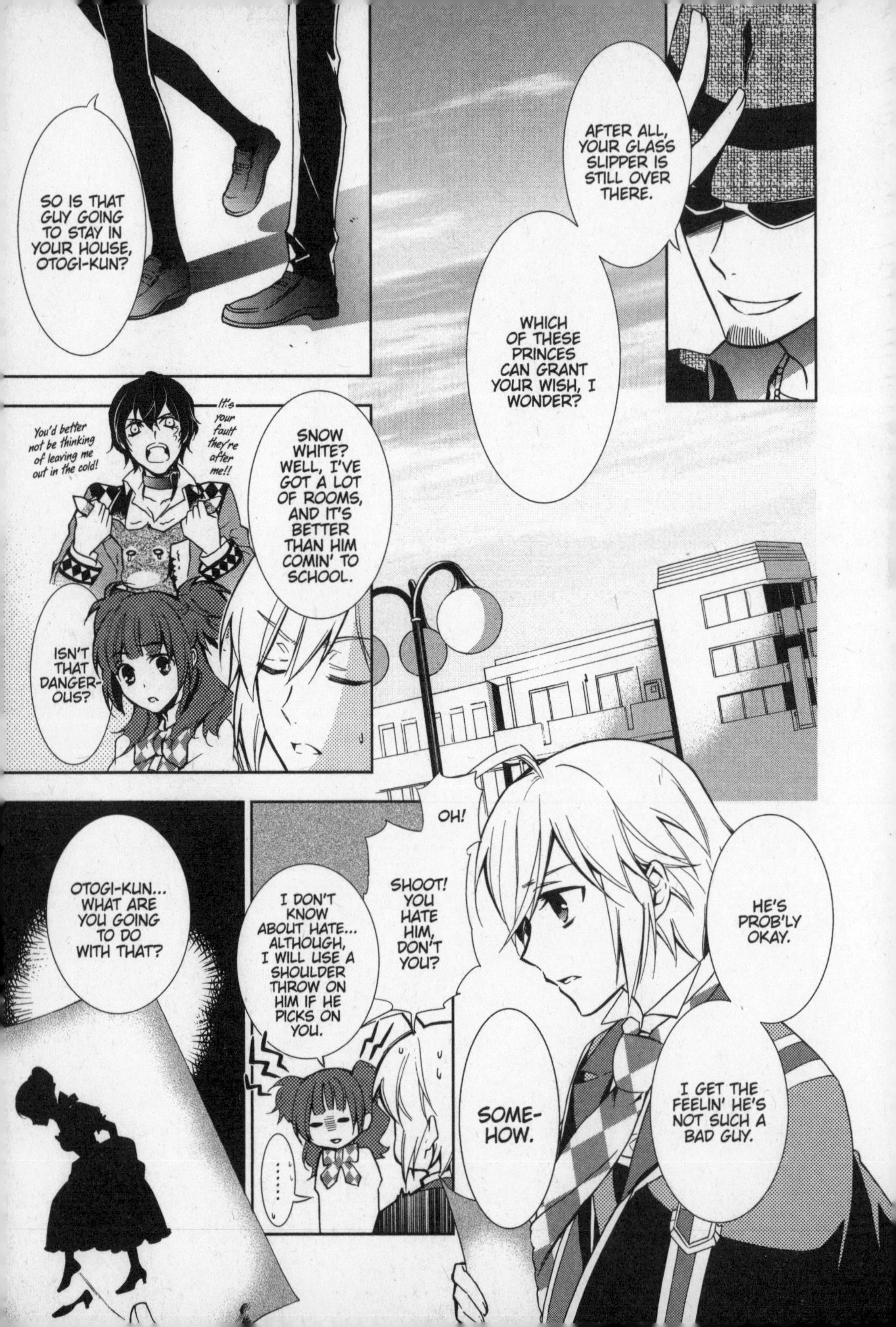
AFTER ALL, YOUR GLASS SLIPPER IS STILL OVER THERE.
WHICH OF THESE PRINCES CAN GRANT YOUR WISH, I WONDER?
SO IS THAT GUY GOING TO STAY IN YOUR HOUSE, OTOGI-KUN?
SNOW WHITE? WELL, I'VE GOT A LOT OF ROOMS, AND IT'S BETTER THAN HIM COMIN' TO SCHOOL.
It's your fault they're after me!!
You'd better not be thinking of leaving me out in the cold!
ISN'T THAT DANGER-OUS?
OH!
HE'S PROB'LY OKAY.
I GET THE FEELIN' HE'S NOT SUCH A BAD GUY.
SOME-HOW.
SHOOT! YOU HATE HIM, DON'T YOU?
I DON'T KNOW ABOUT HATE... ALTHOUGH, I WILL USE A SHOULDER THROW ON HIM IF HE PICKS ON YOU.
......
OTOGI-KUN... WHAT ARE YOU GOING TO DO WITH THAT?

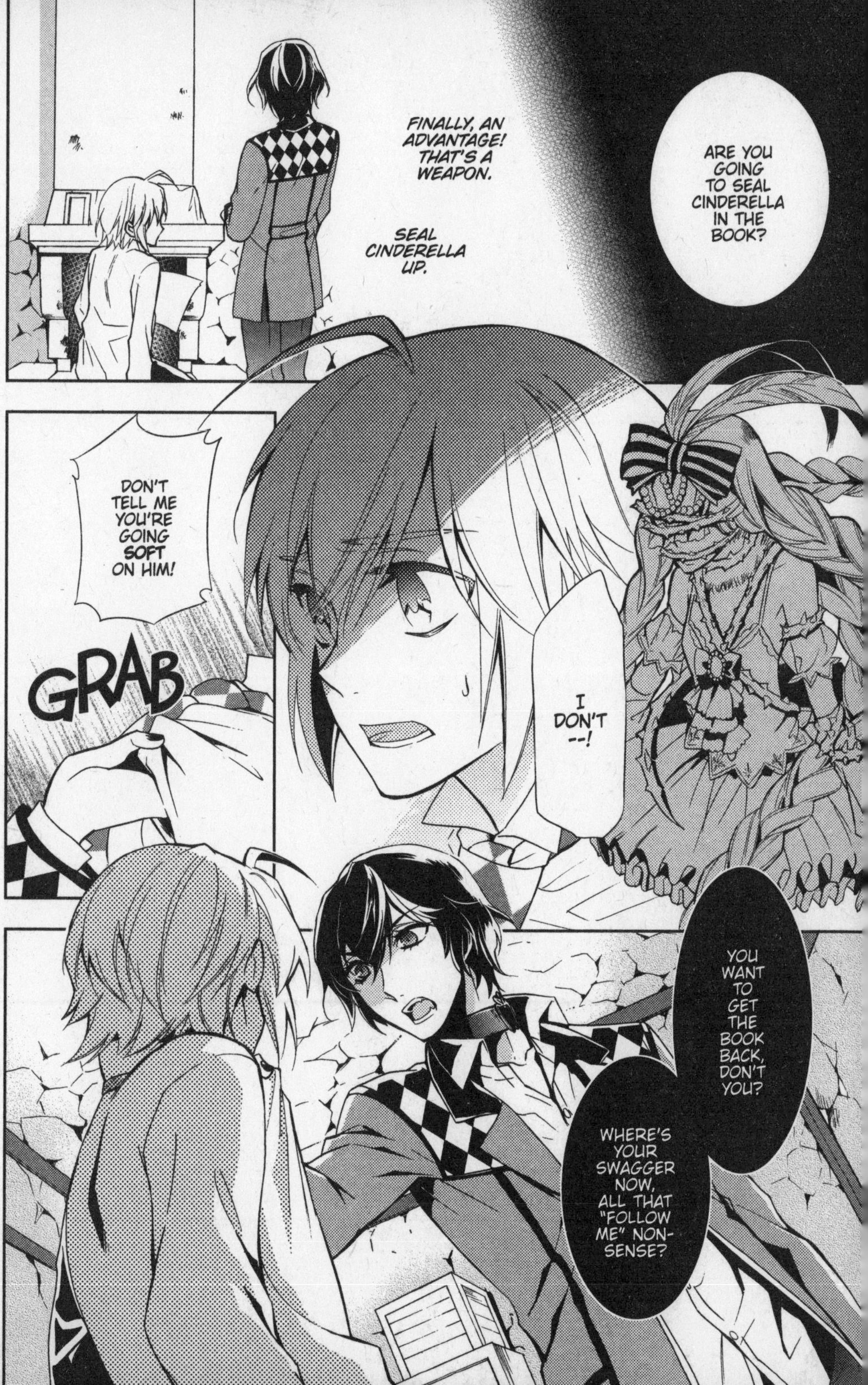
ARE YOU GOING TO SEAL CINDERELLA IN THE BOOK?
FINALLY, AN ADVANTAGE! THAT'S A WEAPON.
SEAL CINDERELLA UP.
I DON'T --!
DON'T TELL ME YOU'RE GOING SOFT ON HIM!
GRAB
YOU WANT TO GET THE BOOK BACK, DON'T YOU?
WHERE'S YOUR SWAGGER NOW, ALL THAT "FOLLOW ME" NON-SENSE?

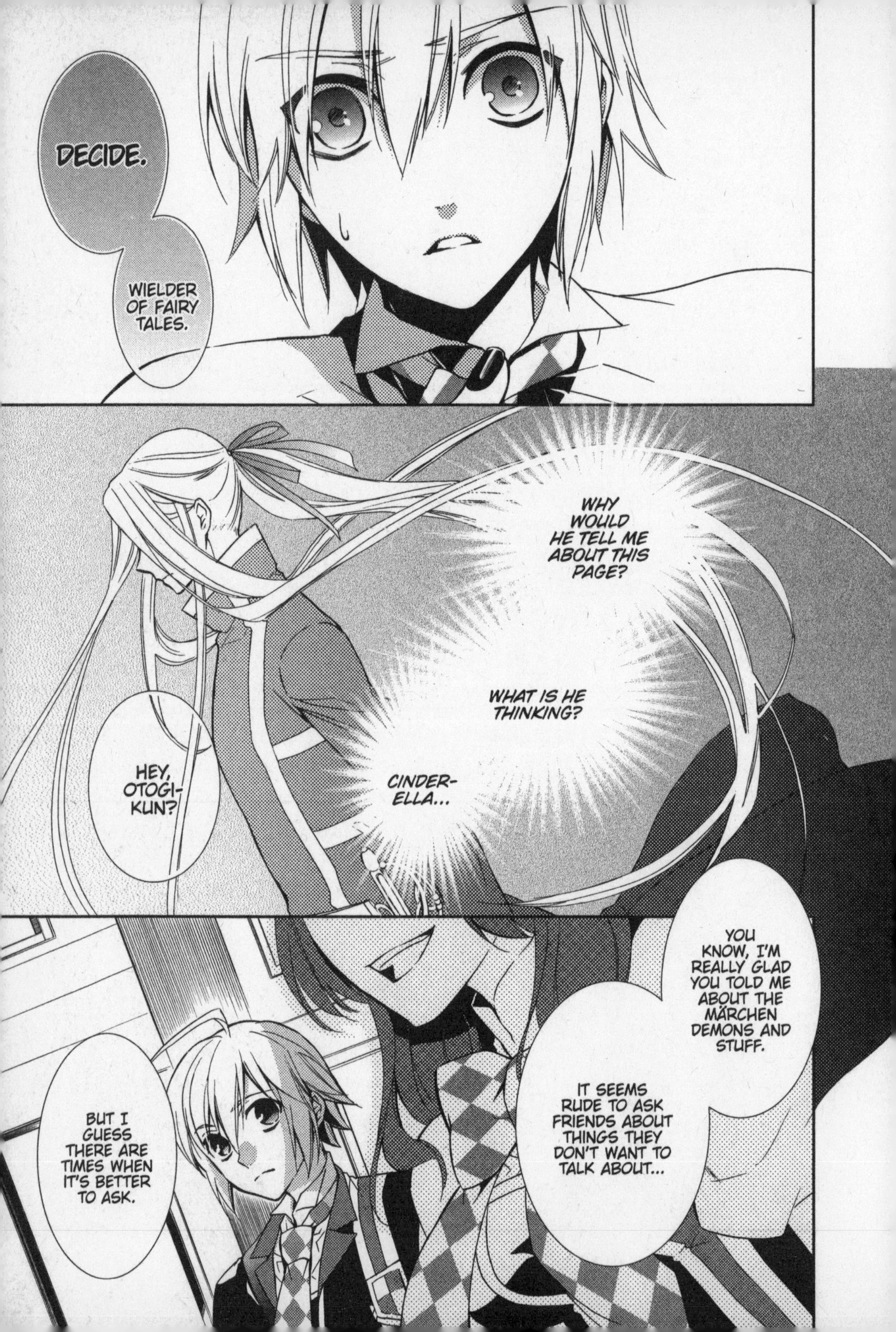
DECIDE.
WIELDER OF FAIRY TALES.
WHY WOULD HE TELL ME ABOUT THIS PAGE?
WHAT IS HE THINKING?
CINDER-ELLA...
HEY, OTOGI-KUN?
YOU KNOW, I'M REALLY GLAD YOU TOLD ME ABOUT THE MÄRCHEN DEMONS AND STUFF.
IT SEEMS RUDE TO ASK FRIENDS ABOUT THINGS THEY DON'T WANT TO TALK ABOUT...
BUT I GUESS THERE ARE TIMES WHEN IT'S BETTER TO ASK.

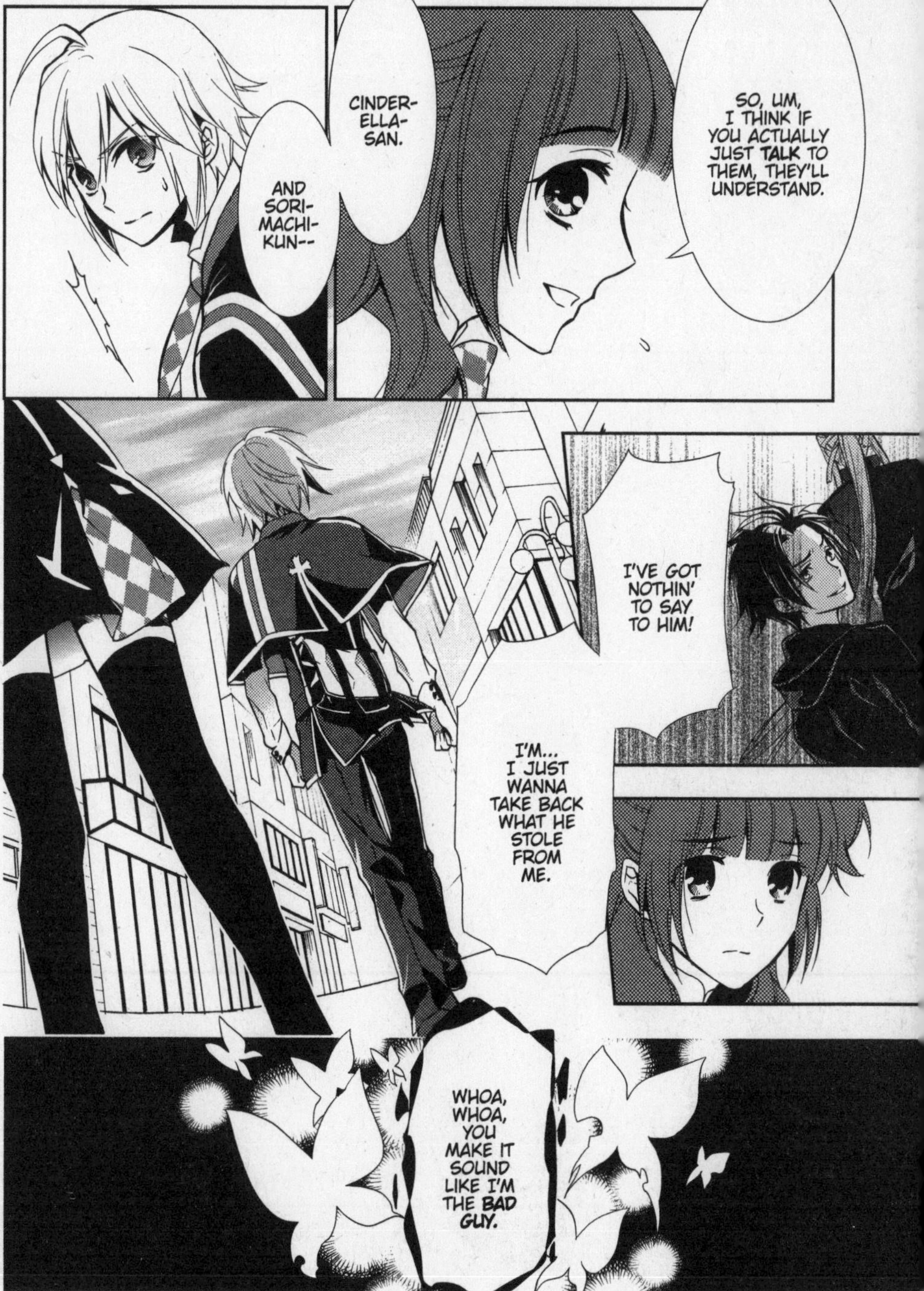
SO, UM, I THINK IF YOU ACTUALLY JUST **TALK** TO THEM, THEY'LL UNDERSTAND.
CINDER-ELLA-SAN.
AND SORI-MACHI-KUN--
I'VE GOT NOTHIN' TO SAY TO HIM!
I'M... I JUST WANNA TAKE BACK WHAT HE STOLE FROM ME.
WHOA, WHOA, YOU MAKE IT SOUND LIKE I'M THE **BAD GUY.**

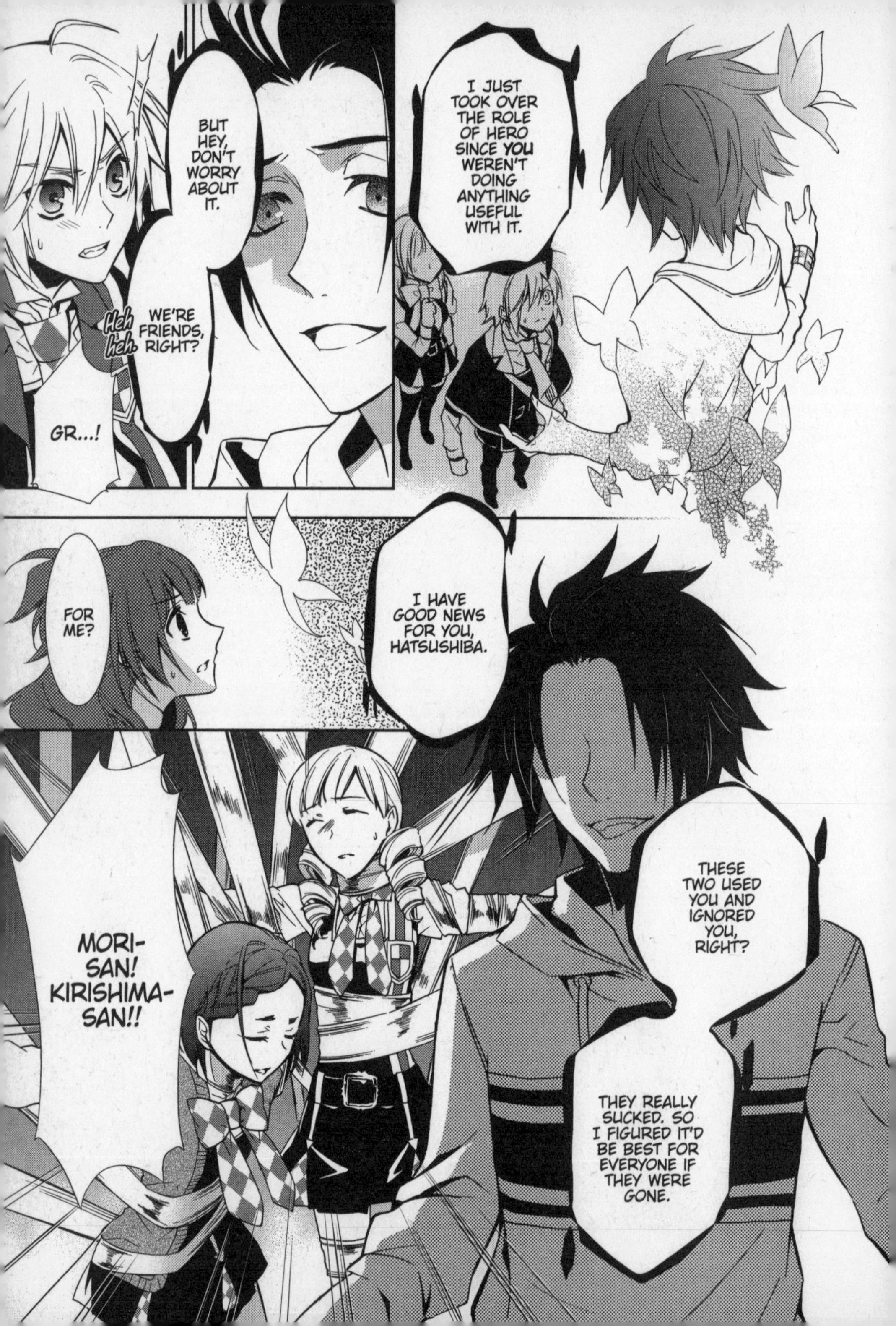
I JUST TOOK OVER THE ROLE OF HERO SINCE YOU WEREN'T DOING ANYTHING USEFUL WITH IT.
BUT HEY, DON'T WORRY ABOUT IT.
WE'RE FRIENDS, RIGHT?
Heh heh
GR...!
I HAVE GOOD NEWS FOR YOU, HATSUSHIBA.
FOR ME?
THESE TWO USED YOU AND IGNORED YOU, RIGHT?
THEY REALLY SUCKED. SO I FIGURED IT'D BE BEST FOR EVERYONE IF THEY WERE GONE.
MORI-SAN! KIRISHIMA-SAN!!

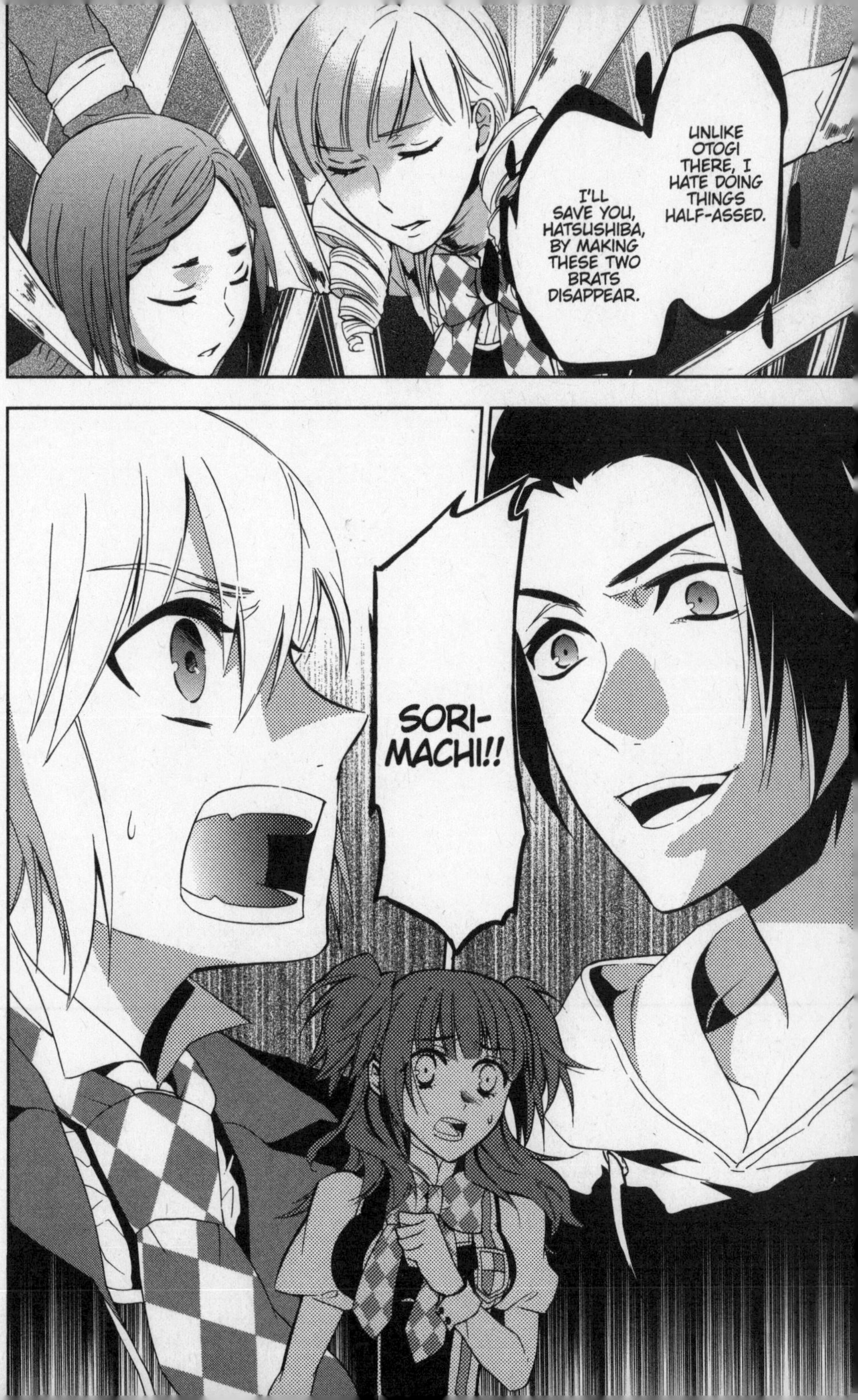
UNLIKE OTOGI THERE, I HATE DOING THINGS HALF-ASSED.
I'LL SAVE YOU, HATSUSHIBA, BY MAKING THESE TWO BRATS DISAPPEAR.
SORI-MACHI!!

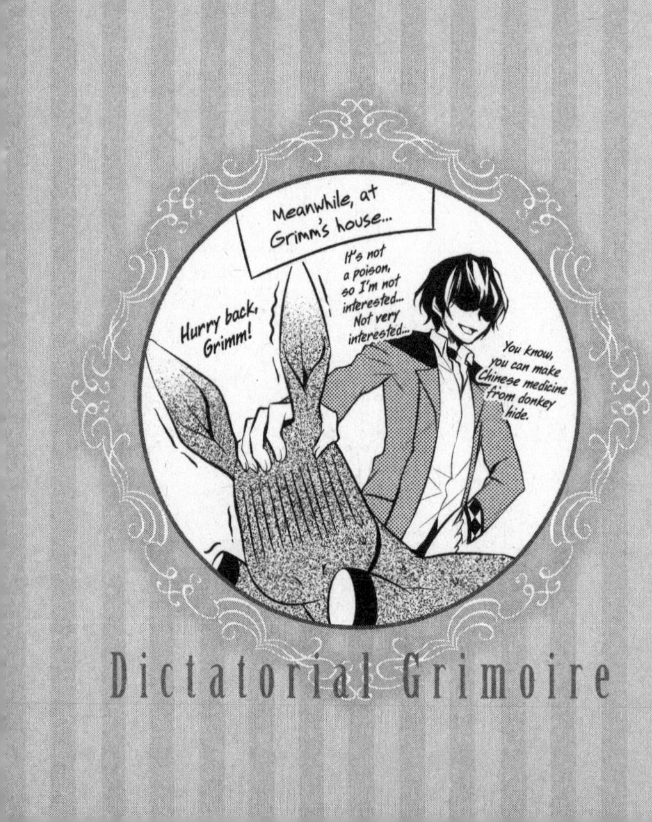
Meanwhile, at Grimm's house...
It's not a poison, so I'm not interested... Not very interested...
You know, you can make Chinese medicine from donkey hide.
Hurry back, Grimm!

Dictatorial Grimoire

独裁グリムワール
Dictatorial Grimoire

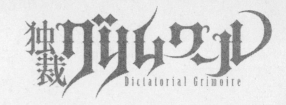

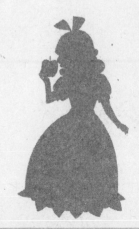

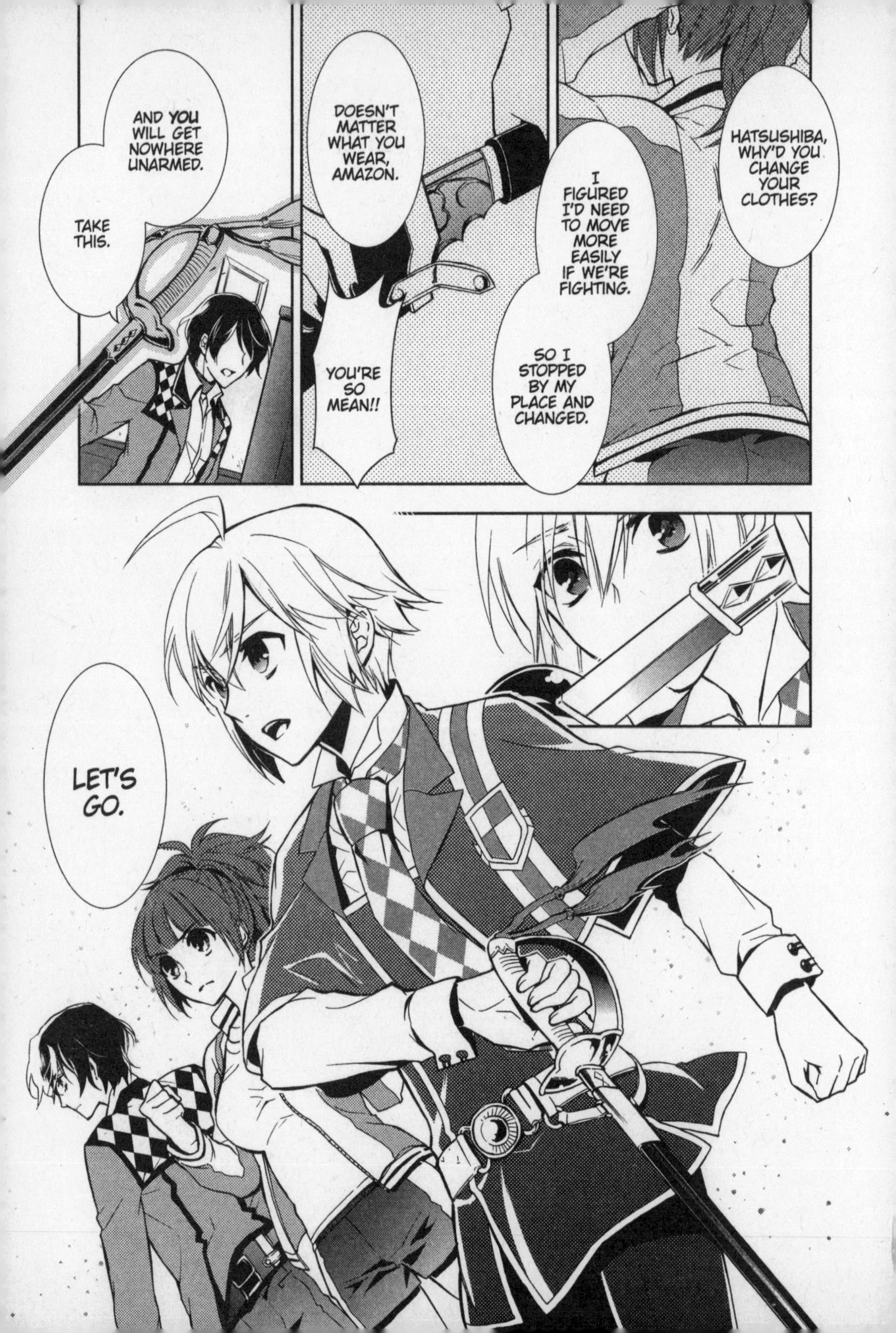
HATSUSHIBA, WHY'D YOU CHANGE YOUR CLOTHES?
I FIGURED I'D NEED TO MOVE MORE EASILY IF WE'RE FIGHTING.
SO I STOPPED BY MY PLACE AND CHANGED.
DOESN'T MATTER WHAT YOU WEAR, AMAZON.
YOU'RE SO MEAN!!
AND YOU WILL GET NOWHERE UNARMED.
TAKE THIS.
LET'S GO.

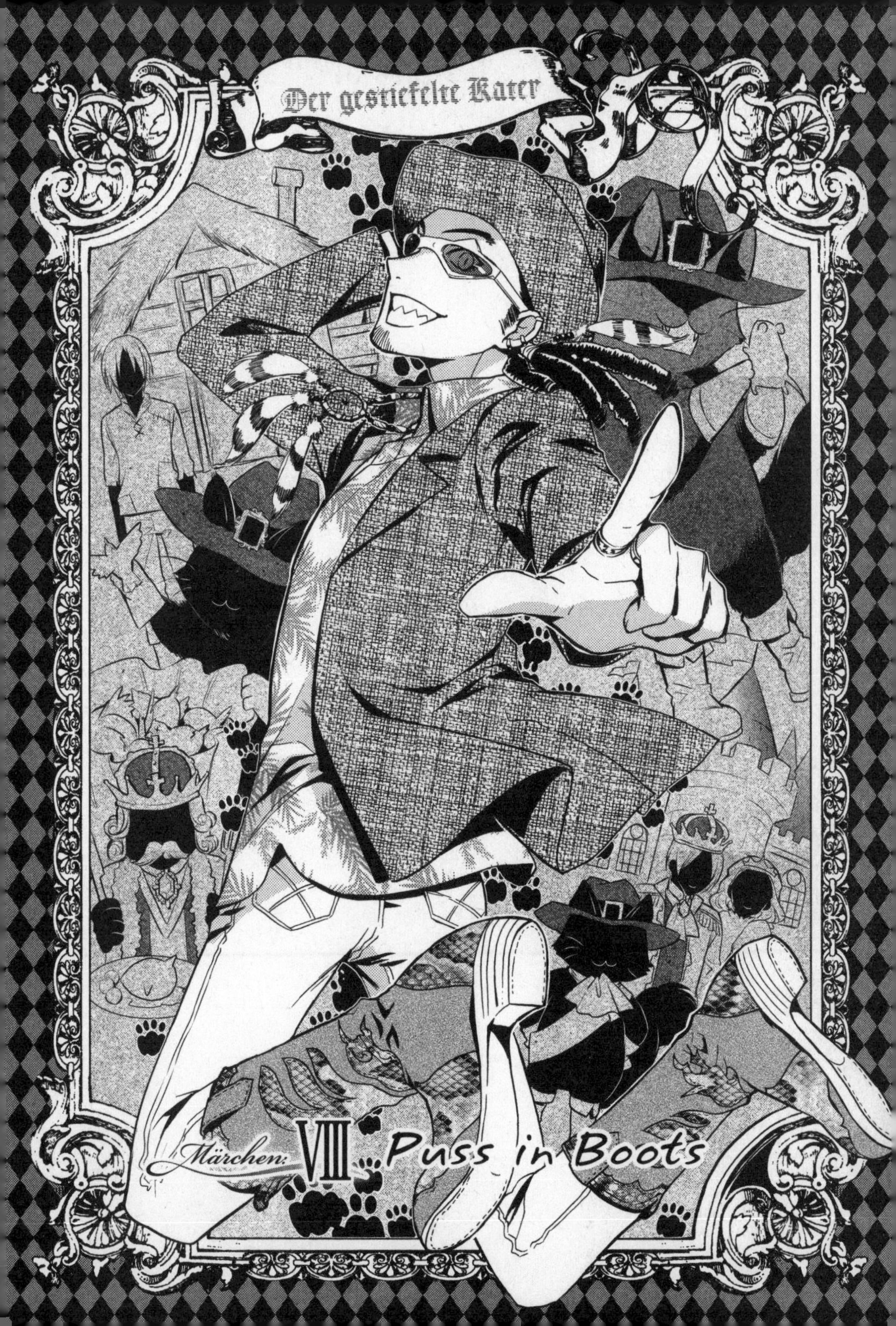
Der gestiefelte Kater
Märchen: VIII Puss in Boots

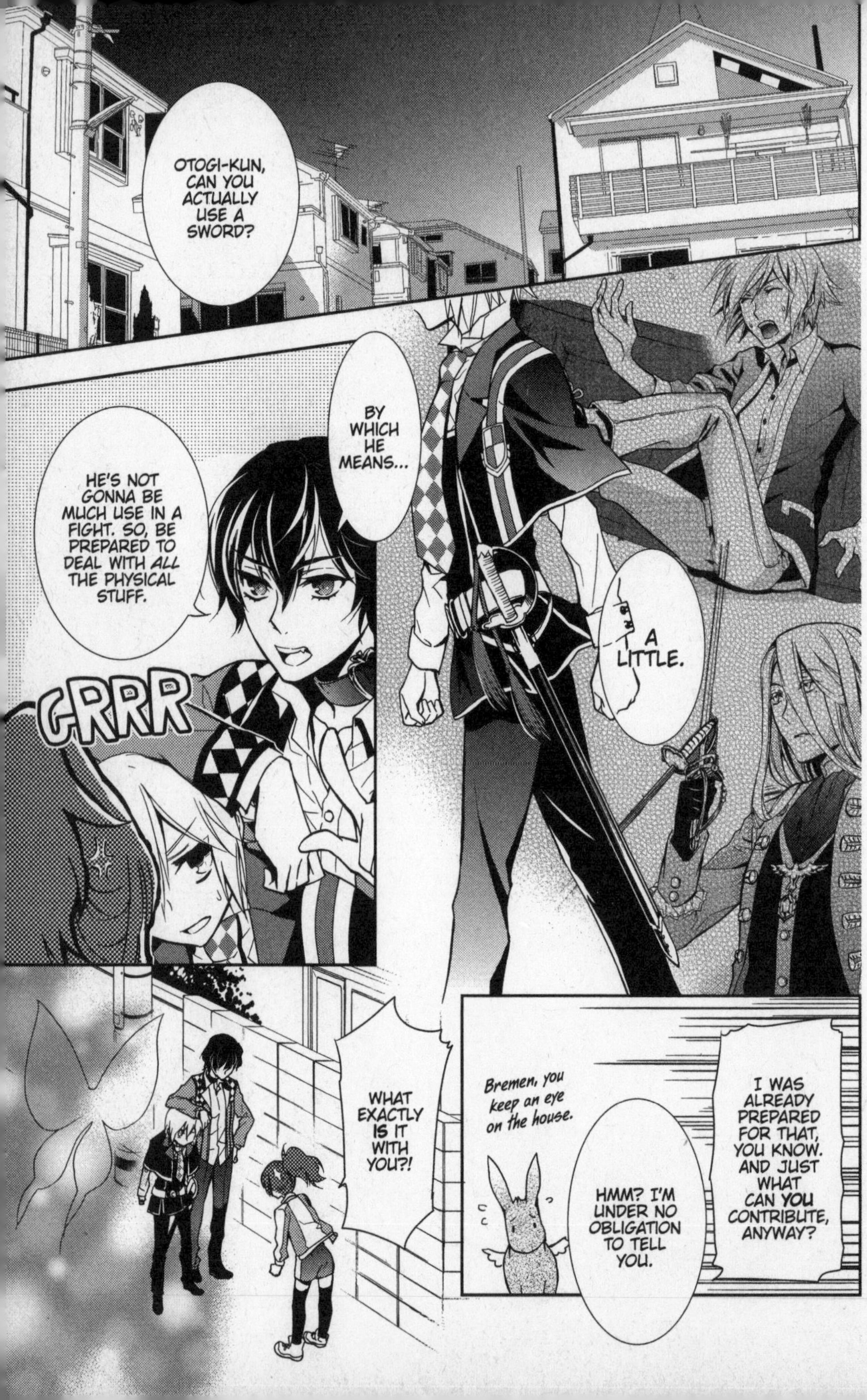
OTOGI-KUN, CAN YOU ACTUALLY USE A SWORD?
A LITTLE.
BY WHICH HE MEANS...
HE'S NOT GONNA BE MUCH USE IN A FIGHT. SO, BE PREPARED TO DEAL WITH *ALL* THE PHYSICAL STUFF.
GRRR
I WAS ALREADY PREPARED FOR THAT, YOU KNOW. AND JUST WHAT CAN **YOU** CONTRIBUTE, ANYWAY?
HMM? I'M UNDER NO OBLIGATION TO TELL YOU.
Bremen, you keep an eye on the house.
WHAT EXACTLY **IS** IT WITH YOU?!

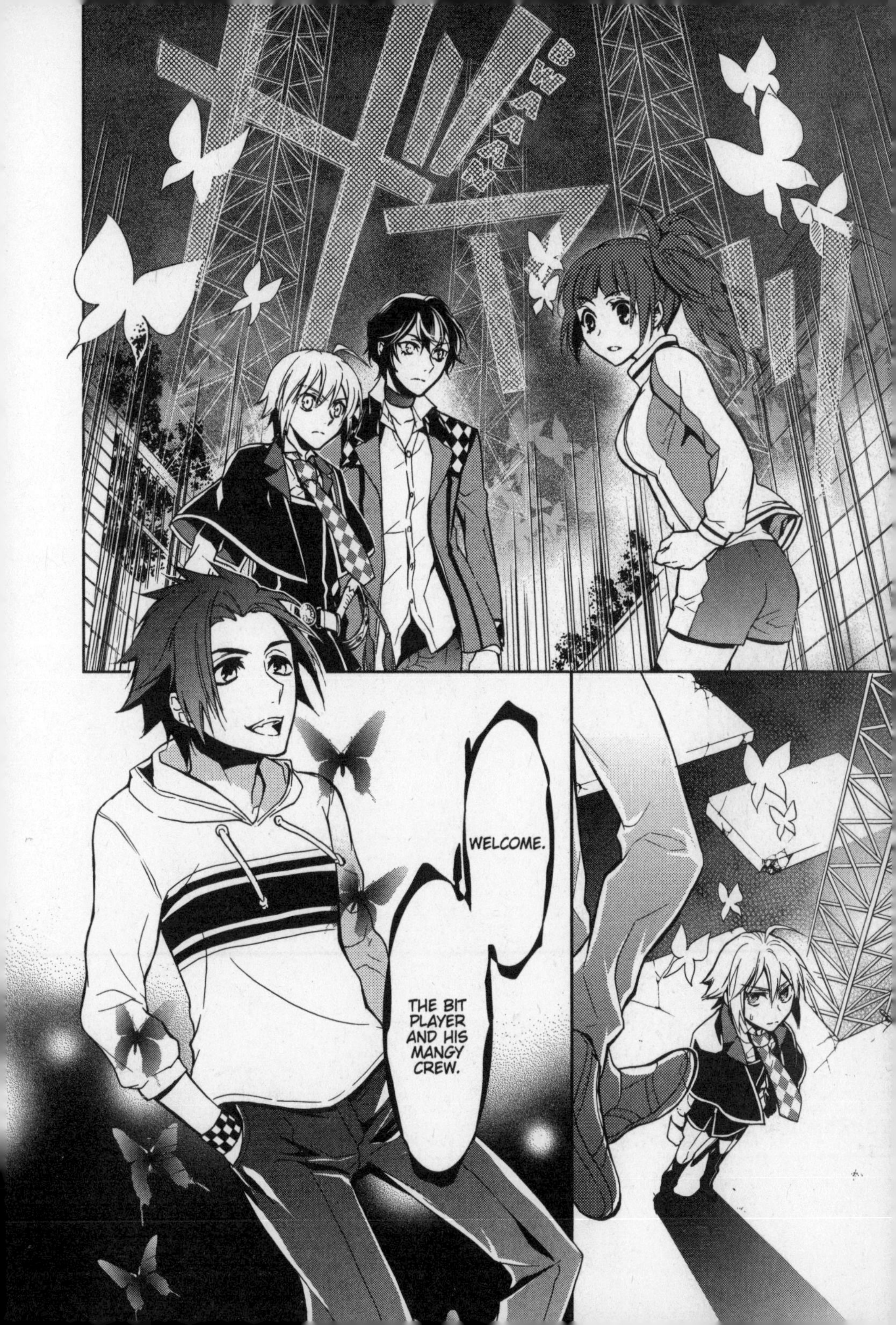
WELCOME.
THE BIT PLAYER AND HIS MANGY CREW.

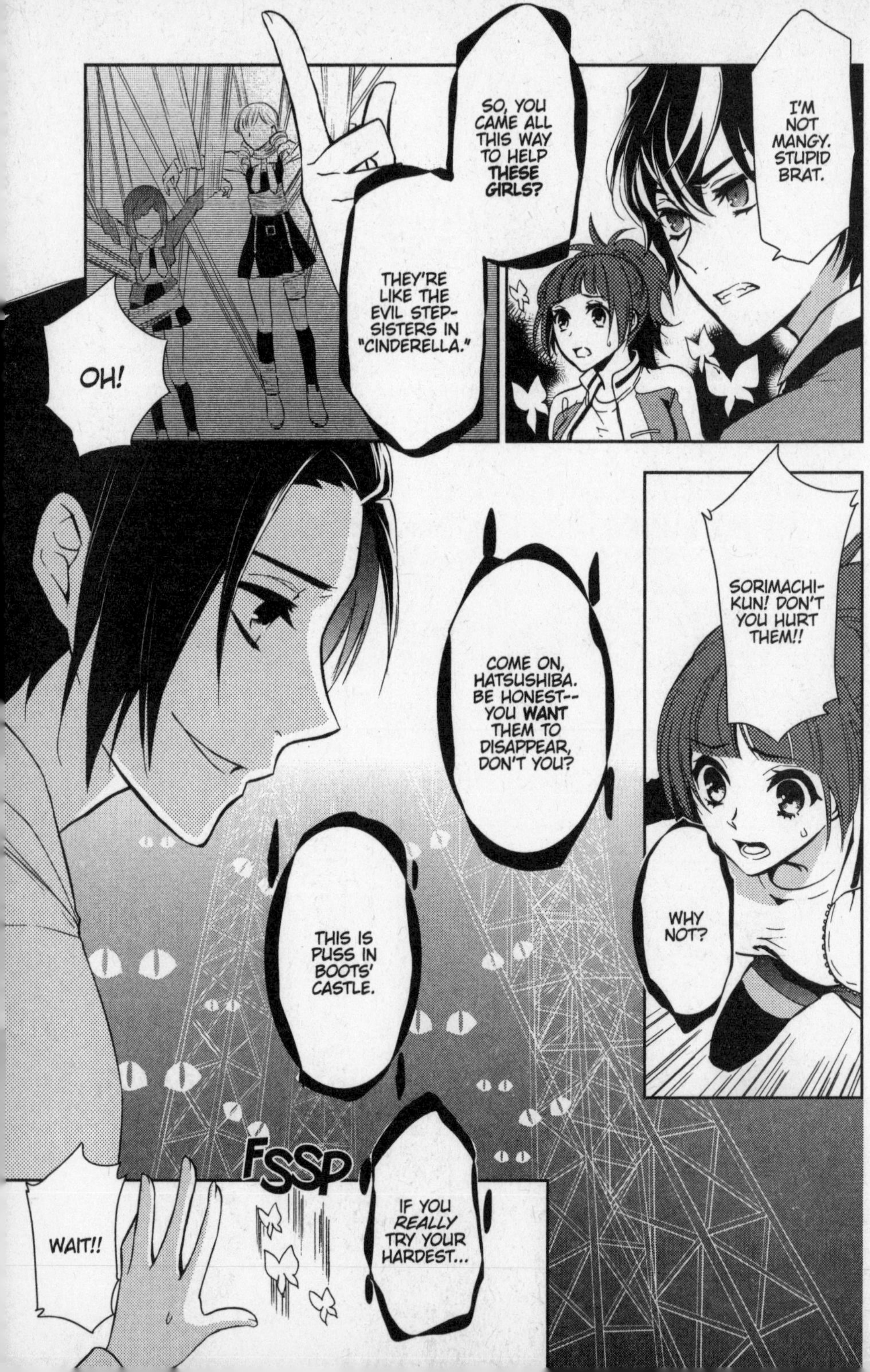
I'M NOT MANGY. STUPID BRAT.
SO, YOU CAME ALL THIS WAY TO HELP THESE GIRLS?
THEY'RE LIKE THE EVIL STEP-SISTERS IN "CINDERELLA."
OH!
SORIMACHI-KUN! DON'T YOU HURT THEM!!
WHY NOT?
COME ON, HATSUSHIBA. BE HONEST--YOU WANT THEM TO DISAPPEAR, DON'T YOU?
THIS IS PUSS IN BOOTS' CASTLE.
FSSP
IF YOU REALLY TRY YOUR HARDEST...
WAIT!!

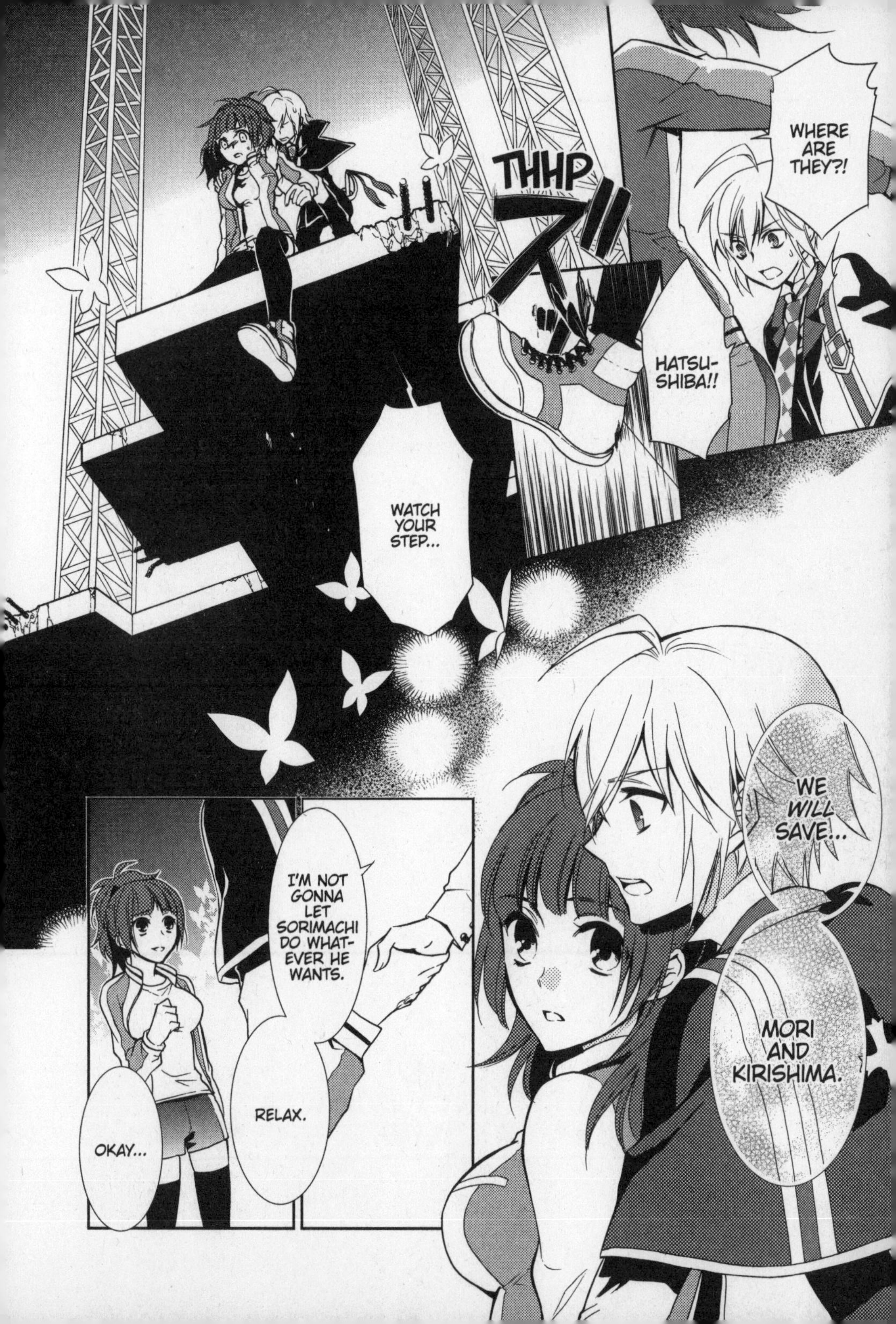
WHERE ARE THEY?!
HATSU-SHIBA!!
THHP
WATCH YOUR STEP...
WE WILL SAVE...
MORI AND KIRISHIMA.
I'M NOT GONNA LET SORIMACHI DO WHAT-EVER HE WANTS.
RELAX.
OKAY...

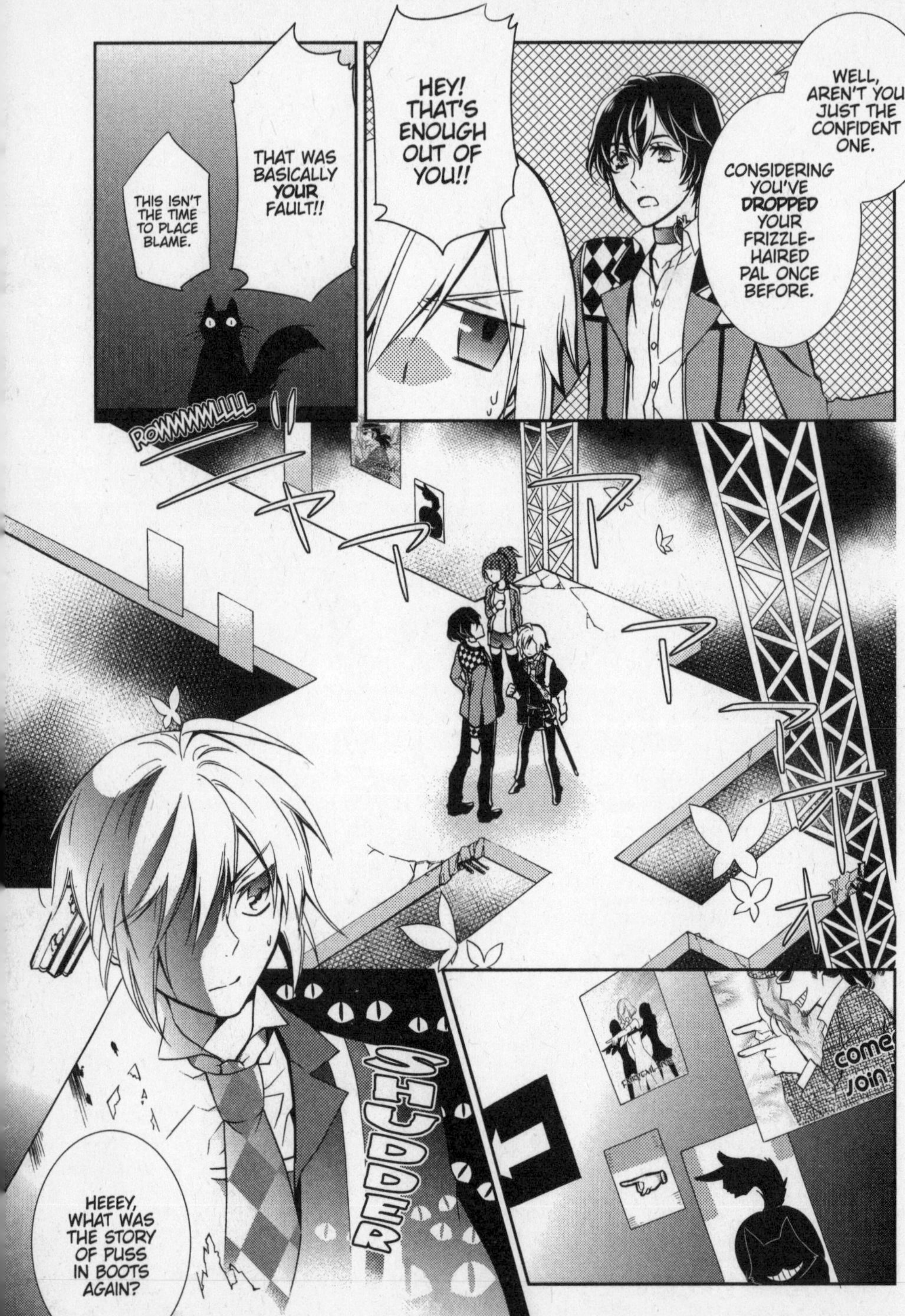

WELL, AREN'T YOU JUST THE CONFIDENT ONE.
CONSIDERING YOU'VE **DROPPED** YOUR FRIZZLE-HAIRED PAL ONCE BEFORE.
HEY! THAT'S ENOUGH OUT OF YOU!!
THAT WAS BASICALLY **YOUR** FAULT!!
THIS ISN'T THE TIME TO PLACE BLAME.
ROWWWWLLLL
come join
SHUDDER
HEEEY, WHAT WAS THE STORY OF PUSS IN BOOTS AGAIN?

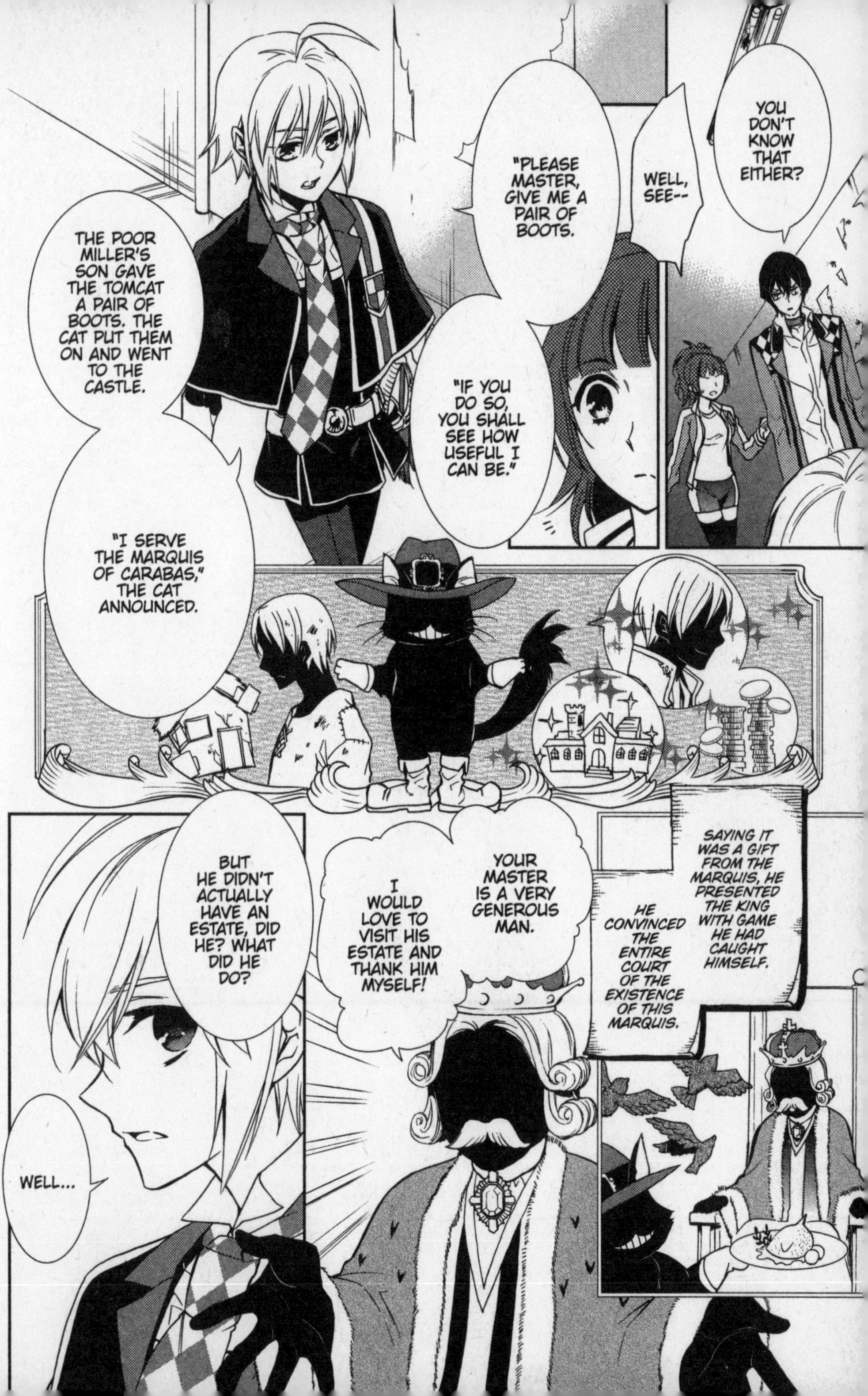
YOU DON'T KNOW THAT EITHER?
WELL, SEE--
"PLEASE MASTER, GIVE ME A PAIR OF BOOTS.
"IF YOU DO SO, YOU SHALL SEE HOW USEFUL I CAN BE."
THE POOR MILLER'S SON GAVE THE TOMCAT A PAIR OF BOOTS. THE CAT PUT THEM ON AND WENT TO THE CASTLE.
"I SERVE THE MARQUIS OF CARABAS," THE CAT ANNOUNCED.
SAYING IT WAS A GIFT FROM THE MARQUIS, HE PRESENTED THE KING WITH GAME HE HAD CAUGHT HIMSELF.
HE CONVINCED THE ENTIRE COURT OF THE EXISTENCE OF THIS MARQUIS.
YOUR MASTER IS A VERY GENEROUS MAN.
I WOULD LOVE TO VISIT HIS ESTATE AND THANK HIM MYSELF!
BUT HE DIDN'T ACTUALLY HAVE AN ESTATE, DID HE? WHAT DID HE DO?
WELL...

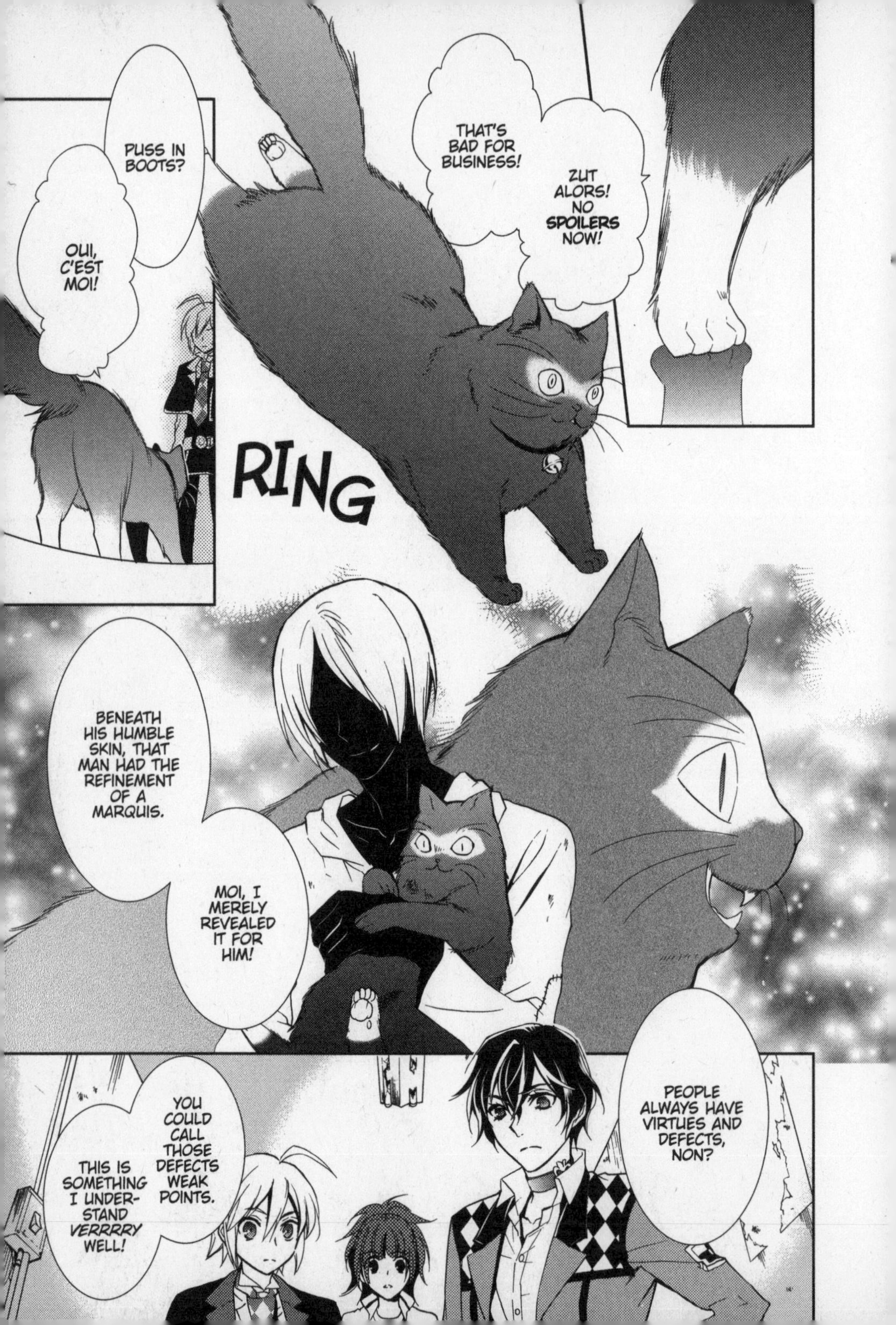
ZUT ALORS! NO SPOILERS NOW!
THAT'S BAD FOR BUSINESS!
PUSS IN BOOTS?
OUI, C'EST MOI!
RING
BENEATH HIS HUMBLE SKIN, THAT MAN HAD THE REFINEMENT OF A MARQUIS.
MOI, I MERELY REVEALED IT FOR HIM!
PEOPLE ALWAYS HAVE VIRTUES AND DEFECTS, NON?
YOU COULD CALL THOSE DEFECTS WEAK POINTS.
THIS IS SOMETHING I UNDERSTAND VERRRRY WELL!

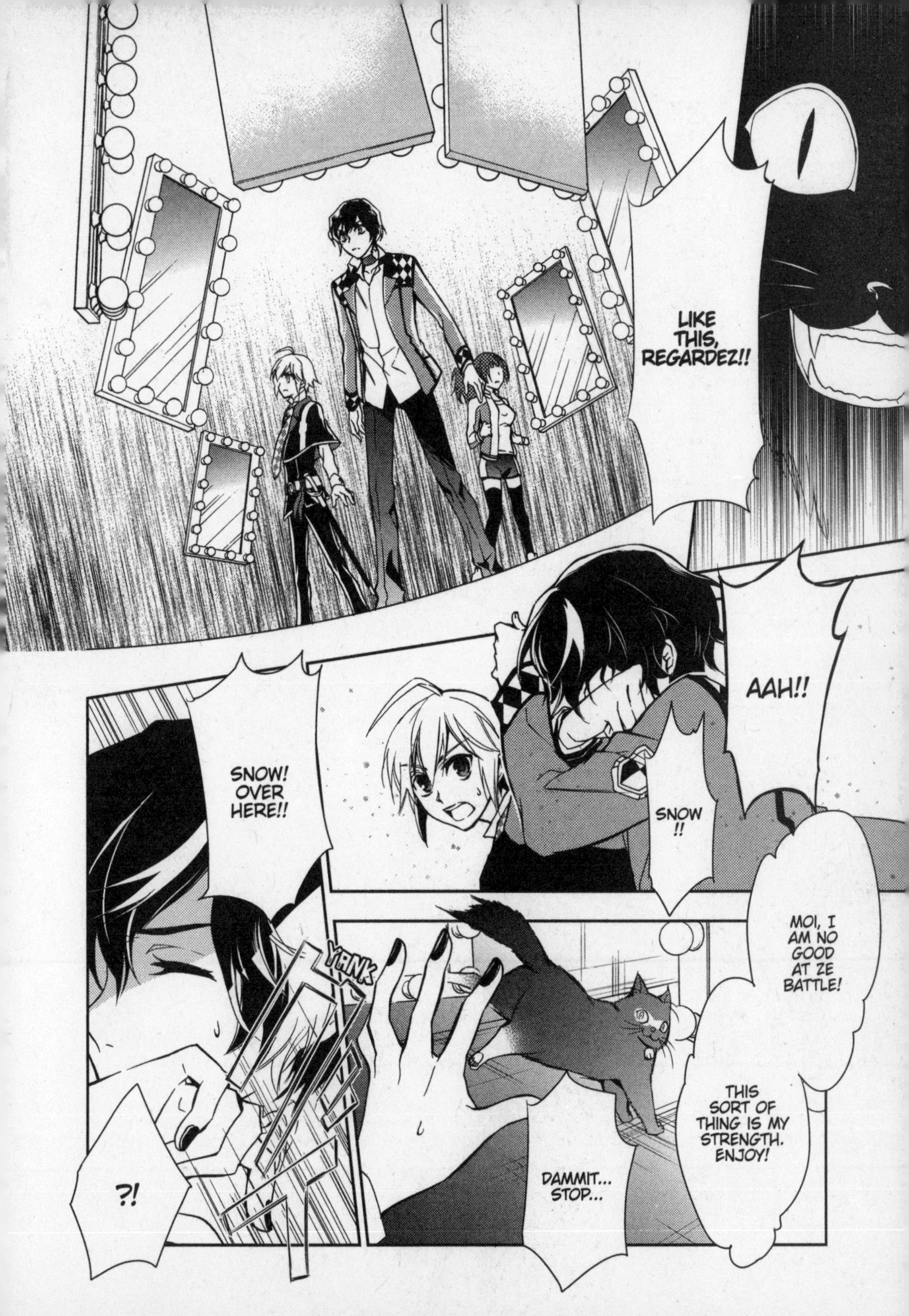
LIKE THIS, REGARDEZ!!
AAH!!
SNOW !!
SNOW! OVER HERE!!
MOI, I AM NO GOOD AT ZE BATTLE!
THIS SORT OF THING IS MY STRENGTH. ENJOY!
DAMMIT... STOP...
YANK
?!

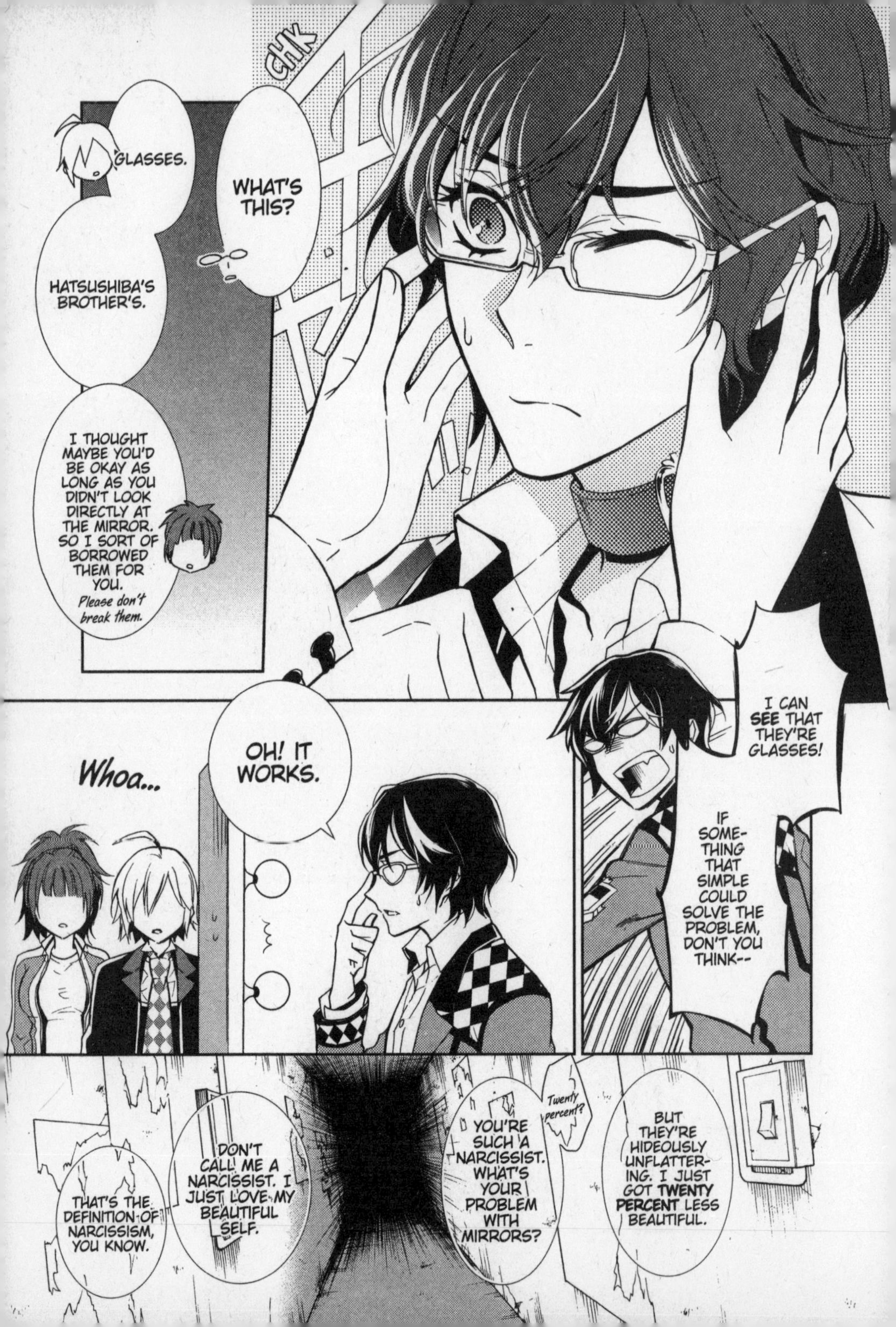

CHK
WHAT'S THIS?
GLASSES.
HATSUSHIBA'S BROTHER'S.
I THOUGHT MAYBE YOU'D BE OKAY AS LONG AS YOU DIDN'T LOOK DIRECTLY AT THE MIRROR. SO I SORT OF BORROWED THEM FOR YOU. *Please don't break them.*
I CAN **SEE** THAT THEY'RE GLASSES!
IF SOMETHING THAT SIMPLE COULD SOLVE THE PROBLEM, DON'T YOU THINK--
OH! IT WORKS.
Whoa...
BUT THEY'RE HIDEOUSLY UNFLATTERING. I JUST GOT **TWENTY PERCENT** LESS BEAUTIFUL.
Twenty percent?
YOU'RE SUCH A NARCISSIST. WHAT'S YOUR PROBLEM WITH MIRRORS?
DON'T CALL ME A NARCISSIST. I JUST LOVE MY BEAUTIFUL SELF.
THAT'S THE DEFINITION OF NARCISSISM, YOU KNOW.

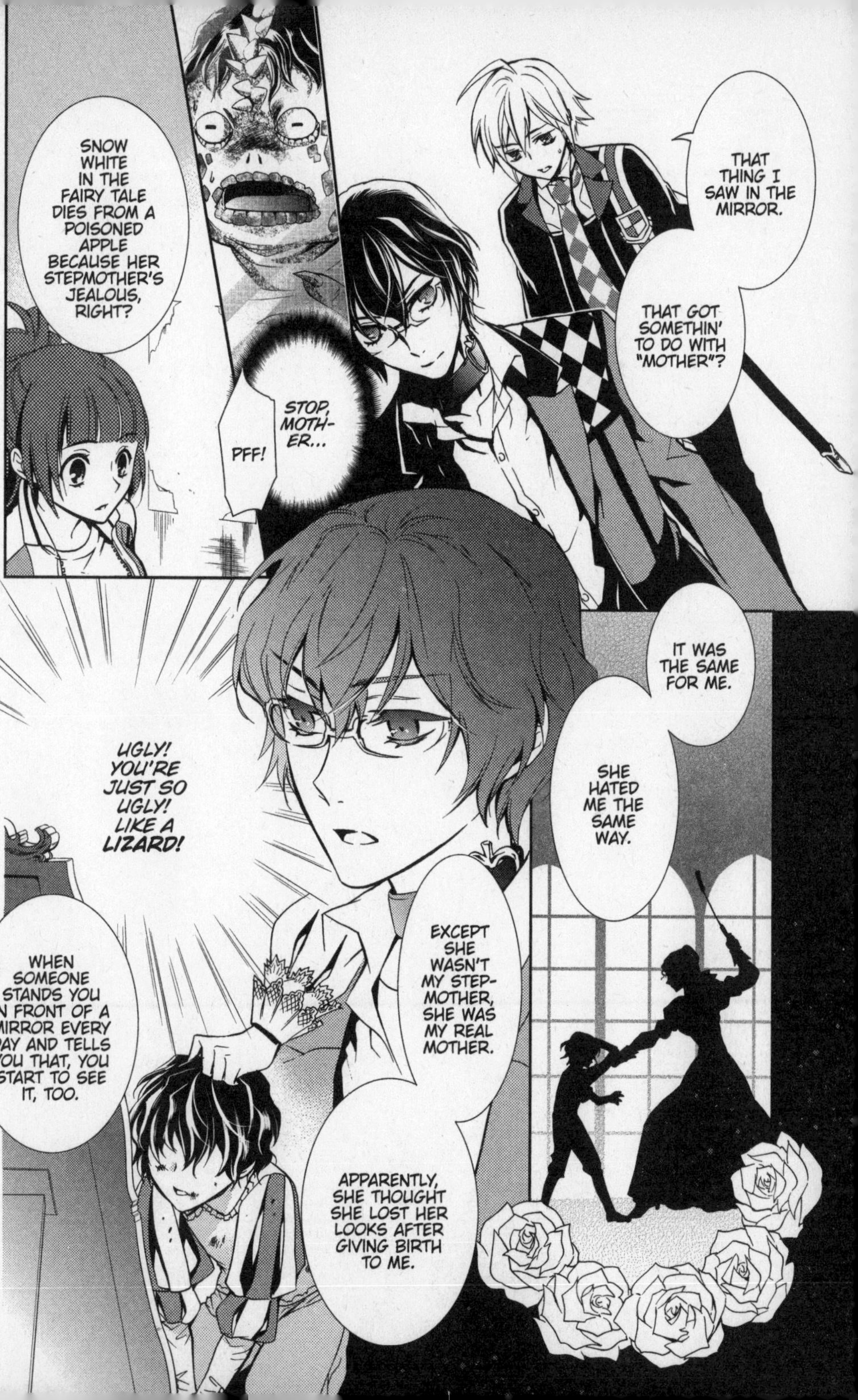
THAT THING I SAW IN THE MIRROR.
THAT GOT SOMETHIN' TO DO WITH "MOTHER"?
SNOW WHITE IN THE FAIRY TALE DIES FROM A POISONED APPLE BECAUSE HER STEPMOTHER'S JEALOUS, RIGHT?
STOP, MOTHER...
PFF!
IT WAS THE SAME FOR ME.
SHE HATED ME THE SAME WAY.
EXCEPT SHE WASN'T MY STEP-MOTHER, SHE WAS MY REAL MOTHER.
APPARENTLY, SHE THOUGHT SHE LOST HER LOOKS AFTER GIVING BIRTH TO ME.
UGLY! YOU'RE JUST SO UGLY! LIKE A LIZARD!
WHEN SOMEONE STANDS YOU IN FRONT OF A MIRROR EVERY DAY AND TELLS YOU THAT, YOU START TO SEE IT, TOO.

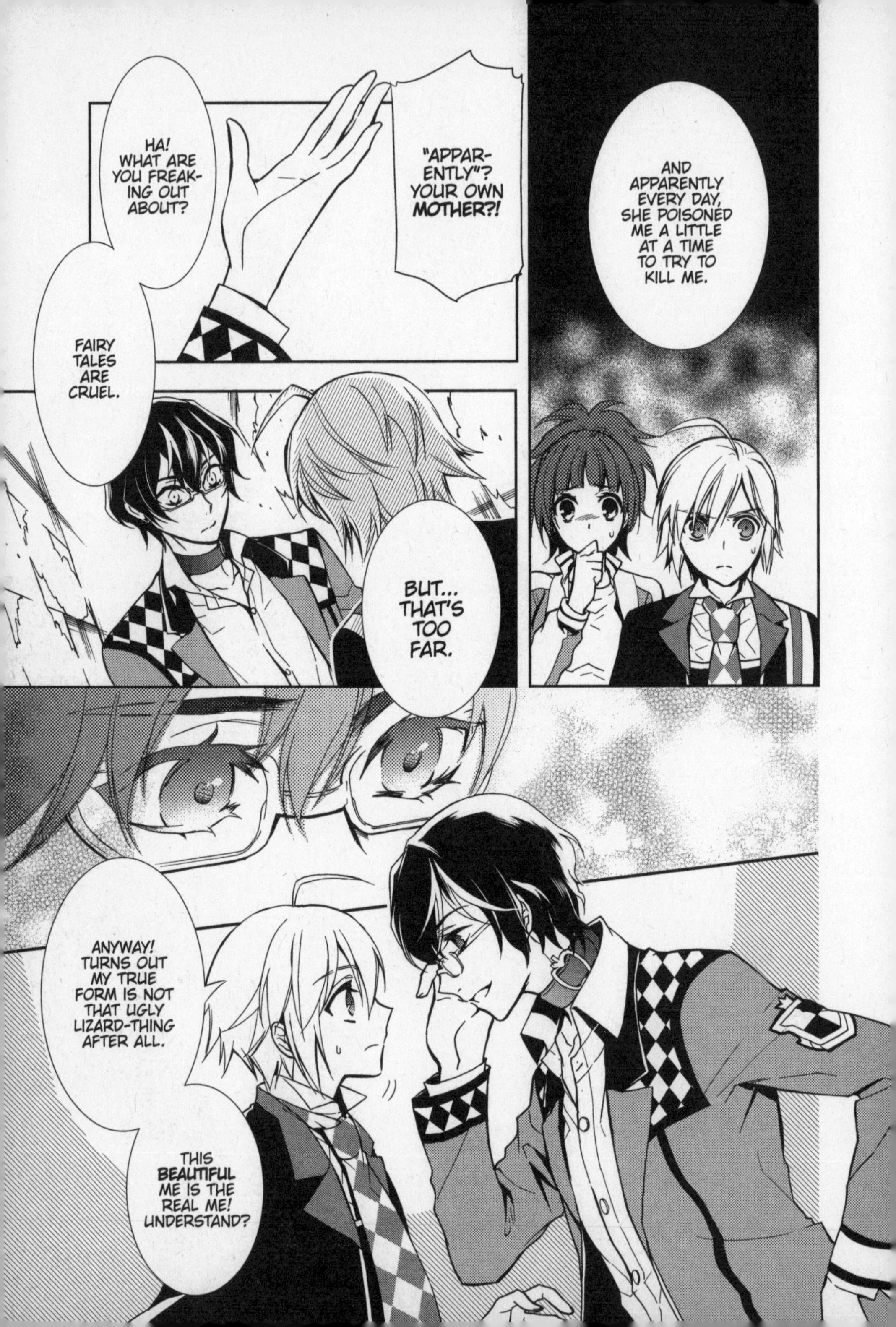
AND APPARENTLY EVERY DAY, SHE POISONED ME A LITTLE AT A TIME TO TRY TO KILL ME.
"APPAR-ENTLY"? YOUR OWN MOTHER?!
HA! WHAT ARE YOU FREAK-ING OUT ABOUT?
FAIRY TALES ARE CRUEL.
BUT... THAT'S TOO FAR.
ANYWAY! TURNS OUT MY TRUE FORM IS NOT THAT UGLY LIZARD-THING AFTER ALL.
THIS BEAUTIFUL ME IS THE REAL ME! UNDERSTAND?

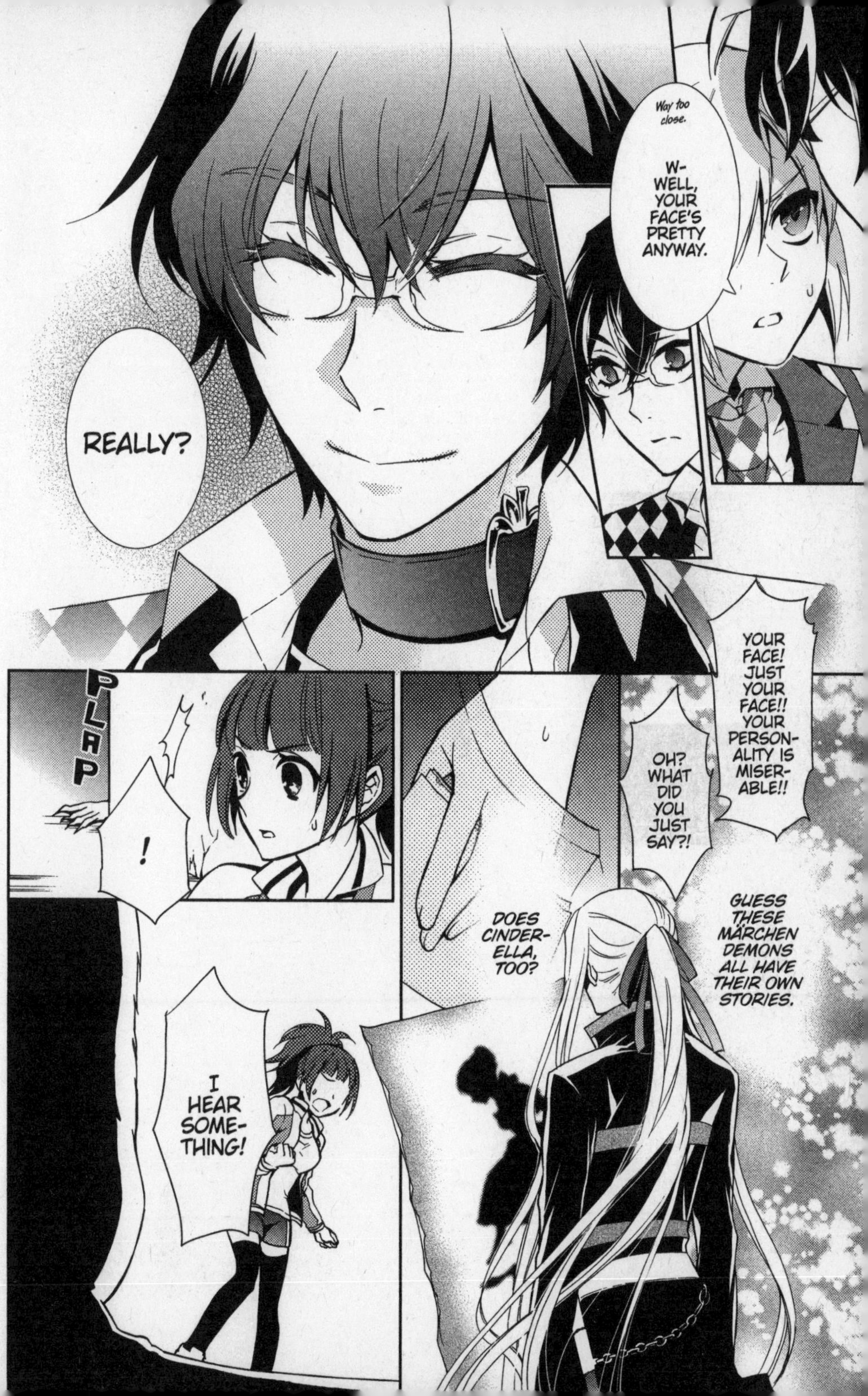

Way too close.
W-WELL, YOUR FACE'S PRETTY ANYWAY.
REALLY?
YOUR FACE! JUST YOUR FACE!! YOUR PERSON-ALITY IS MISER-ABLE!!
OH? WHAT DID YOU JUST SAY?!
GUESS THESE MÄRCHEN DEMONS ALL HAVE THEIR OWN STORIES.
DOES CINDER-ELLA, TOO?
PLAP
!
I HEAR SOME-THING!

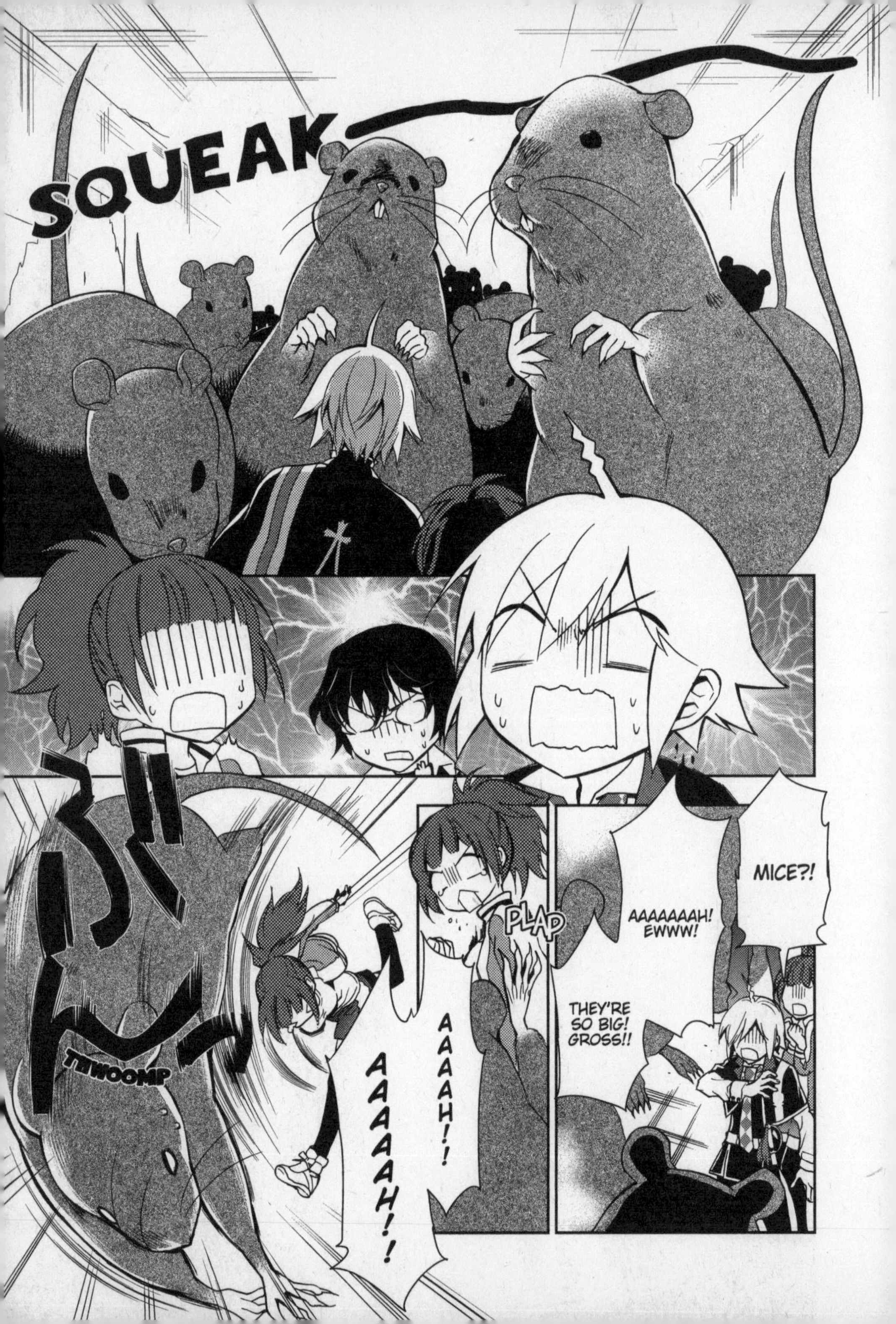

SQUEAK
MICE?!
AAAAAAAH! EWWW!
THEY'RE SO BIG! GROSS!!
PLAP
AAAAAH!!
AAAAAAH!!
TWWOOMP

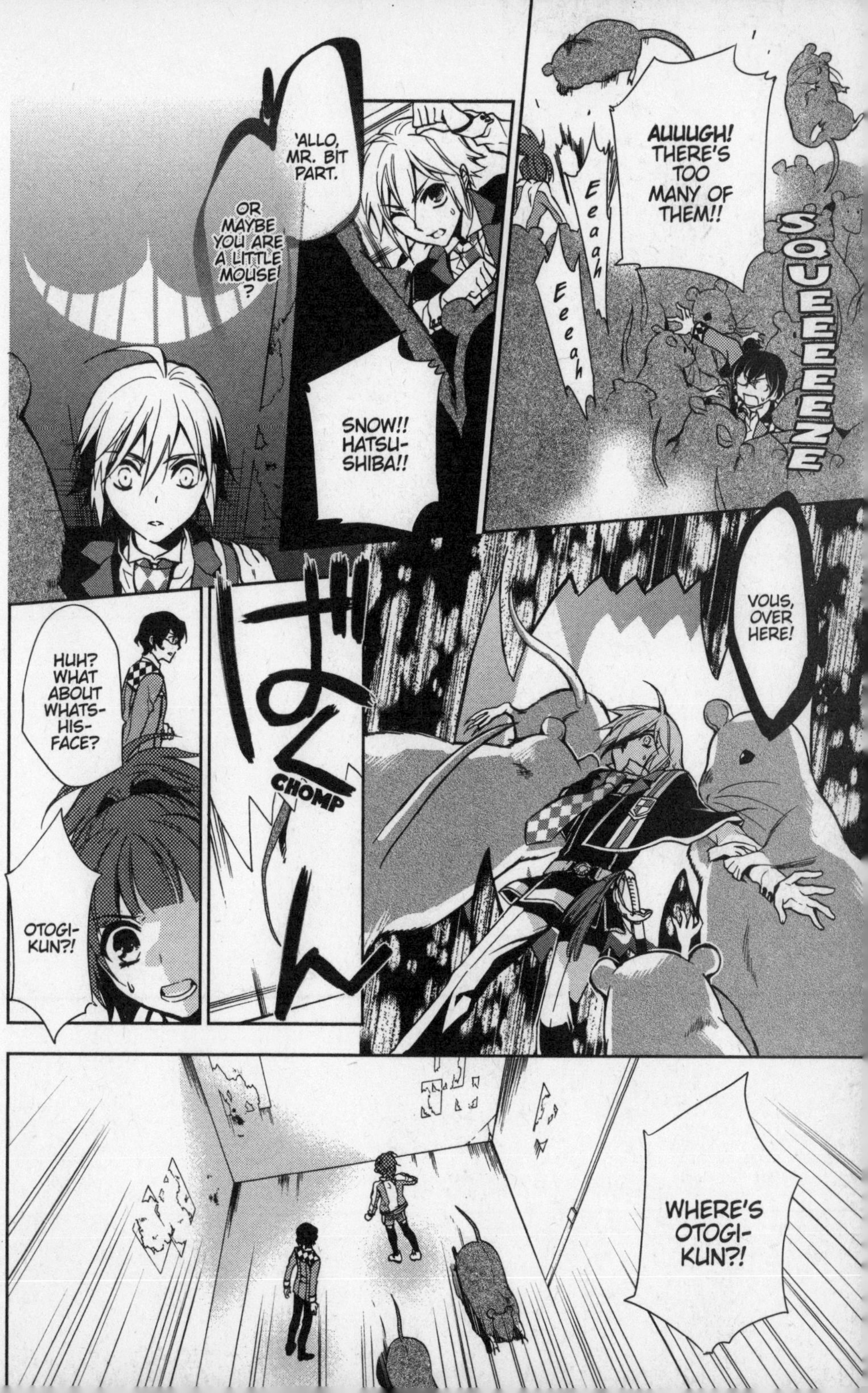
AUUUGH! THERE'S TOO MANY OF THEM!!
Eeeah
Eeeah
SQUEEEEEZE
'ALLO, MR. BIT PART.
OR MAYBE YOU ARE A LITTLE MOUSE!?
SNOW!! HATSU-SHIBA!!
VOUS, OVER HERE!
CHOMP
HUH? WHAT ABOUT WHATS-HIS-FACE?
OTOGI-KUN?!
WHERE'S OTOGI-KUN?!

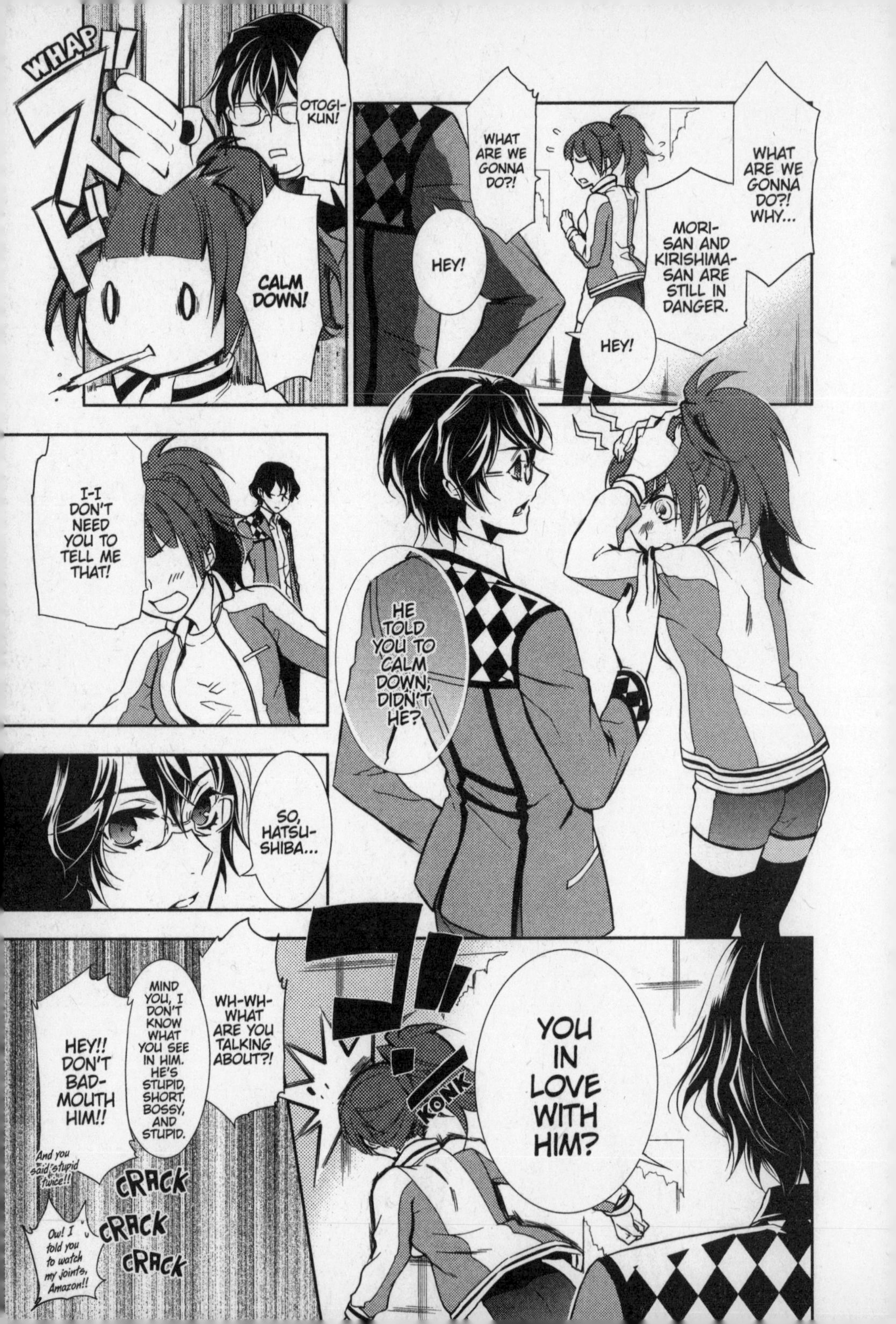
WHAT ARE WE GONNA DO?! WHY...
MORI-SAN AND KIRISHIMA-SAN ARE STILL IN DANGER.
WHAT ARE WE GONNA DO?!
HEY!
HEY!
WHAP
OTOGI-KUN!
CALM DOWN!
HE TOLD YOU TO CALM DOWN, DIDN'T HE?
I-I DON'T NEED YOU TO TELL ME THAT!
SO, HATSUSHIBA...
YOU IN LOVE WITH HIM?
KONK
WH-WH-WHAT ARE YOU TALKING ABOUT?!
MIND YOU, I DON'T KNOW WHAT YOU SEE IN HIM. HE'S STUPID, SHORT, BOSSY, AND STUPID.
HEY!! DON'T BAD-MOUTH HIM!!
And you said stupid twice!!
CRACK
CRACK
CRACK
Ow! I told you to watch my joints, Amazon!!

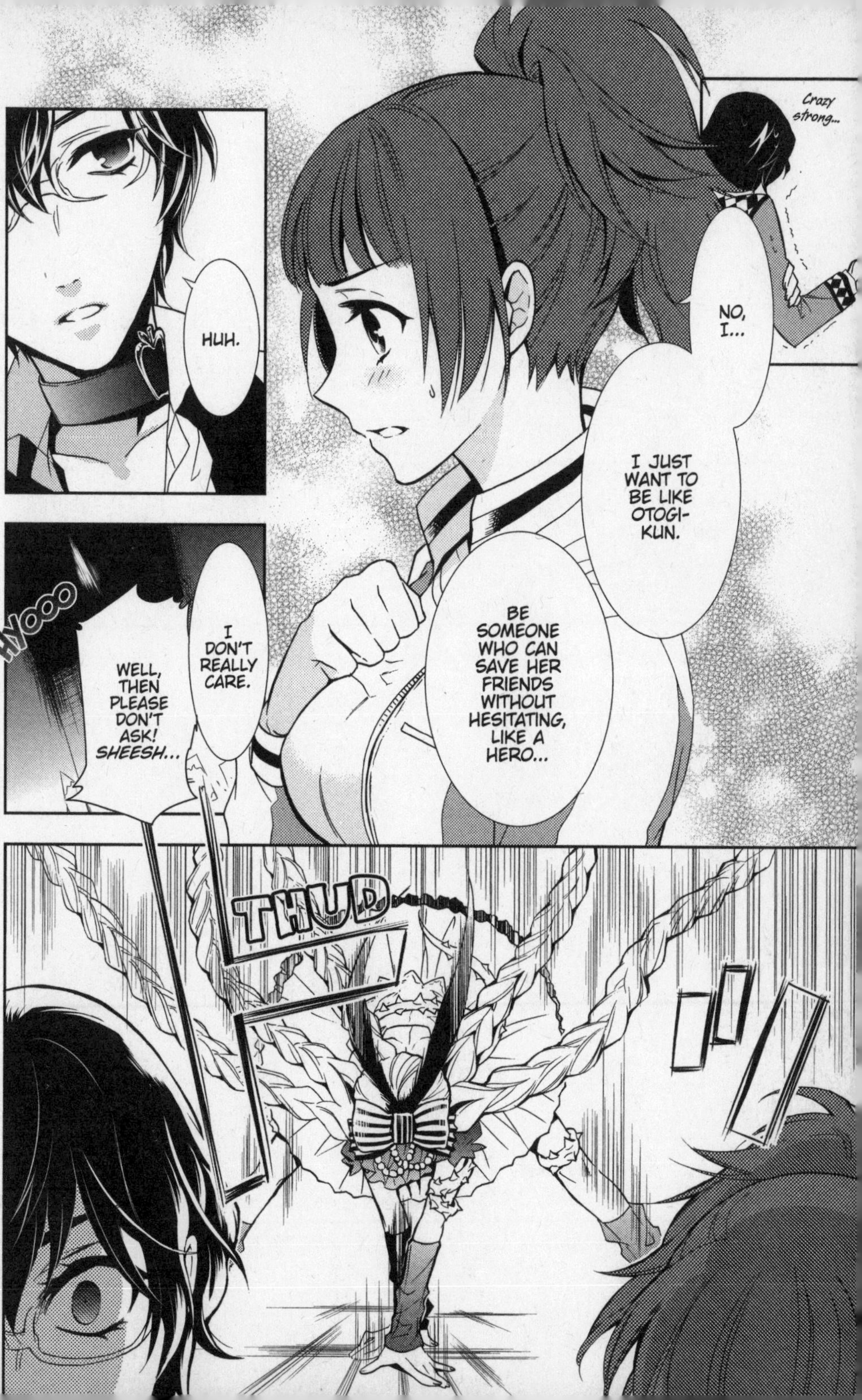
Crazy strong...
NO, I...
I JUST WANT TO BE LIKE OTOGI-KUN.
BE SOMEONE WHO CAN SAVE HER FRIENDS WITHOUT HESITATING, LIKE A HERO...
HUH.
I DON'T REALLY CARE.
WELL, THEN PLEASE DON'T ASK! SHEESH...
HYOOO
THUD

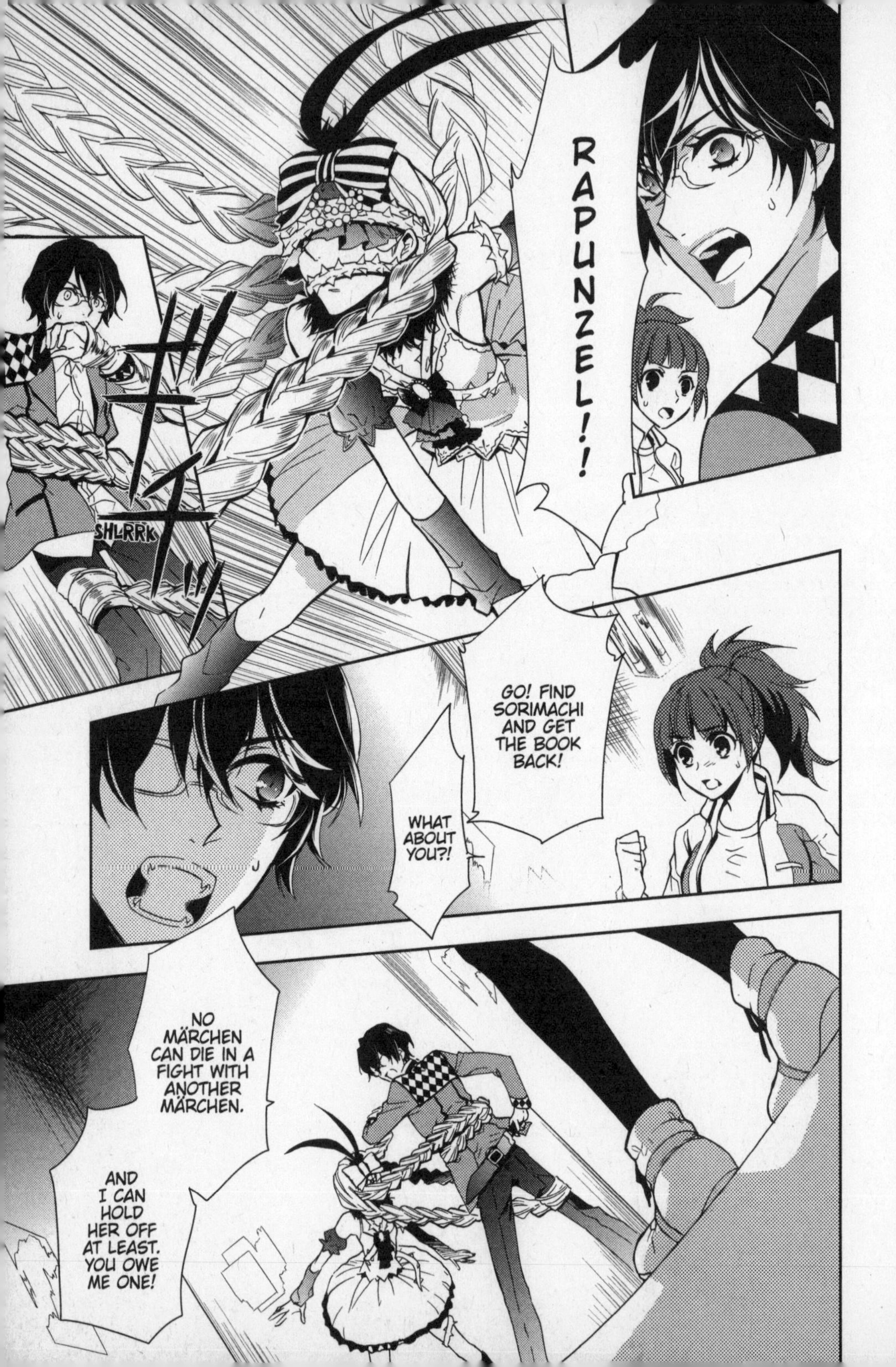
RAPUNZEL!!
SHLRRK
GO! FIND SORIMACHI AND GET THE BOOK BACK!
WHAT ABOUT YOU?!
NO MÄRCHEN CAN DIE IN A FIGHT WITH ANOTHER MÄRCHEN.
AND I CAN HOLD HER OFF AT LEAST. YOU OWE ME ONE!

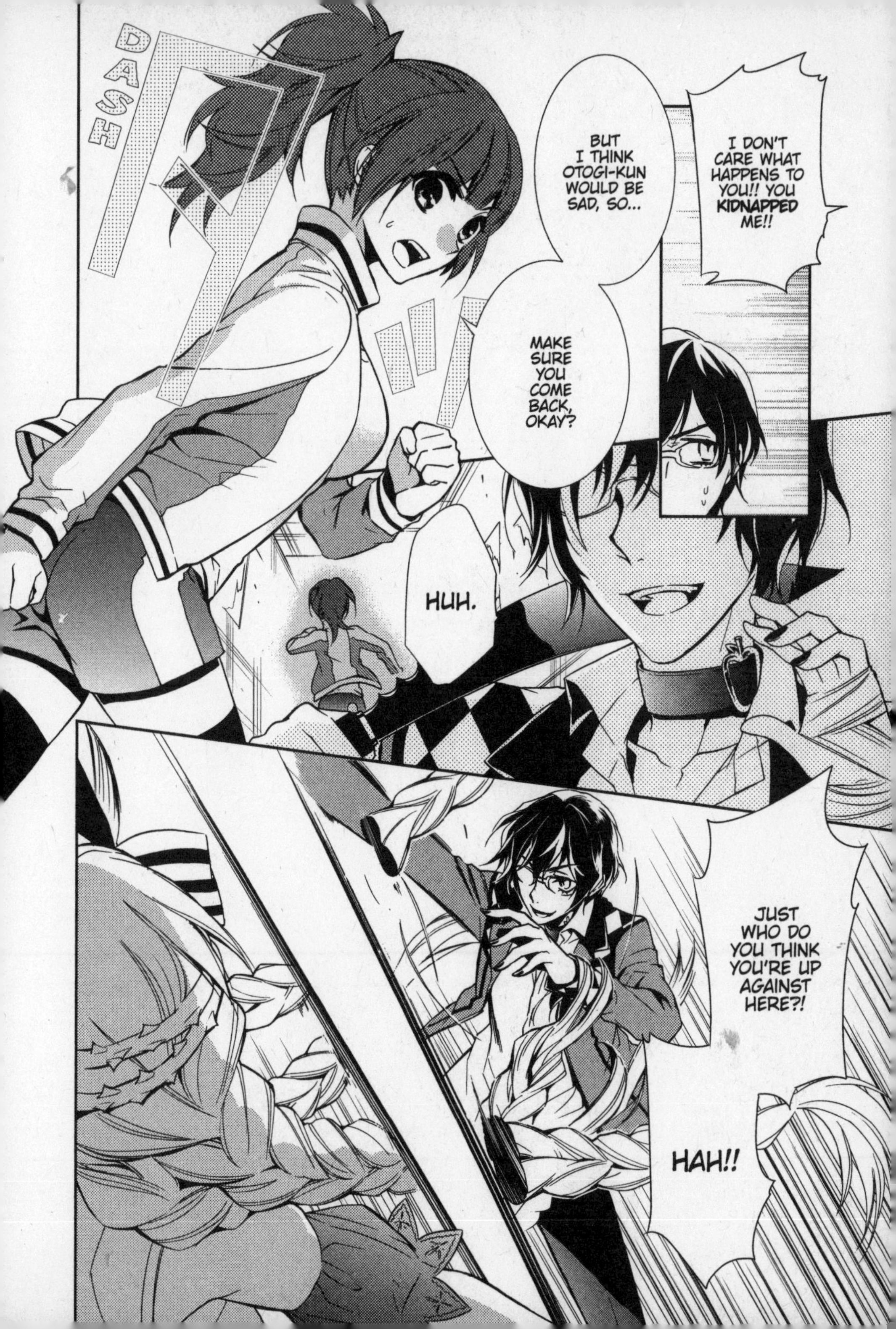
I DON'T CARE WHAT HAPPENS TO YOU!! YOU KIDNAPPED ME!!
BUT I THINK OTOGI-KUN WOULD BE SAD, SO...
MAKE SURE YOU COME BACK, OKAY?
DASH
HUH.
JUST WHO DO YOU THINK YOU'RE UP AGAINST HERE?!
HAH!!

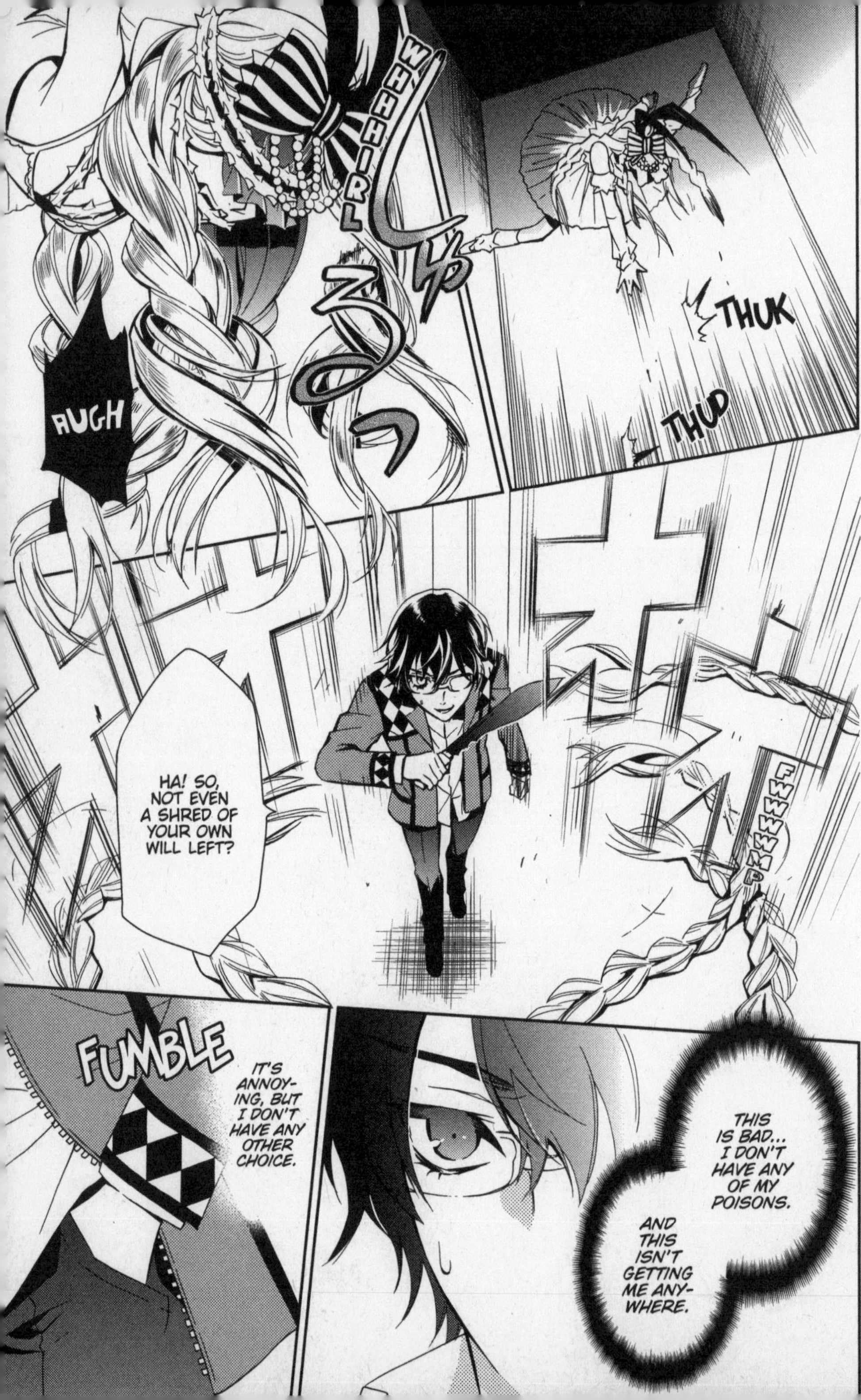
THUK
THUD
WHHHIRL
AUGH
FWWWWMP
HA! SO, NOT EVEN A SHRED OF YOUR OWN WILL LEFT?
THIS IS BAD... I DON'T HAVE ANY OF MY POISONS.
AND THIS ISN'T GETTING ME ANY-WHERE.
FUMBLE
IT'S ANNOY-ING, BUT I DON'T HAVE ANY OTHER CHOICE.

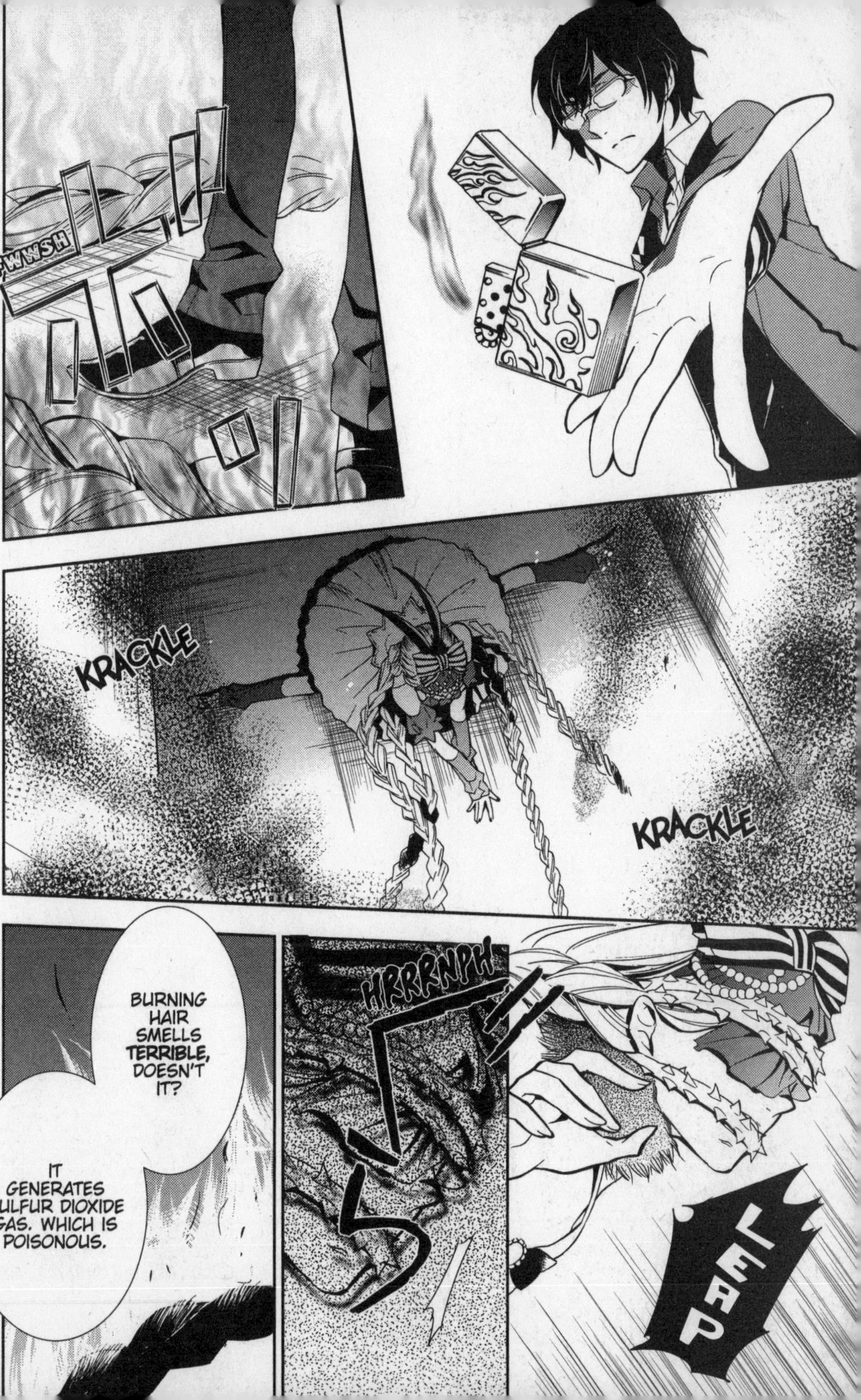
FWWSH
KRACKLE
KRACKLE
HRRRNPH
LEAP
BURNING HAIR SMELLS TERRIBLE, DOESN'T IT?
IT GENERATES SULFUR DIOXIDE GAS. WHICH IS POISONOUS.

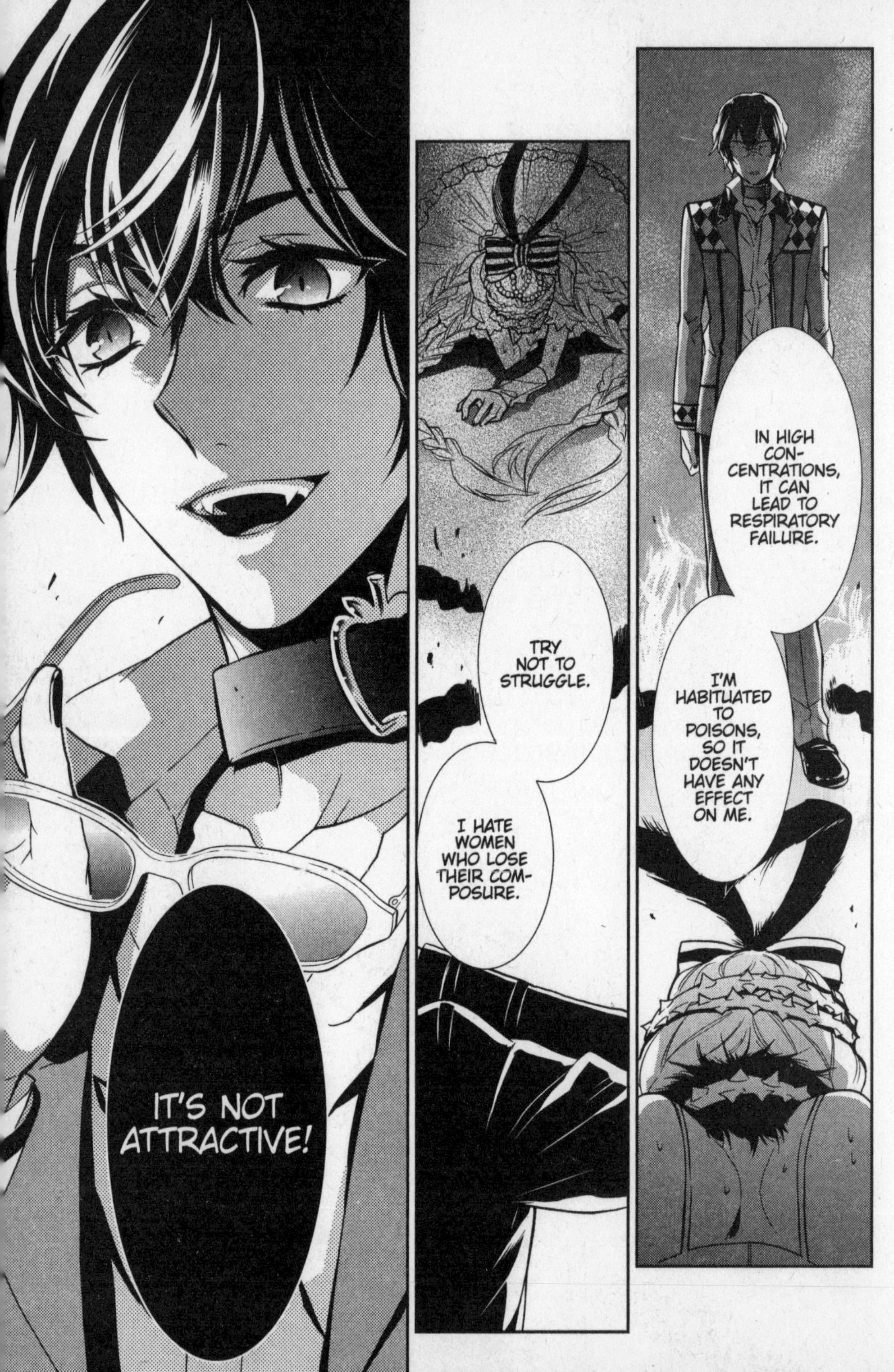
IN HIGH CON-CENTRATIONS, IT CAN LEAD TO RESPIRATORY FAILURE.
I'M HABITUATED TO POISONS, SO IT DOESN'T HAVE ANY EFFECT ON ME.
TRY NOT TO STRUGGLE.
I HATE WOMEN WHO LOSE THEIR COM-POSURE.
IT'S NOT ATTRACTIVE!

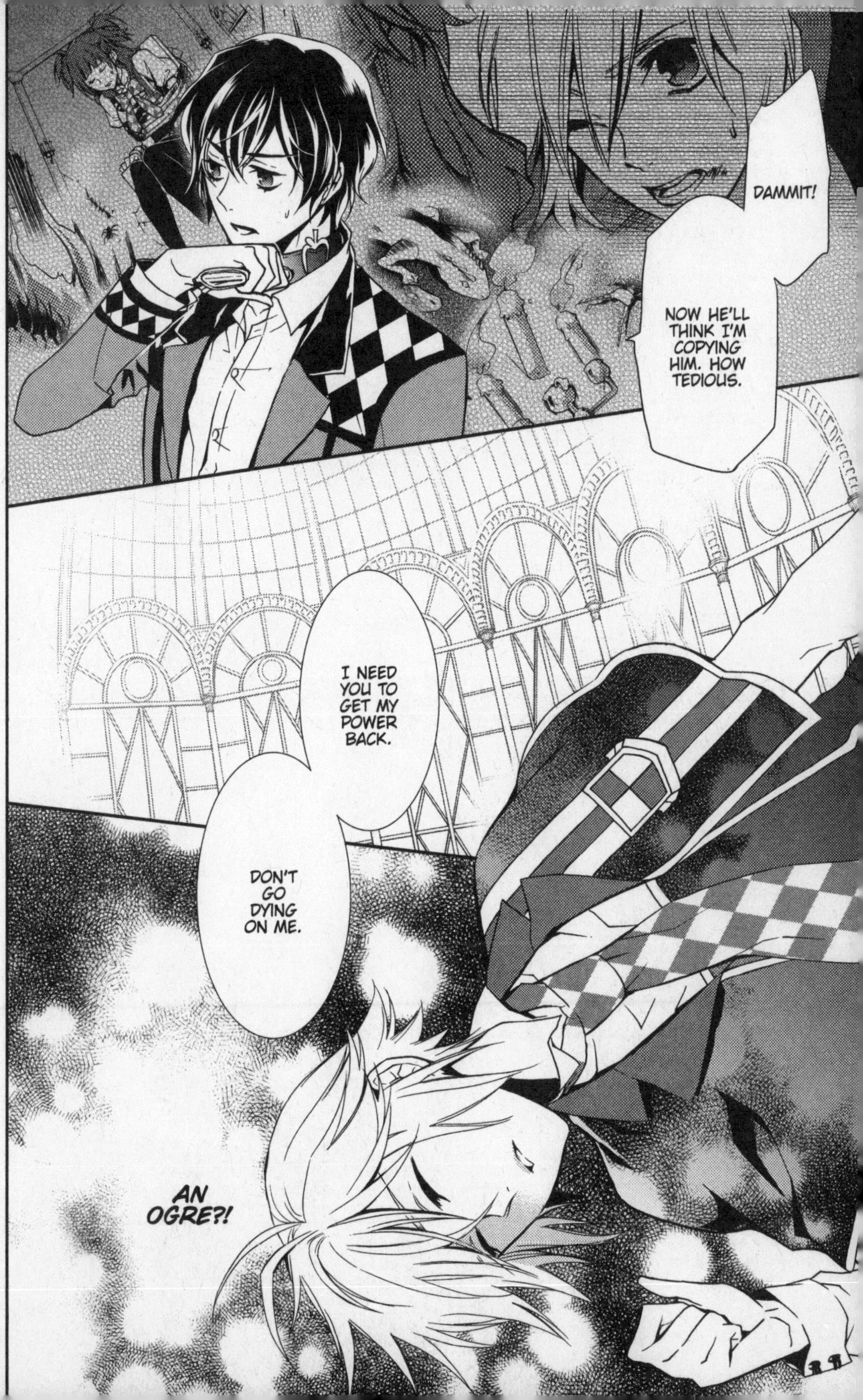
DAMMIT!
NOW HE'LL THINK I'M COPYING HIM. HOW TEDIOUS.
I NEED YOU TO GET MY POWER BACK.
DON'T GO DYING ON ME.
AN OGRE?!

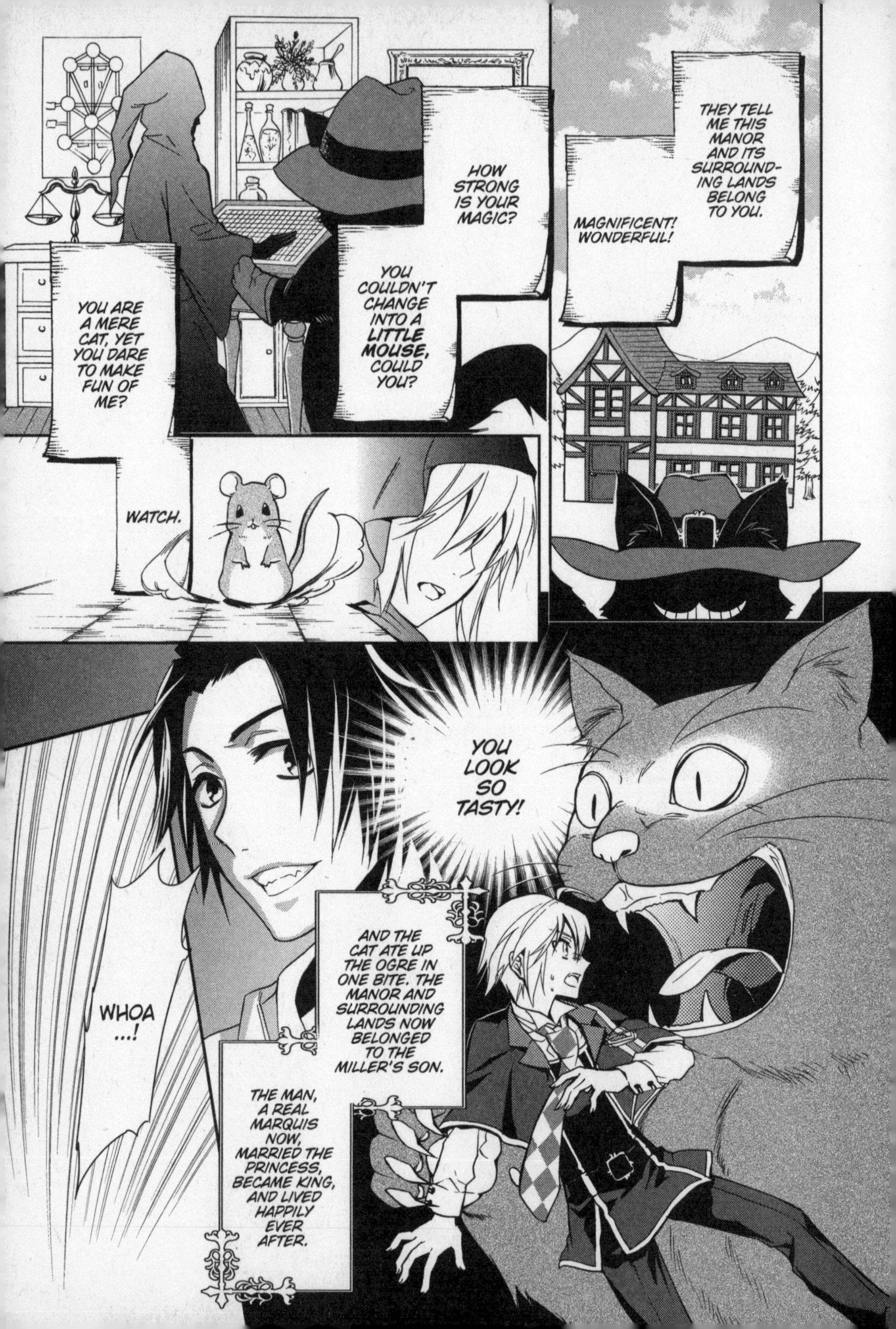

THEY TELL ME THIS MANOR AND ITS SURROUNDING LANDS BELONG TO YOU.
MAGNIFICENT! WONDERFUL!
HOW STRONG IS YOUR MAGIC?
YOU COULDN'T CHANGE INTO A **LITTLE MOUSE,** COULD YOU?
YOU ARE A MERE CAT, YET YOU DARE TO MAKE FUN OF ME?
WATCH.
YOU LOOK SO TASTY!
AND THE CAT ATE UP THE OGRE IN ONE BITE. THE MANOR AND SURROUNDING LANDS NOW BELONGED TO THE MILLER'S SON.
THE MAN, A REAL MARQUIS NOW, MARRIED THE PRINCESS, BECAME KING, AND LIVED HAPPILY EVER AFTER.
WHOA ...!

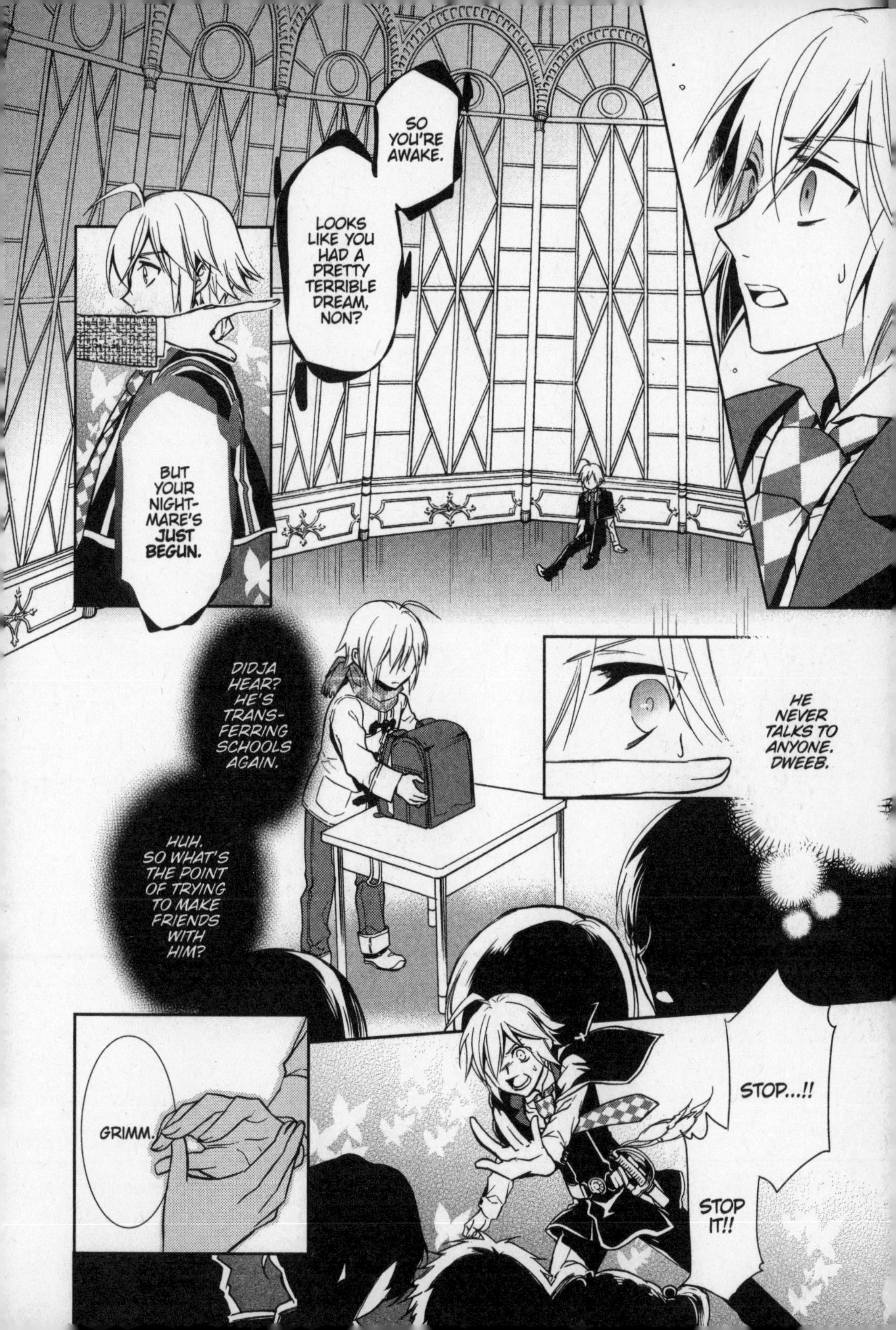

SO YOU'RE AWAKE.
LOOKS LIKE YOU HAD A PRETTY TERRIBLE DREAM, NON?
BUT YOUR NIGHT-MARE'S **JUST BEGUN.**
HE NEVER TALKS TO ANYONE. DWEEB.
DIDJA HEAR? HE'S TRANS-FERRING SCHOOLS AGAIN.
HUH. SO WHAT'S THE POINT OF TRYING TO MAKE FRIENDS WITH HIM?
STOP...!!
STOP IT!!
GRIMM.

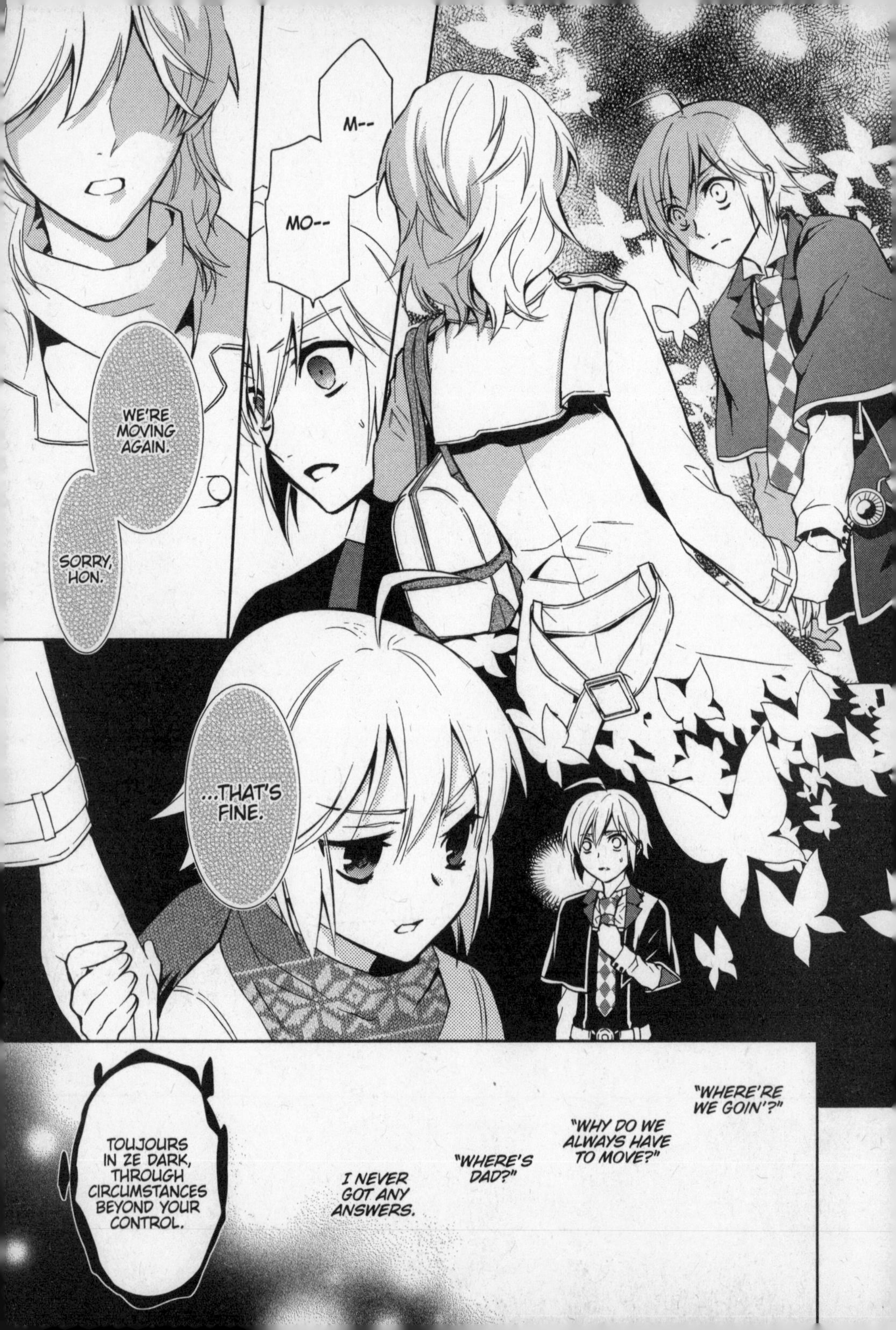
M-- MO--
WE'RE MOVING AGAIN.
SORRY, HON.
...THAT'S FINE.
"WHERE'RE WE GOIN'?"
"WHY DO WE ALWAYS HAVE TO MOVE?"
"WHERE'S DAD?"
I NEVER GOT ANY ANSWERS.
TOUJOURS IN ZE DARK, THROUGH CIRCUMSTANCES BEYOND YOUR CONTROL.

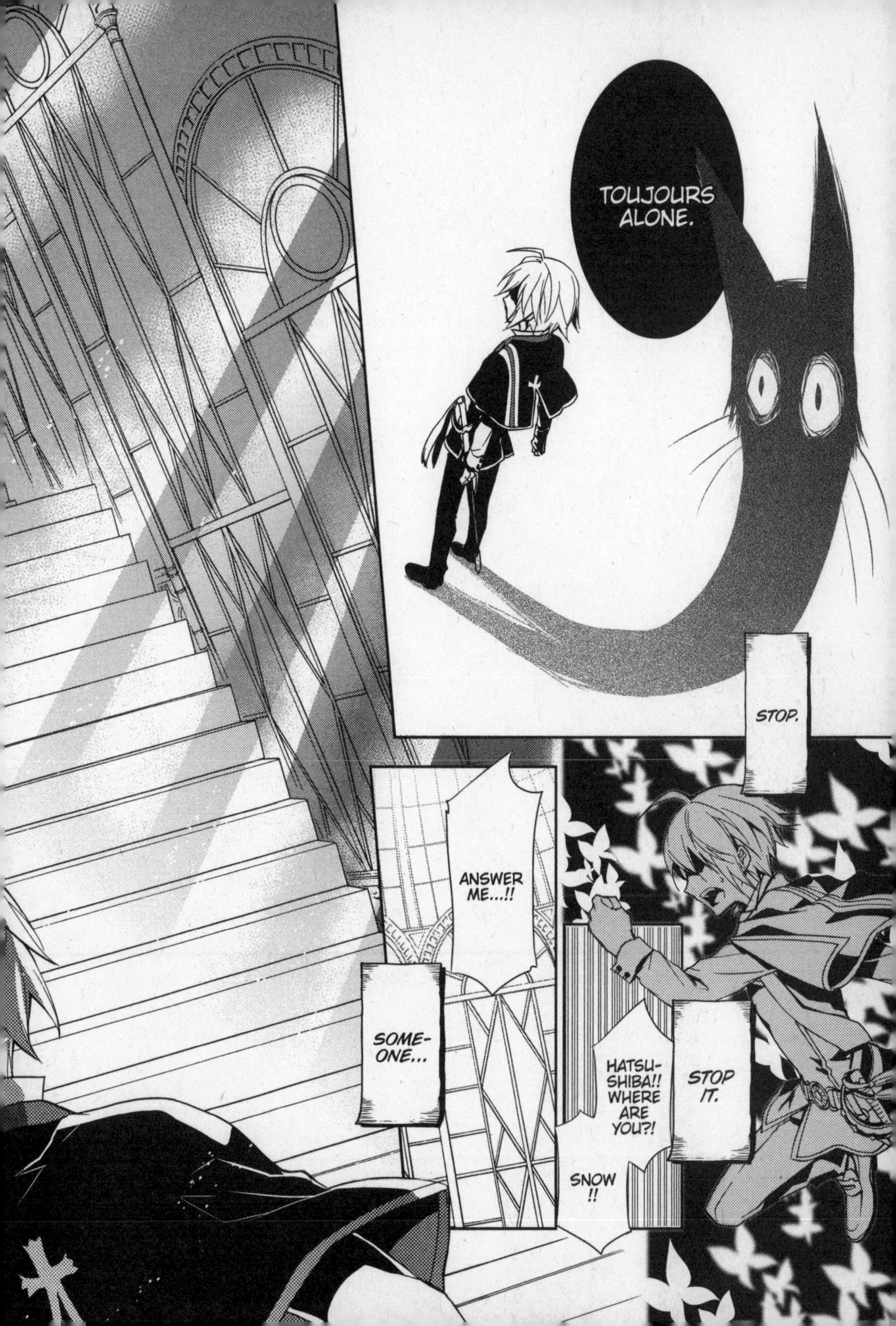
TOUJOURS ALONE.
STOP.
STOP IT.
HATSU-SHIBA!! WHERE ARE YOU?!
SNOW !!
ANSWER ME...!!
SOME-ONE...

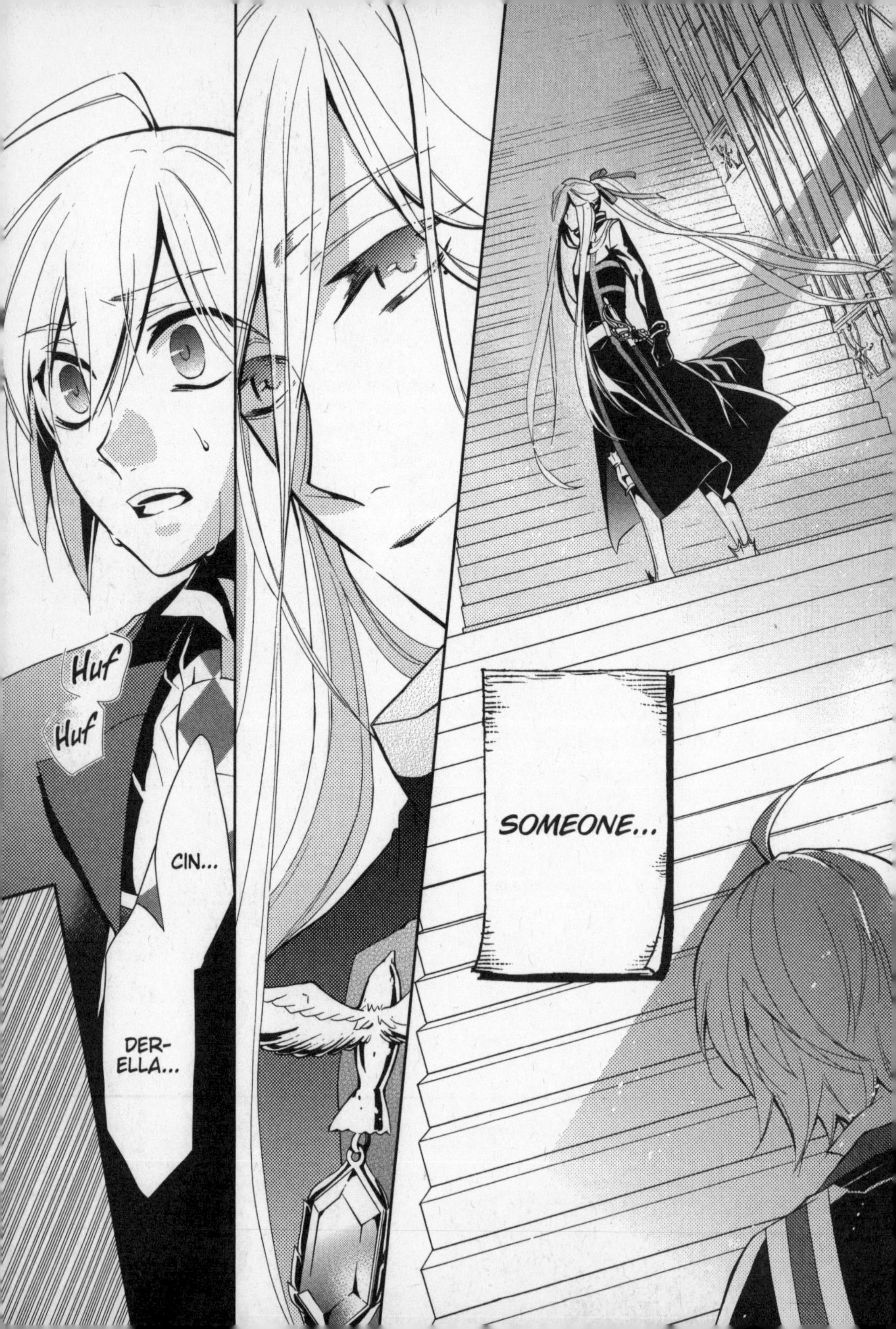
SOMEONE...
Huf
Huf
CIN...
DER-
ELLA...

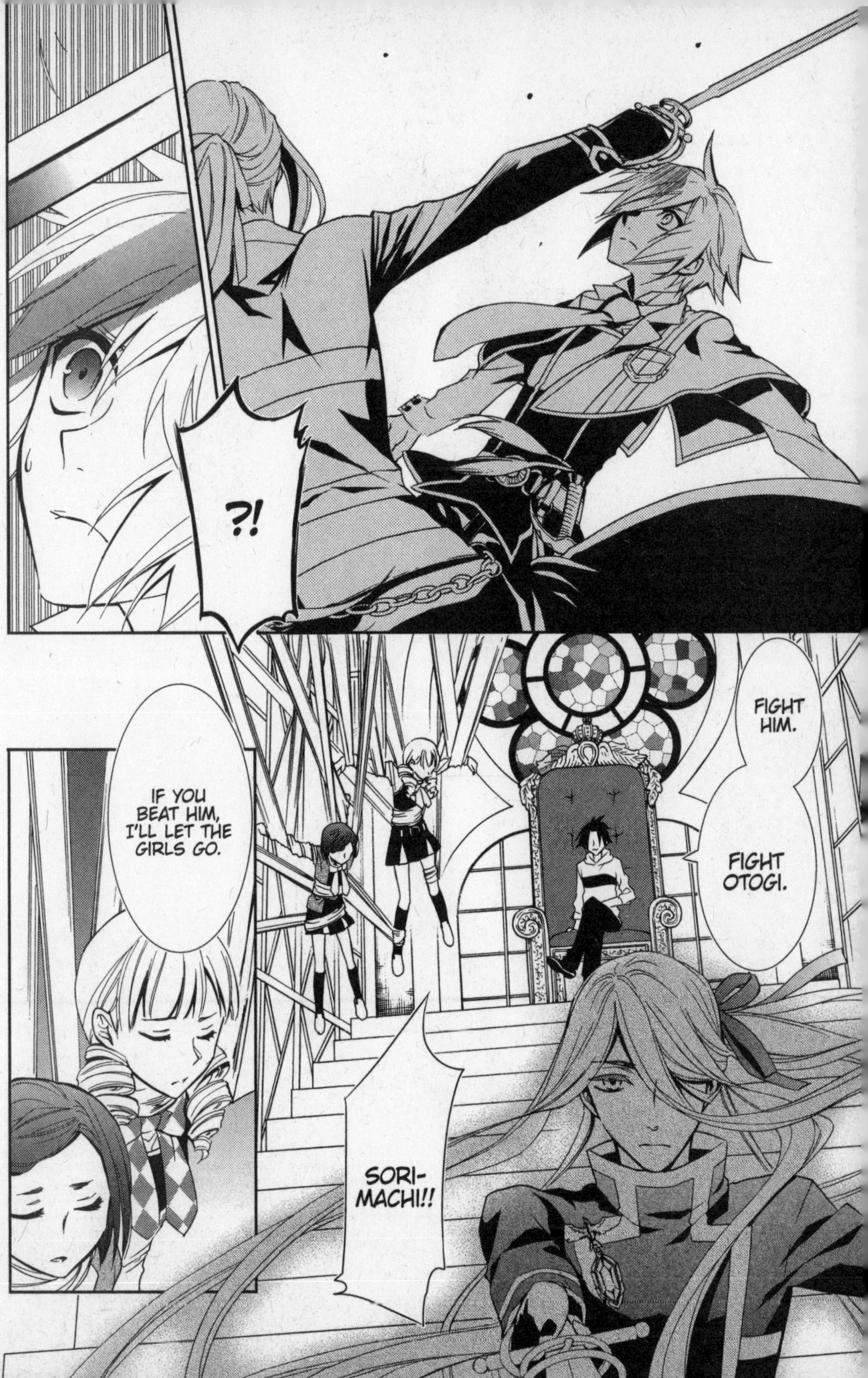
?!
FIGHT HIM.
FIGHT OTOGI.
IF YOU BEAT HIM, I'LL LET THE GIRLS GO.
SORI-MACHI!!

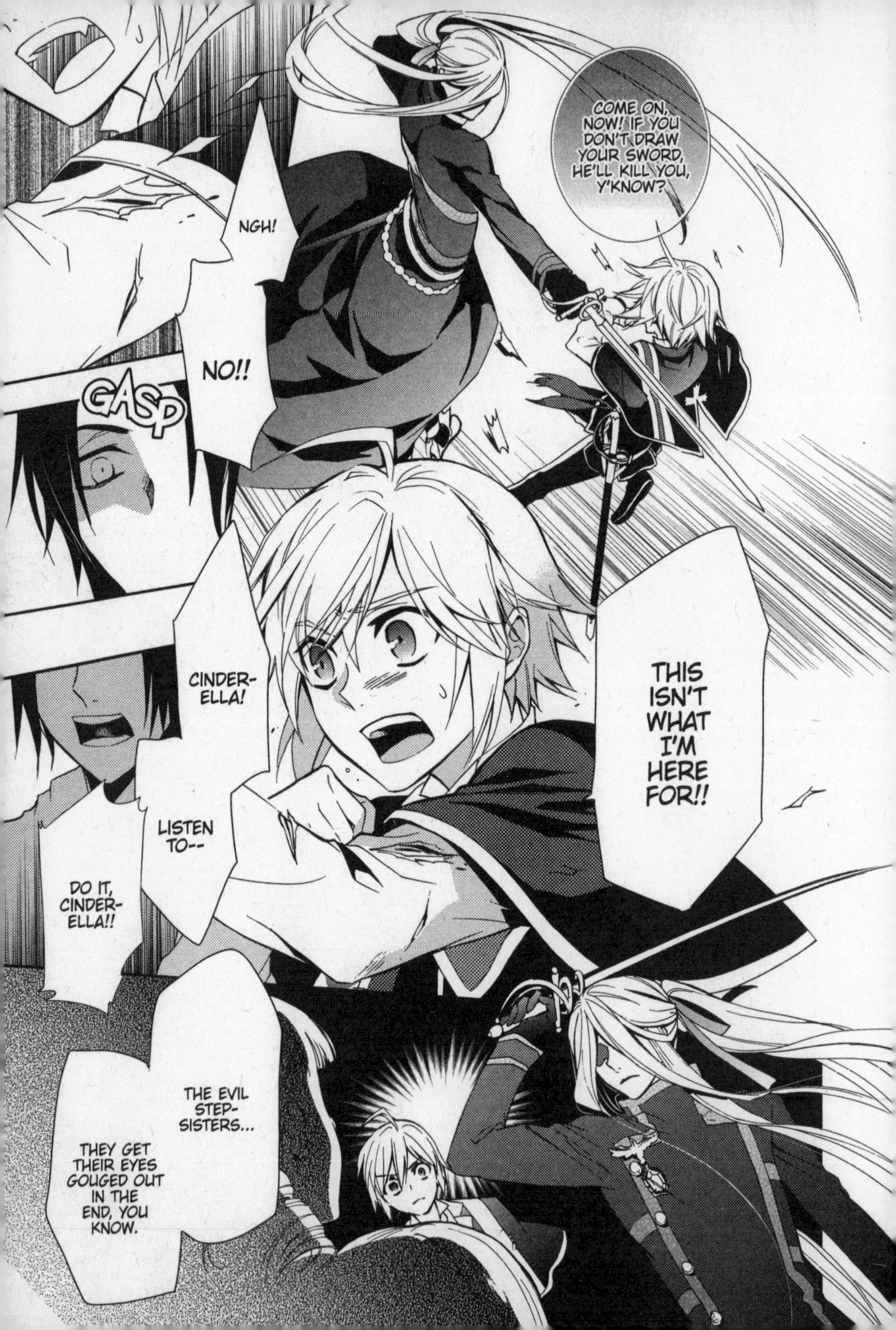

COME ON, NOW! IF YOU DON'T DRAW YOUR SWORD, HE'LL KILL YOU, Y'KNOW?
NGH!
NO!!
GASP
THIS ISN'T WHAT I'M HERE FOR!!
CINDER-ELLA!
LISTEN TO--
DO IT, CINDER-ELLA!!
THE EVIL STEP-SISTERS...
THEY GET THEIR EYES GOUGED OUT IN THE END, YOU KNOW.

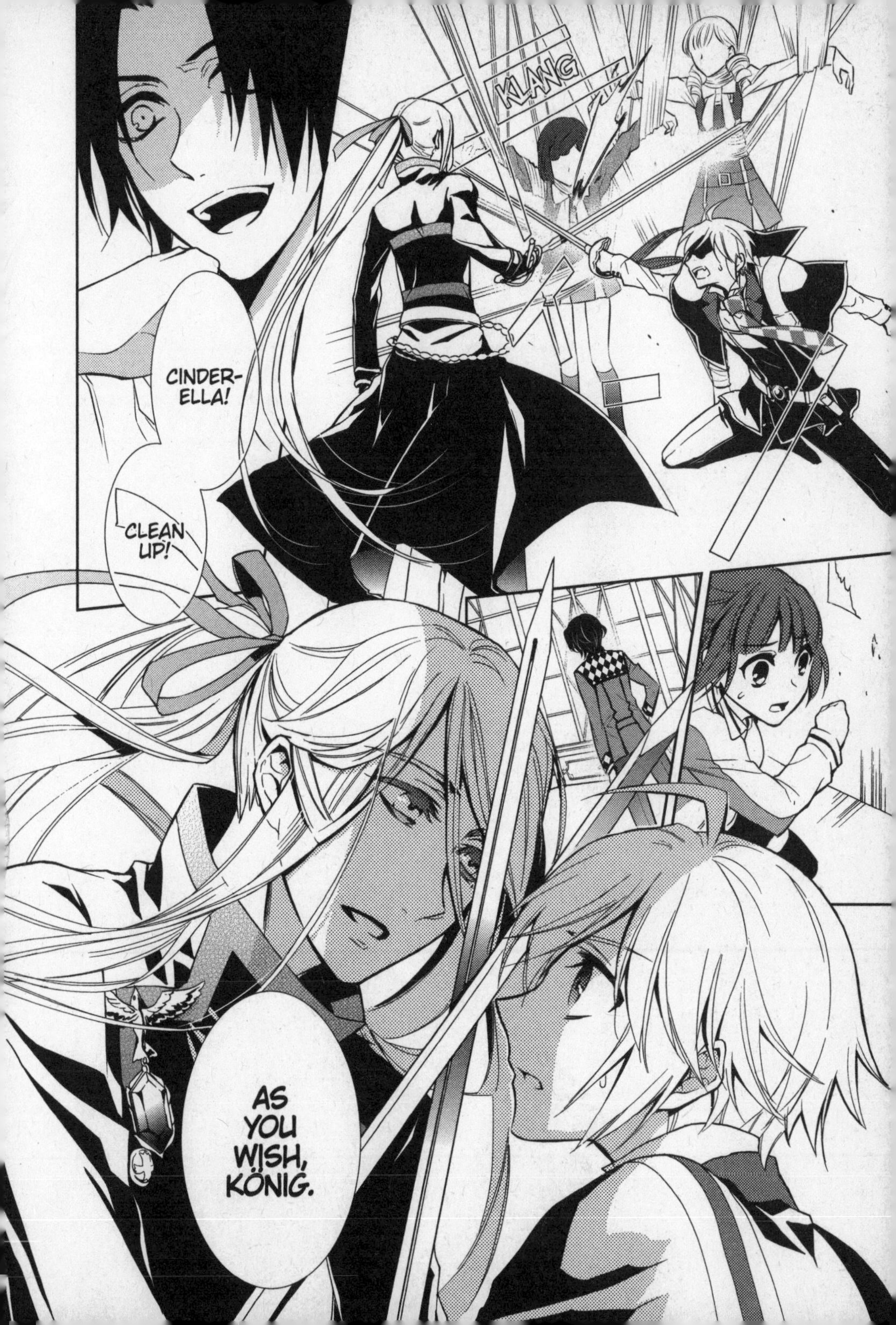
KLANG
CINDER-ELLA!
CLEAN UP!
AS YOU WISH, KÖNIG.

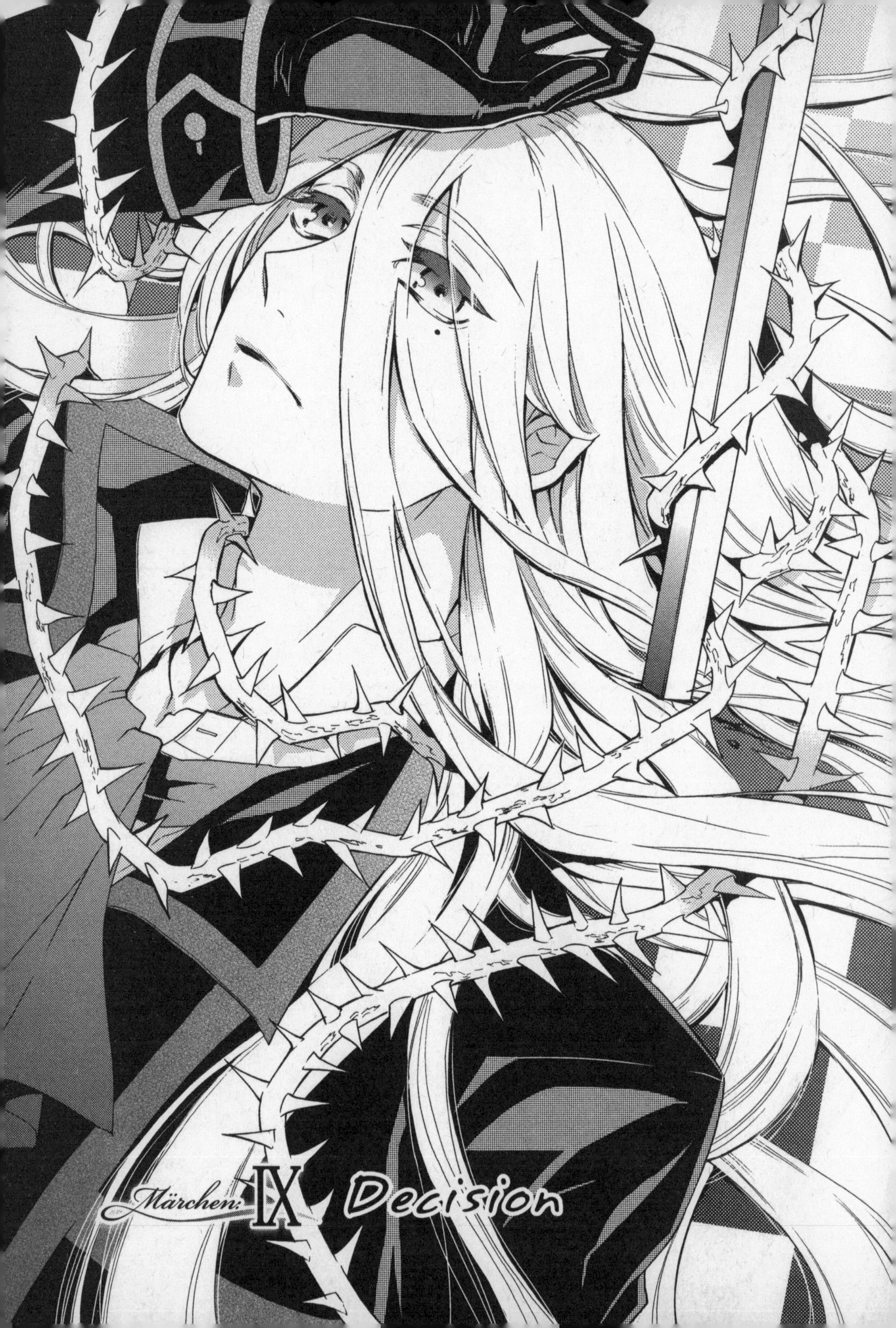
Märchen: IX Decision

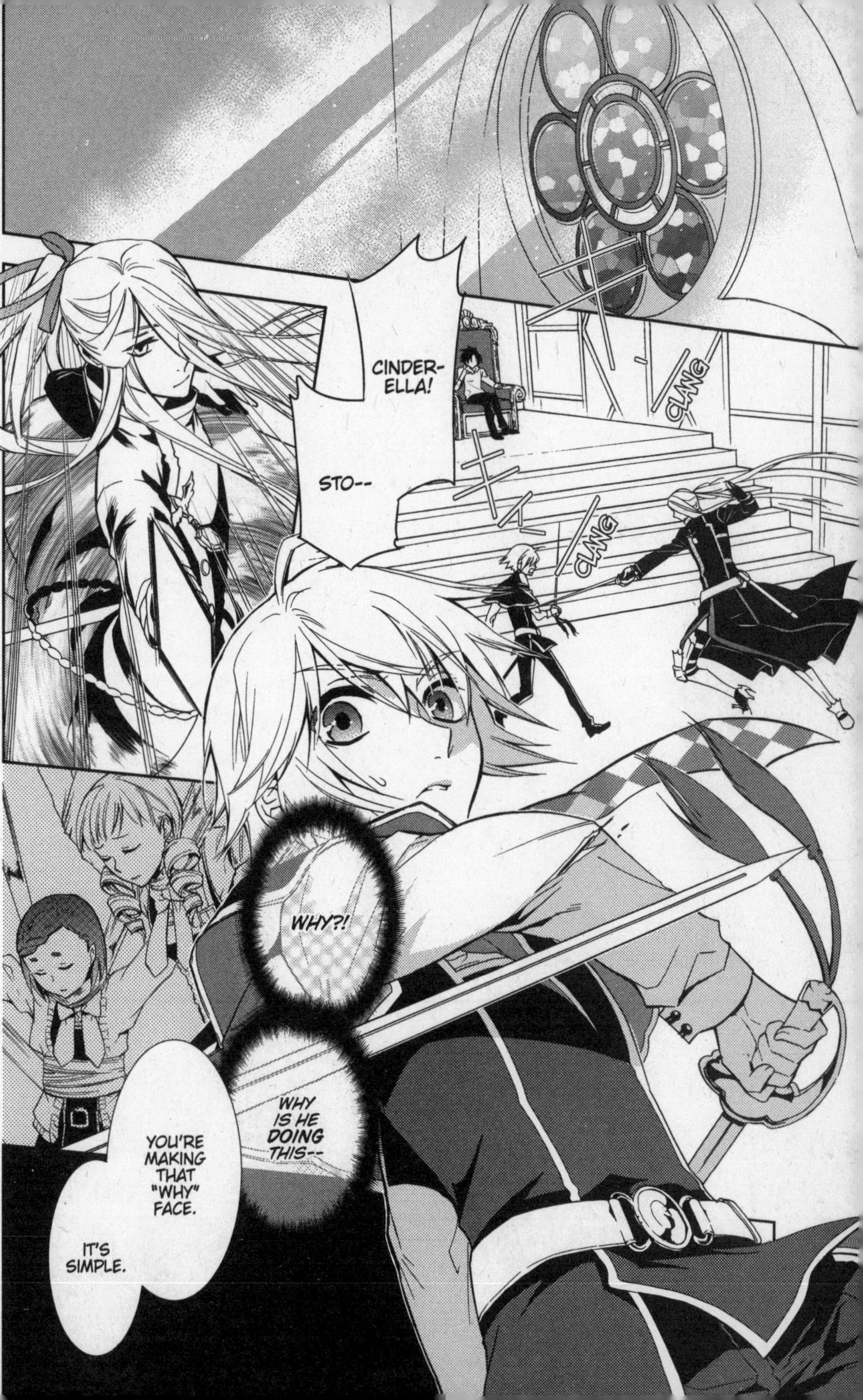
CLANG
CINDER-ELLA!
STO--
CLANG
WHY?!
WHY IS HE DOING THIS--
YOU'RE MAKING THAT "WHY" FACE.
IT'S SIMPLE.

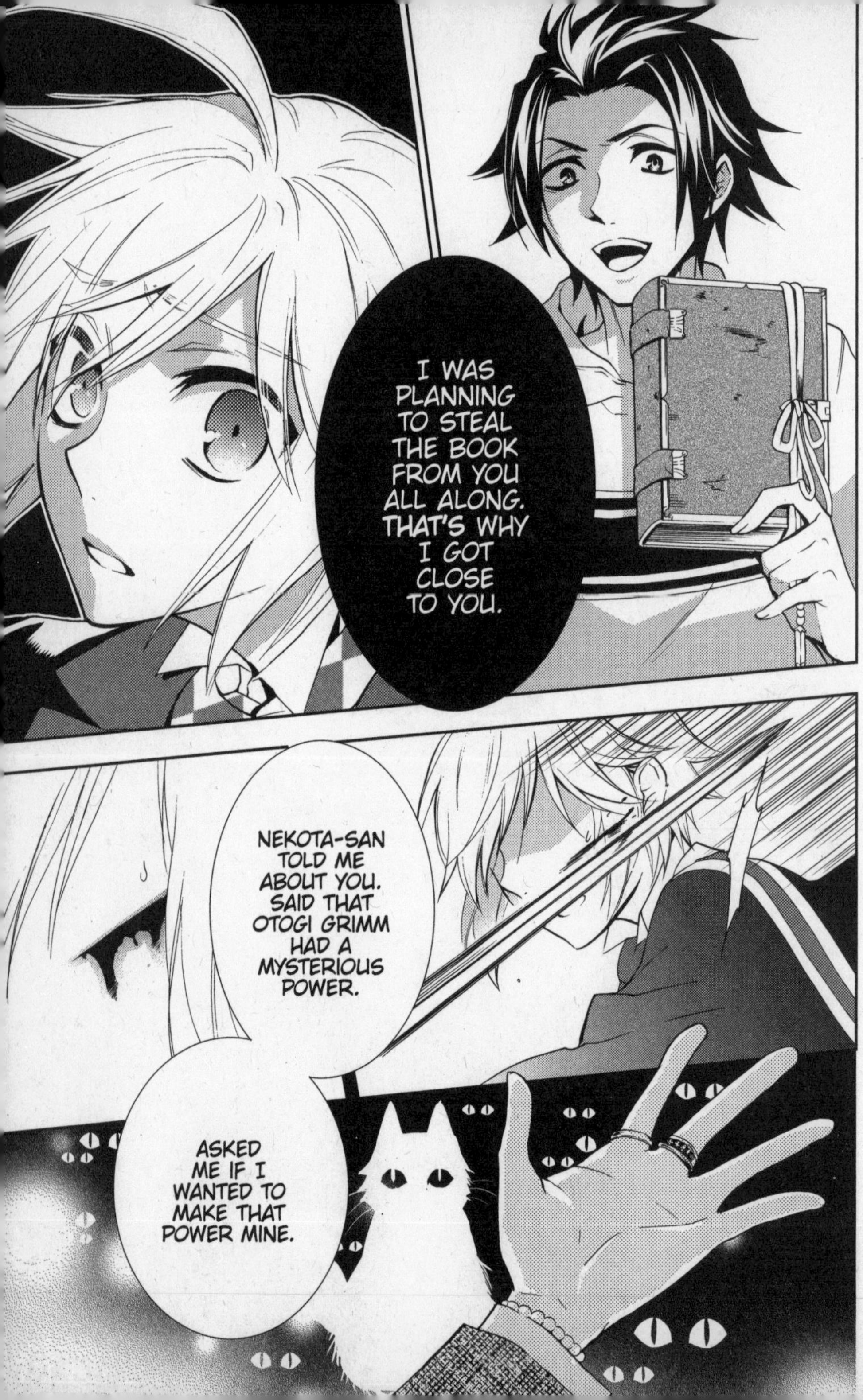
I WAS PLANNING TO STEAL THE BOOK FROM YOU ALL ALONG. THAT'S WHY I GOT CLOSE TO YOU.
NEKOTA-SAN TOLD ME ABOUT YOU. SAID THAT OTOGI GRIMM HAD A MYSTERIOUS POWER.
ASKED ME IF I WANTED TO MAKE THAT POWER MINE.

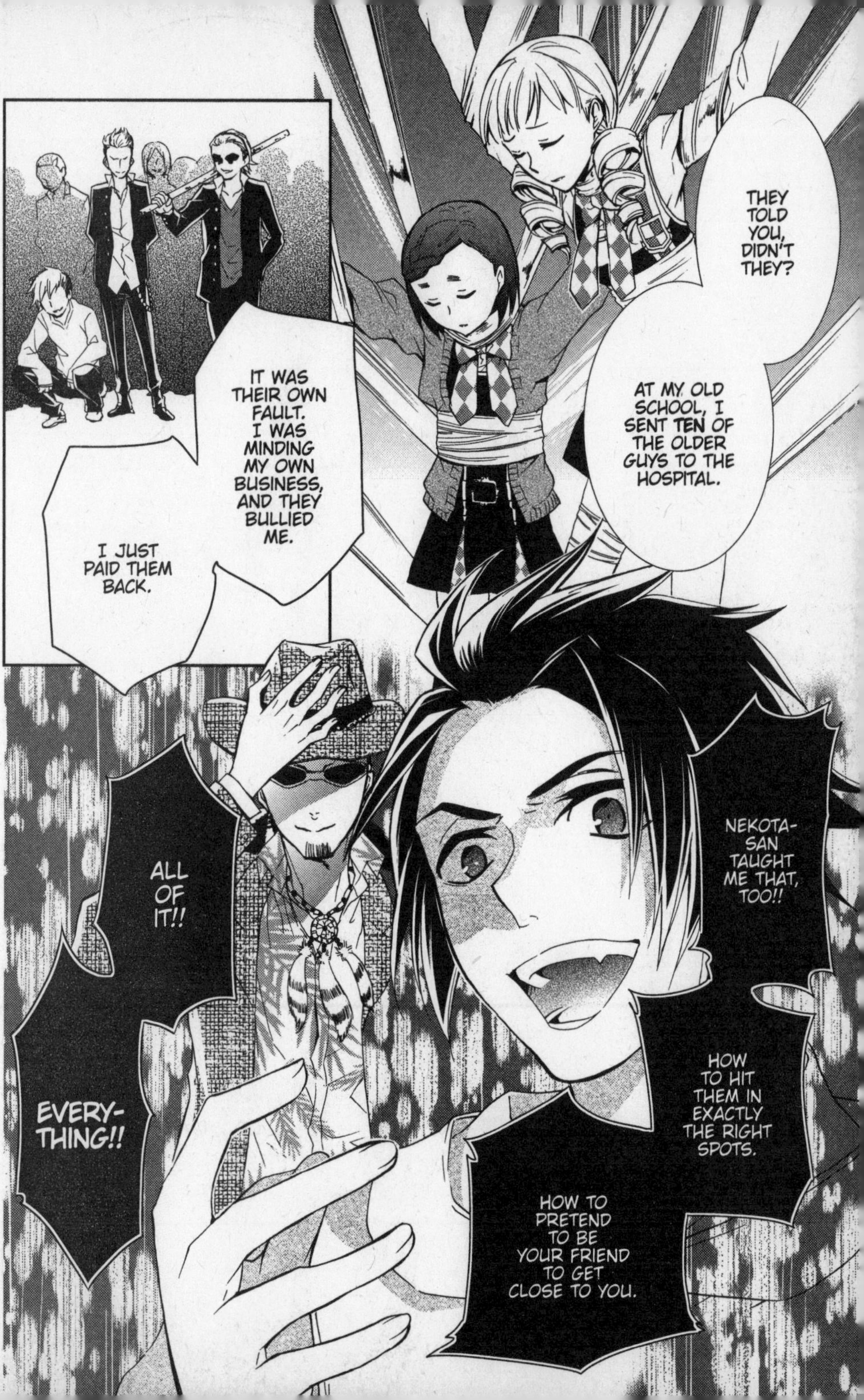
THEY TOLD YOU, DIDN'T THEY?
AT MY OLD SCHOOL, I SENT TEN OF THE OLDER GUYS TO THE HOSPITAL.
IT WAS THEIR OWN FAULT. I WAS MINDING MY OWN BUSINESS, AND THEY BULLIED ME.
I JUST PAID THEM BACK.
NEKOTA-SAN TAUGHT ME THAT, TOO!!
HOW TO HIT THEM IN EXACTLY THE RIGHT SPOTS.
HOW TO PRETEND TO BE YOUR FRIEND TO GET CLOSE TO YOU.
ALL OF IT!!
EVERY-THING!!

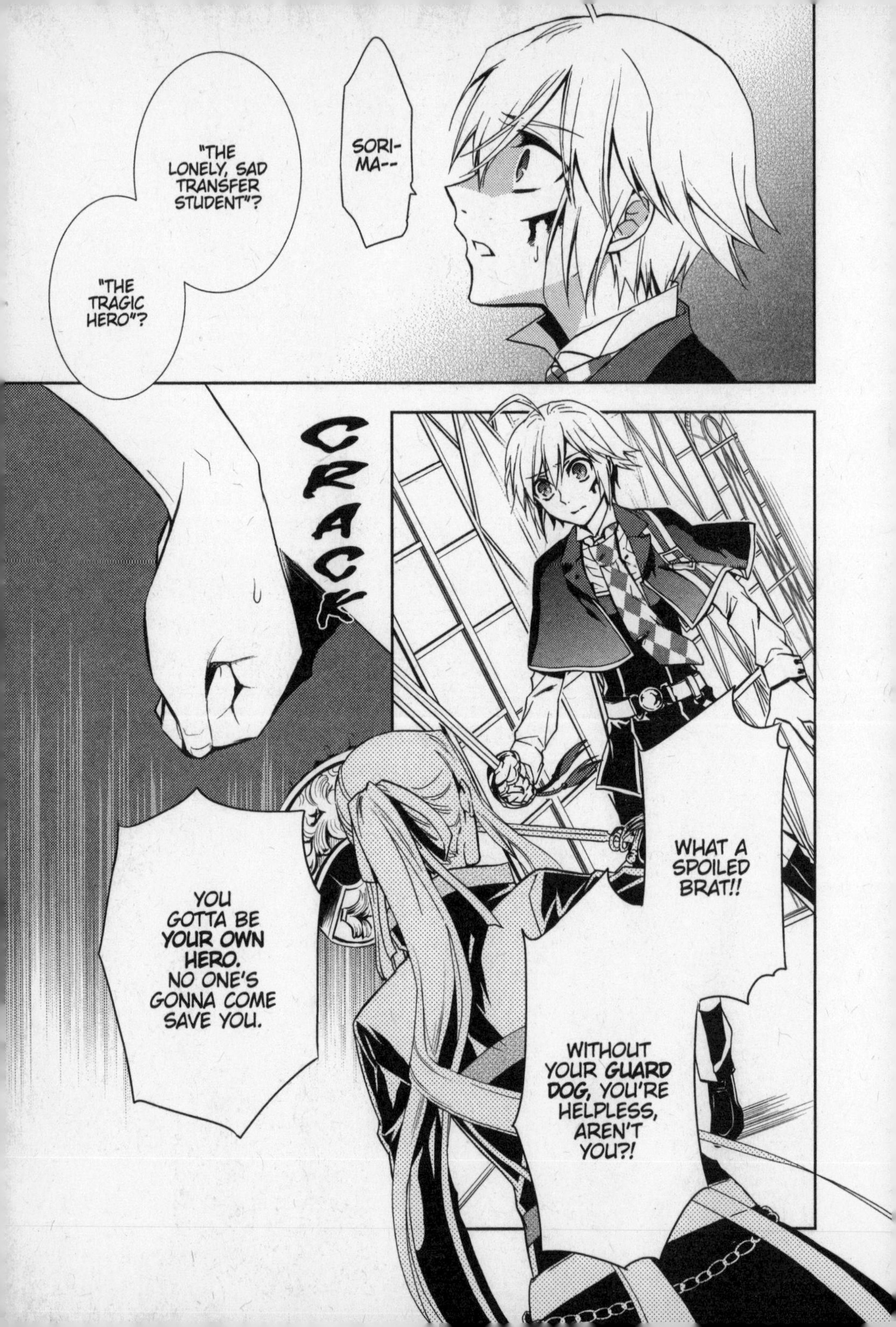
SORI-MA--
"THE LONELY, SAD TRANSFER STUDENT"?
"THE TRAGIC HERO"?
WHAT A SPOILED BRAT!!
WITHOUT YOUR GUARD DOG, YOU'RE HELPLESS, AREN'T YOU?!
CRACK
YOU GOTTA BE YOUR OWN HERO. NO ONE'S GONNA COME SAVE YOU.

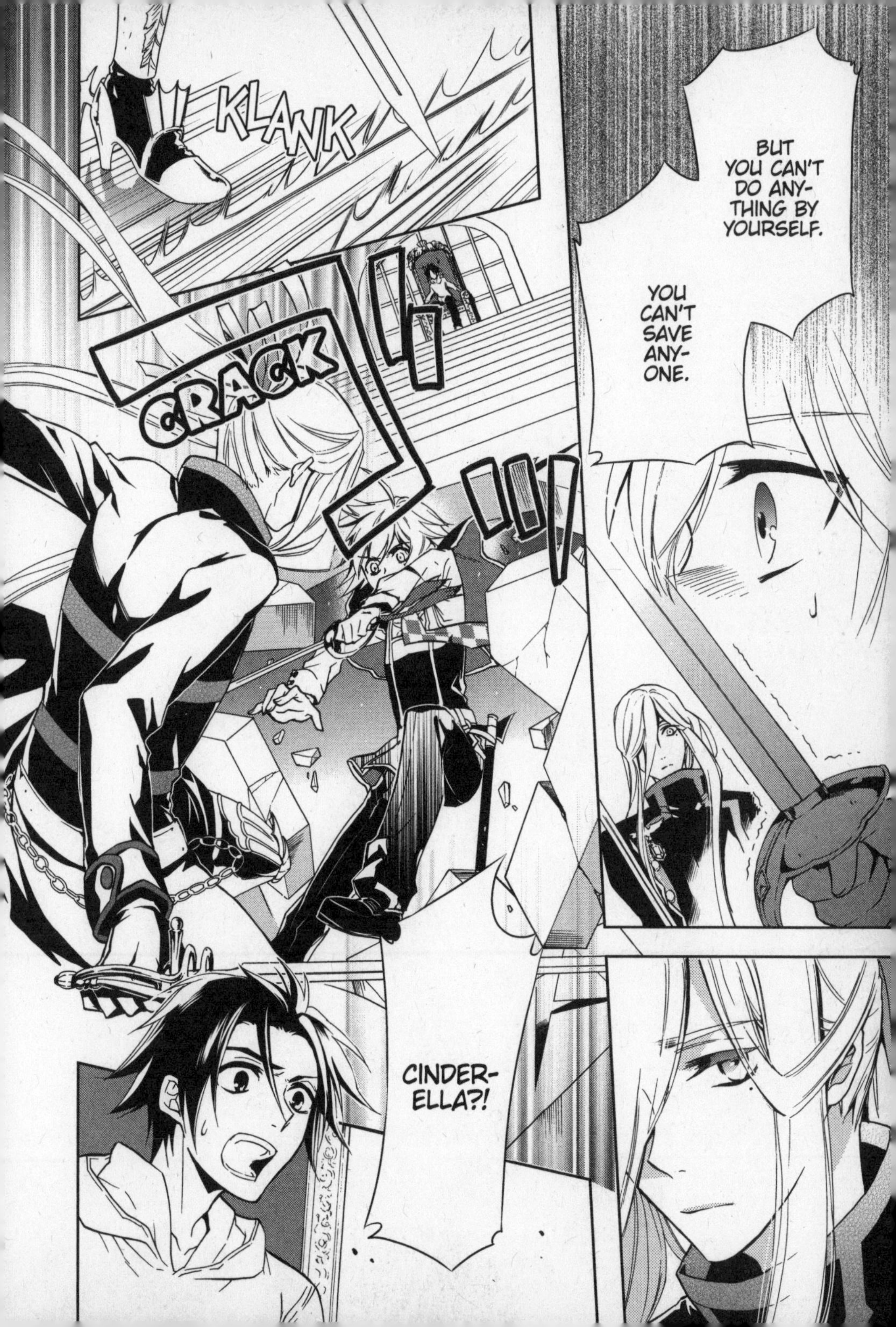
BUT YOU CAN'T DO ANY-THING BY YOURSELF.
YOU CAN'T SAVE ANY-ONE.
KLANK
CRACK
CINDER-ELLA?!

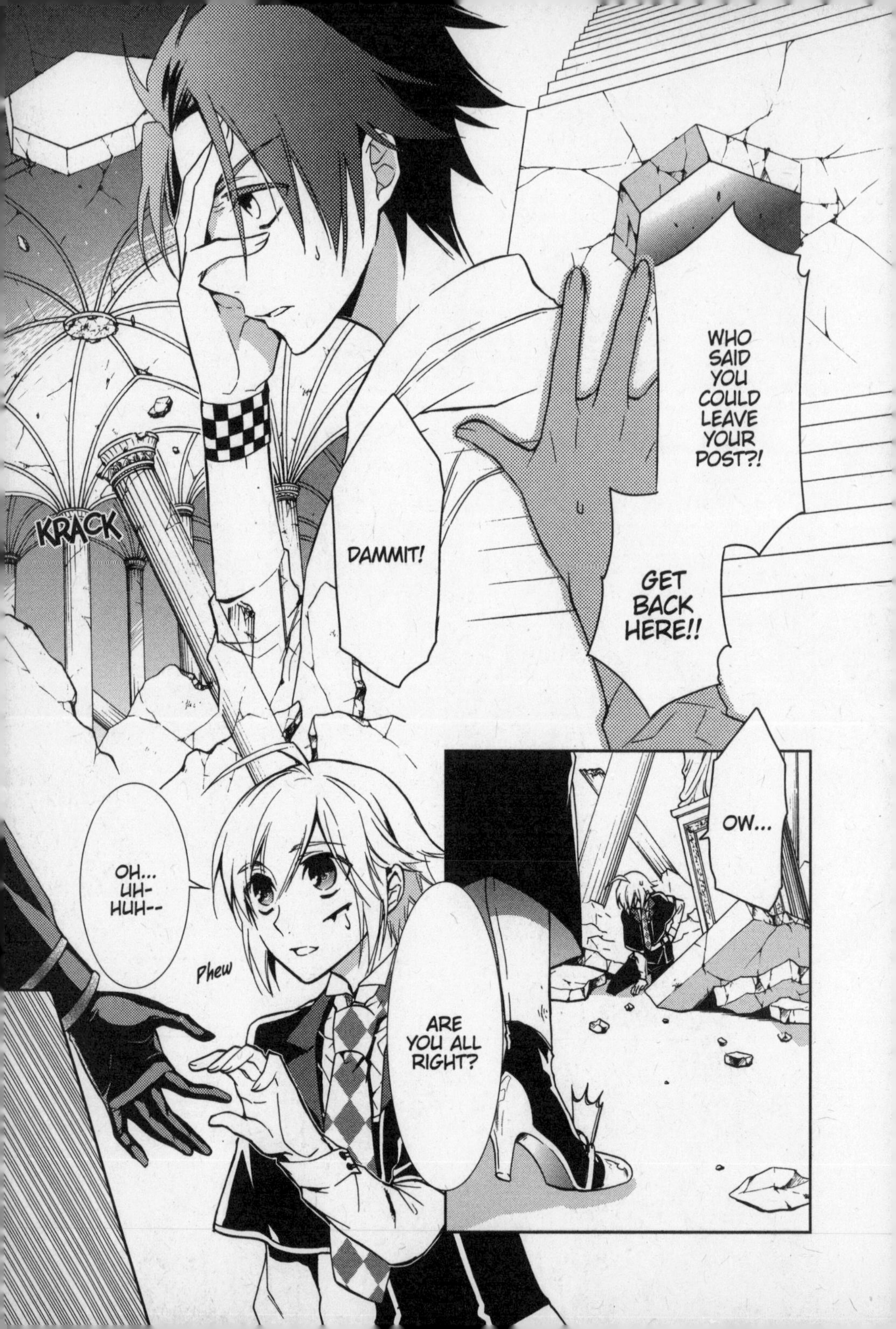
WHO SAID YOU COULD LEAVE YOUR POST?!
GET BACK HERE!!
DAMMIT!
KRACK
OW...
ARE YOU ALL RIGHT?
OH... UH-HUH--
Phew

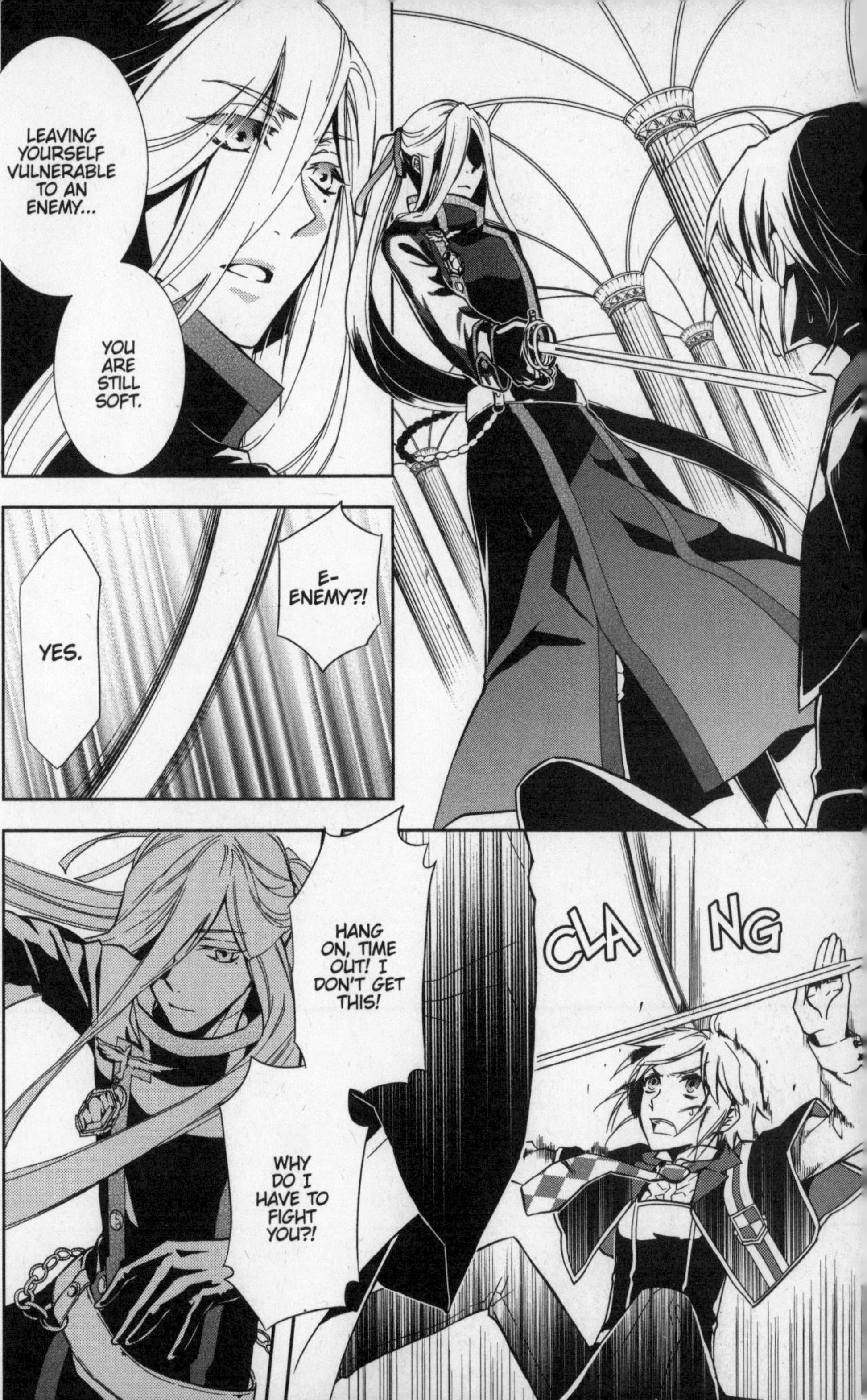
LEAVING YOURSELF VULNERABLE TO AN ENEMY...
YOU ARE STILL SOFT.
E-ENEMY?!
YES.
CLANG
HANG ON, TIME OUT! I DON'T GET THIS!
WHY DO I HAVE TO FIGHT YOU?!

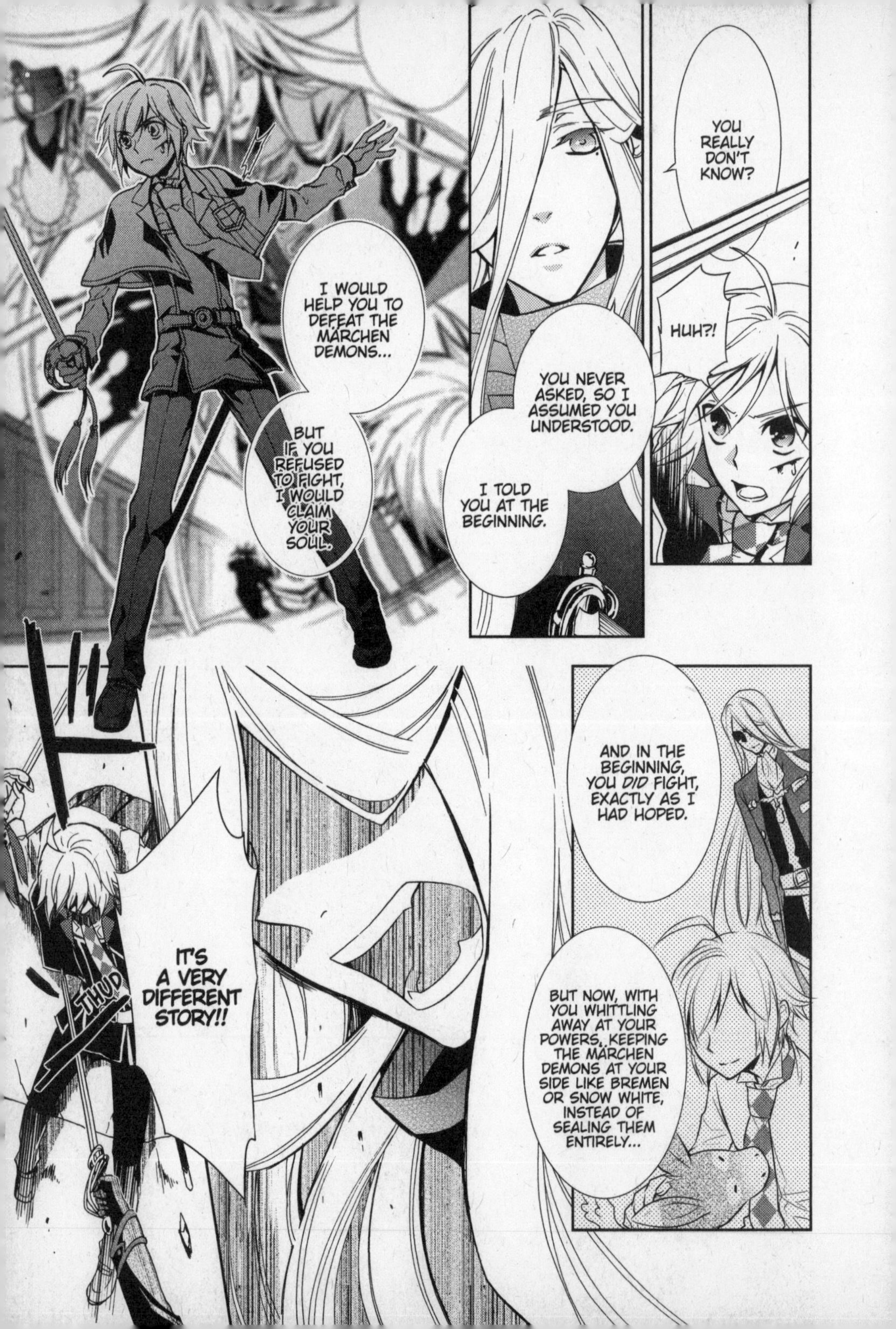
YOU REALLY DON'T KNOW?
HUH?!
YOU NEVER ASKED, SO I ASSUMED YOU UNDERSTOOD.
I TOLD YOU AT THE BEGINNING.
I WOULD HELP YOU TO DEFEAT THE MÄRCHEN DEMONS...
BUT IF YOU REFUSED TO FIGHT, I WOULD CLAIM YOUR SOUL.
AND IN THE BEGINNING, YOU *DID* FIGHT, EXACTLY AS I HAD HOPED.
BUT NOW, WITH YOU WHITTLING AWAY AT YOUR POWERS, KEEPING THE MÄRCHEN DEMONS AT YOUR SIDE LIKE BREMEN OR SNOW WHITE, INSTEAD OF SEALING THEM ENTIRELY...
IT'S A VERY DIFFERENT STORY!!
THUD

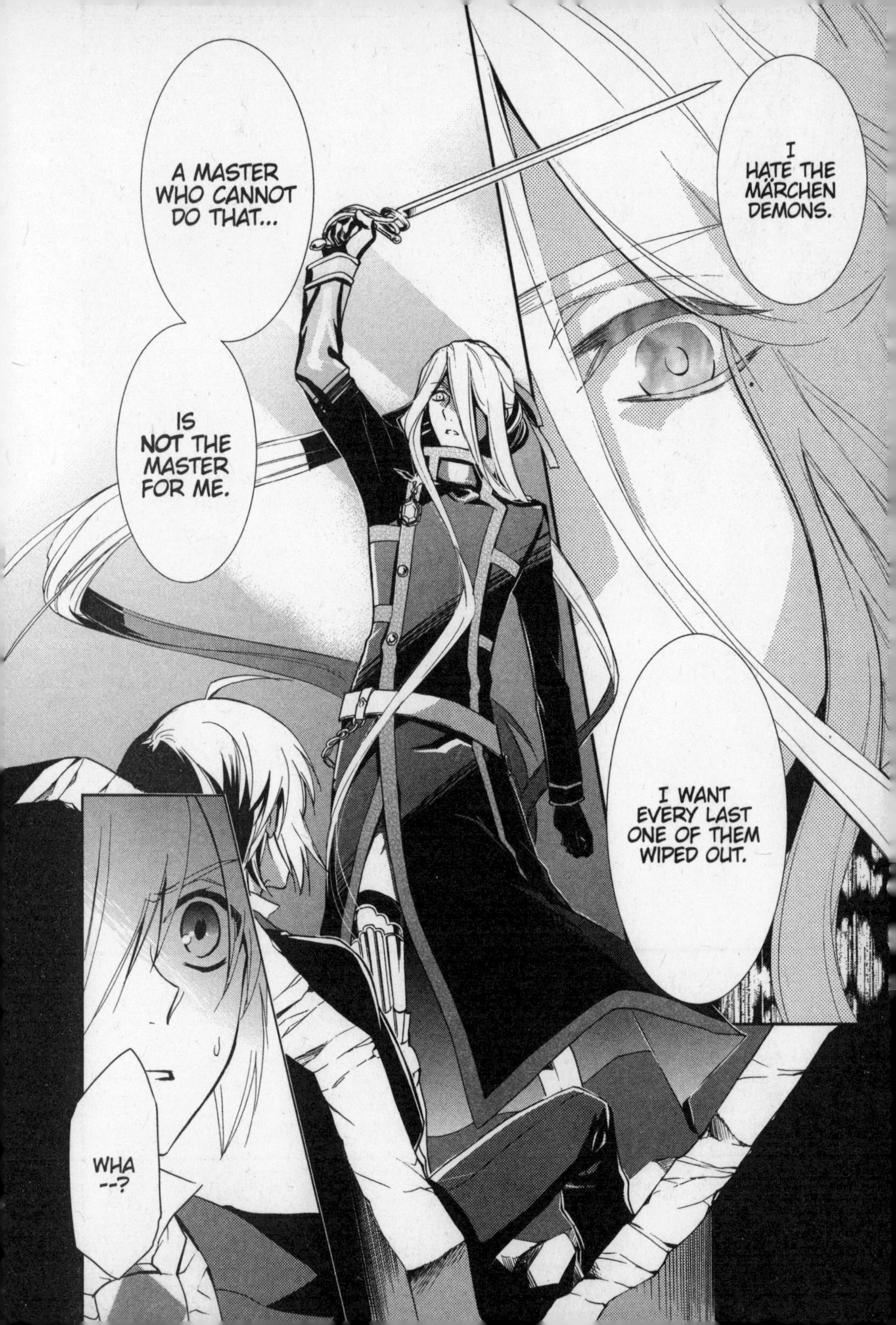
I HATE THE MÄRCHEN DEMONS.
I WANT EVERY LAST ONE OF THEM WIPED OUT.
A MASTER WHO CANNOT DO THAT...
IS NOT THE MASTER FOR ME.
WHA --?

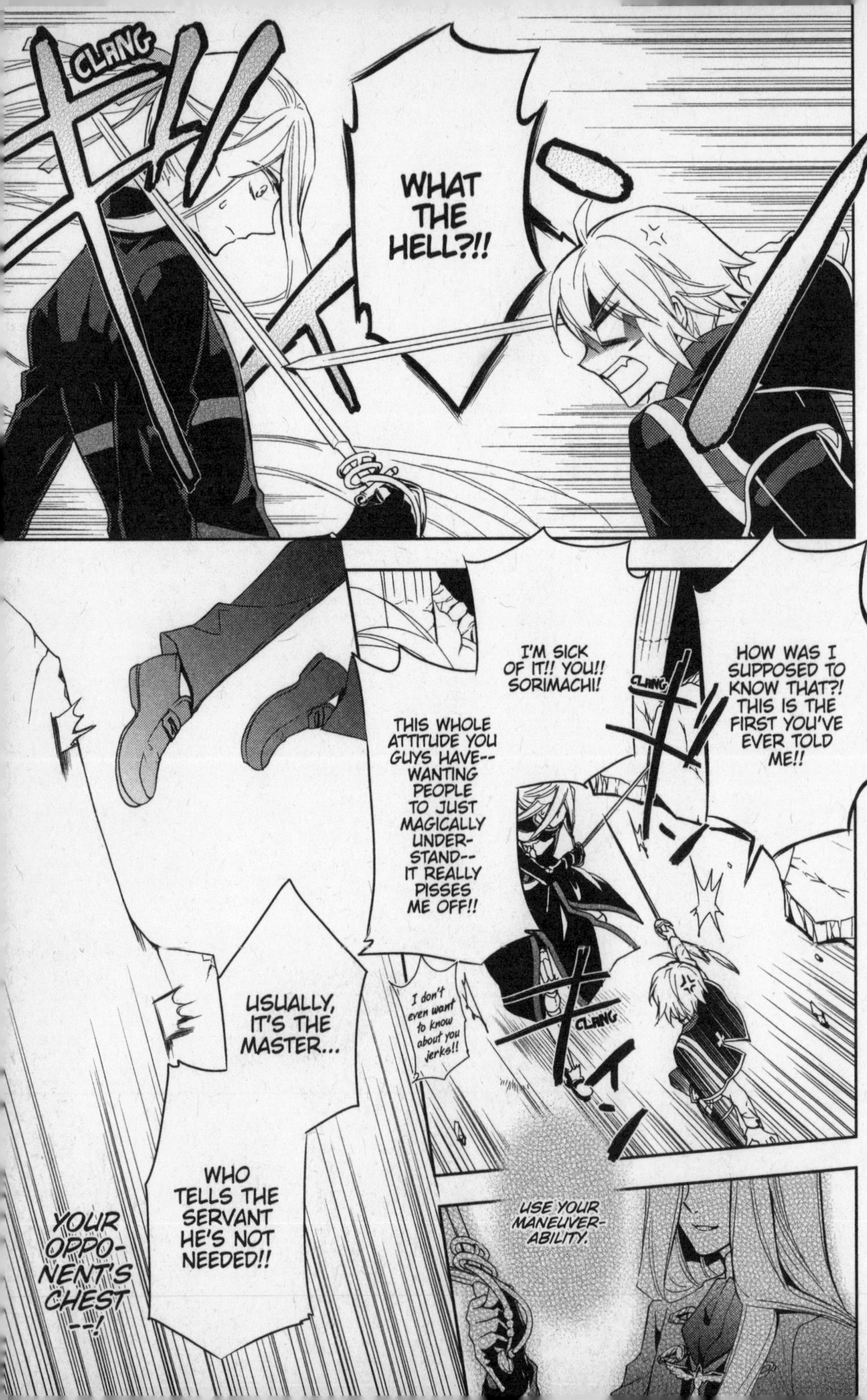
CLANG
WHAT THE HELL?!!
HOW WAS I SUPPOSED TO KNOW THAT?! THIS IS THE FIRST YOU'VE EVER TOLD ME!!
CLANG
I'M SICK OF IT!! YOU!! SORIMACHI!
THIS WHOLE ATTITUDE YOU GUYS HAVE-- WANTING PEOPLE TO JUST MAGICALLY UNDER-STAND-- IT REALLY PISSES ME OFF!!
I don't even want to know about you jerks!!
CLANG
USE YOUR MANEUVER-ABILITY.
USUALLY, IT'S THE MASTER...
WHO TELLS THE SERVANT HE'S NOT NEEDED!!
YOUR OPPO-NENT'S CHEST --!

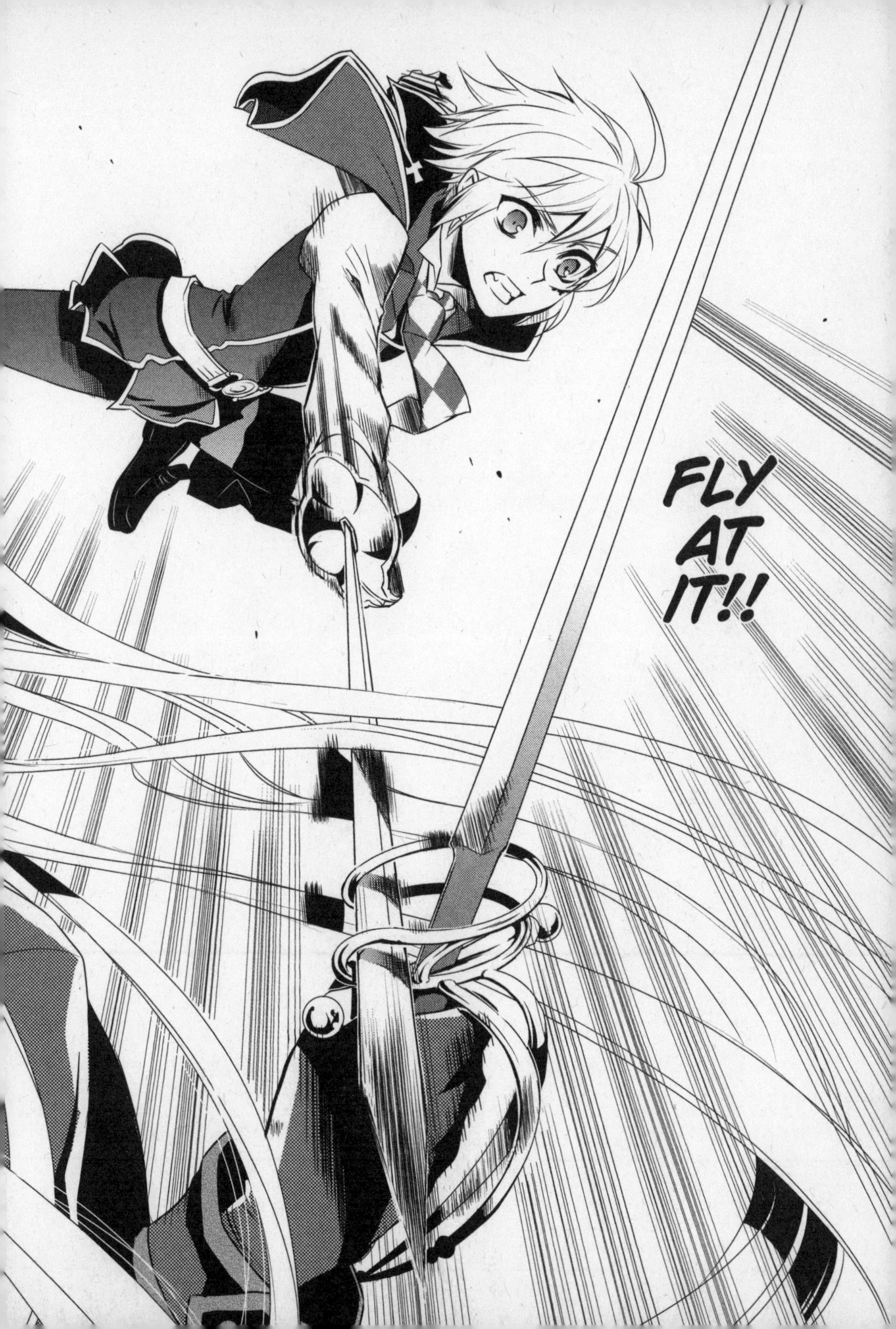
FLY AT IT!!

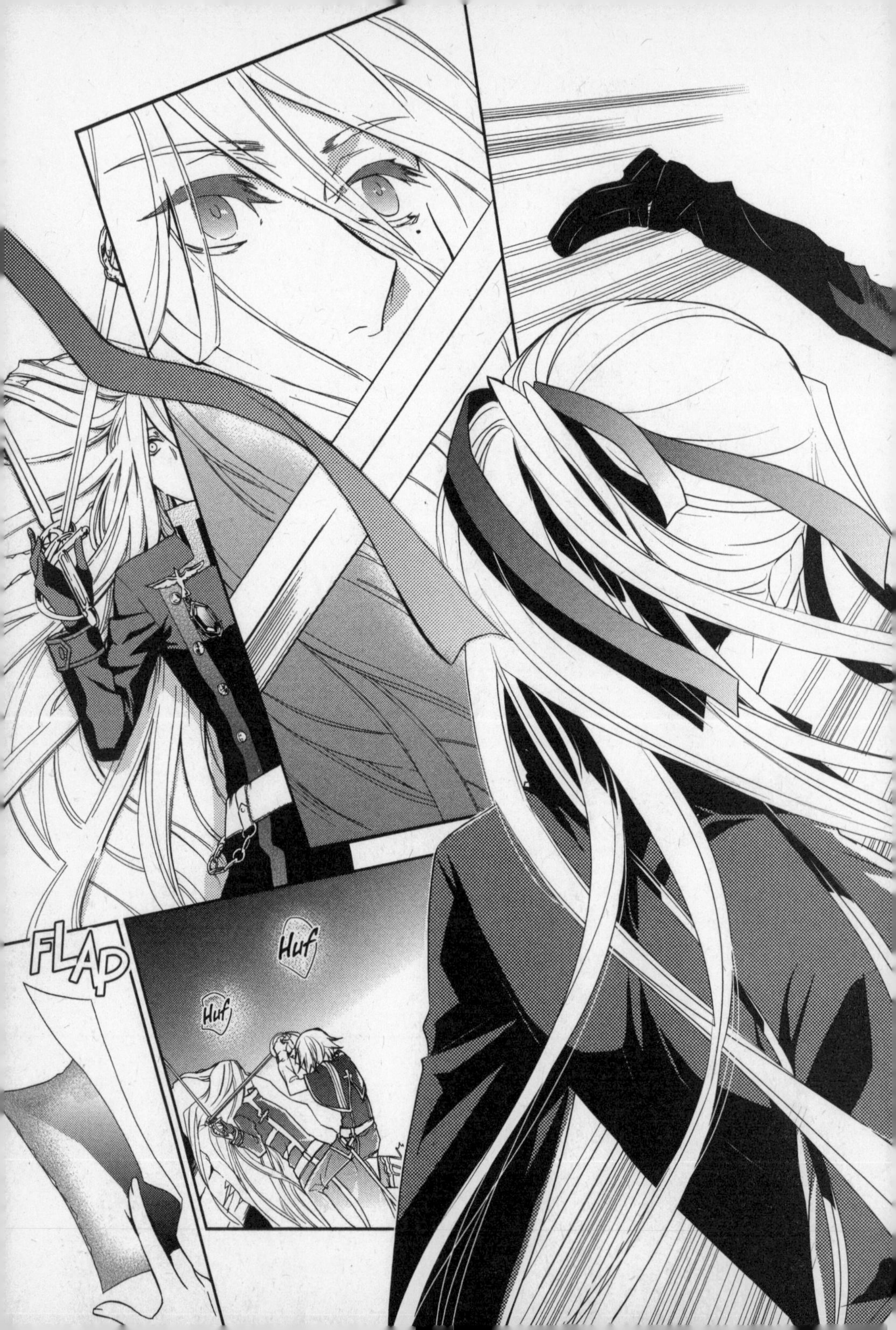
Huf
Huf
FLAP

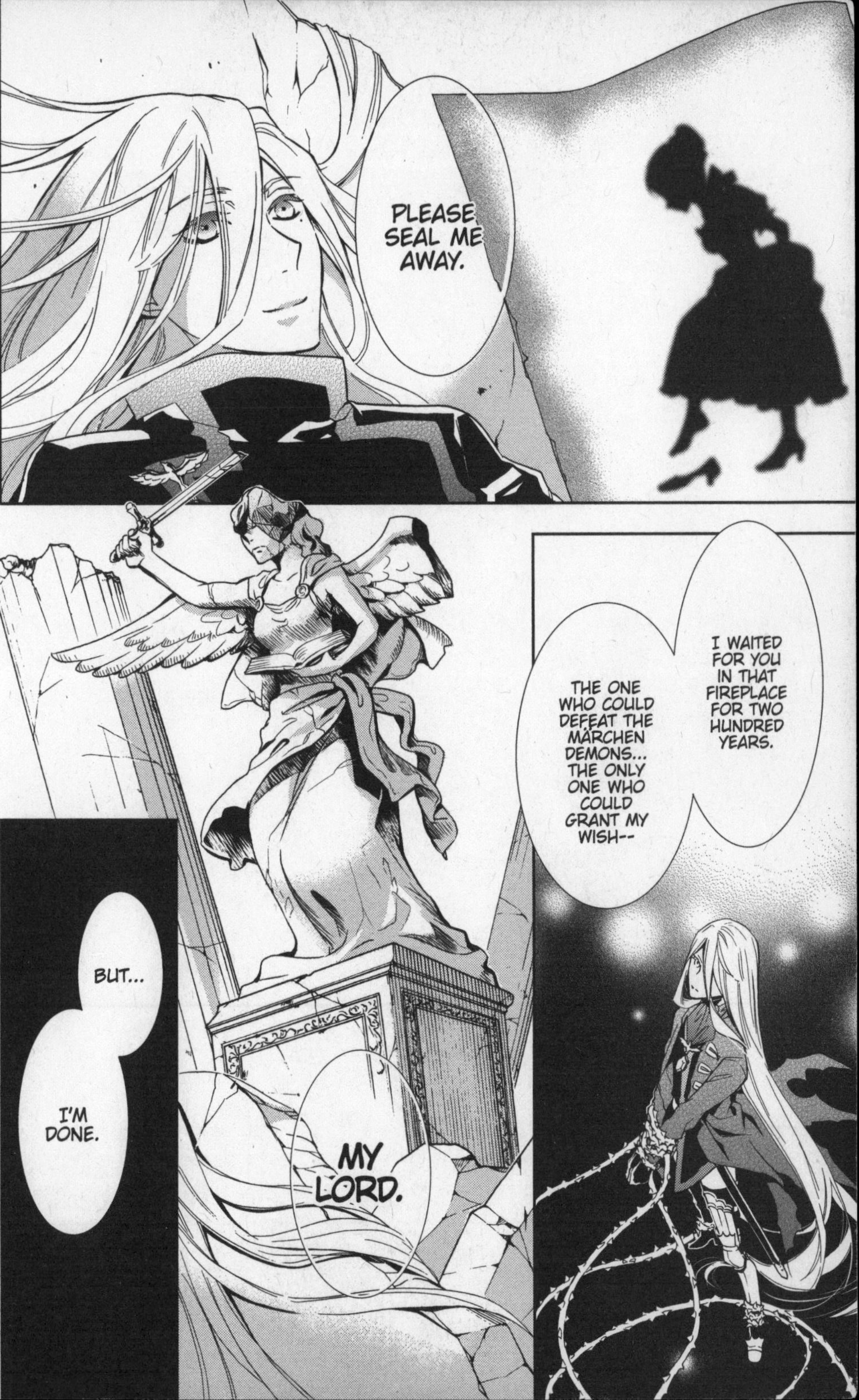
PLEASE SEAL ME AWAY.
I WAITED FOR YOU IN THAT FIREPLACE FOR TWO HUNDRED YEARS.
THE ONE WHO COULD DEFEAT THE MÄRCHEN DEMONS... THE ONLY ONE WHO COULD GRANT MY WISH--
MY LORD.
BUT...
I'M DONE.

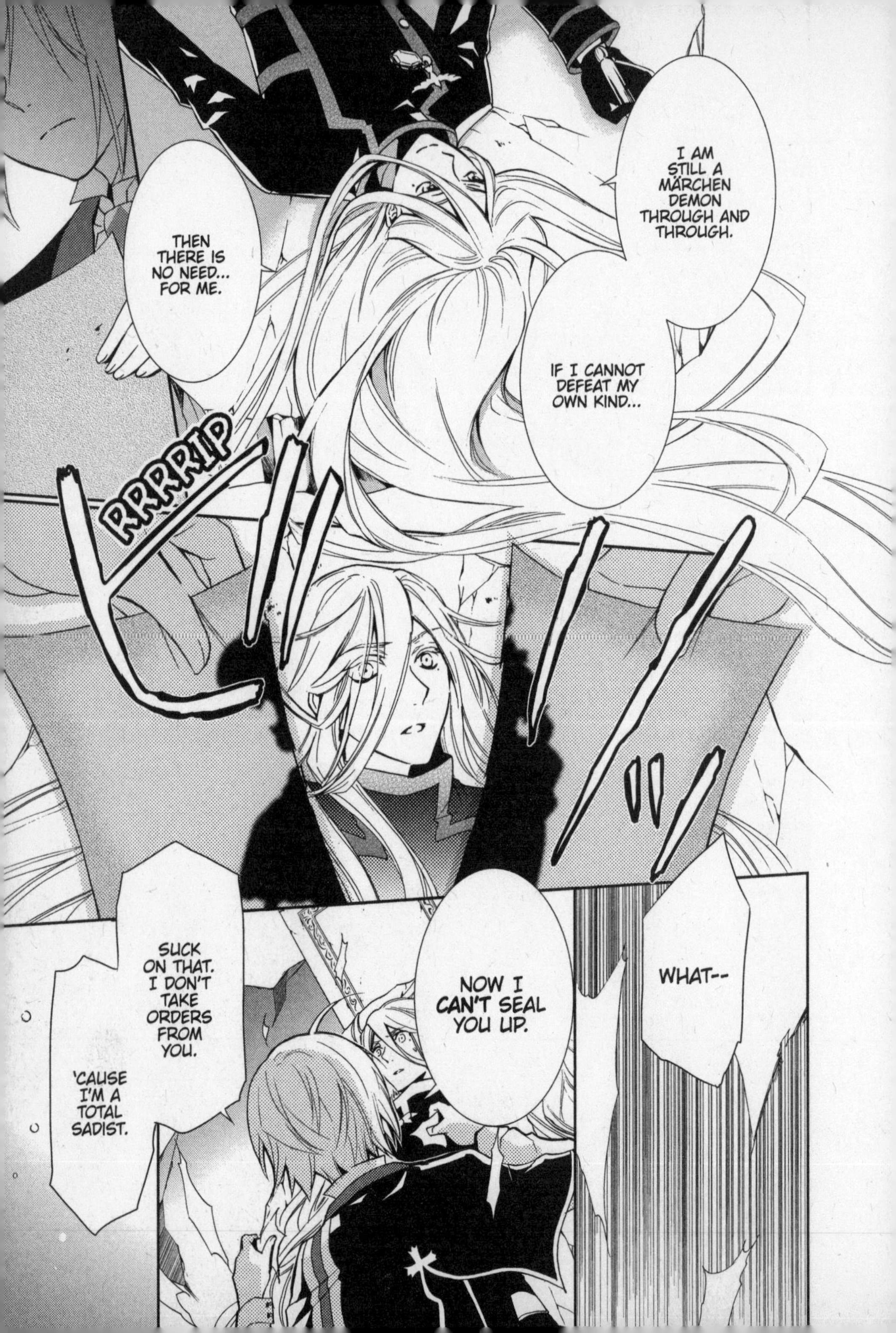
I AM STILL A MÄRCHEN DEMON THROUGH AND THROUGH.
IF I CANNOT DEFEAT MY OWN KIND...
THEN THERE IS NO NEED... FOR ME.
RRRRIP
WHAT--
NOW I CAN'T SEAL YOU UP.
SUCK ON THAT. I DON'T TAKE ORDERS FROM YOU.
'CAUSE I'M A TOTAL SADIST.

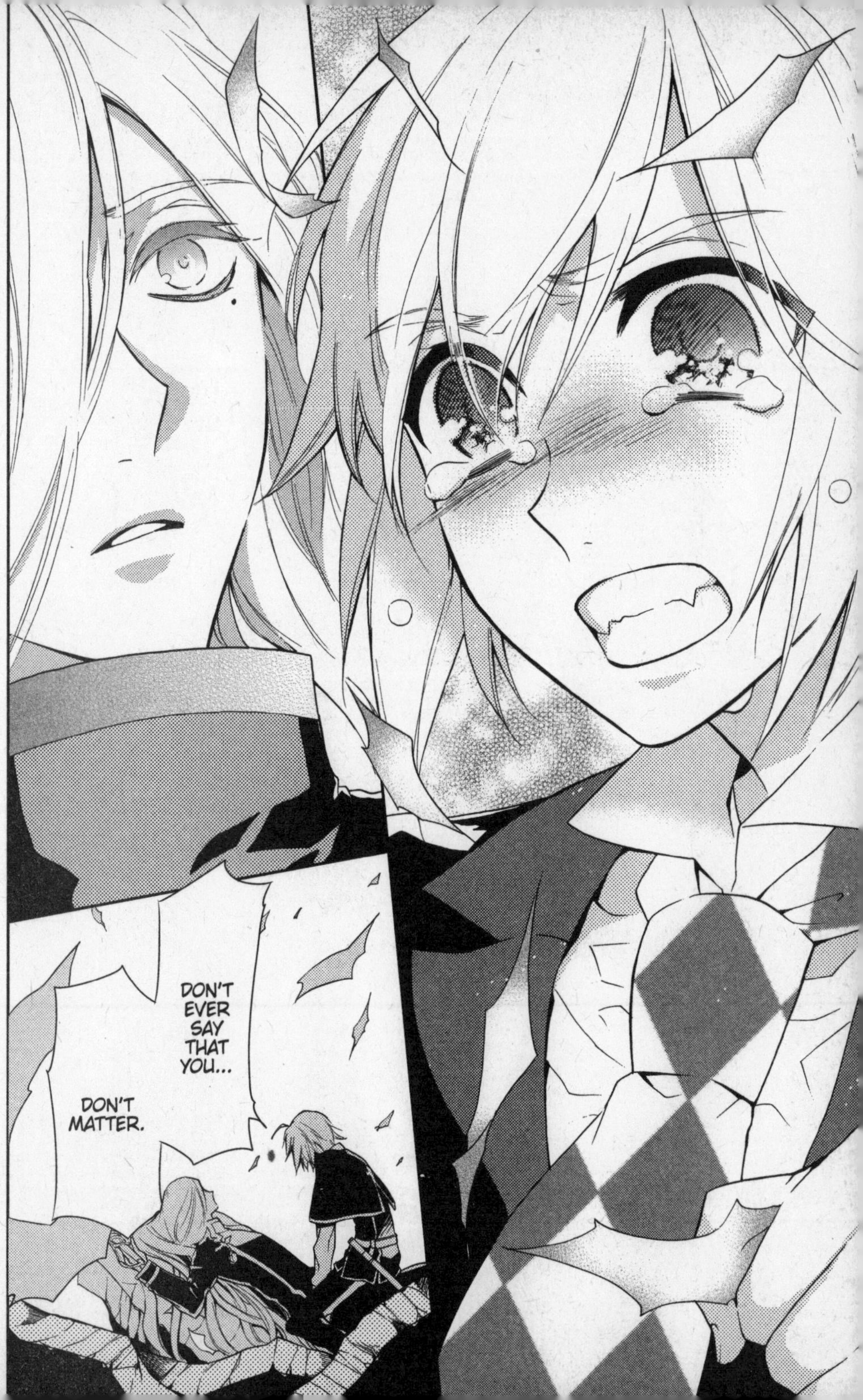
DON'T EVER SAY THAT YOU...
DON'T MATTER.

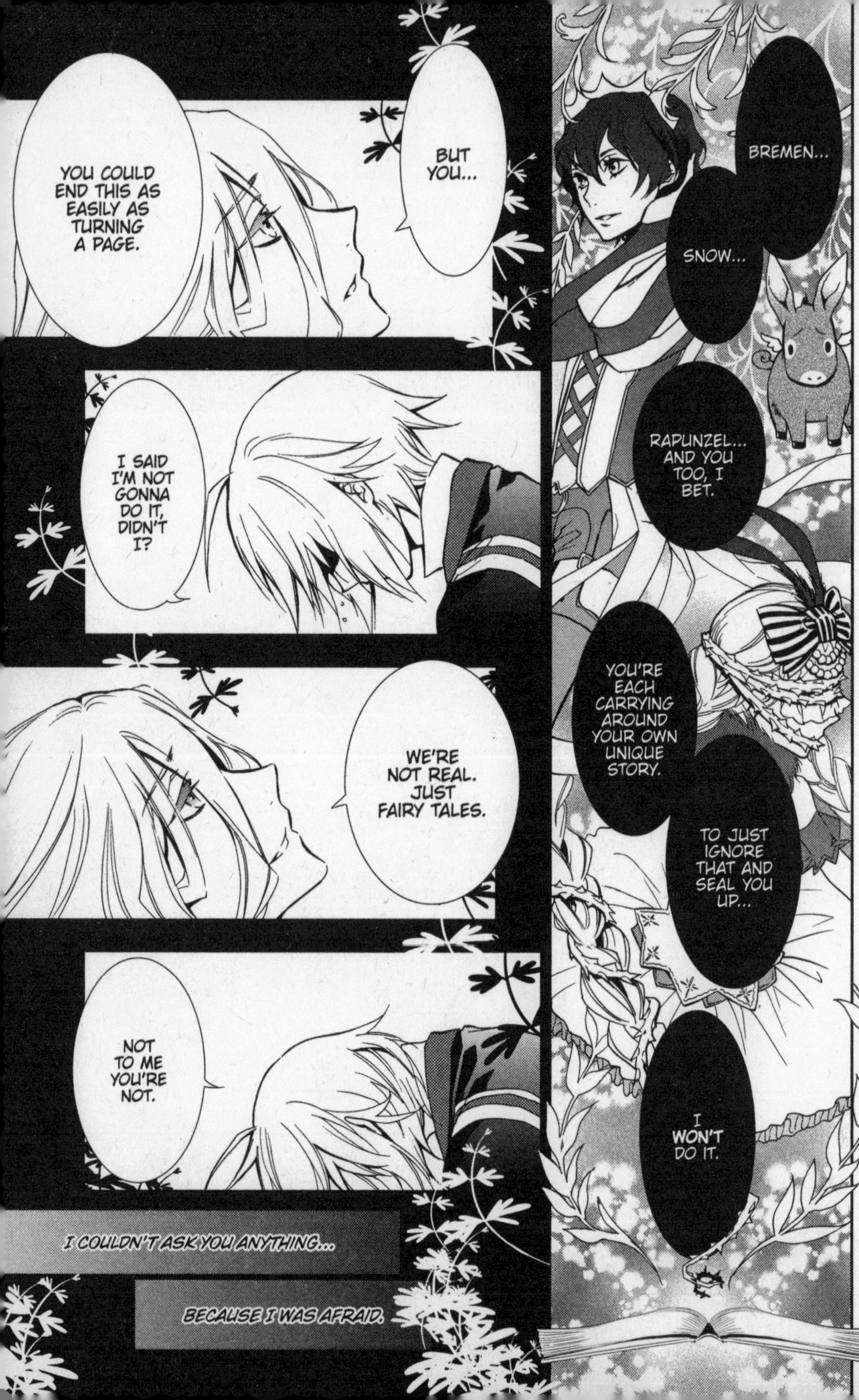
BREMEN...
SNOW...
RAPUNZEL... AND YOU TOO, I BET.
YOU'RE EACH CARRYING AROUND YOUR OWN UNIQUE STORY.
TO JUST IGNORE THAT AND SEAL YOU UP...
I WON'T DO IT.
BUT YOU...
YOU COULD END THIS AS EASILY AS TURNING A PAGE.
I SAID I'M NOT GONNA DO IT, DIDN'T I?
WE'RE NOT REAL. JUST FAIRY TALES.
NOT TO ME YOU'RE NOT.
I COULDN'T ASK YOU ANYTHING...
BECAUSE I WAS AFRAID.

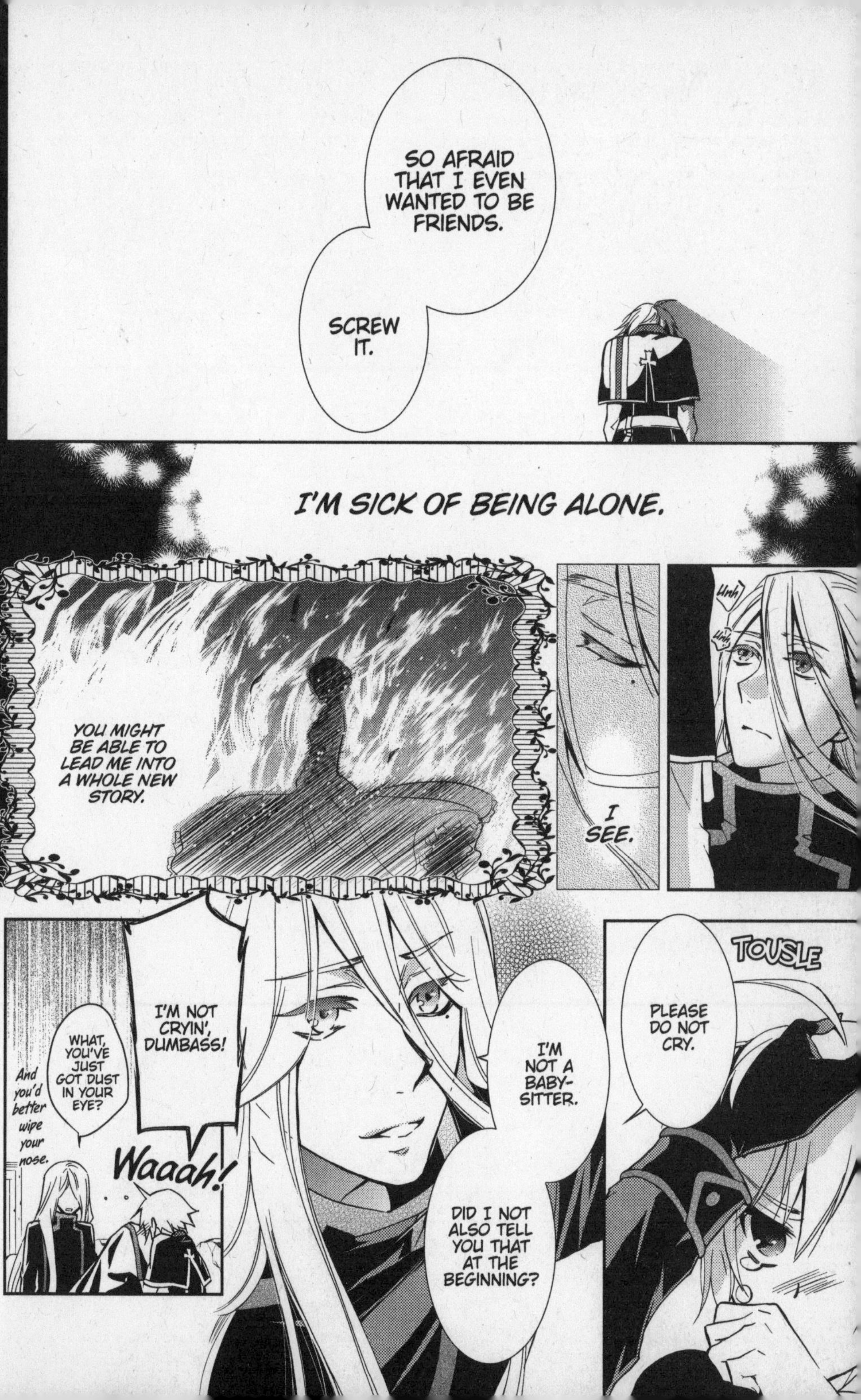
SO AFRAID THAT I EVEN WANTED TO BE FRIENDS.
SCREW IT.
I'M SICK OF BEING ALONE.
Unh
Unh
I SEE.
YOU MIGHT BE ABLE TO LEAD ME INTO A WHOLE NEW STORY.
TOUSLE
PLEASE DO NOT CRY.
I'M NOT A BABY-SITTER.
DID I NOT ALSO TELL YOU THAT AT THE BEGINNING?
I'M NOT CRYIN', DUMBASS!
WHAT, YOU'VE JUST GOT DUST IN YOUR EYE?
And you'd better wipe your nose.
Waaah!

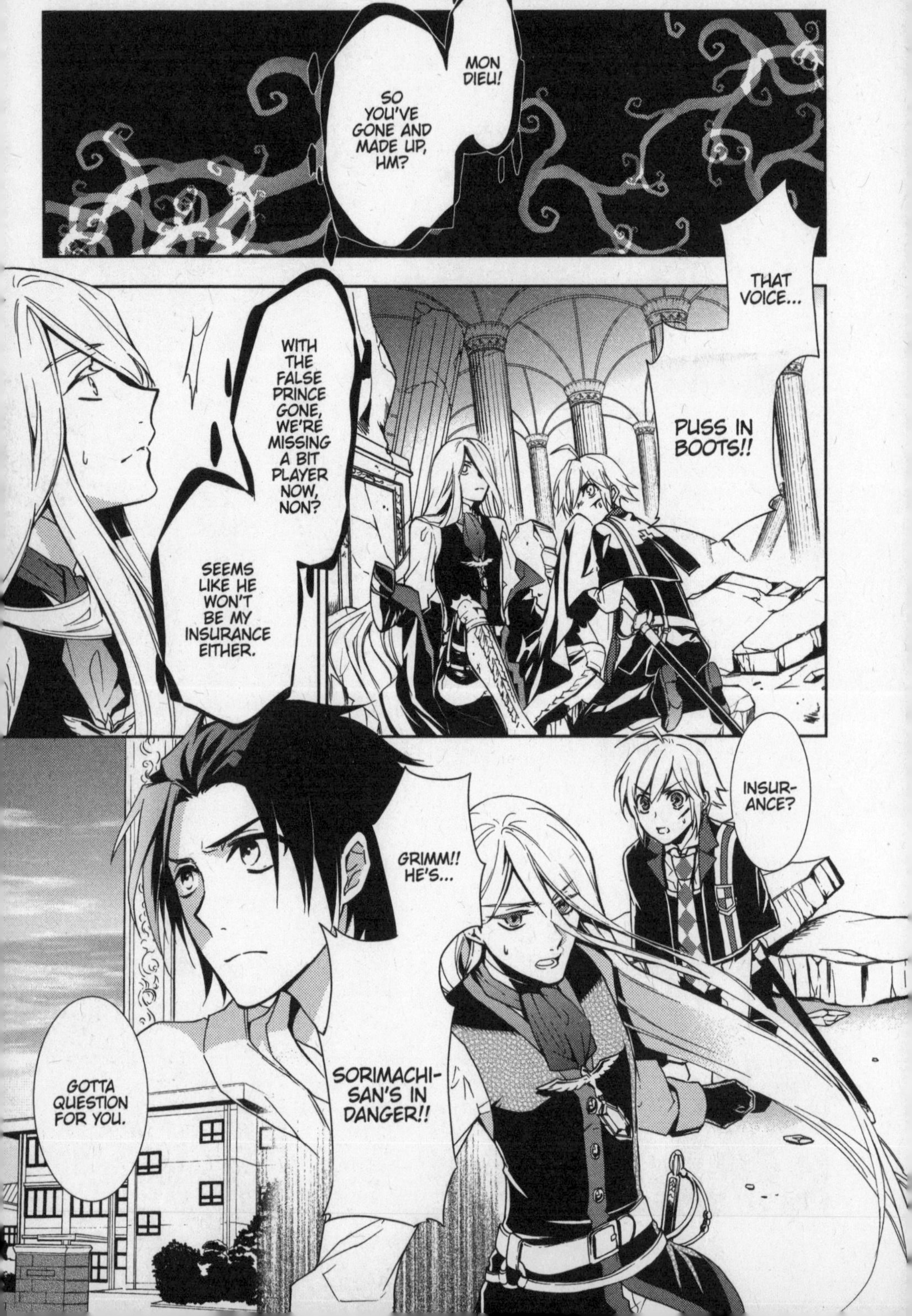
MON DIEU!
SO YOU'VE GONE AND MADE UP, HM?
THAT VOICE...
PUSS IN BOOTS!!
WITH THE FALSE PRINCE GONE, WE'RE MISSING A BIT PLAYER NOW, NON?
SEEMS LIKE HE WON'T BE MY INSURANCE EITHER.
INSUR-ANCE?
GRIMM!! HE'S...
SORIMACHI-SAN'S IN DANGER!!
GOTTA QUESTION FOR YOU.

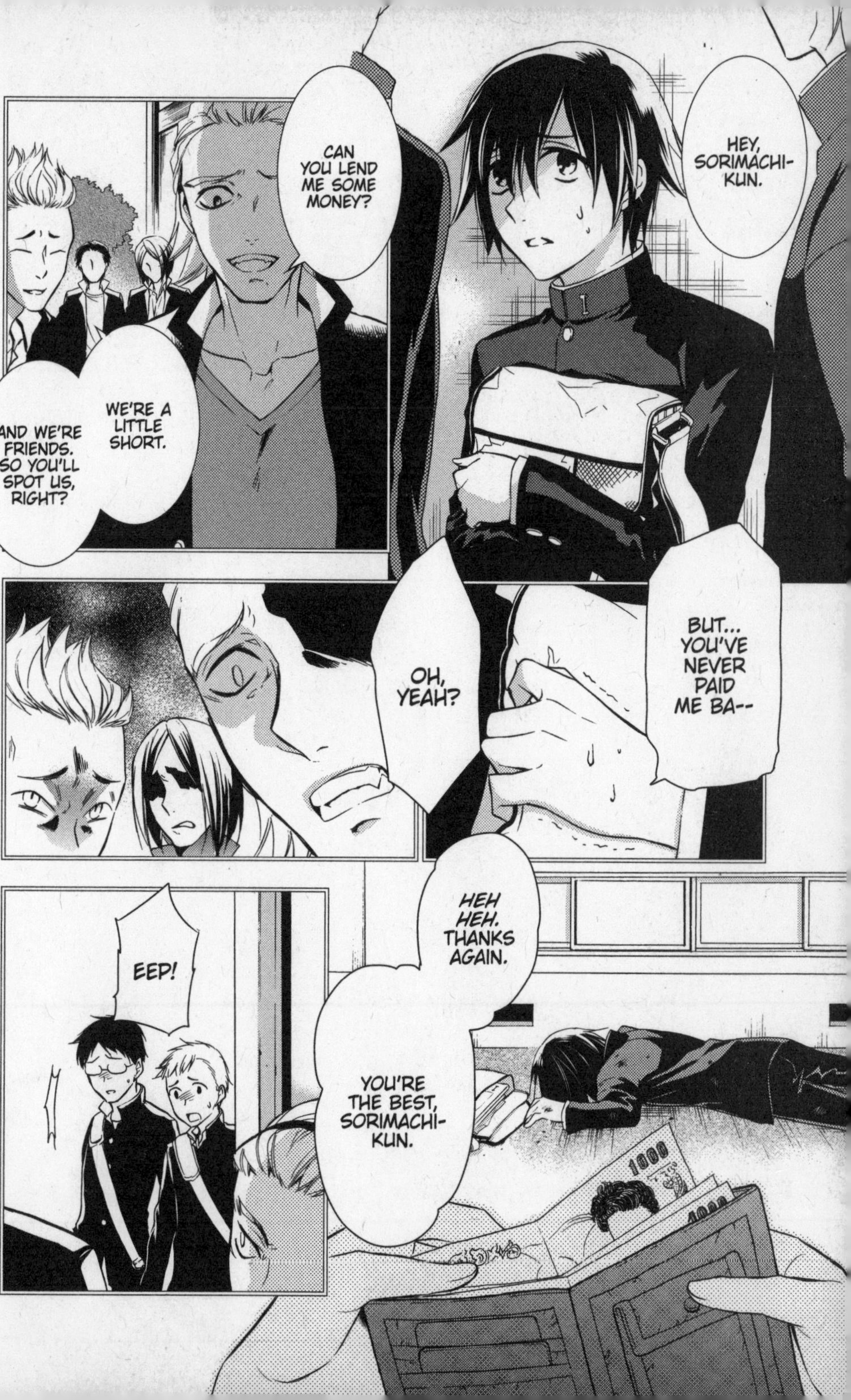
HEY, SORIMACHI-KUN.
CAN YOU LEND ME SOME MONEY?
WE'RE A LITTLE SHORT.
AND WE'RE FRIENDS. SO YOU'LL SPOT US, RIGHT?
BUT... YOU'VE NEVER PAID ME BA--
OH, YEAH?
HEH HEH. THANKS AGAIN.
YOU'RE THE BEST, SORIMACHI-KUN.
EEP!

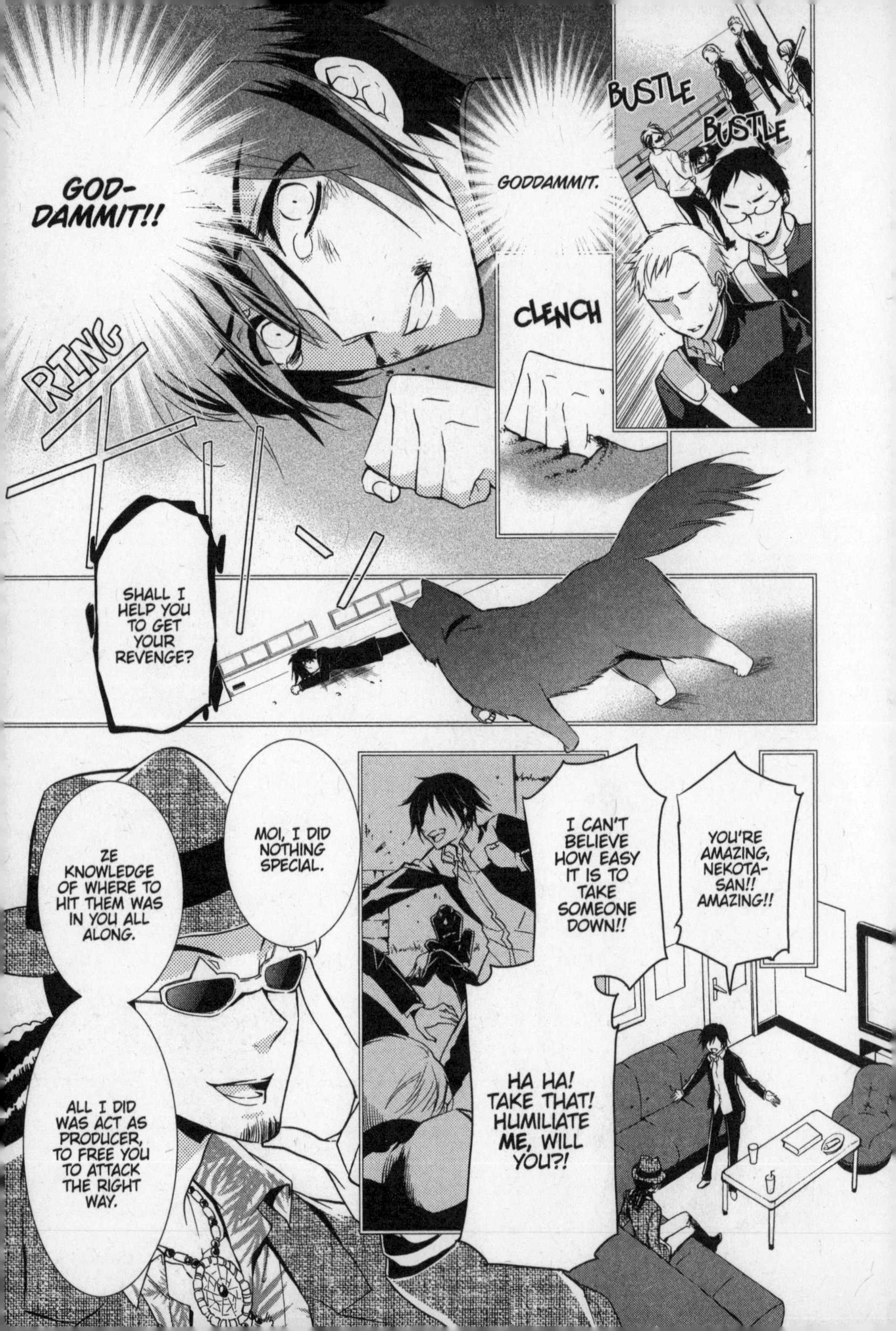

BUSTLE
BUSTLE
CLENCH
GODDAMMIT.
GOD-DAMMIT!!
RING
SHALL I HELP YOU TO GET YOUR REVENGE?
YOU'RE AMAZING, NEKOTA-SAN!! AMAZING!!
I CAN'T BELIEVE HOW EASY IT IS TO TAKE SOMEONE DOWN!!
HA HA! TAKE THAT! HUMILIATE ME, WILL YOU?!
MOI, I DID NOTHING SPECIAL.
ZE KNOWLEDGE OF WHERE TO HIT THEM WAS IN YOU ALL ALONG.
ALL I DID WAS ACT AS PRODUCER, TO FREE YOU TO ATTACK THE RIGHT WAY.

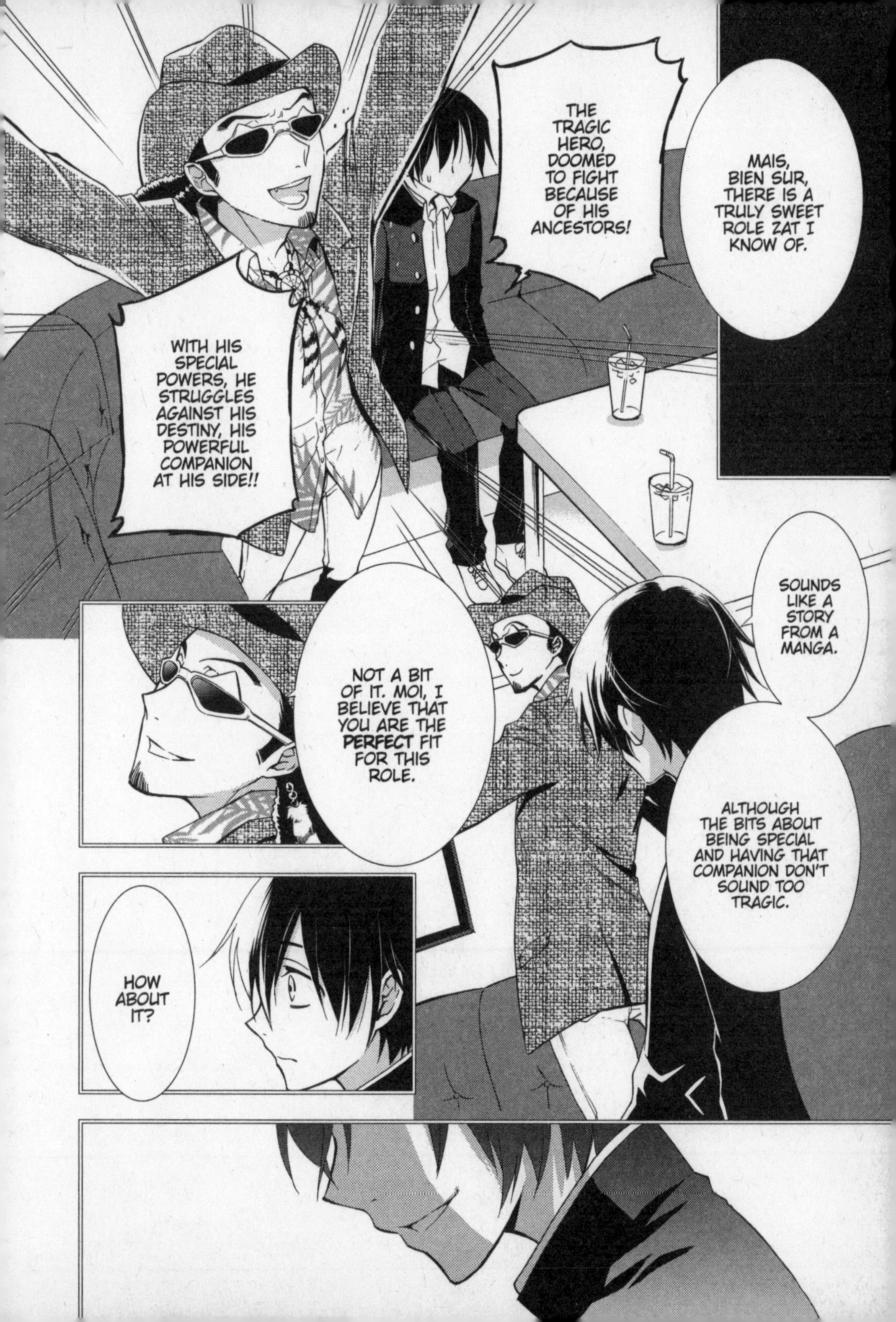
MAIS, BIEN SUR, THERE IS A TRULY SWEET ROLE ZAT I KNOW OF.
THE TRAGIC HERO, DOOMED TO FIGHT BECAUSE OF HIS ANCESTORS!
WITH HIS SPECIAL POWERS, HE STRUGGLES AGAINST HIS DESTINY, HIS POWERFUL COMPANION AT HIS SIDE!!
SOUNDS LIKE A STORY FROM A MANGA.
ALTHOUGH THE BITS ABOUT BEING SPECIAL AND HAVING THAT COMPANION DON'T SOUND TOO TRAGIC.
NOT A BIT OF IT. MOI, I BELIEVE THAT YOU ARE THE PERFECT FIT FOR THIS ROLE.
HOW ABOUT IT?

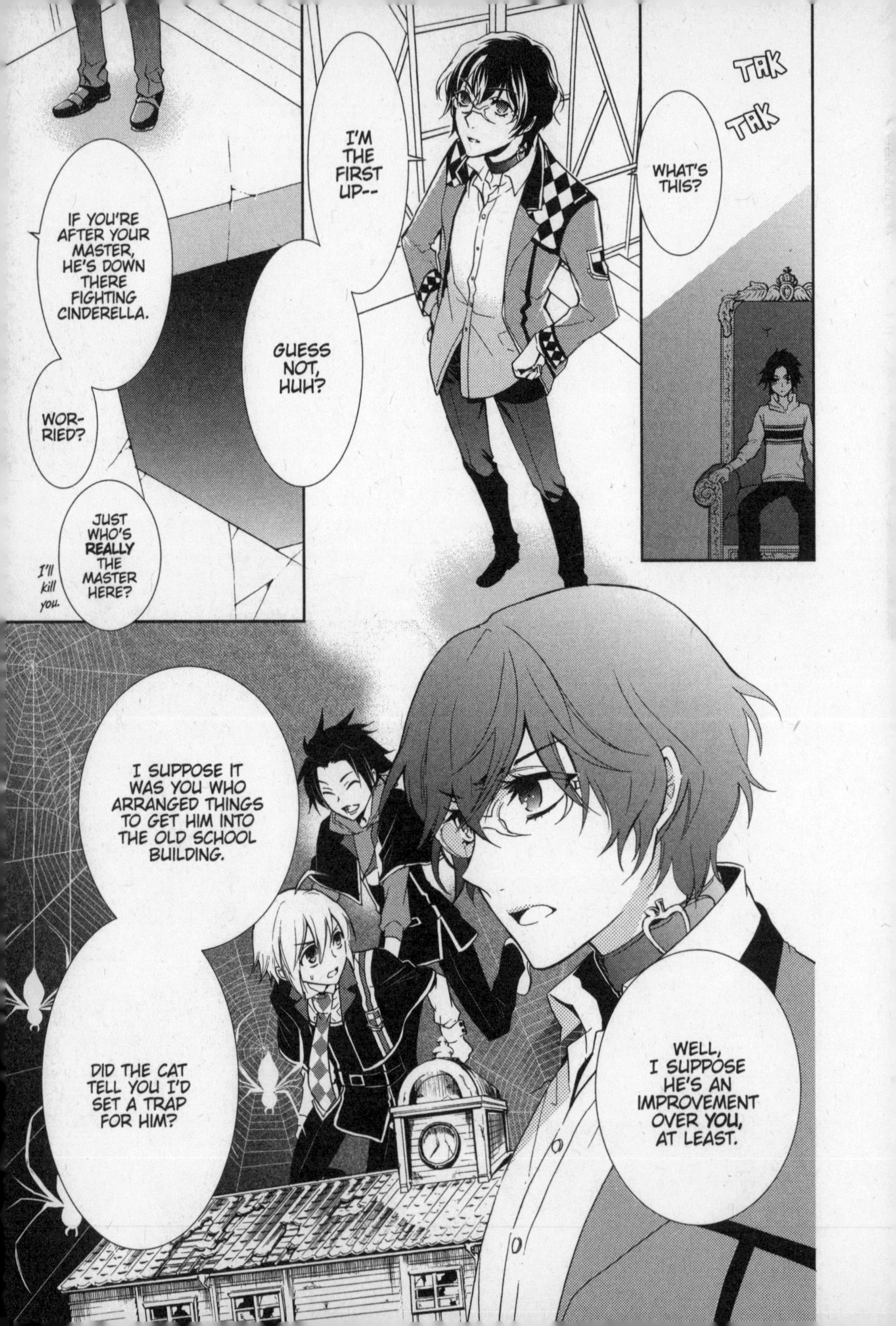
TAK
TAK
WHAT'S THIS?
I'M THE FIRST UP--
GUESS NOT, HUH?
IF YOU'RE AFTER YOUR MASTER, HE'S DOWN THERE FIGHTING CINDERELLA.
WOR-RIED?
JUST WHO'S **REALLY** THE MASTER HERE?
I'll kill you.
WELL, I SUPPOSE HE'S AN IMPROVEMENT OVER **YOU**, AT LEAST.
I SUPPOSE IT WAS YOU WHO ARRANGED THINGS TO GET HIM INTO THE OLD SCHOOL BUILDING.
DID THE CAT TELL YOU I'D SET A TRAP FOR HIM?

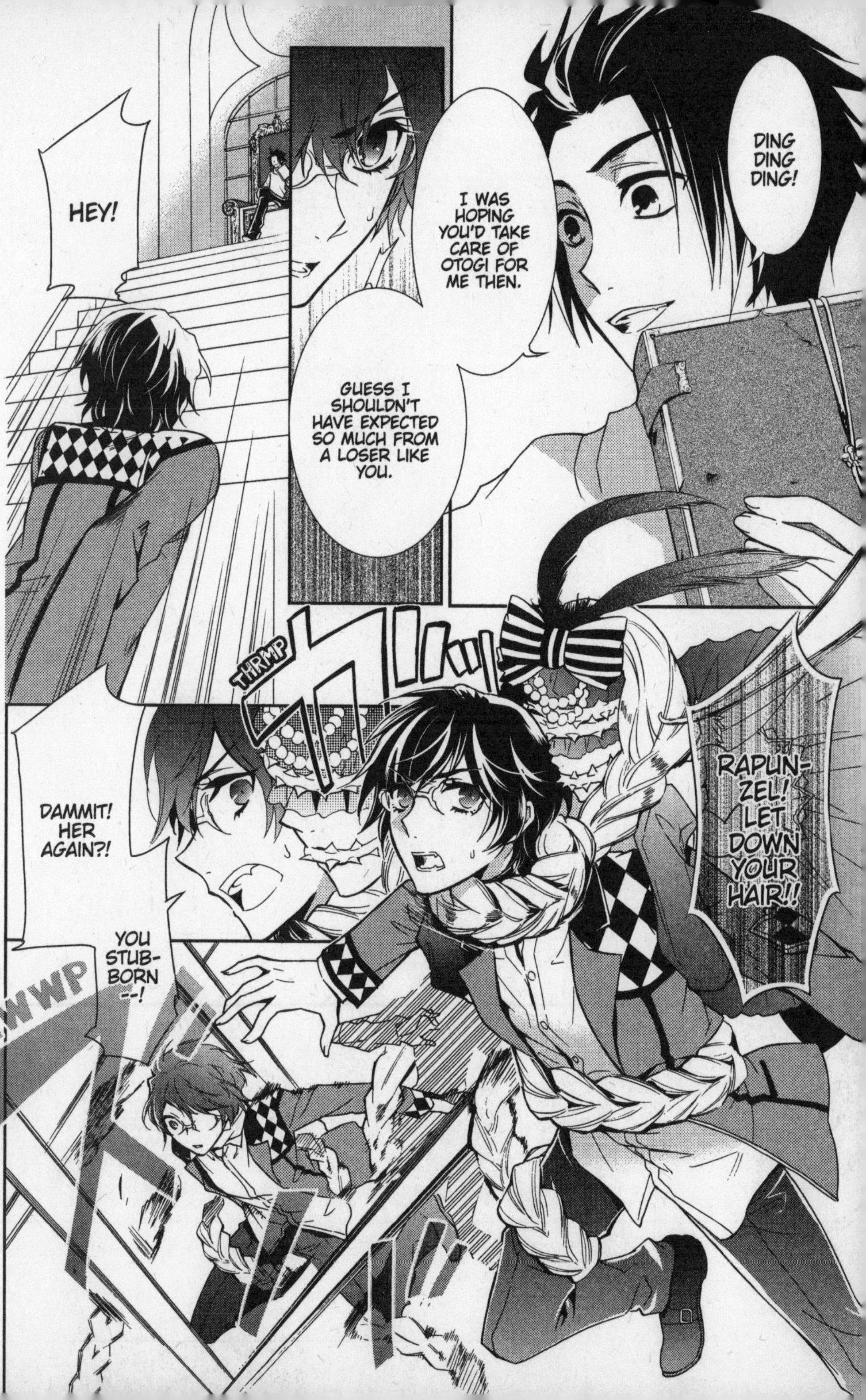
DING DING DING!
I WAS HOPING YOU'D TAKE CARE OF OTOGI FOR ME THEN.
GUESS I SHOULDN'T HAVE EXPECTED SO MUCH FROM A LOSER LIKE YOU.
HEY!
THRMP
RAPUN-ZEL! LET DOWN YOUR HAIR!!
DAMMIT! HER AGAIN?!
YOU STUB-BORN --!
SHWWP

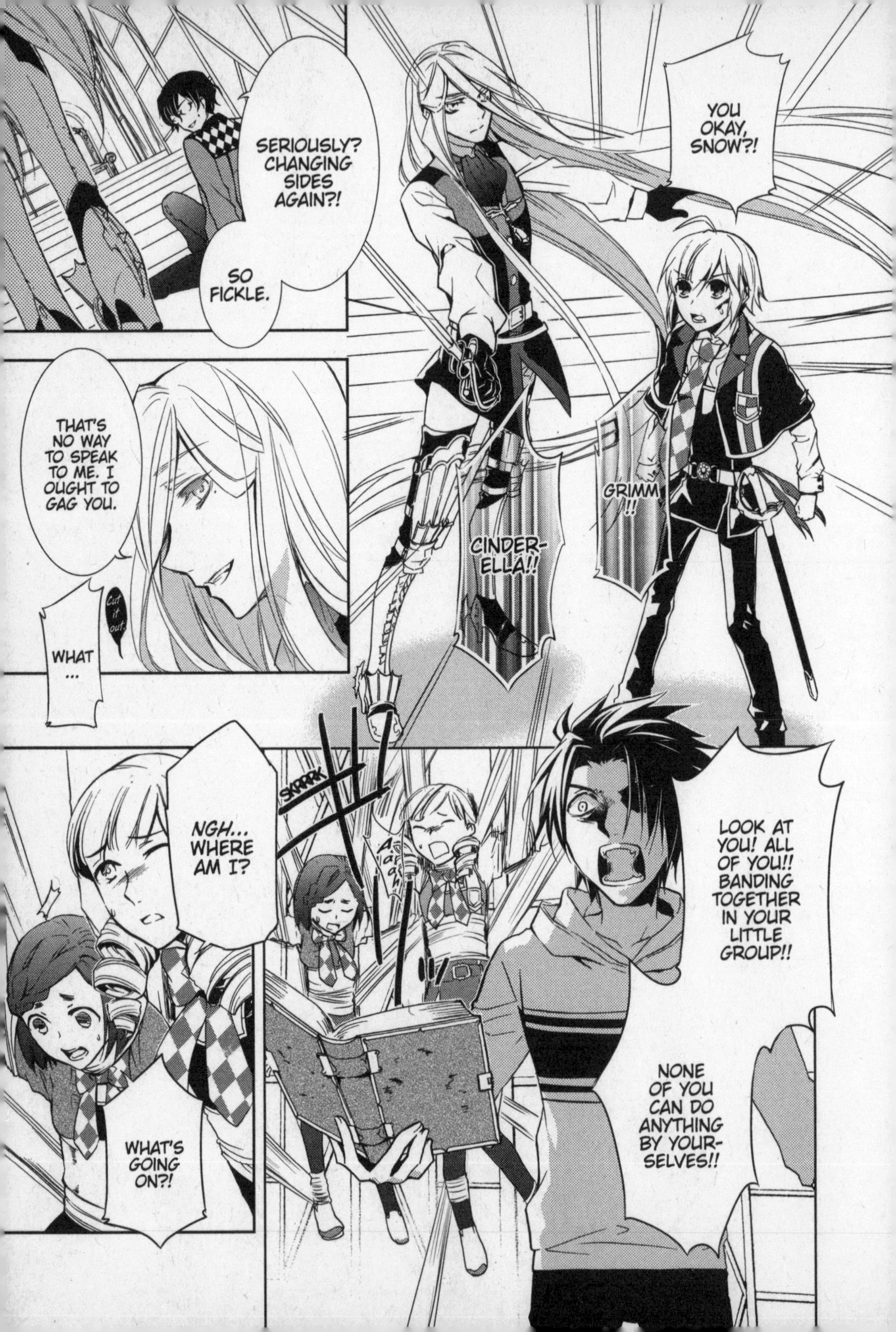
YOU OKAY, SNOW?!
GRIMM!!
CINDER-ELLA!!
SERIOUSLY? CHANGING SIDES AGAIN?!
SO FICKLE.
THAT'S NO WAY TO SPEAK TO ME. I OUGHT TO GAG YOU.
Cut it out.
WHAT ...
LOOK AT YOU! ALL OF YOU!! BANDING TOGETHER IN YOUR LITTLE GROUP!!
NONE OF YOU CAN DO ANYTHING BY YOUR-SELVES!!
SKRRRK
NGH... WHERE AM I?
WHAT'S GOING ON?!

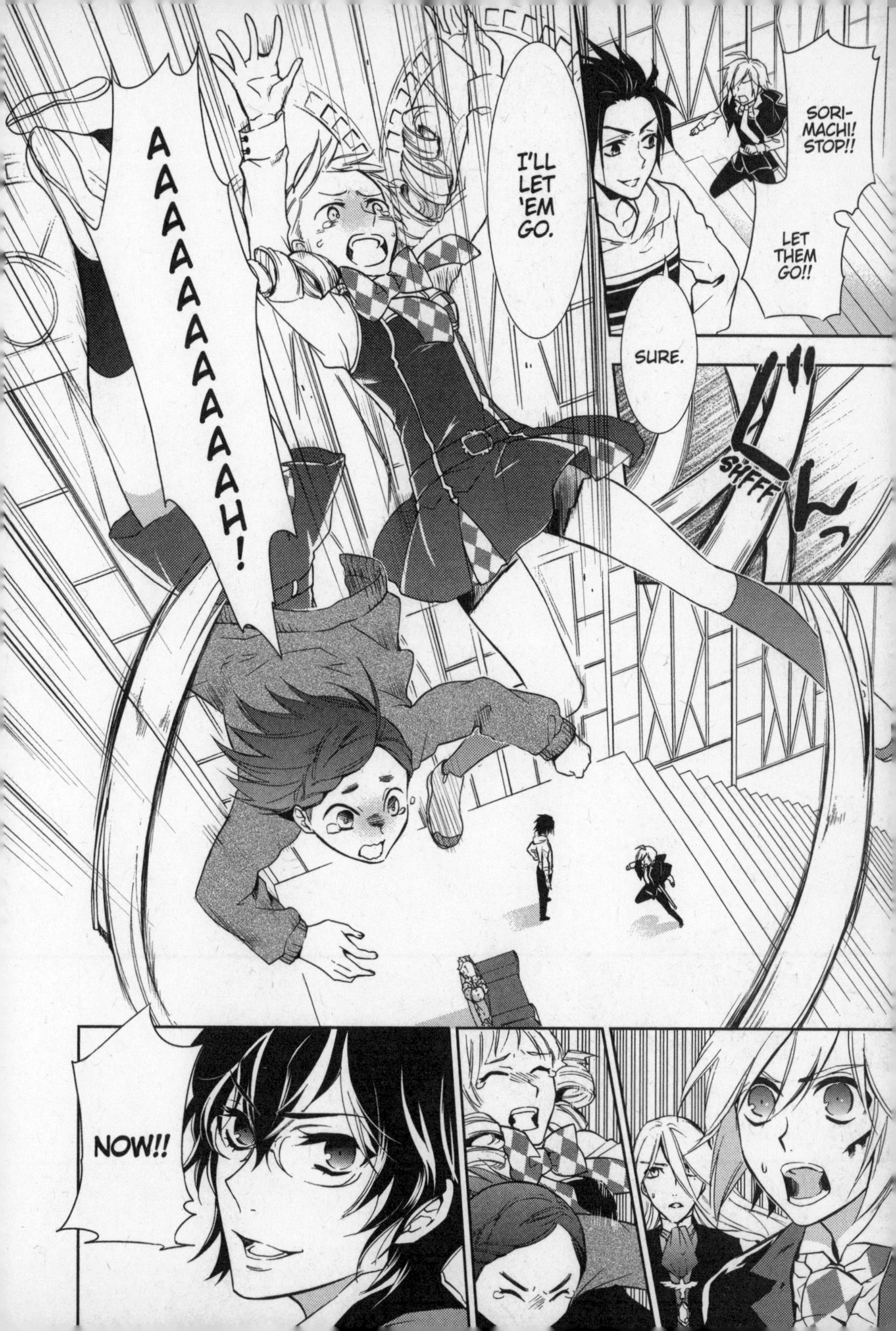
SORI-MACHI! STOP!!
LET THEM GO!!
SURE.
I'LL LET 'EM GO.
SHFFF
AAAAAAAAAAH!
NOW!!

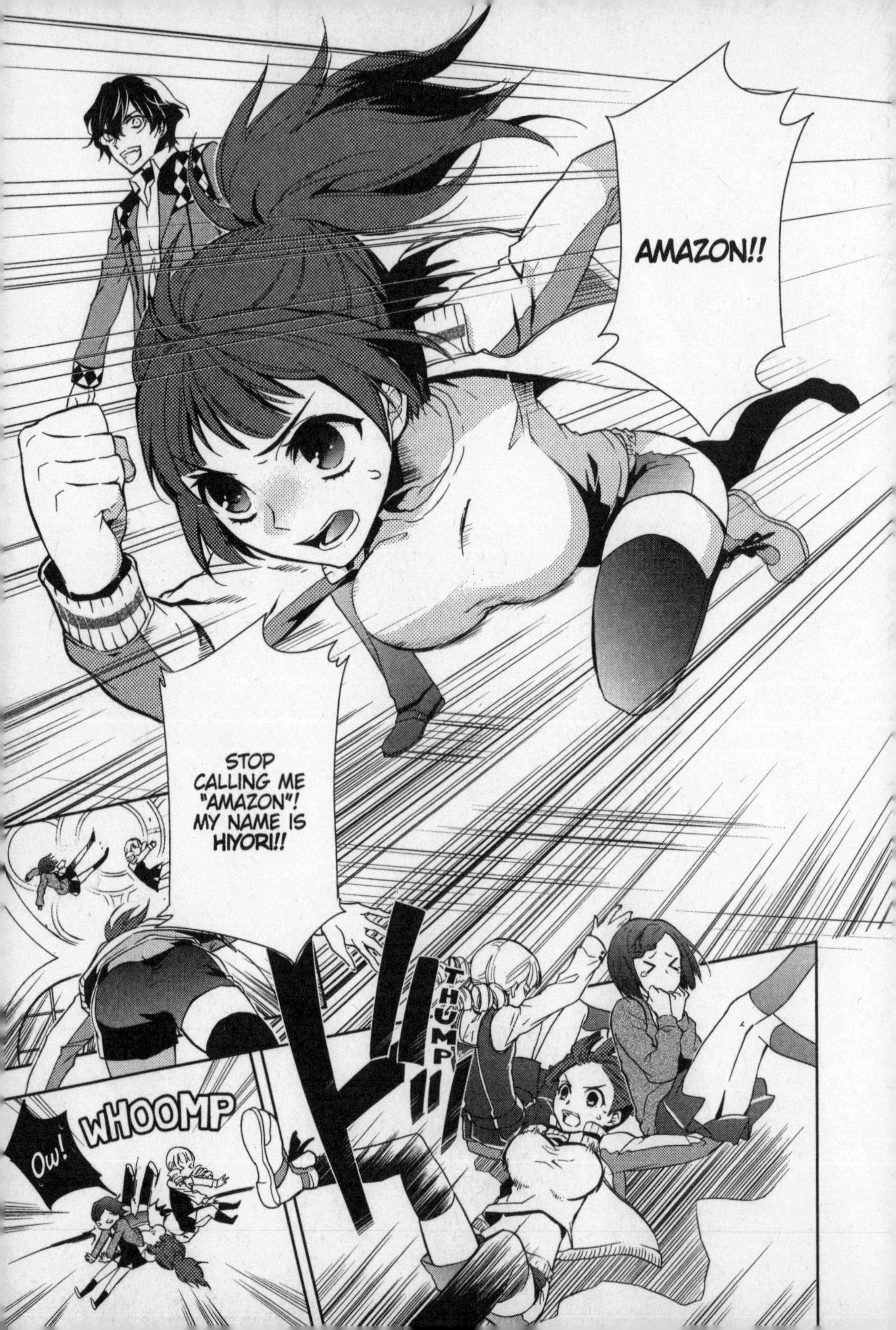
AMAZON!!
STOP CALLING ME "AMAZON"! MY NAME IS HIYORI!!
THUMP!!
wHOOMP
Ow!

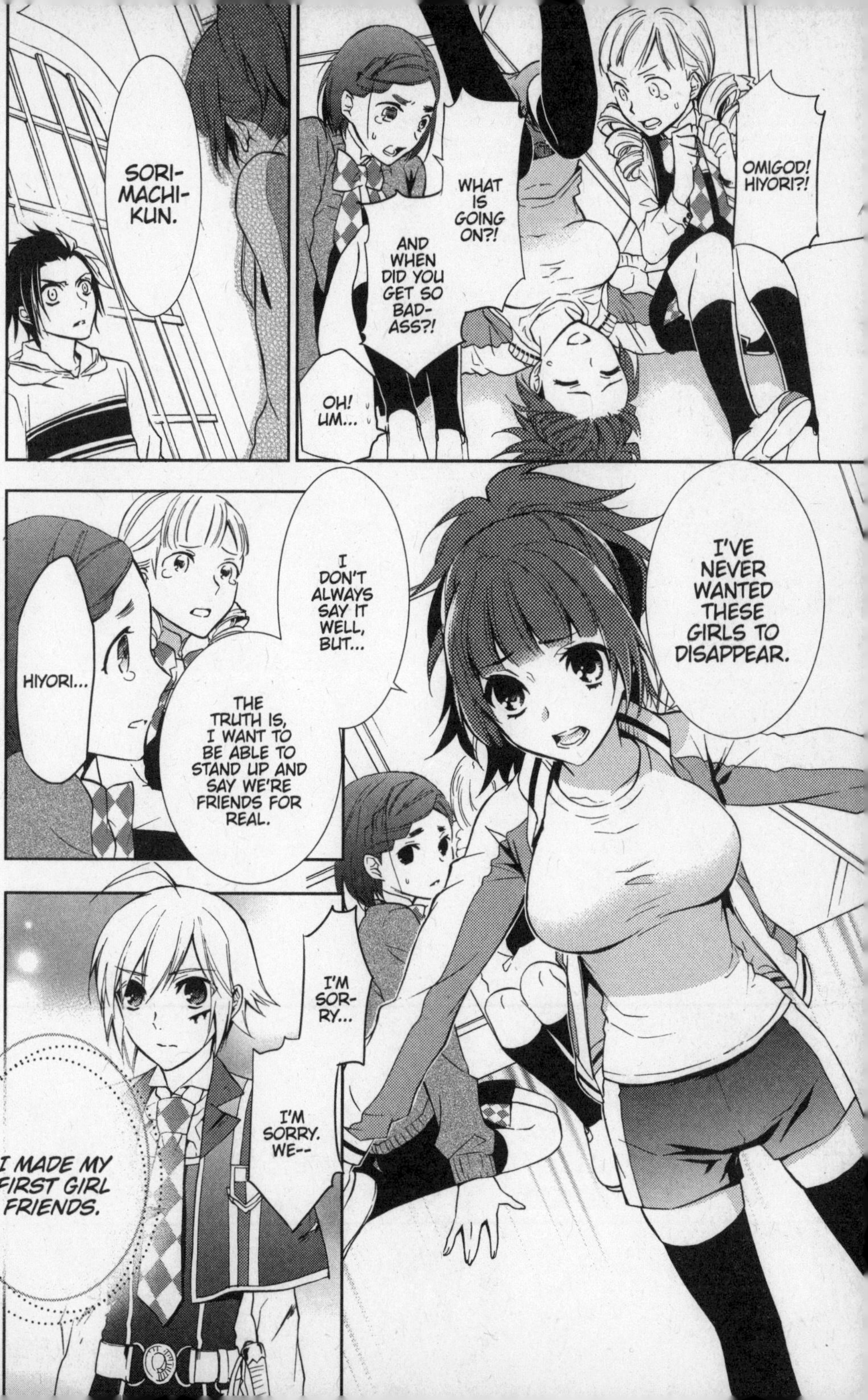
OMIGOD! HIYORI?!
WHAT IS GOING ON?!
AND WHEN DID YOU GET SO BAD-ASS?!
OH! UM...
SORI-MACHI-KUN.
I'VE NEVER WANTED THESE GIRLS TO DISAPPEAR.
I DON'T ALWAYS SAY IT WELL, BUT...
THE TRUTH IS, I WANT TO BE ABLE TO STAND UP AND SAY WE'RE FRIENDS FOR REAL.
HIYORI...
I'M SOR-RY...
I'M SORRY. WE--
I MADE MY FIRST GIRL FRIENDS.

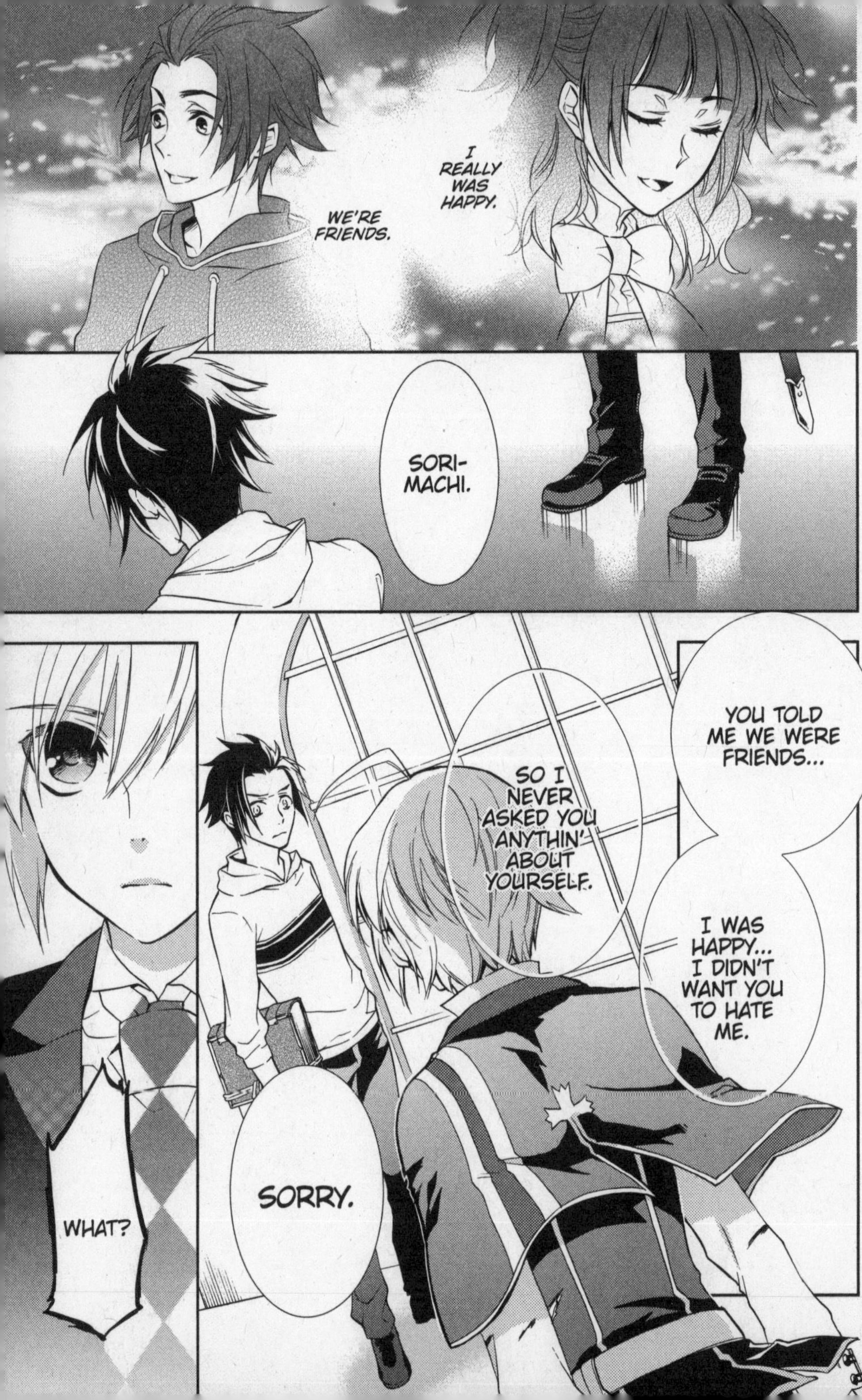
I REALLY WAS HAPPY.
WE'RE FRIENDS.
SORI-MACHI.
YOU TOLD ME WE WERE FRIENDS...
SO I NEVER ASKED YOU ANYTHIN' ABOUT YOURSELF.
I WAS HAPPY... I DIDN'T WANT YOU TO HATE ME.
SORRY.
WHAT?

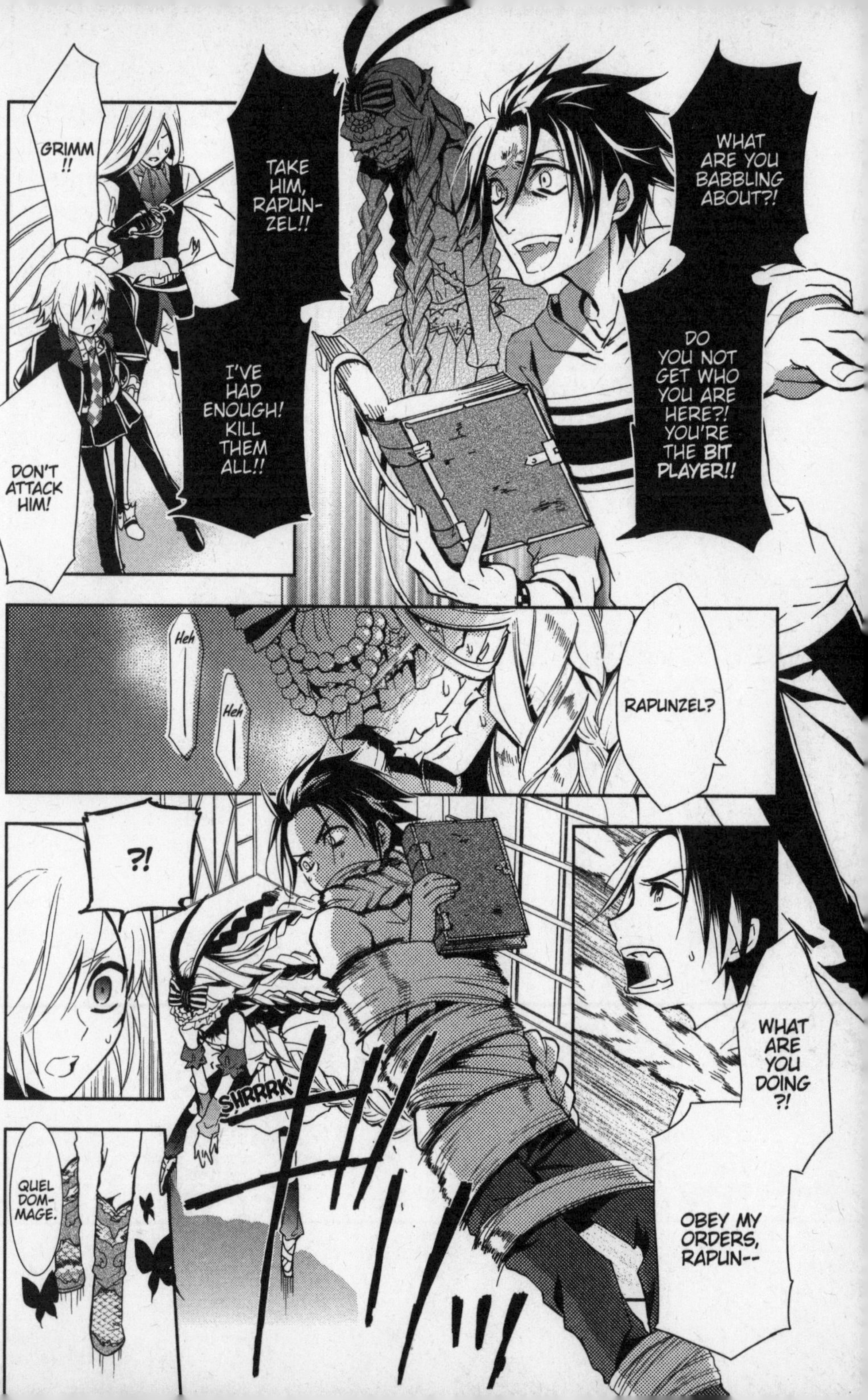
WHAT ARE YOU BABBLING ABOUT?!
DO YOU NOT GET WHO YOU ARE HERE?! YOU'RE THE **BIT PLAYER**!!
TAKE HIM, RAPUN-ZEL!!
I'VE HAD ENOUGH! KILL THEM ALL!!
GRIMM!!
DON'T ATTACK HIM!
RAPUNZEL?
Heh
Heh
WHAT ARE YOU DOING?!
OBEY MY ORDERS, RAPUN--
SHRRRK
?!
QUEL DOM-MAGE.

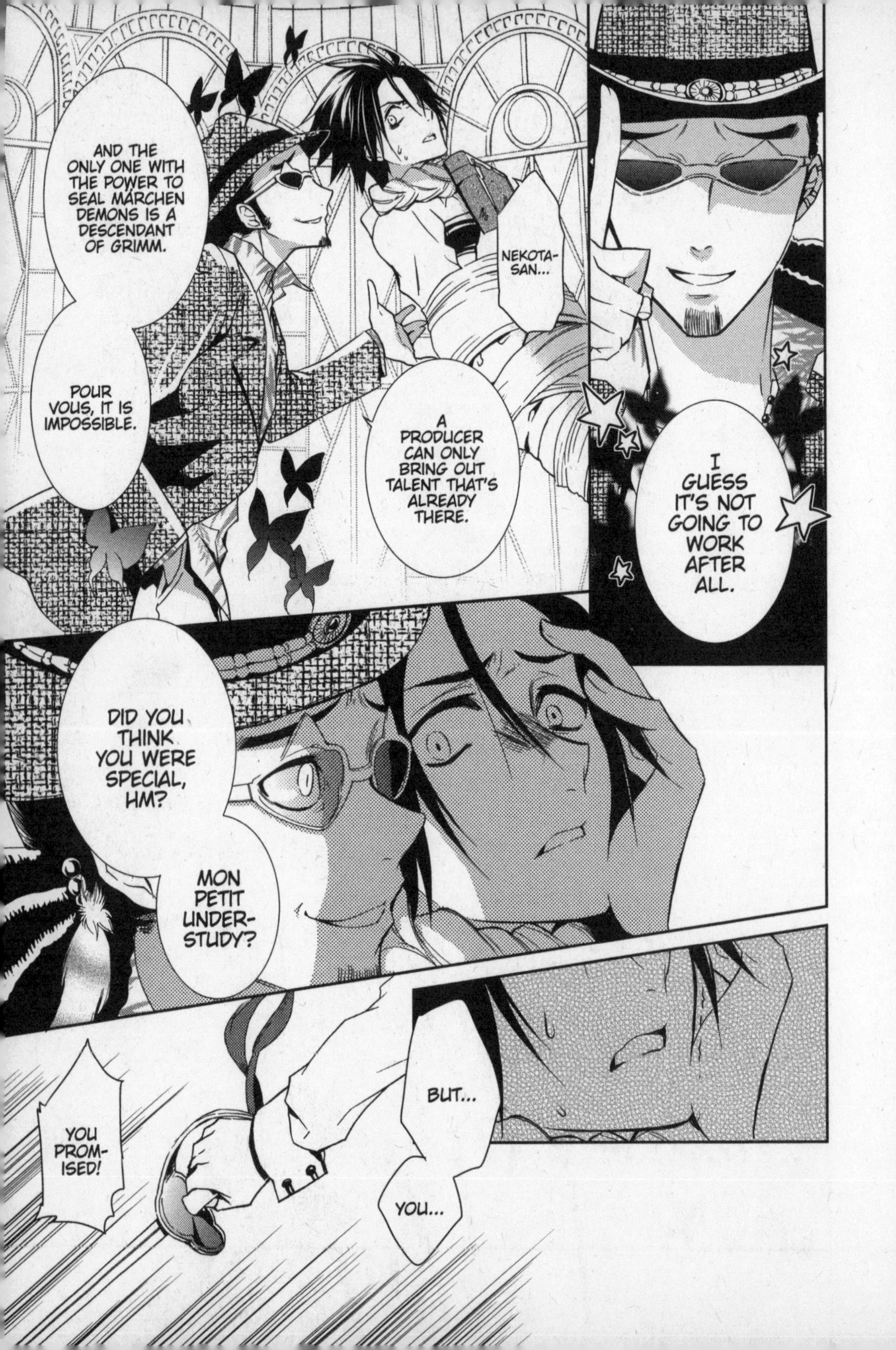
I GUESS IT'S NOT GOING TO WORK AFTER ALL.
NEKOTA-SAN...
A PRODUCER CAN ONLY BRING OUT TALENT THAT'S ALREADY THERE.
AND THE ONLY ONE WITH THE POWER TO SEAL MÄRCHEN DEMONS IS A DESCENDANT OF GRIMM.
POUR VOUS, IT IS IMPOSSIBLE.
DID YOU THINK YOU WERE SPECIAL, HM?
MON PETIT UNDER-STUDY?
BUT...
YOU...
YOU PROM-ISED!

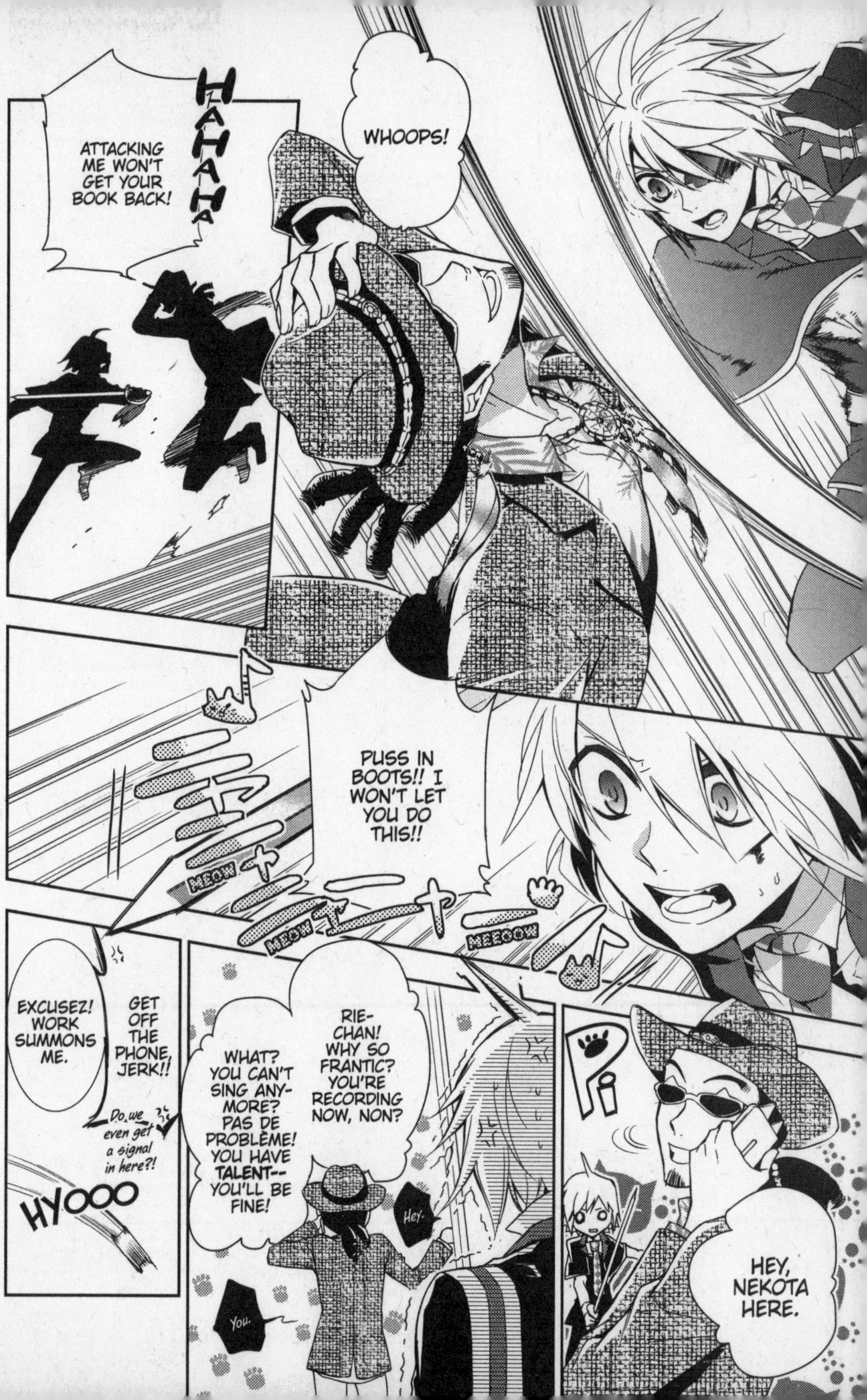
WHOOPS!
HAHAHAHA
ATTACKING ME WON'T GET YOUR BOOK BACK!
PUSS IN BOOTS!! I WON'T LET YOU DO THIS!!
MEEOOW
MEOW
MEOW
Pi
HEY, NEKOTA HERE.
RIE-CHAN! WHY SO FRANTIC? YOU'RE RECORDING NOW, NON?
WHAT? YOU CAN'T SING ANY-MORE? PAS DE PROBLÈME! YOU HAVE **TALENT**-- YOU'LL BE FINE!
Hey.
You.
GET OFF THE PHONE, JERK!!
EXCUSEZ! WORK SUMMONS ME.
Do we even get a signal in here?!
HYOOO

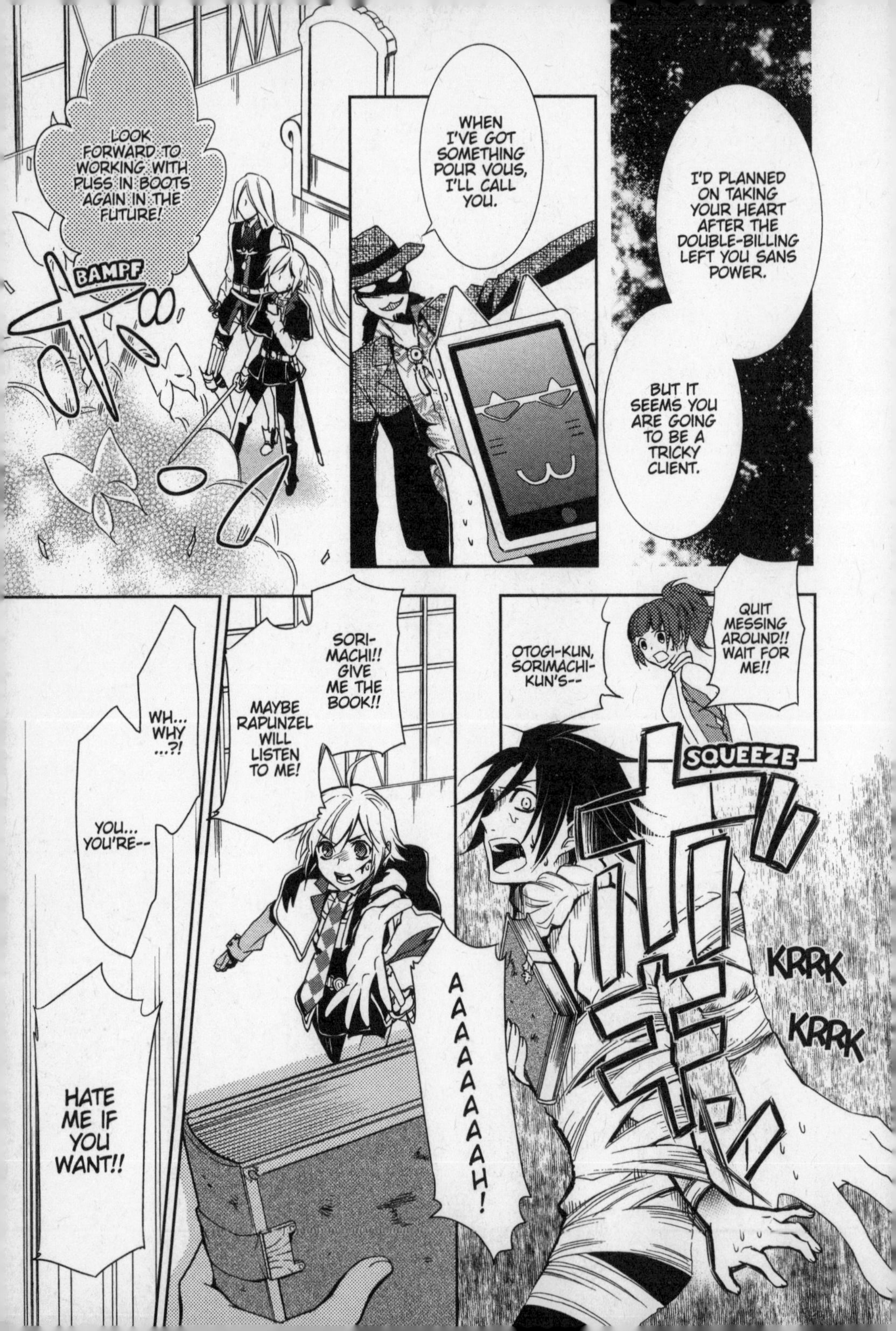
I'D PLANNED ON TAKING YOUR HEART AFTER THE DOUBLE-BILLING LEFT YOU SANS POWER.
BUT IT SEEMS YOU ARE GOING TO BE A TRICKY CLIENT.
WHEN I'VE GOT SOMETHING POUR VOUS, I'LL CALL YOU.
LOOK FORWARD TO WORKING WITH PUSS IN BOOTS AGAIN IN THE FUTURE!
BAMPF
QUIT MESSING AROUND!! WAIT FOR ME!!
OTOGI-KUN, SORIMACHI-KUN'S--
SQUEEZE
KRRK
KRRK
SORI-MACHI!! GIVE ME THE BOOK!!
MAYBE RAPUNZEL WILL LISTEN TO ME!
AAAAAAAAAAH!
WH... WHY ...?!
YOU... YOU'RE--
HATE ME IF YOU WANT!!

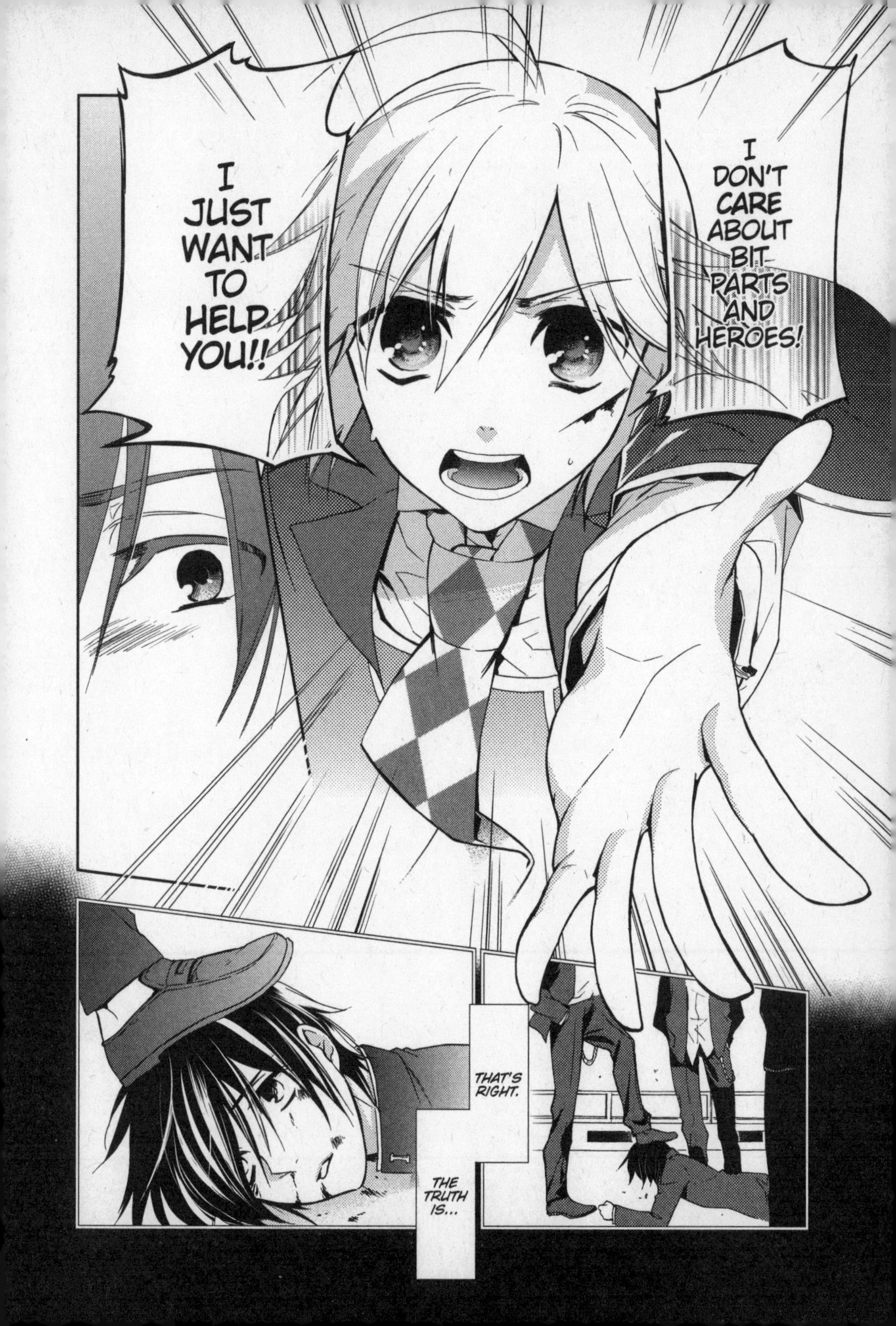
I DON'T CARE ABOUT BIT PARTS AND HEROES!
I JUST WANT TO HELP YOU!!
THAT'S RIGHT.
THE TRUTH IS...

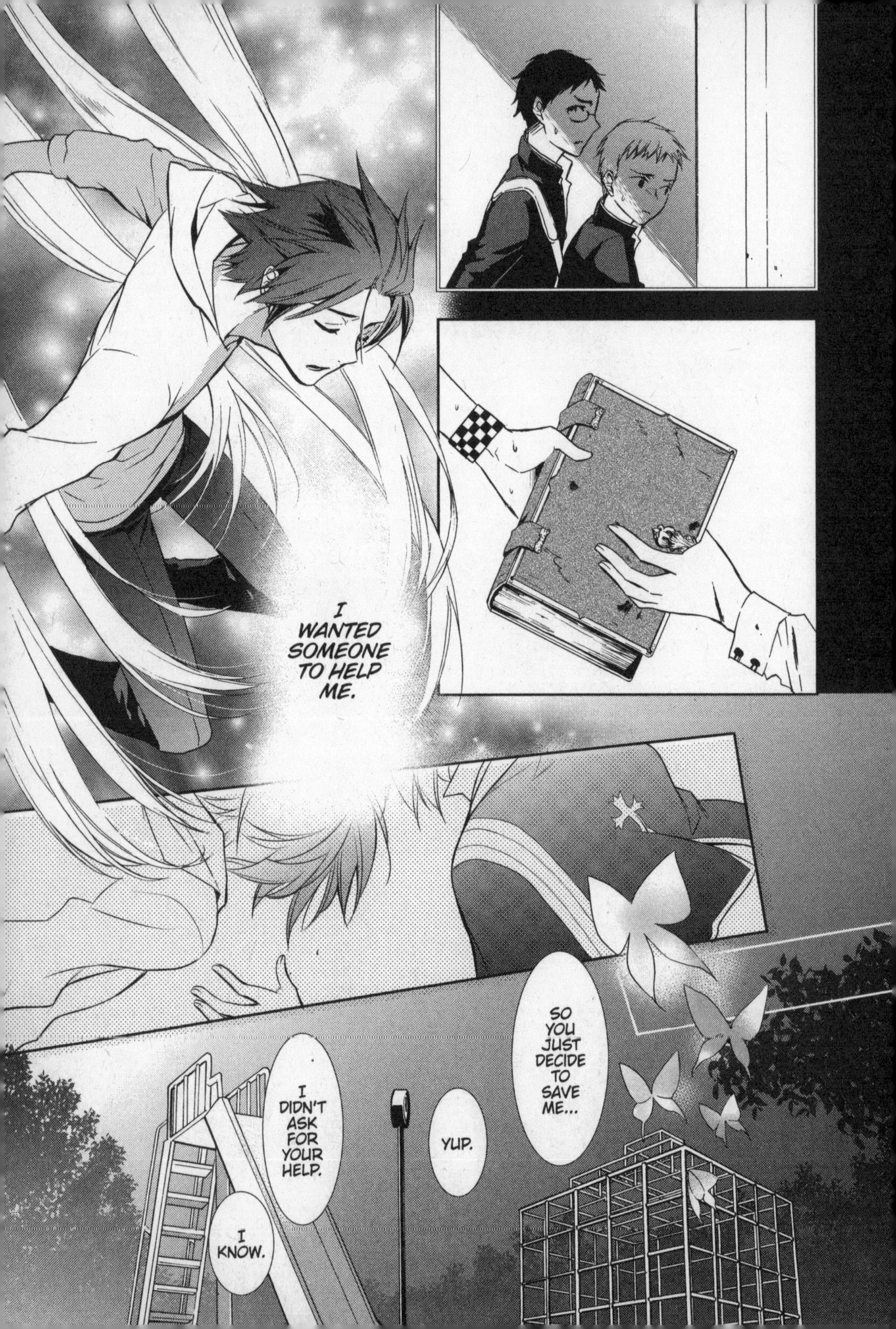
I WANTED SOMEONE TO HELP ME.
SO YOU JUST DECIDE TO SAVE ME...
YUP.
I DIDN'T ASK FOR YOUR HELP.
I KNOW.

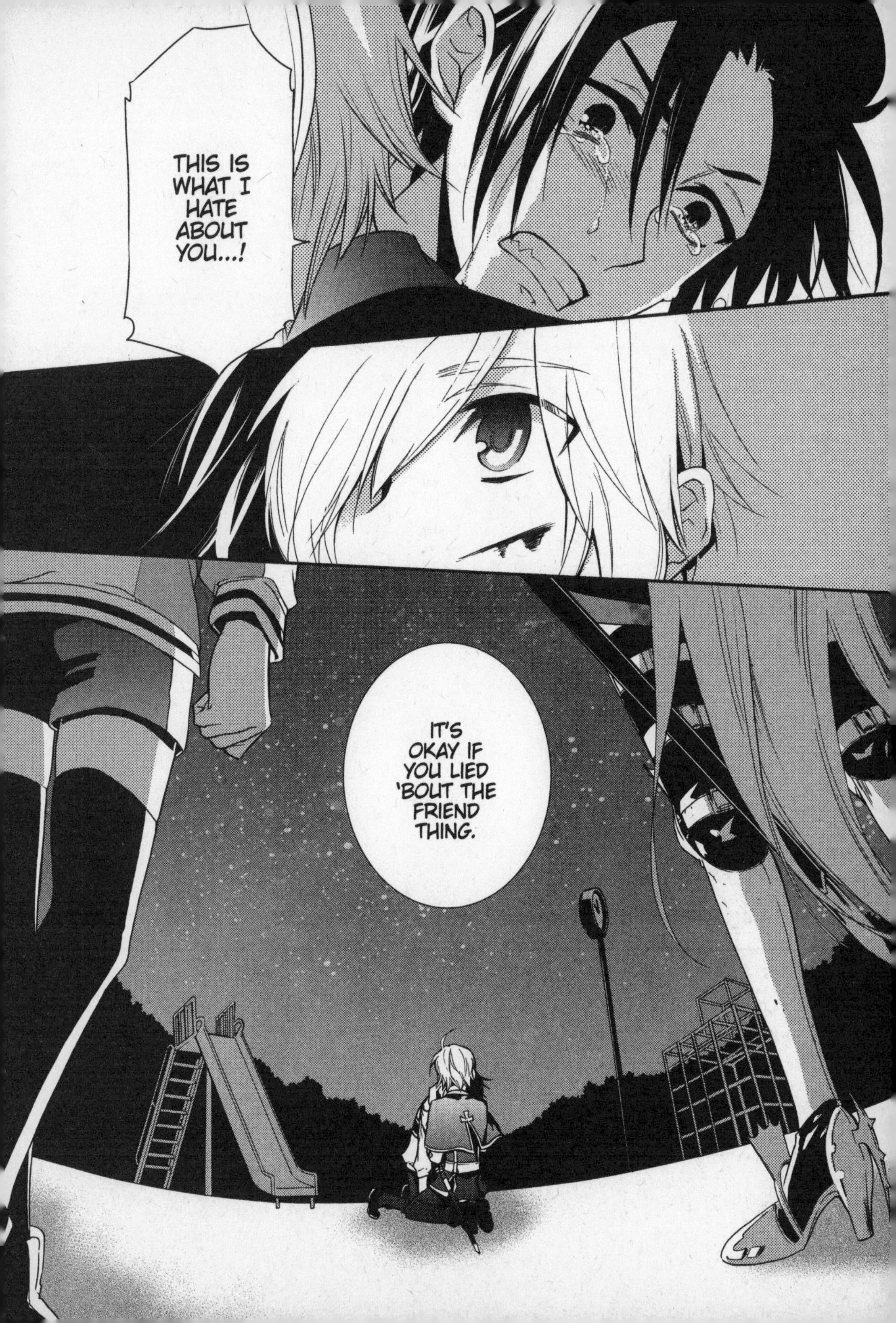
THIS IS WHAT I HATE ABOUT YOU...!
IT'S OKAY IF YOU LIED 'BOUT THE FRIEND THING.

Dictatorial Grimoire

独裁グリムワール
Dictatorial Grimoire

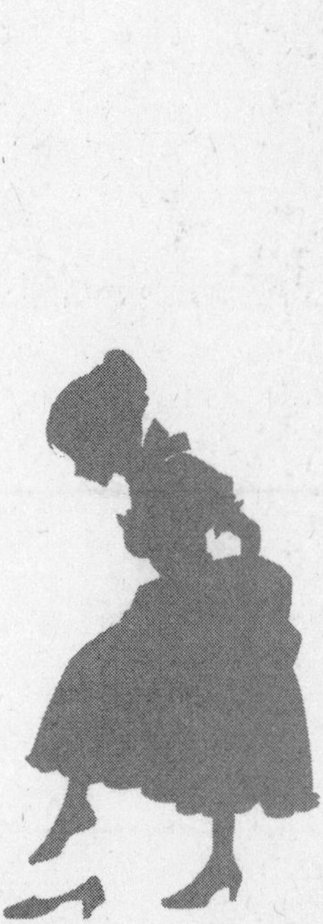

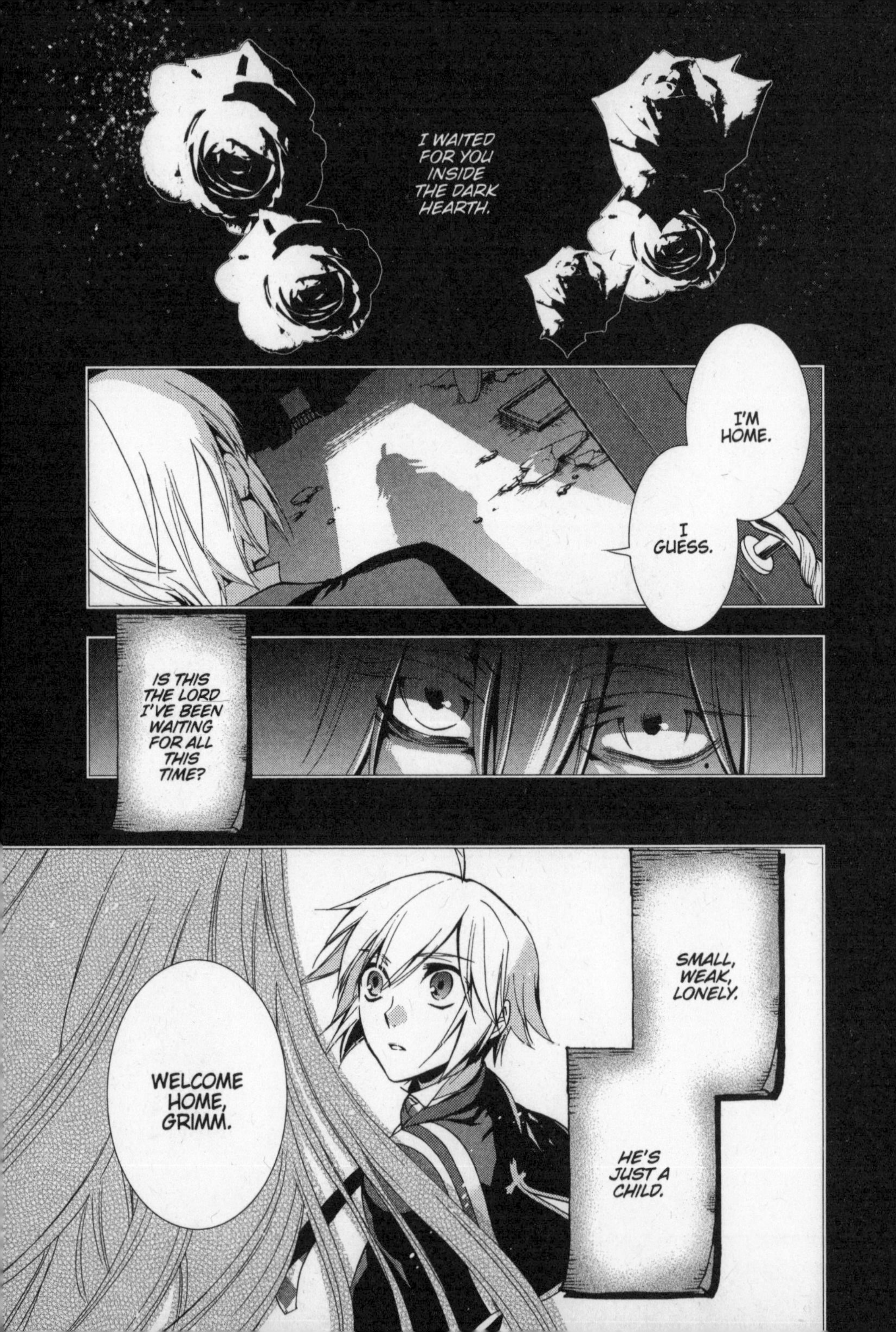
I WAITED FOR YOU INSIDE THE DARK HEARTH.
I'M HOME.
I GUESS.
IS THIS THE LORD I'VE BEEN WAITING FOR ALL THIS TIME?
SMALL, WEAK, LONELY.
HE'S JUST A CHILD.
WELCOME HOME, GRIMM.

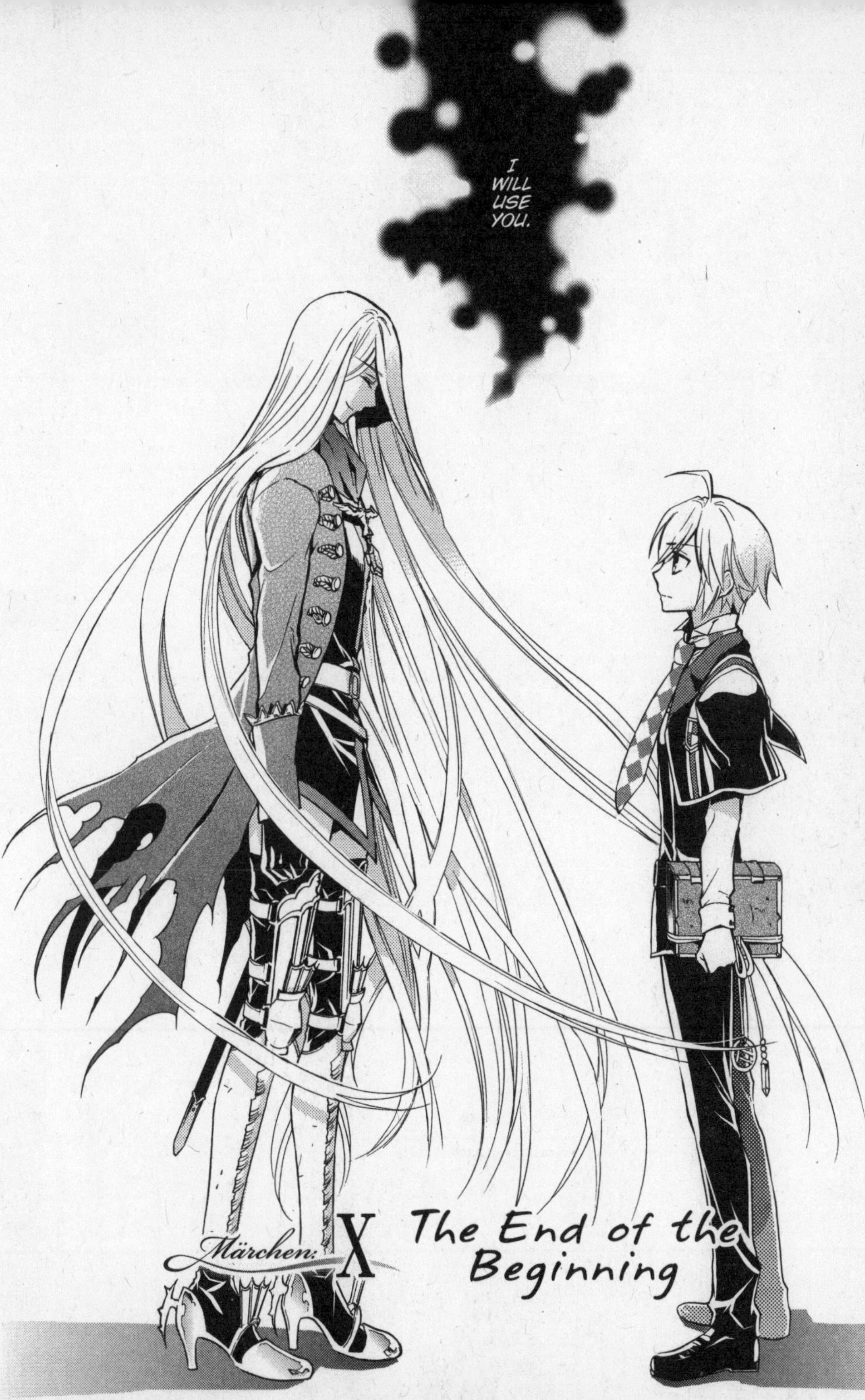
I WILL USE YOU.
Märchen: X The End of the Beginning

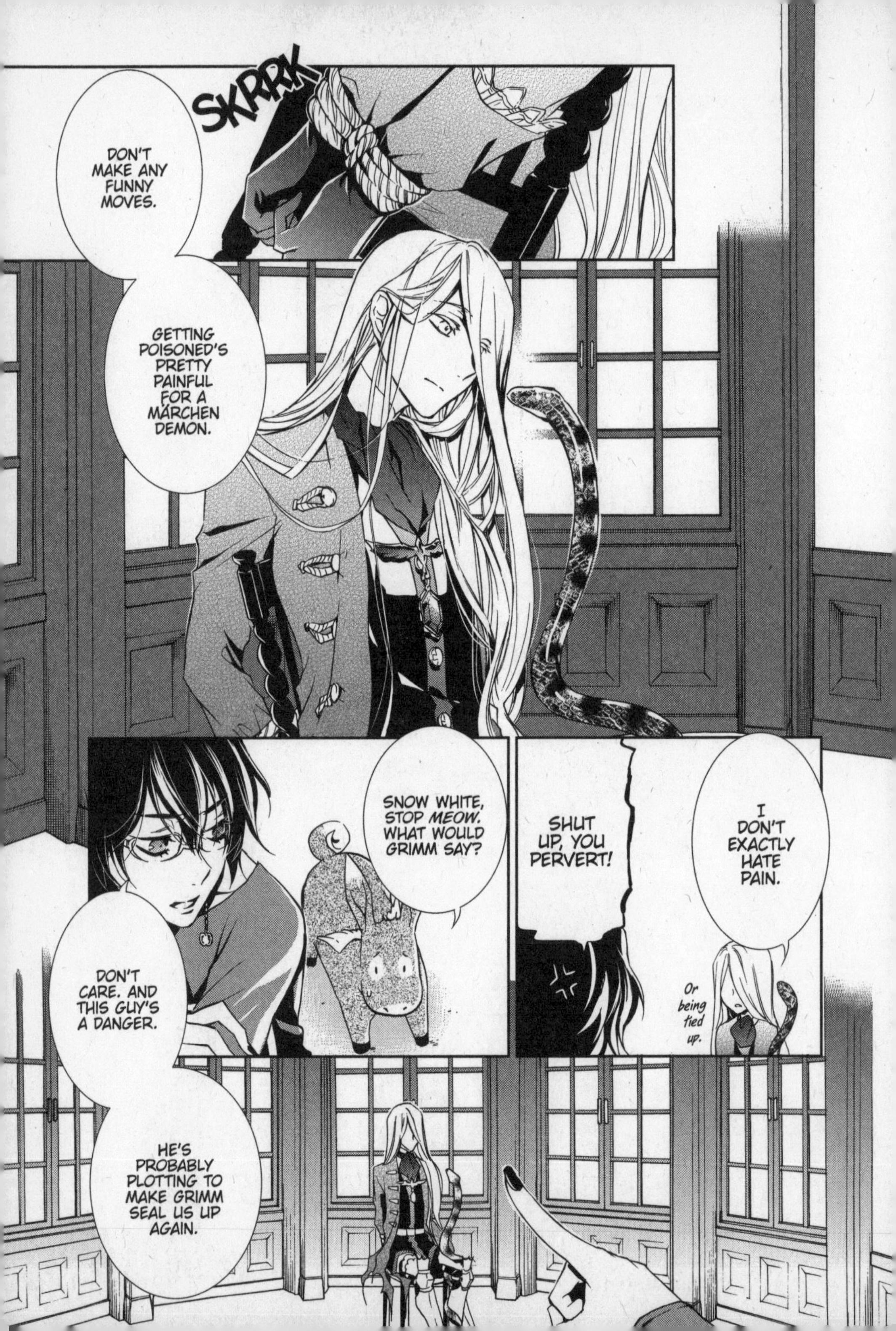
SKRRK
DON'T MAKE ANY FUNNY MOVES.
GETTING POISONED'S PRETTY PAINFUL FOR A MÄRCHEN DEMON.
I DON'T EXACTLY HATE PAIN.
SHUT UP, YOU PERVERT!
Or being tied up.
SNOW WHITE, STOP *MEOW*. WHAT WOULD GRIMM SAY?
DON'T CARE. AND THIS GUY'S A DANGER.
HE'S PROBABLY PLOTTING TO MAKE GRIMM SEAL US UP AGAIN.

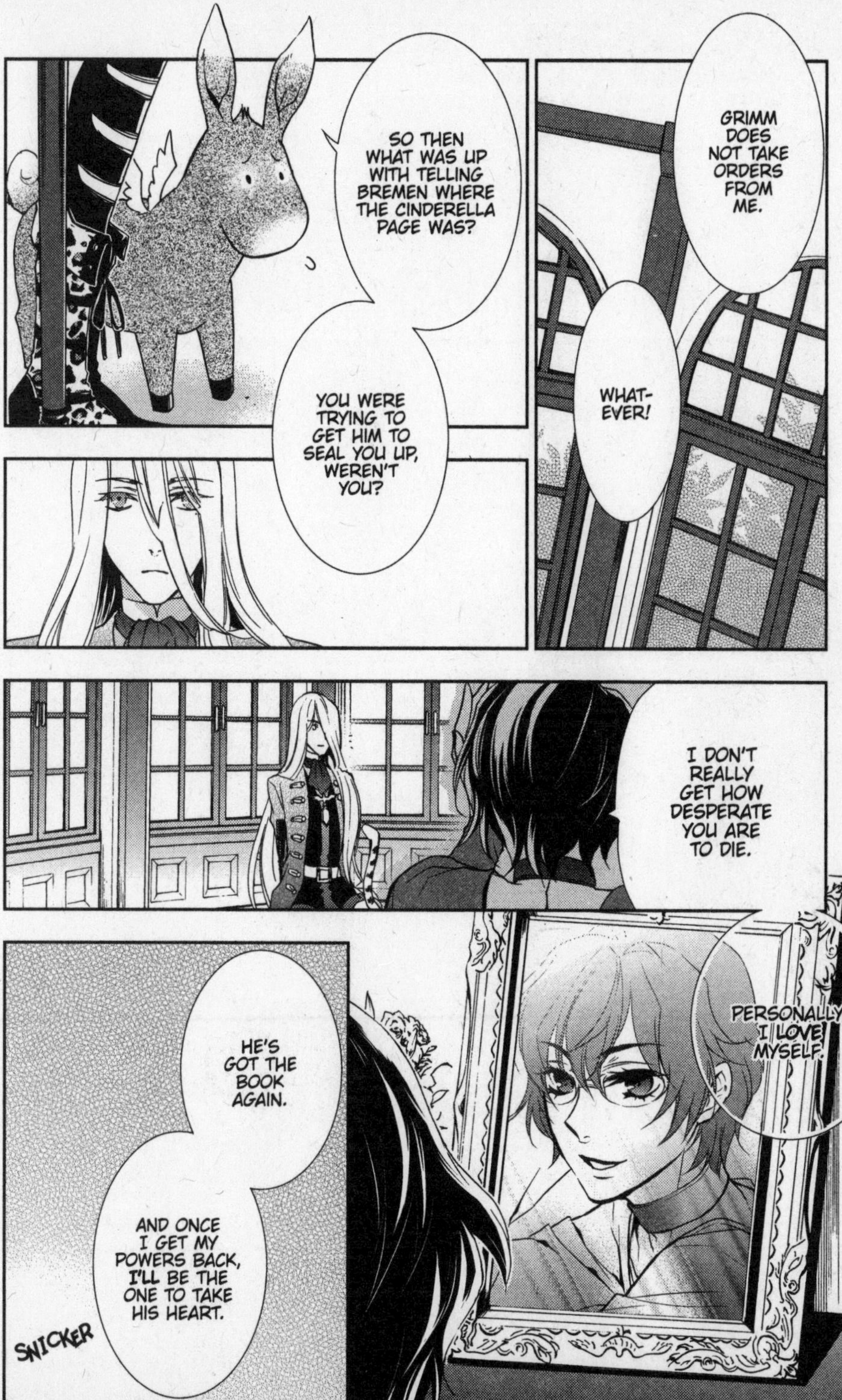
GRIMM DOES NOT TAKE ORDERS FROM ME.
WHAT-EVER!
SO THEN WHAT WAS UP WITH TELLING BREMEN WHERE THE CINDERELLA PAGE WAS?
YOU WERE TRYING TO GET HIM TO SEAL YOU UP, WEREN'T YOU?
I DON'T REALLY GET HOW DESPERATE YOU ARE TO DIE.
PERSONALLY, I LOVE MYSELF.
HE'S GOT THE BOOK AGAIN.
AND ONCE I GET MY POWERS BACK, **I'LL** BE THE ONE TO TAKE HIS HEART.
SNICKER

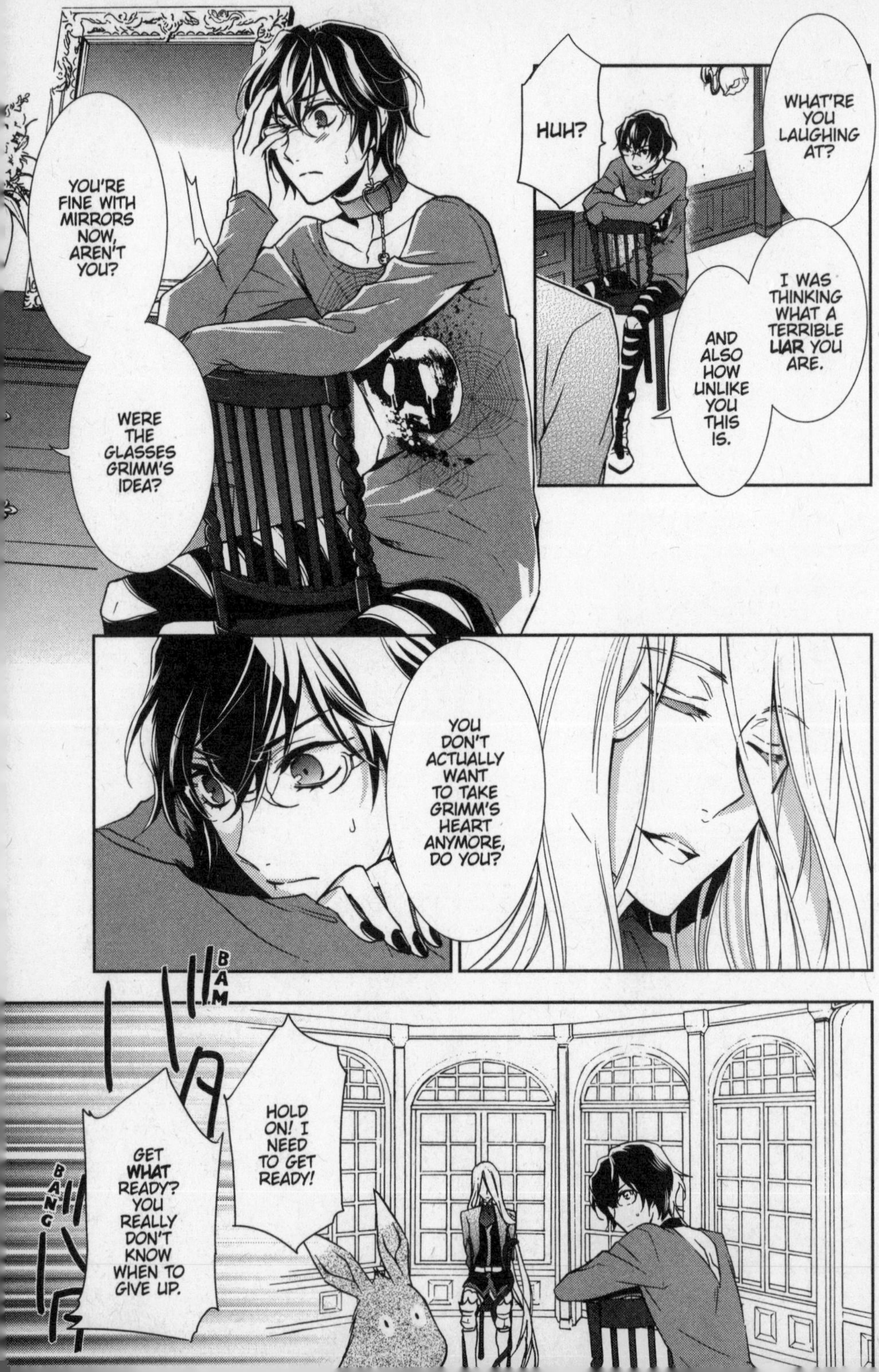
WHAT'RE YOU LAUGHING AT?
HUH?
I WAS THINKING WHAT A TERRIBLE LIAR YOU ARE.
AND ALSO HOW UNLIKE YOU THIS IS.
YOU'RE FINE WITH MIRRORS NOW, AREN'T YOU?
WERE THE GLASSES GRIMM'S IDEA?
YOU DON'T ACTUALLY WANT TO TAKE GRIMM'S HEART ANYMORE, DO YOU?
BAM
HOLD ON! I NEED TO GET READY!
GET WHAT READY? YOU REALLY DON'T KNOW WHEN TO GIVE UP.
BANG

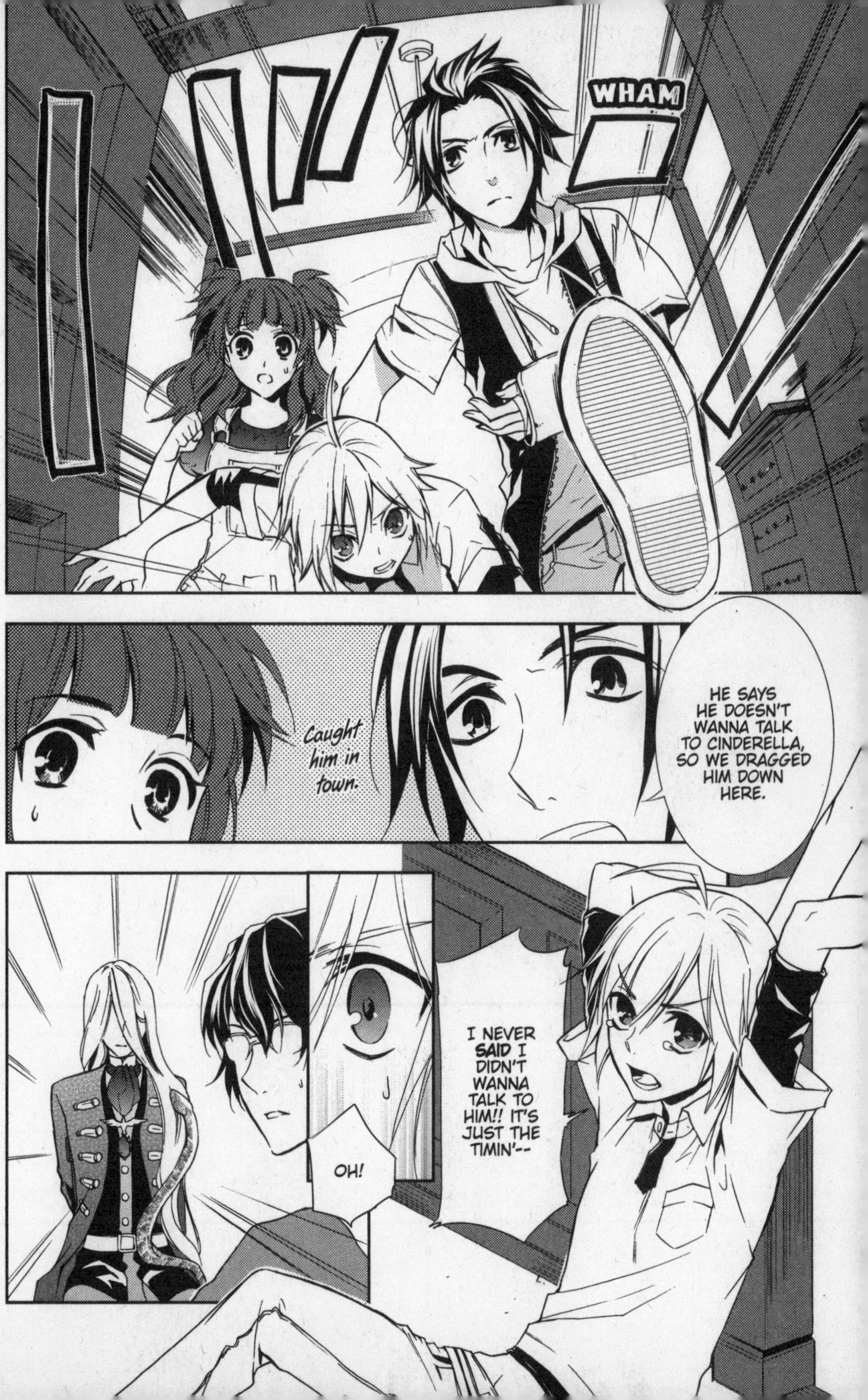
WHAM
HE SAYS HE DOESN'T WANNA TALK TO CINDERELLA, SO WE DRAGGED HIM DOWN HERE.
Caught him in town.
I NEVER SAID I DIDN'T WANNA TALK TO HIM!! IT'S JUST THE TIMIN'--
OH!

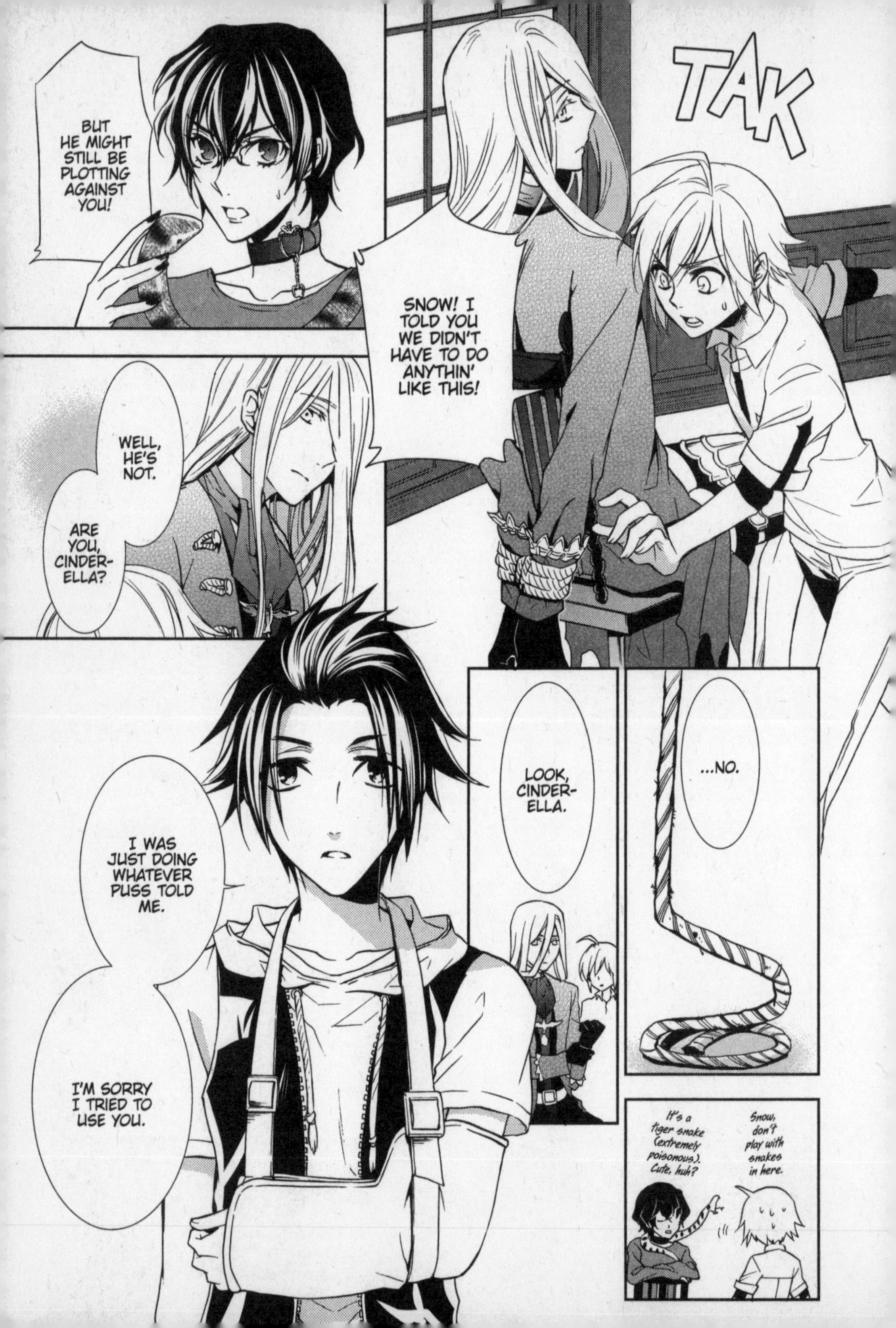
TAK
SNOW! I TOLD YOU WE DIDN'T HAVE TO DO ANYTHIN' LIKE THIS!
BUT HE MIGHT STILL BE PLOTTING AGAINST YOU!
WELL, HE'S NOT.
ARE YOU, CINDER-ELLA?
...NO.
Snow, don't play with snakes in here.
It's a tiger snake (extremely poisonous). Cute, huh?
LOOK, CINDER-ELLA.
I WAS JUST DOING WHATEVER PUSS TOLD ME.
I'M SORRY I TRIED TO USE YOU.

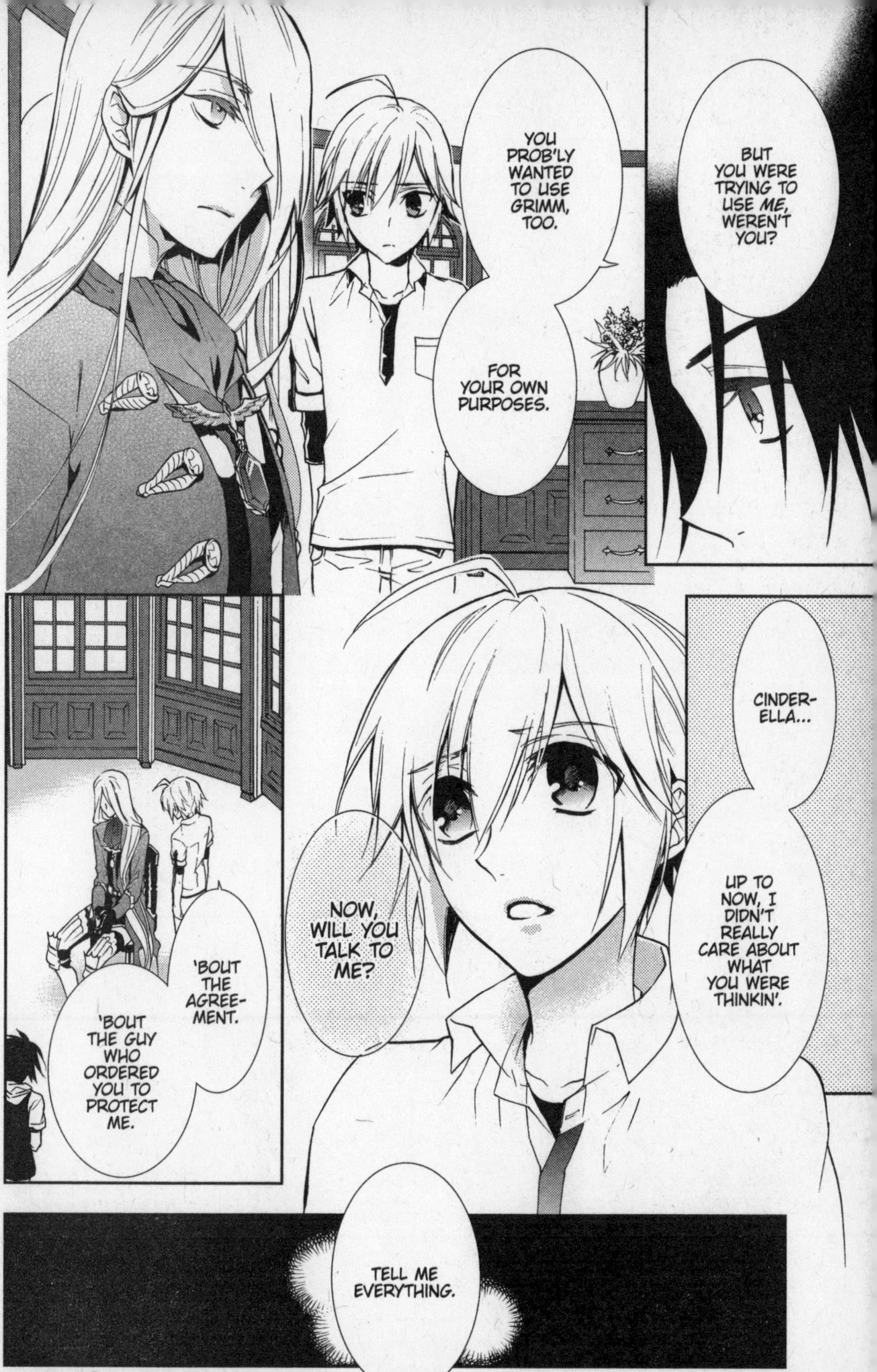
BUT YOU WERE TRYING TO USE *ME*, WEREN'T YOU?
YOU PROB'LY WANTED TO USE GRIMM, TOO.
FOR YOUR OWN PURPOSES.
CINDERELLA...
UP TO NOW, I DIDN'T REALLY CARE ABOUT WHAT YOU WERE THINKIN'.
NOW, WILL YOU TALK TO ME?
'BOUT THE AGREEMENT.
'BOUT THE GUY WHO ORDERED YOU TO PROTECT ME.
TELL ME EVERYTHING.

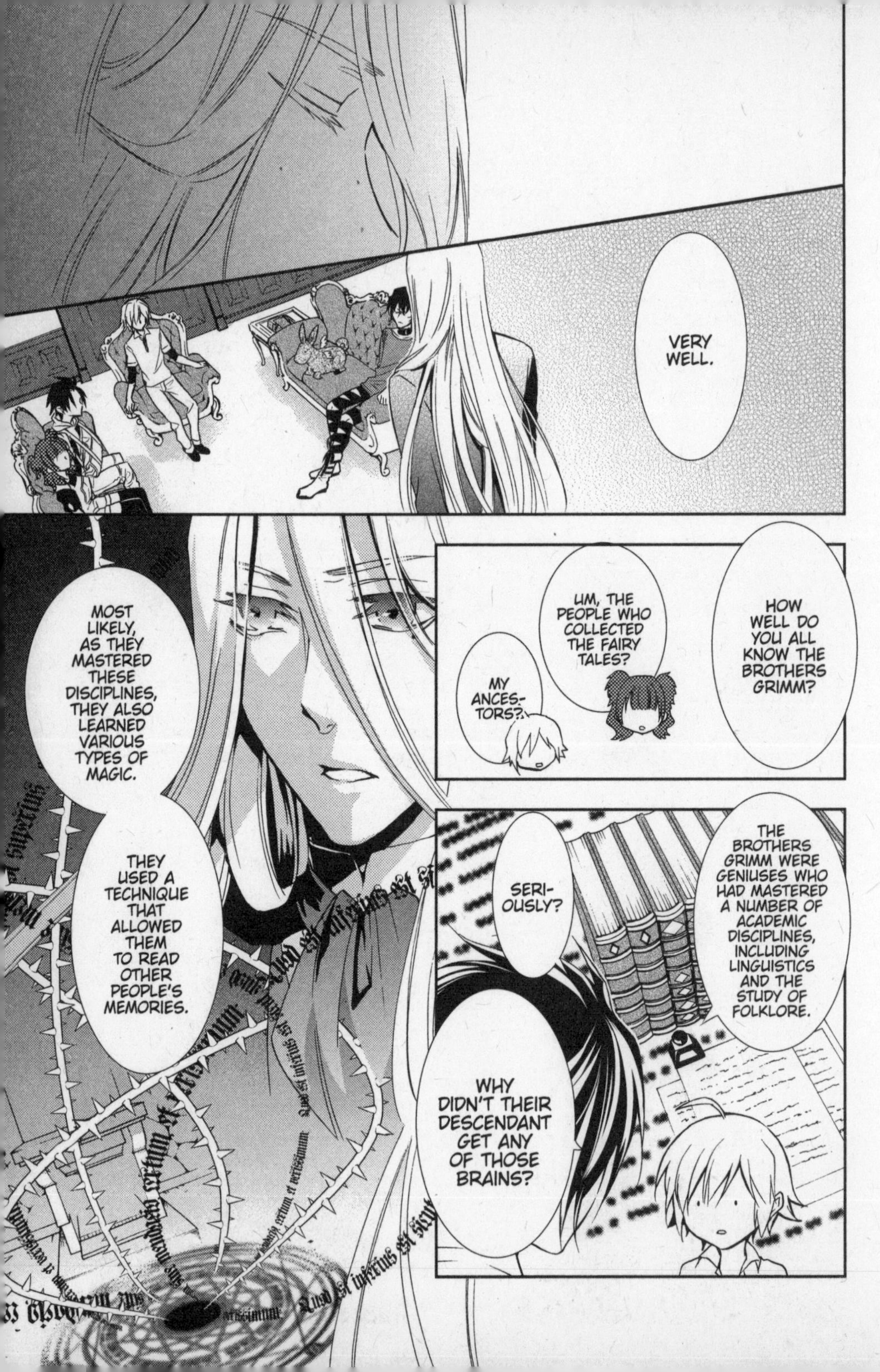
VERY WELL.
HOW WELL DO YOU ALL KNOW THE BROTHERS GRIMM?
UM, THE PEOPLE WHO COLLECTED THE FAIRY TALES?
MY ANCESTORS?
THE BROTHERS GRIMM WERE GENIUSES WHO HAD MASTERED A NUMBER OF ACADEMIC DISCIPLINES, INCLUDING LINGUISTICS AND THE STUDY OF FOLKLORE.
SERIOUSLY?
WHY DIDN'T THEIR DESCENDANT GET ANY OF THOSE BRAINS?
MOST LIKELY, AS THEY MASTERED THESE DISCIPLINES, THEY ALSO LEARNED VARIOUS TYPES OF MAGIC.
THEY USED A TECHNIQUE THAT ALLOWED THEM TO READ OTHER PEOPLE'S MEMORIES.

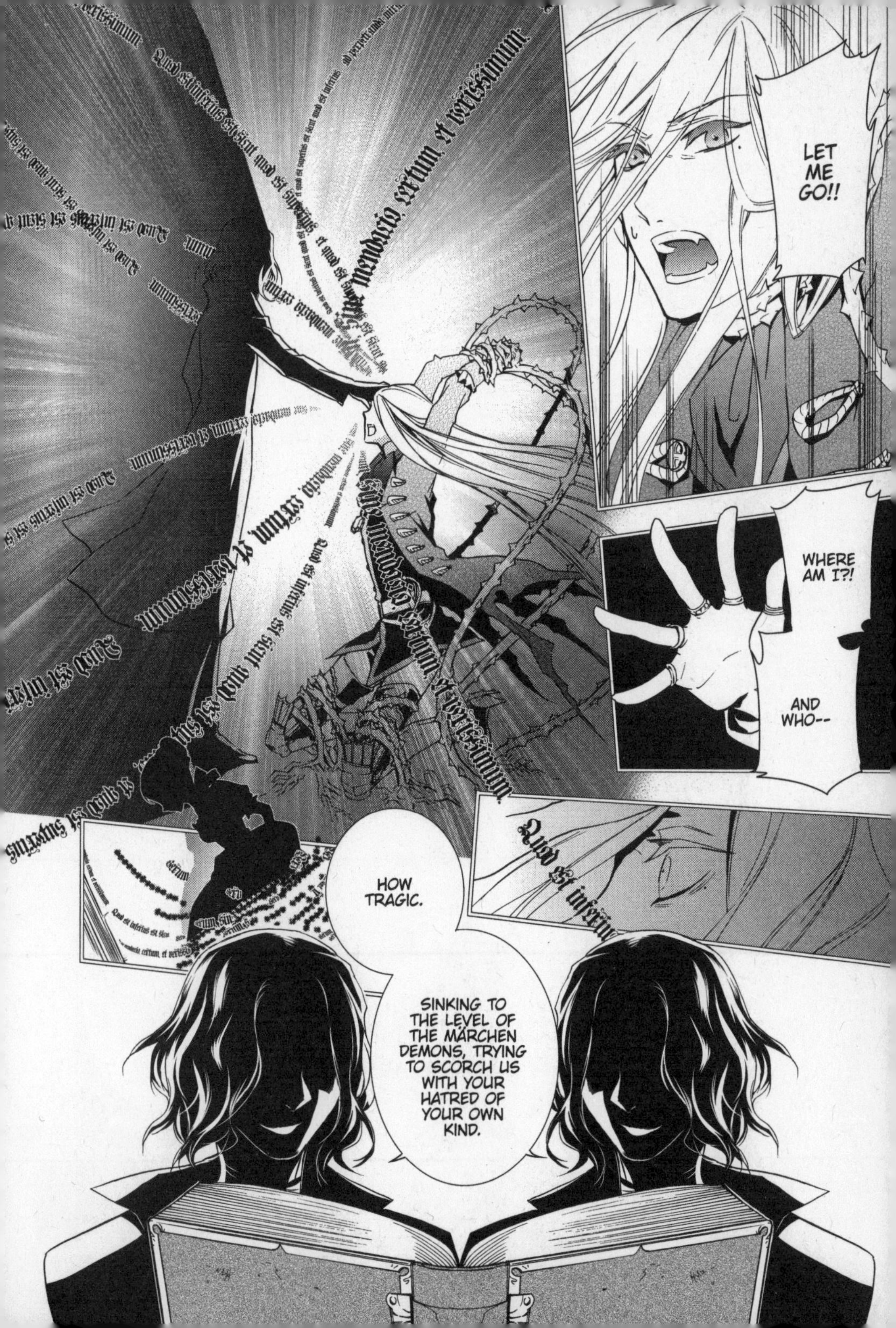
LET ME GO!!
WHERE AM I?!
AND WHO--
HOW TRAGIC.
SINKING TO THE LEVEL OF THE MÄRCHEN DEMONS, TRYING TO SCORCH US WITH YOUR HATRED OF YOUR OWN KIND.

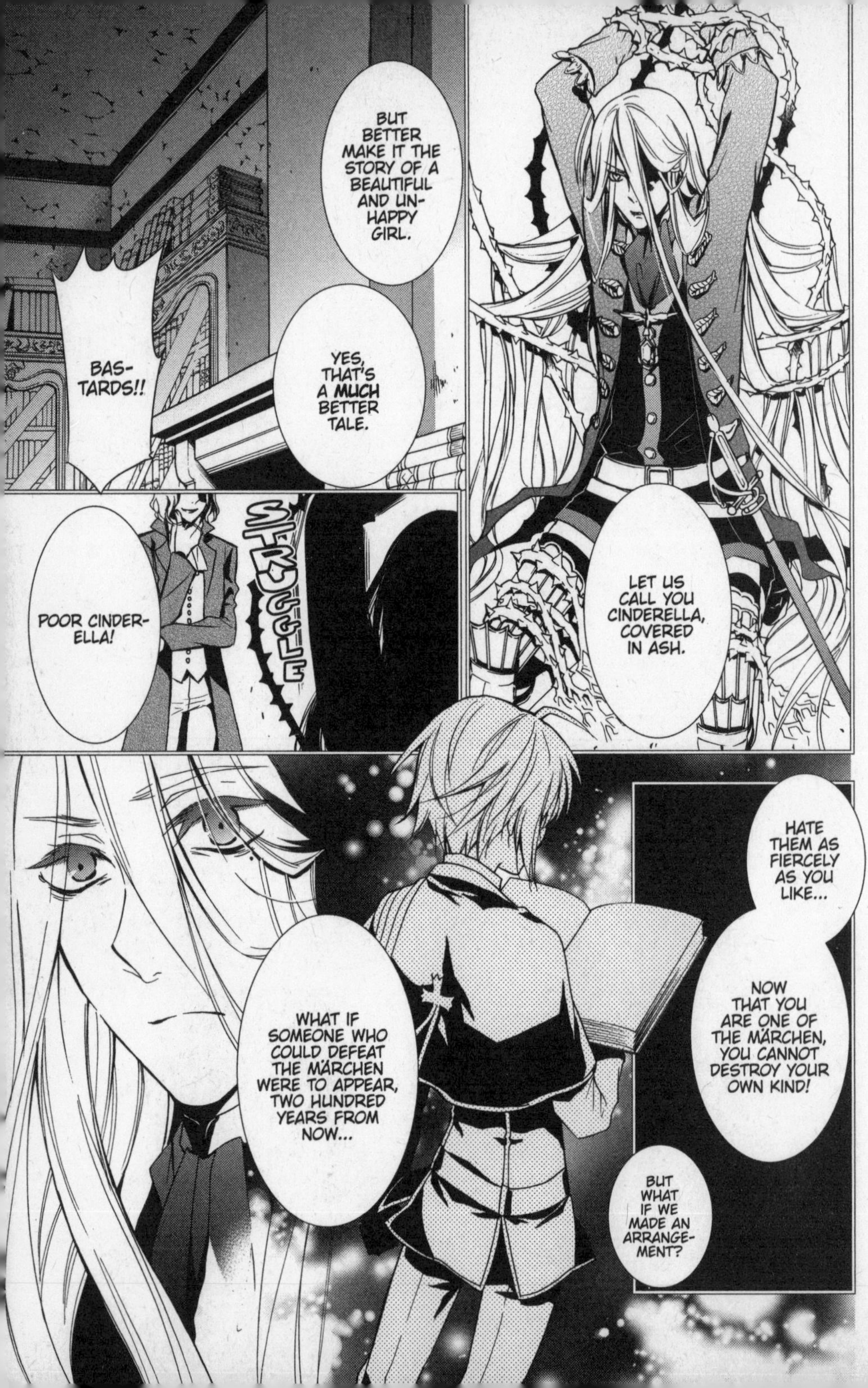
LET US CALL YOU CINDERELLA, COVERED IN ASH.
BUT BETTER MAKE IT THE STORY OF A BEAUTIFUL AND UNHAPPY GIRL.
YES, THAT'S A **MUCH** BETTER TALE.
BASTARDS!!
STRUGGLE
POOR CINDERELLA!
HATE THEM AS FIERCELY AS YOU LIKE...
NOW THAT YOU ARE ONE OF THE MÄRCHEN, YOU CANNOT DESTROY YOUR OWN KIND!
BUT WHAT IF WE MADE AN ARRANGEMENT?
WHAT IF SOMEONE WHO COULD DEFEAT THE MÄRCHEN WERE TO APPEAR, TWO HUNDRED YEARS FROM NOW...

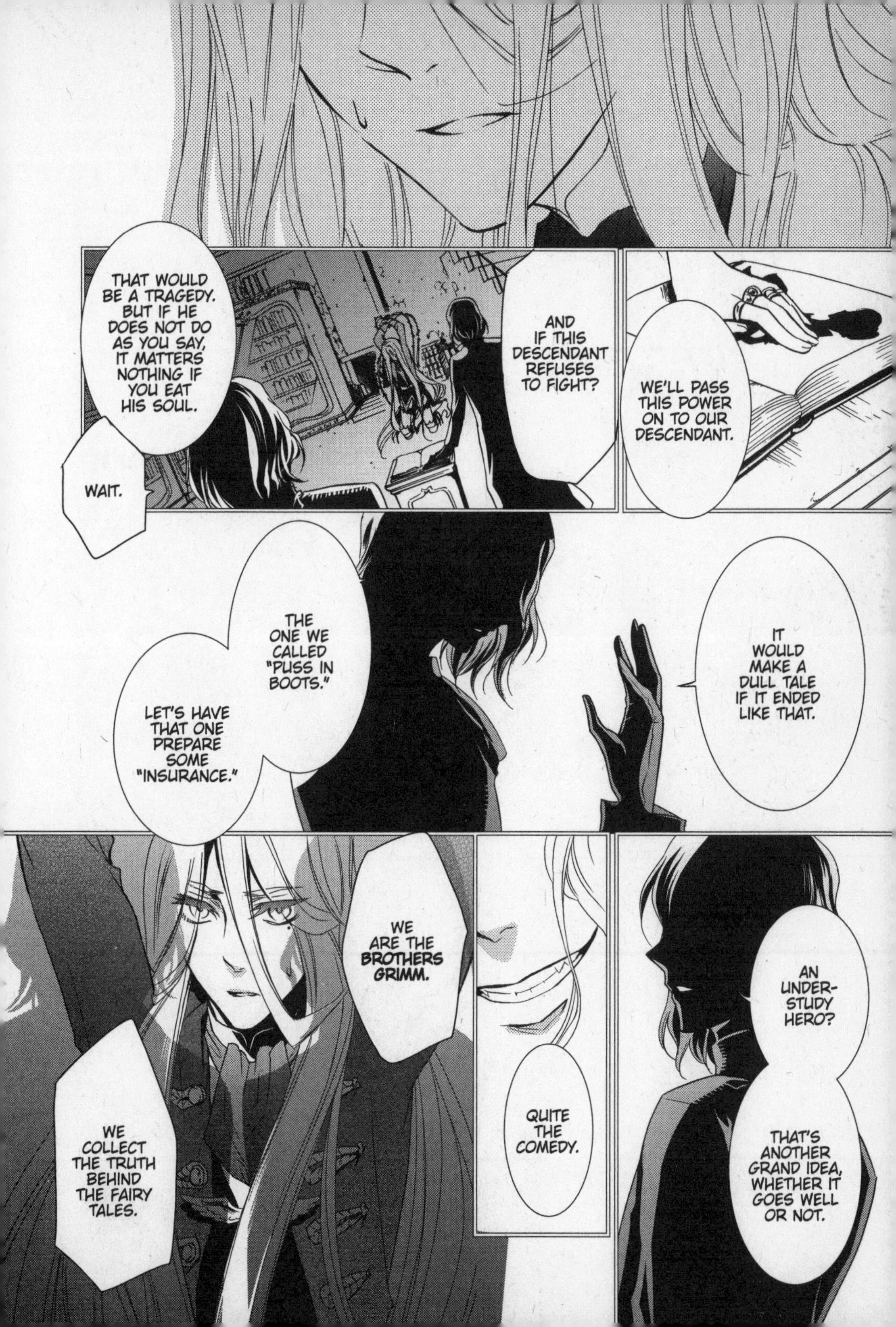
WE'LL PASS THIS POWER ON TO OUR DESCENDANT.
AND IF THIS DESCENDANT REFUSES TO FIGHT?
THAT WOULD BE A TRAGEDY. BUT IF HE DOES NOT DO AS YOU SAY, IT MATTERS NOTHING IF YOU EAT HIS SOUL.
WAIT.
IT WOULD MAKE A DULL TALE IF IT ENDED LIKE THAT.
THE ONE WE CALLED "PUSS IN BOOTS."
LET'S HAVE THAT ONE PREPARE SOME "INSURANCE."
AN UNDER-STUDY HERO?
THAT'S ANOTHER GRAND IDEA, WHETHER IT GOES WELL OR NOT.
QUITE THE COMEDY.
WE ARE THE **BROTHERS GRIMM.**
WE COLLECT THE TRUTH BEHIND THE FAIRY TALES.

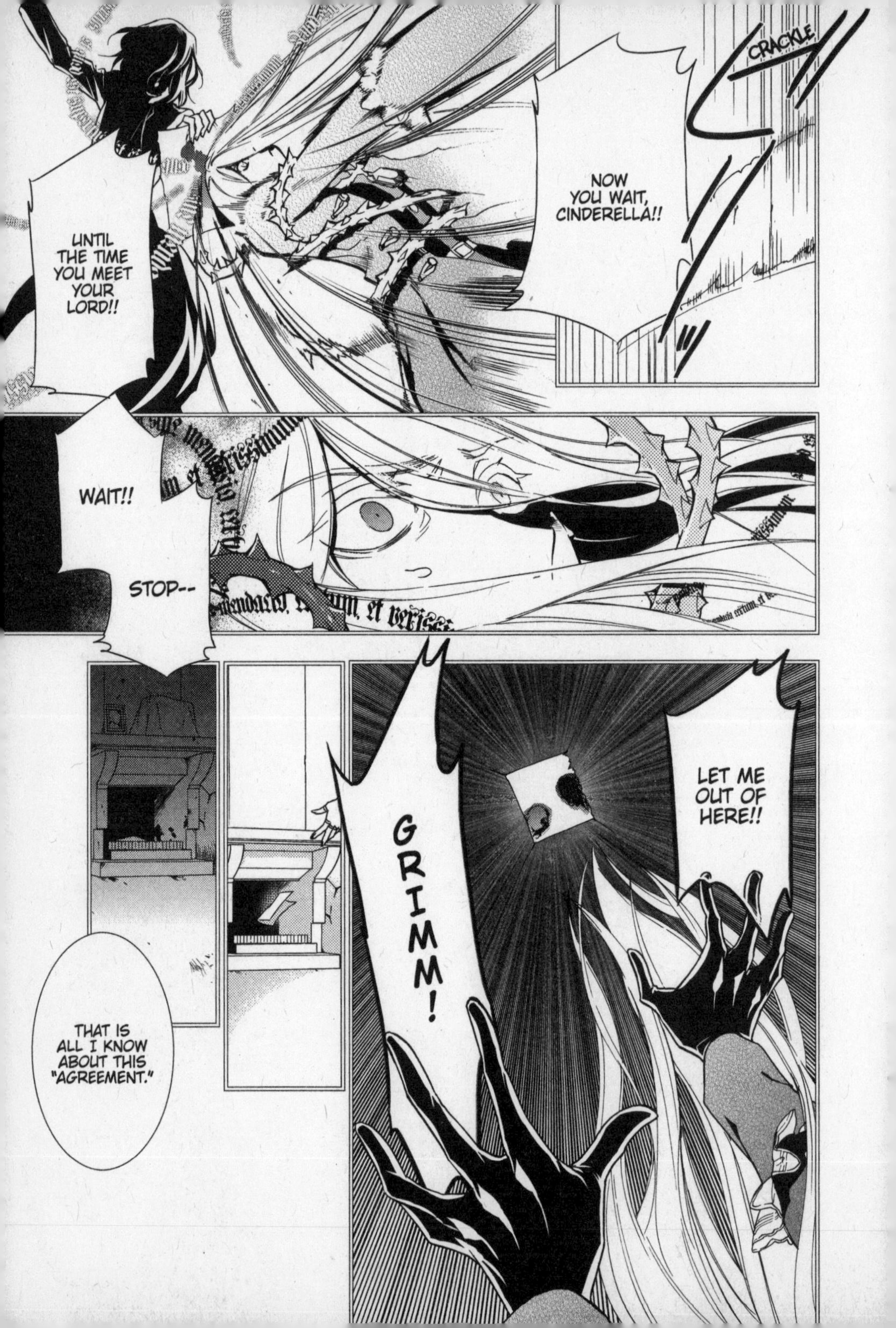
CRACKLE
NOW YOU WAIT, CINDERELLA!!
UNTIL THE TIME YOU MEET YOUR LORD!!
WAIT!!
STOP--
LET ME OUT OF HERE!!
GRIMM!
THAT IS ALL I KNOW ABOUT THIS "AGREEMENT."

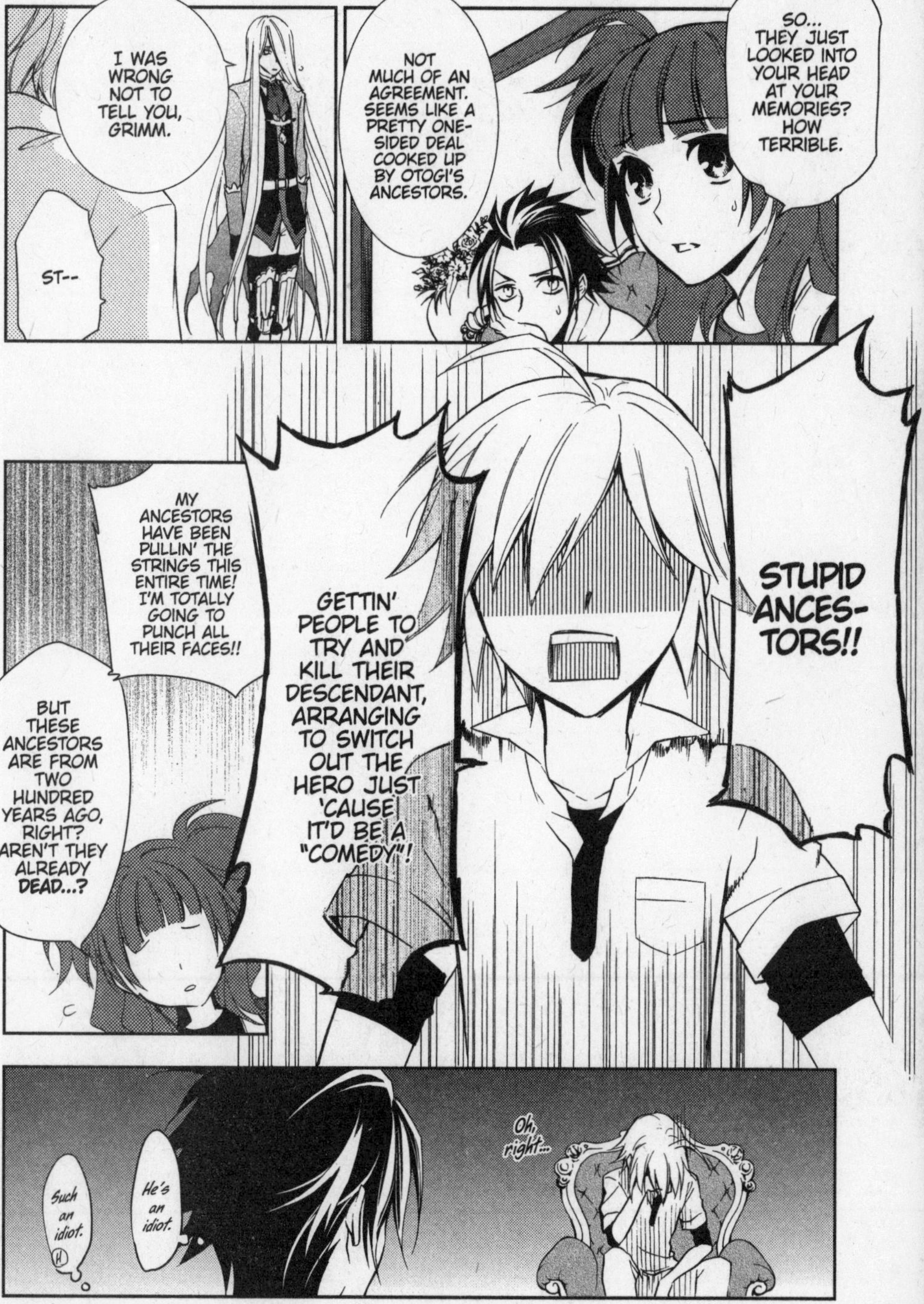
SO... THEY JUST LOOKED INTO YOUR HEAD AT YOUR MEMORIES? HOW TERRIBLE.
NOT MUCH OF AN AGREEMENT. SEEMS LIKE A PRETTY ONE-SIDED DEAL COOKED UP BY OTOGI'S ANCESTORS.
I WAS WRONG NOT TO TELL YOU, GRIMM.
ST--
STUPID ANCESTORS!!
GETTIN' PEOPLE TO TRY AND KILL THEIR DESCENDANT, ARRANGING TO SWITCH OUT THE HERO JUST 'CAUSE IT'D BE A "COMEDY"!
MY ANCESTORS HAVE BEEN PULLIN' THE STRINGS THIS ENTIRE TIME! I'M TOTALLY GOING TO PUNCH ALL THEIR FACES!!
BUT THESE ANCESTORS ARE FROM TWO HUNDRED YEARS AGO, RIGHT? AREN'T THEY ALREADY DEAD...?
Oh, right...
He's an idiot.
Such an idiot.

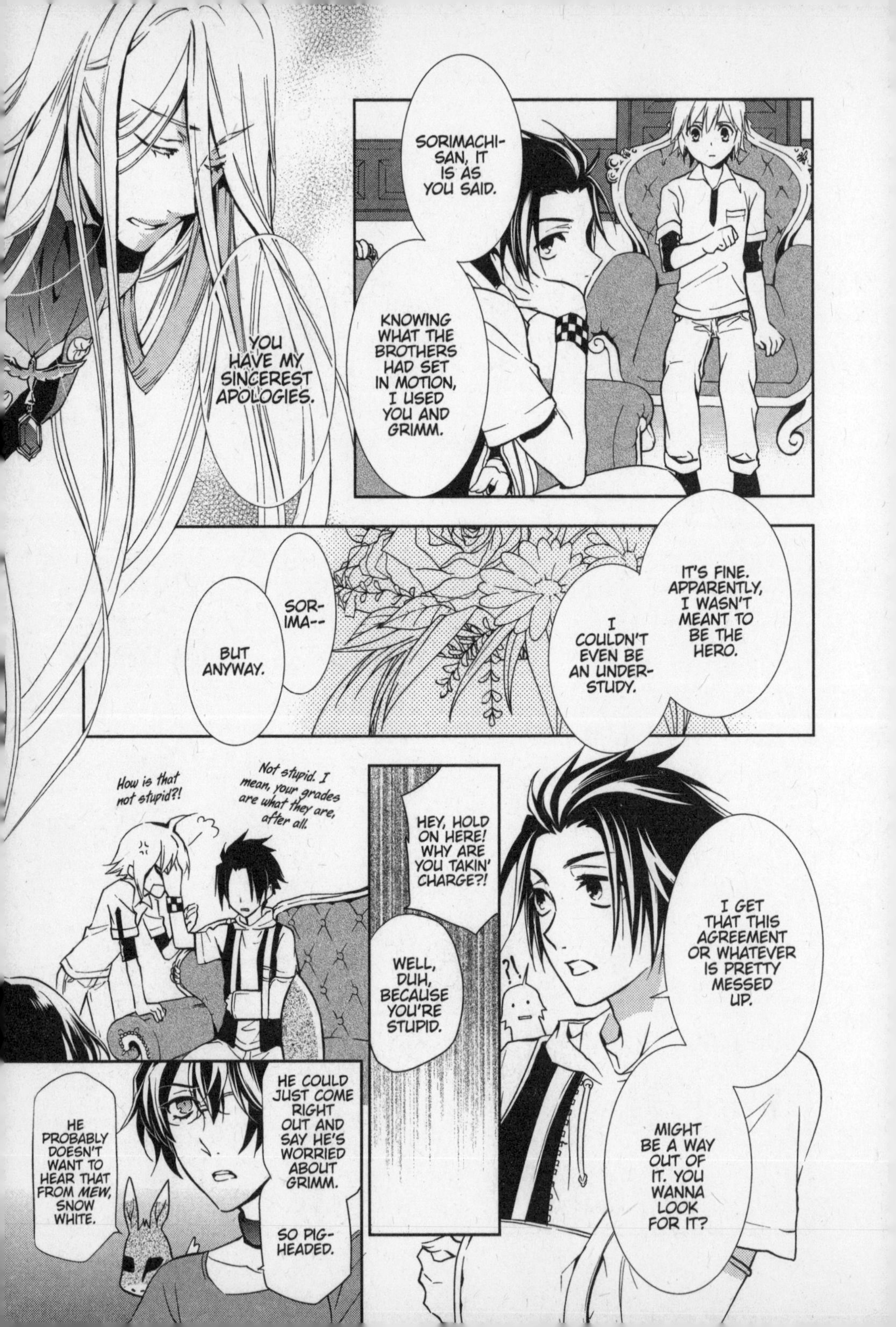
SORIMACHI-SAN, IT IS AS YOU SAID.
KNOWING WHAT THE BROTHERS HAD SET IN MOTION, I USED YOU AND GRIMM.
YOU HAVE MY SINCEREST APOLOGIES.
IT'S FINE. APPARENTLY, I WASN'T MEANT TO BE THE HERO.
I COULDN'T EVEN BE AN UNDER-STUDY.
SOR-IMA--
BUT ANYWAY.
I GET THAT THIS AGREEMENT OR WHATEVER IS PRETTY MESSED UP.
MIGHT BE A WAY OUT OF IT. YOU WANNA LOOK FOR IT?
HEY, HOLD ON HERE! WHY ARE YOU TAKIN' CHARGE?!
?!
WELL, DUH, BECAUSE YOU'RE STUPID.
Not stupid. I mean, your grades are what they are, after all.
How is that not stupid?!
HE COULD JUST COME RIGHT OUT AND SAY HE'S WORRIED ABOUT GRIMM.
HE PROBABLY DOESN'T WANT TO HEAR THAT FROM MEW, SNOW WHITE.
SO PIG-HEADED.

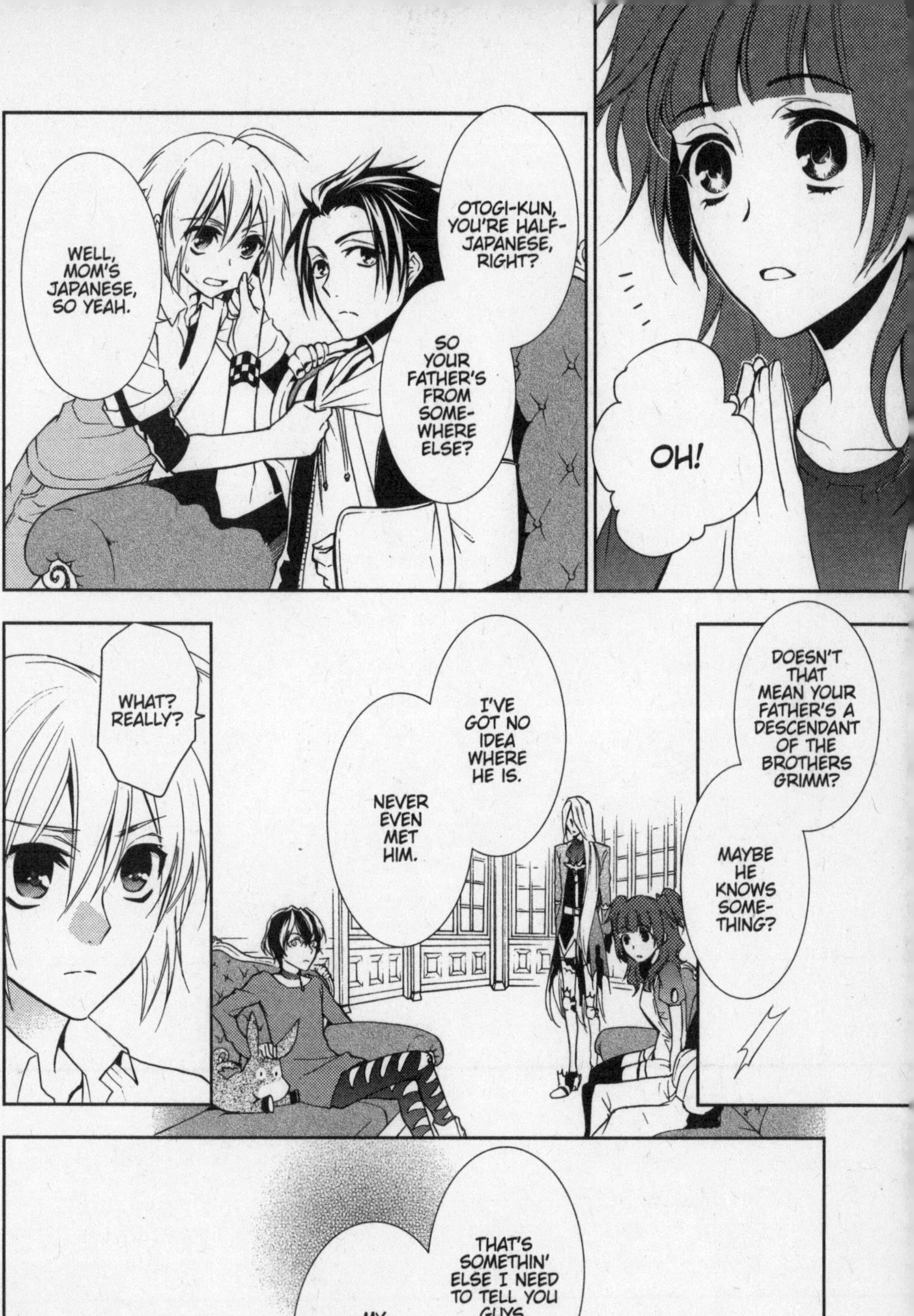
OH!
OTOGI-KUN, YOU'RE HALF-JAPANESE, RIGHT?
SO YOUR FATHER'S FROM SOME-WHERE ELSE?
WELL, MOM'S JAPANESE, SO YEAH.
DOESN'T THAT MEAN YOUR FATHER'S A DESCENDANT OF THE BROTHERS GRIMM?
MAYBE HE KNOWS SOME-THING?
I'VE GOT NO IDEA WHERE HE IS.
NEVER EVEN MET HIM.
WHAT? REALLY?
THAT'S SOMETHIN' ELSE I NEED TO TELL YOU GUYS.
MY "FAMILY CIRCUM-STANCES."

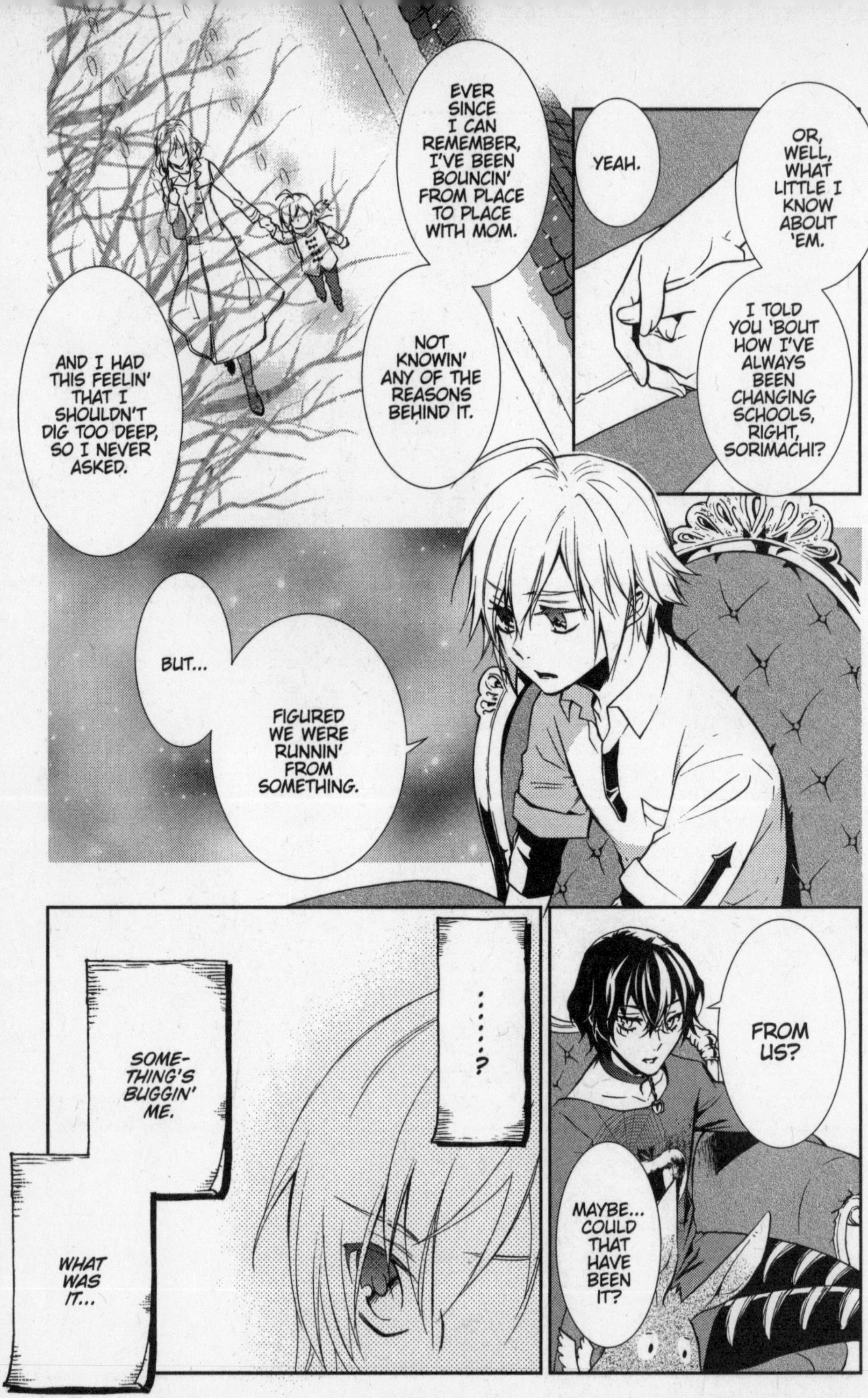
OR, WELL, WHAT LITTLE I KNOW ABOUT 'EM.
YEAH.
I TOLD YOU 'BOUT HOW I'VE ALWAYS BEEN CHANGING SCHOOLS, RIGHT, SORIMACHI?
EVER SINCE I CAN REMEMBER, I'VE BEEN BOUNCIN' FROM PLACE TO PLACE WITH MOM.
NOT KNOWIN' ANY OF THE REASONS BEHIND IT.
AND I HAD THIS FEELIN' THAT I SHOULDN'T DIG TOO DEEP, SO I NEVER ASKED.
BUT...
FIGURED WE WERE RUNNIN' FROM SOMETHING.
FROM US?
MAYBE... COULD THAT HAVE BEEN IT?
......?
SOME-THING'S BUGGIN' ME.
WHAT WAS IT...

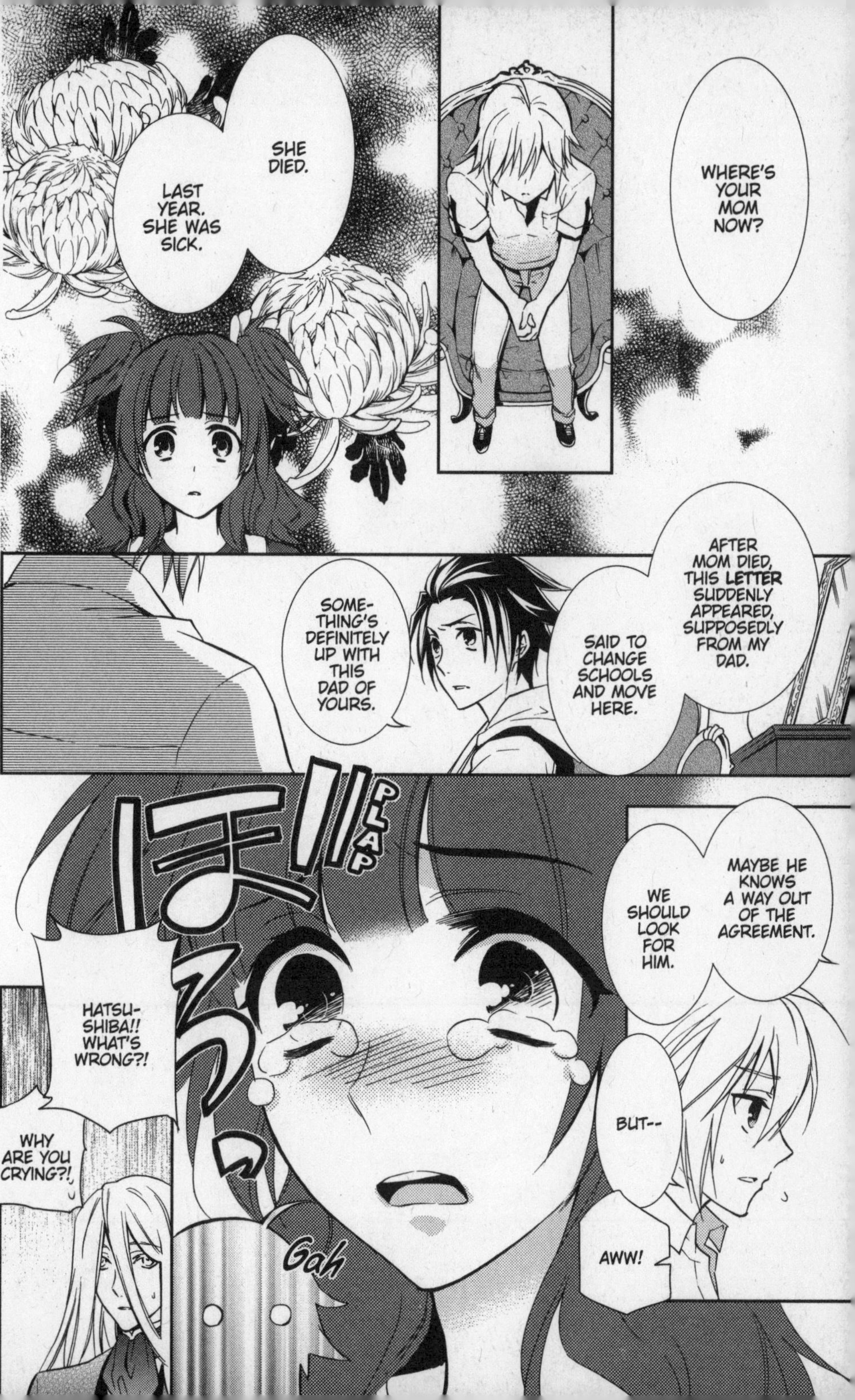
WHERE'S YOUR MOM NOW?
SHE DIED.
LAST YEAR. SHE WAS SICK.
AFTER MOM DIED, THIS LETTER SUDDENLY APPEARED, SUPPOSEDLY FROM MY DAD.
SAID TO CHANGE SCHOOLS AND MOVE HERE.
SOME-THING'S DEFINITELY UP WITH THIS DAD OF YOURS.
MAYBE HE KNOWS A WAY OUT OF THE AGREEMENT.
WE SHOULD LOOK FOR HIM.
BUT--
AWW!
PLAP
Gah
HATSU-SHIBA!! WHAT'S WRONG?!
WHY ARE YOU CRYING?!

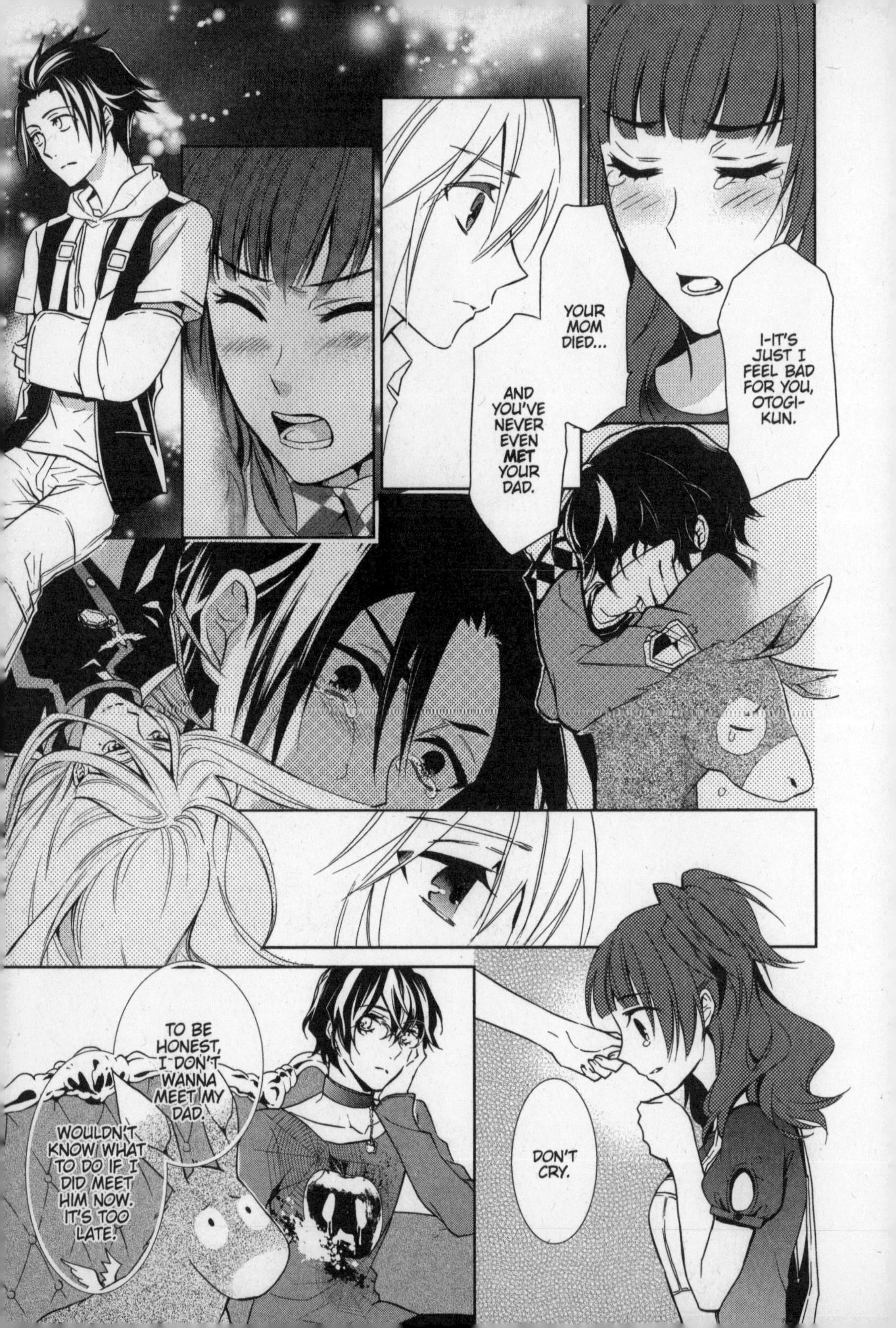
I-IT'S JUST I FEEL BAD FOR YOU, OTOGI-KUN.
YOUR MOM DIED...
AND YOU'VE NEVER EVEN MET YOUR DAD.
DON'T CRY.
TO BE HONEST, I DON'T WANNA MEET MY DAD.
WOULDN'T KNOW WHAT TO DO IF I DID MEET HIM NOW. IT'S TOO LATE.

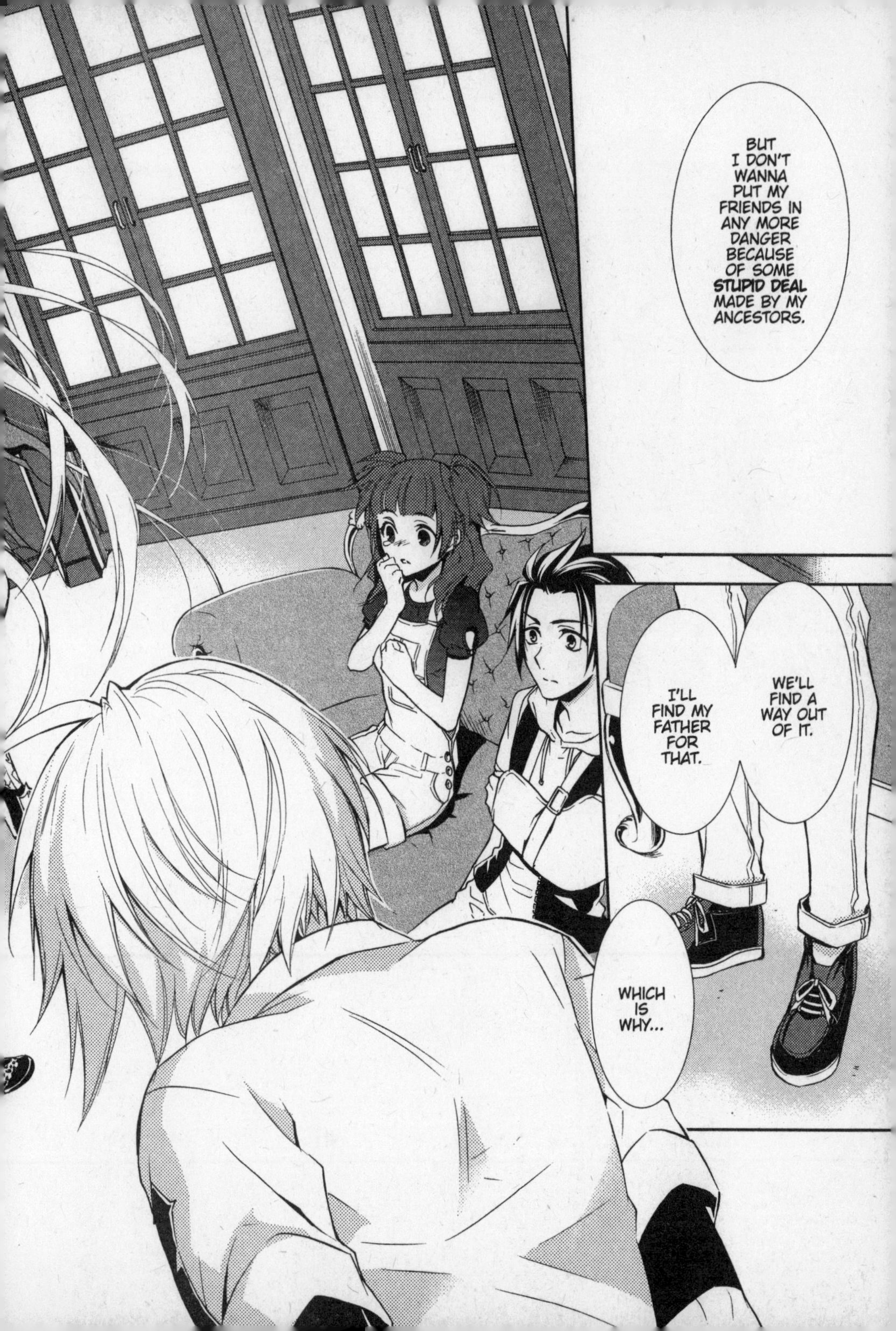
BUT I DON'T WANNA PUT MY FRIENDS IN ANY MORE DANGER BECAUSE OF SOME **STUPID DEAL** MADE BY MY ANCESTORS.
WE'LL FIND A WAY OUT OF IT.
I'LL FIND MY FATHER FOR THAT.
WHICH IS WHY...

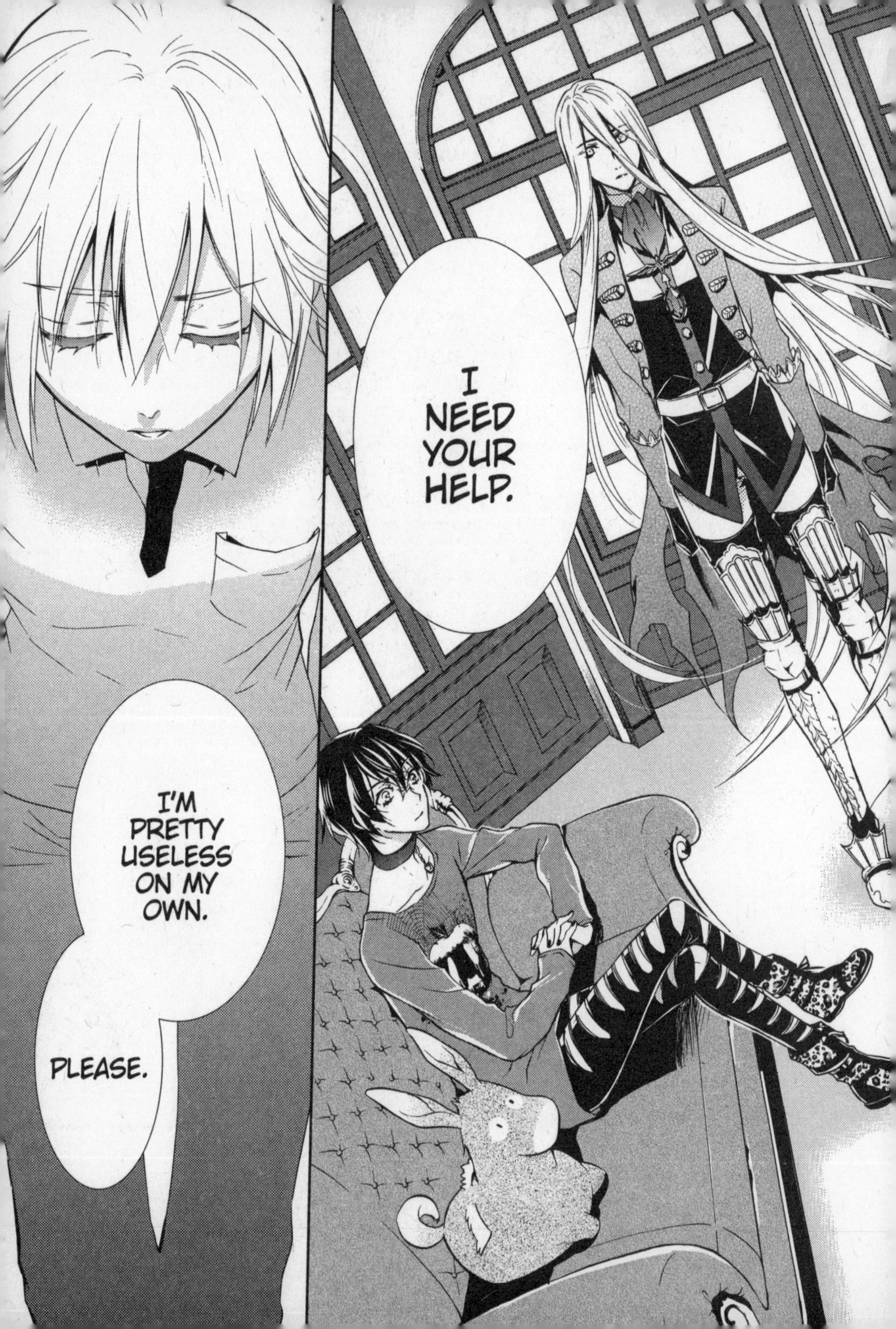
I NEED YOUR HELP.
I'M PRETTY USELESS ON MY OWN.
PLEASE.

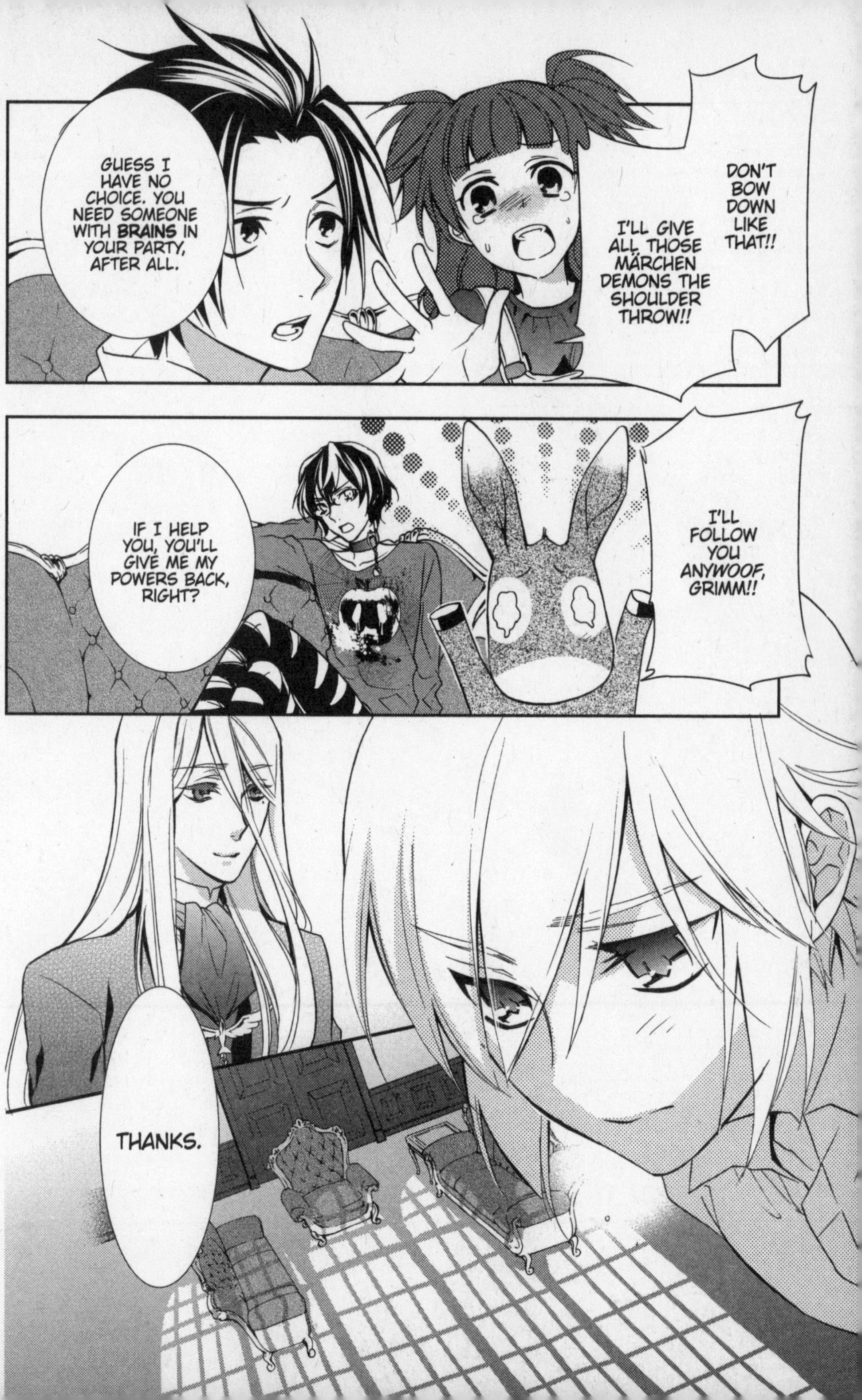
DON'T BOW DOWN LIKE THAT!!
I'LL GIVE ALL THOSE MÄRCHEN DEMONS THE SHOULDER THROW!!
GUESS I HAVE NO CHOICE. YOU NEED SOMEONE WITH **BRAINS** IN YOUR PARTY, AFTER ALL.
I'LL FOLLOW YOU ANYWOOF, GRIMM!!
IF I HELP YOU, YOU'LL GIVE ME MY POWERS BACK, RIGHT?
THANKS.

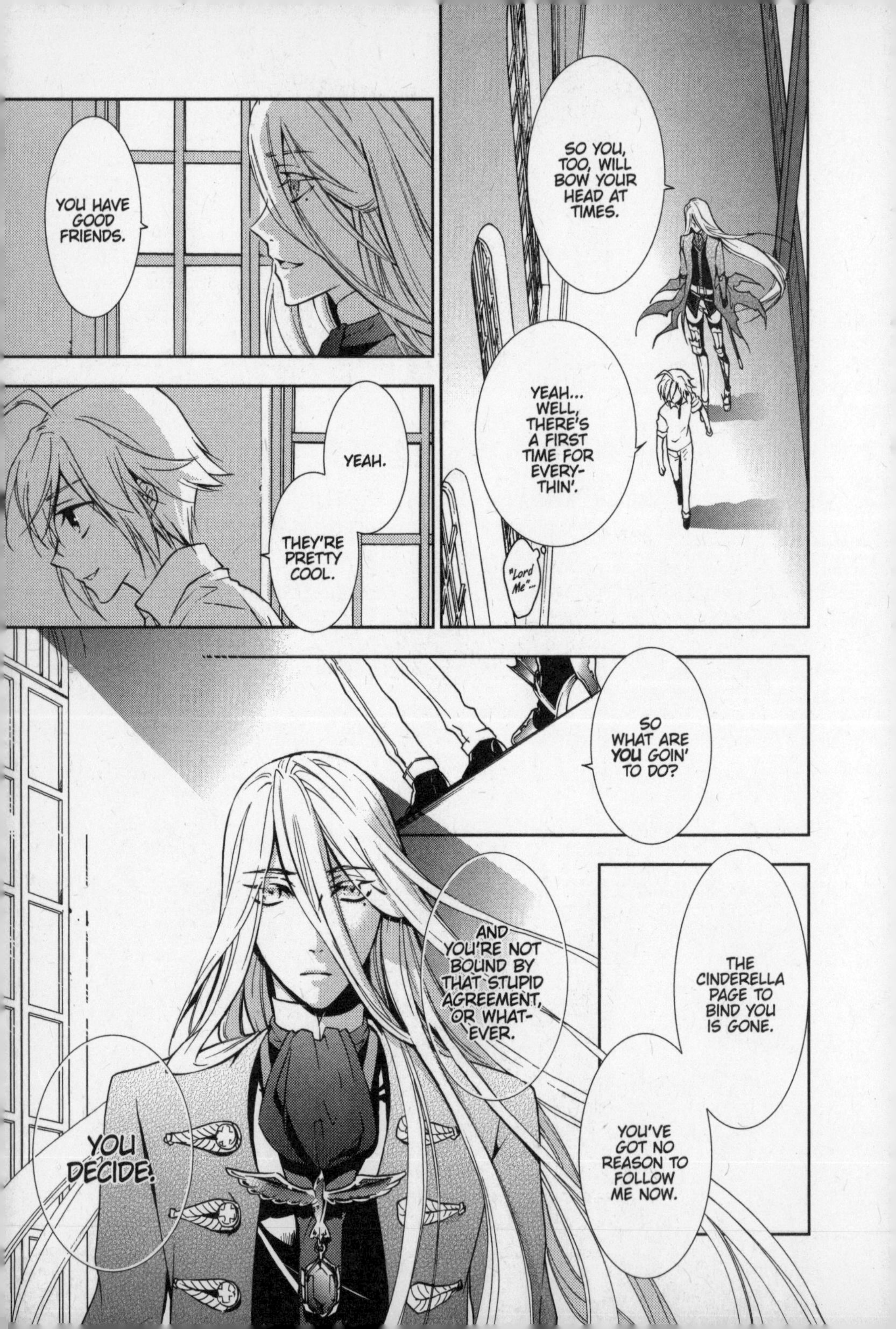
SO YOU, TOO, WILL BOW YOUR HEAD AT TIMES.
YEAH... WELL, THERE'S A FIRST TIME FOR EVERY-THIN'.
"Lord Me"...
YOU HAVE GOOD FRIENDS.
YEAH.
THEY'RE PRETTY COOL.
SO WHAT ARE YOU GOIN' TO DO?
THE CINDERELLA PAGE TO BIND YOU IS GONE.
YOU'VE GOT NO REASON TO FOLLOW ME NOW.
AND YOU'RE NOT BOUND BY THAT STUPID AGREEMENT, OR WHAT-EVER.
YOU DECIDE.

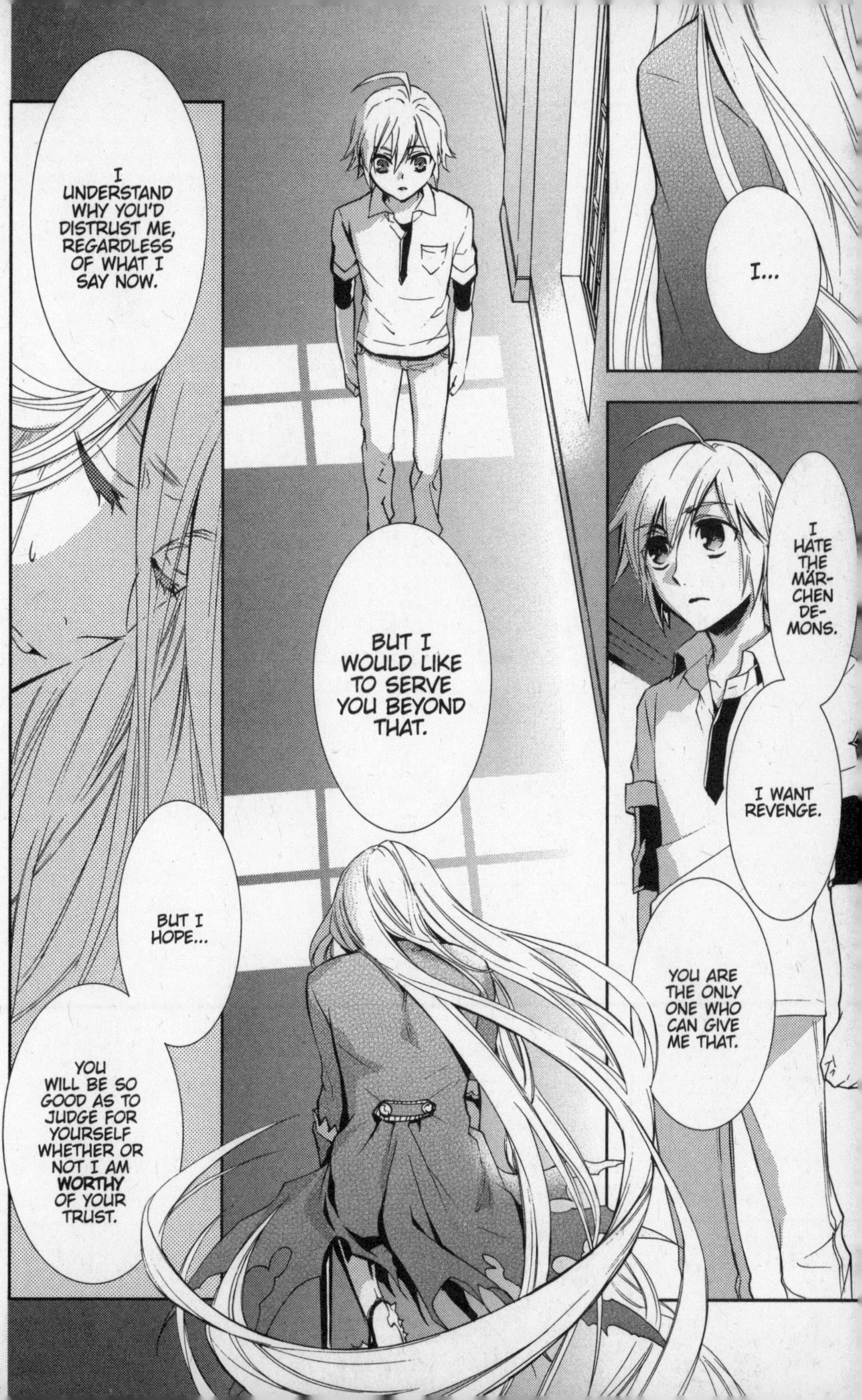
I...
I HATE THE MÄRCHEN DEMONS.
I WANT REVENGE.
YOU ARE THE ONLY ONE WHO CAN GIVE ME THAT.
I UNDERSTAND WHY YOU'D DISTRUST ME, REGARDLESS OF WHAT I SAY NOW.
BUT I WOULD LIKE TO SERVE YOU BEYOND THAT.
BUT I HOPE...
YOU WILL BE SO GOOD AS TO JUDGE FOR YOURSELF WHETHER OR NOT I AM **WORTHY** OF YOUR TRUST.

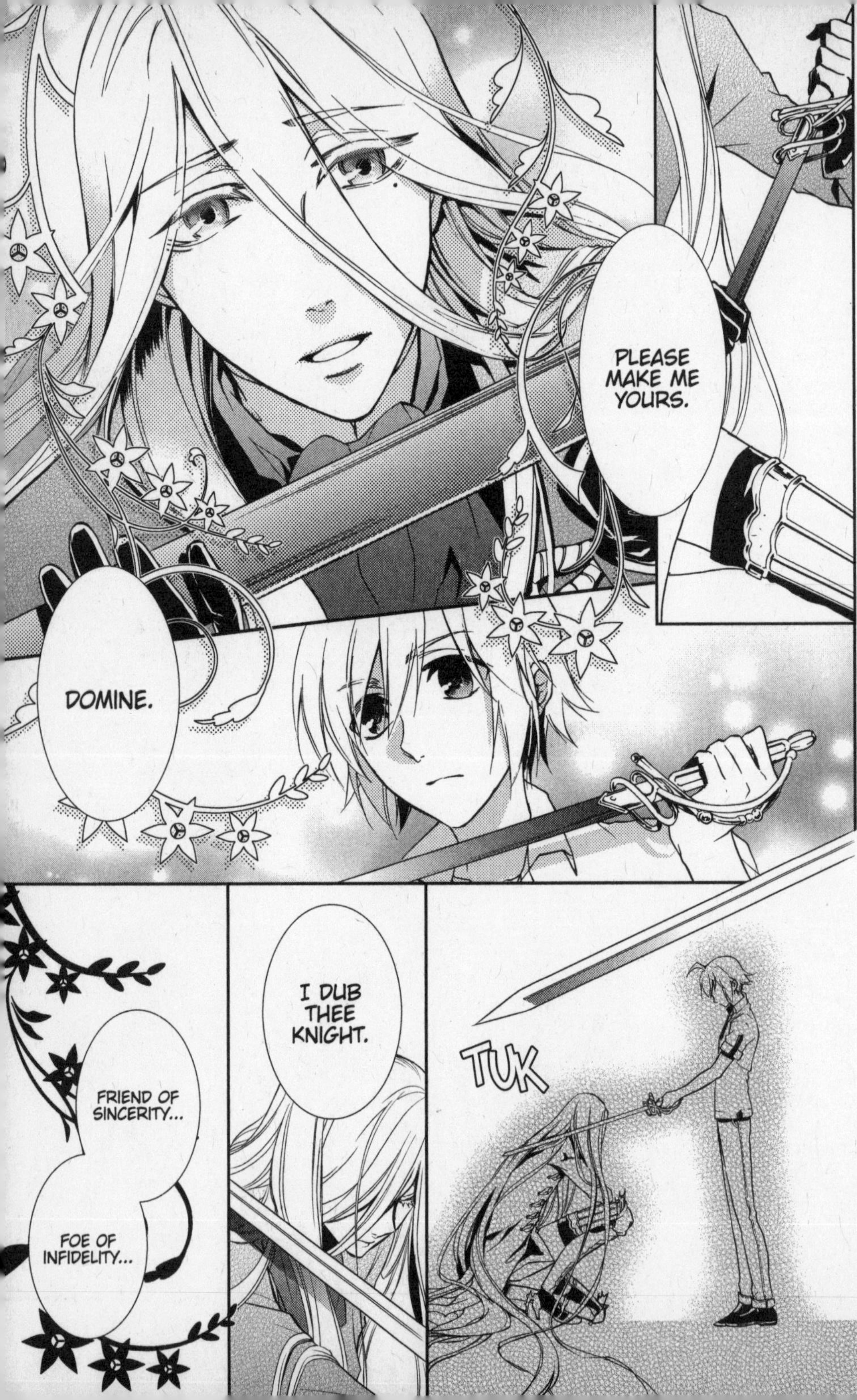
PLEASE MAKE ME YOURS.
DOMINE.
TUK
I DUB THEE KNIGHT.
FRIEND OF SINCERITY...
FOE OF INFIDELITY...

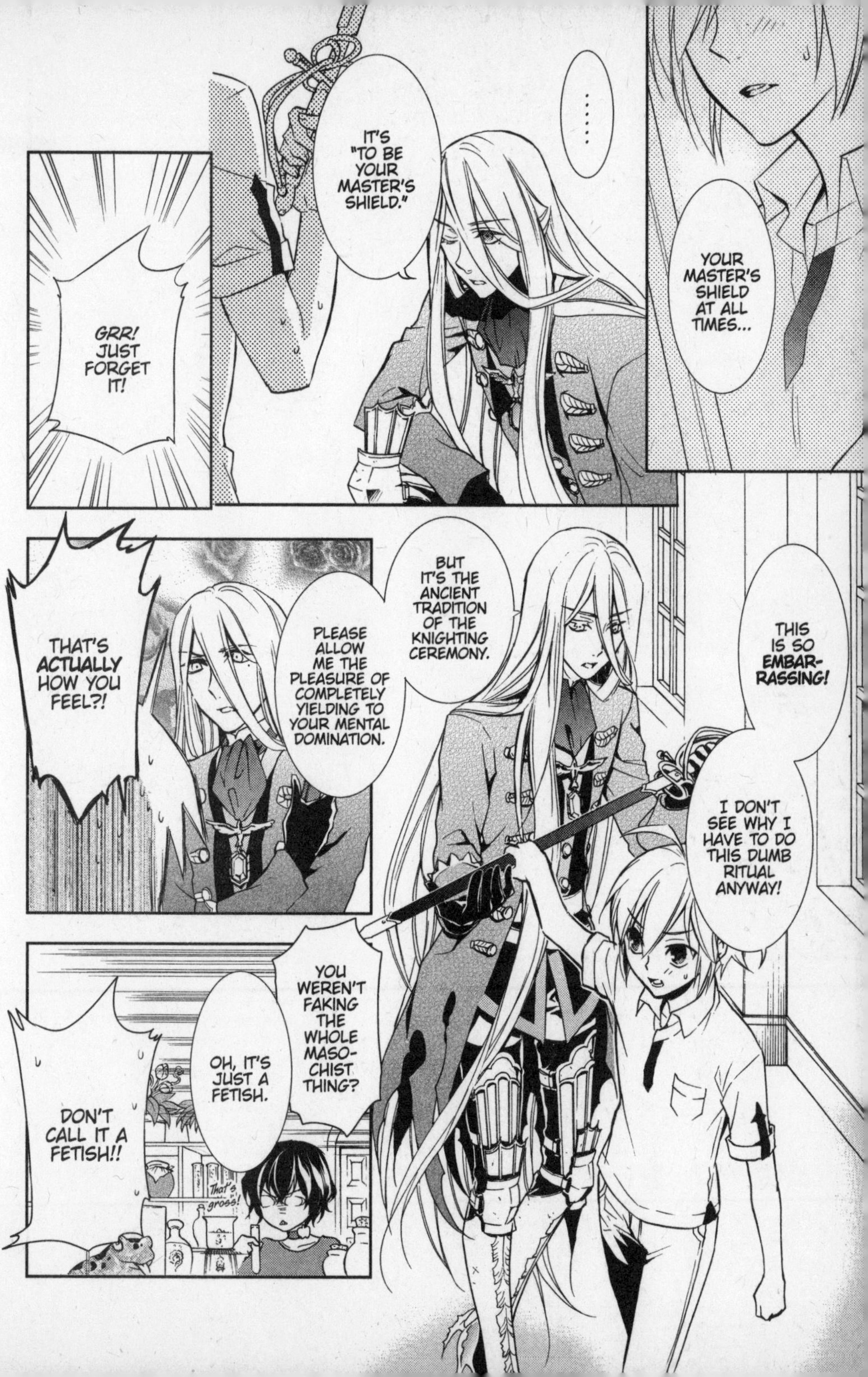
YOUR MASTER'S SHIELD AT ALL TIMES...
......
IT'S "TO BE YOUR MASTER'S SHIELD."
GRR! JUST FORGET IT!
THIS IS SO EMBARRASSING!
I DON'T SEE WHY I HAVE TO DO THIS DUMB RITUAL ANYWAY!
BUT IT'S THE ANCIENT TRADITION OF THE KNIGHTING CEREMONY.
PLEASE ALLOW ME THE PLEASURE OF COMPLETELY YIELDING TO YOUR MENTAL DOMINATION.
THAT'S ACTUALLY HOW YOU FEEL?!
YOU WEREN'T FAKING THE WHOLE MASOCHIST THING?
OH, IT'S JUST A FETISH.
DON'T CALL IT A FETISH!!
That's gross!

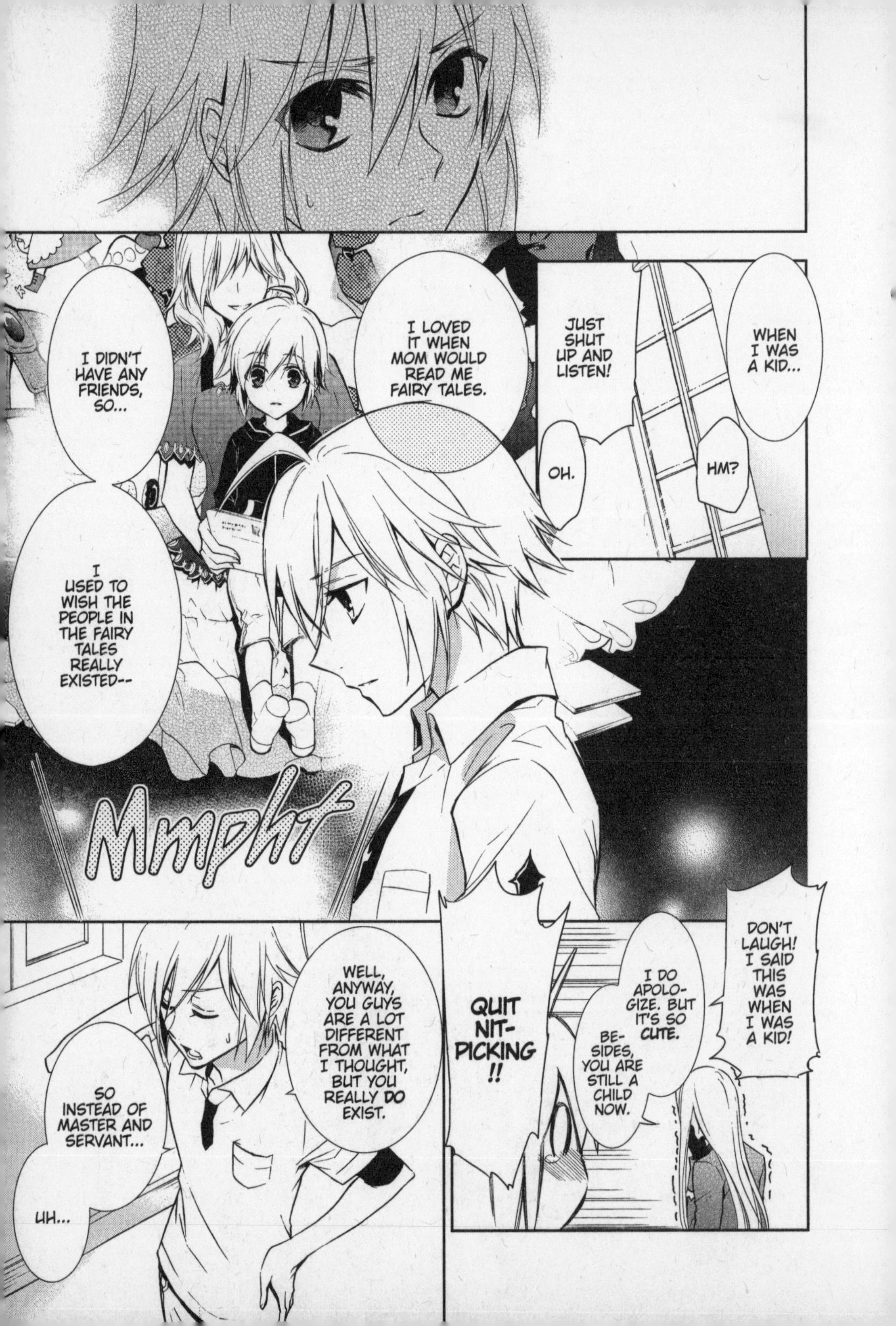
WHEN I WAS A KID...
HM?
JUST SHUT UP AND LISTEN!
OH.
I LOVED IT WHEN MOM WOULD READ ME FAIRY TALES.
I DIDN'T HAVE ANY FRIENDS, SO...
I USED TO WISH THE PEOPLE IN THE FAIRY TALES REALLY EXISTED--
Mmpht
DON'T LAUGH! I SAID THIS WAS WHEN I WAS A KID!
I DO APOLOGIZE. BUT IT'S SO CUTE.
BESIDES, YOU ARE STILL A CHILD NOW.
QUIT NIT-PICKING!!
WELL, ANYWAY, YOU GUYS ARE A LOT DIFFERENT FROM WHAT I THOUGHT, BUT YOU REALLY DO EXIST.
SO INSTEAD OF MASTER AND SERVANT...
UH...

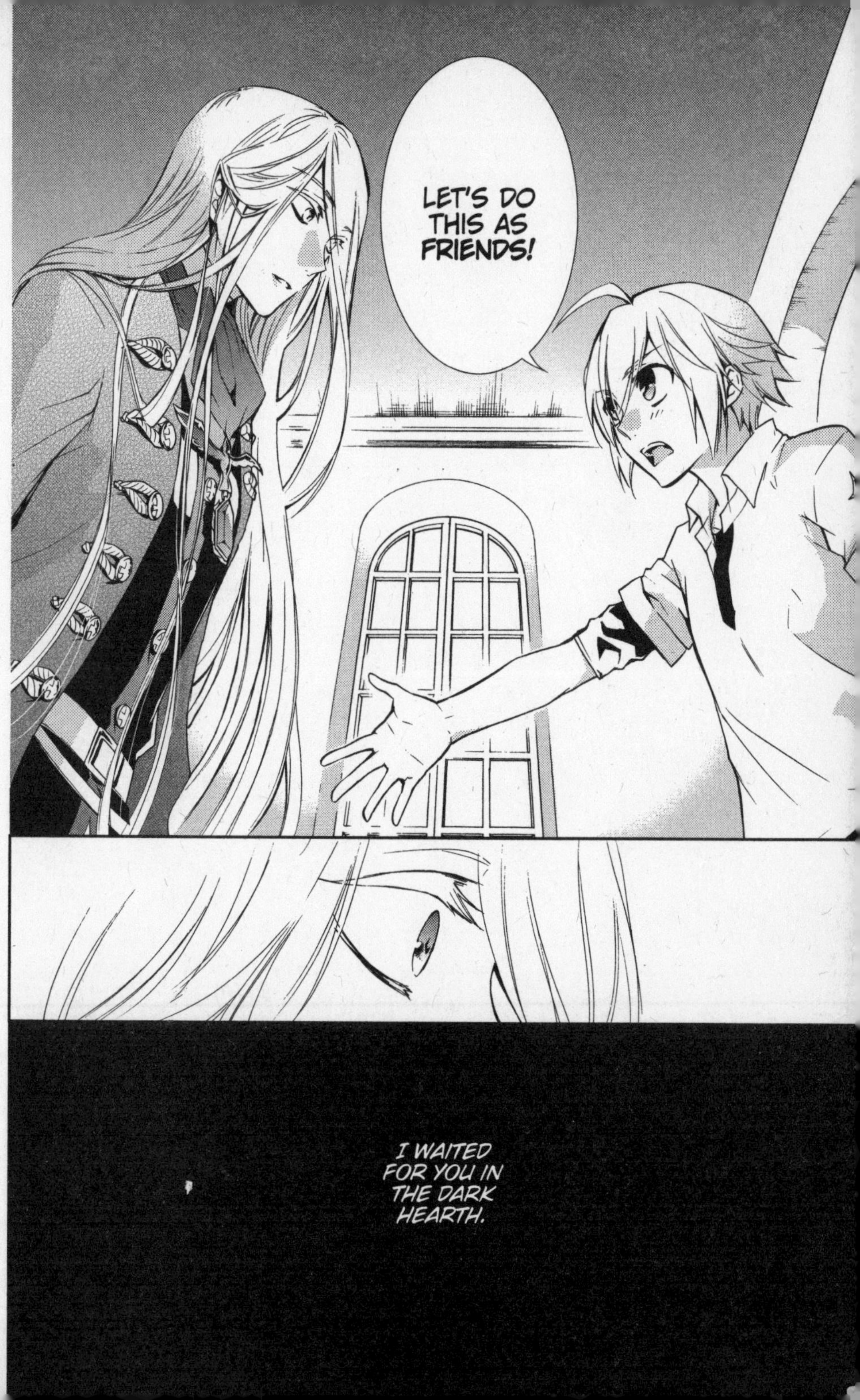
LET'S DO THIS AS FRIENDS!
I WAITED FOR YOU IN THE DARK HEARTH.

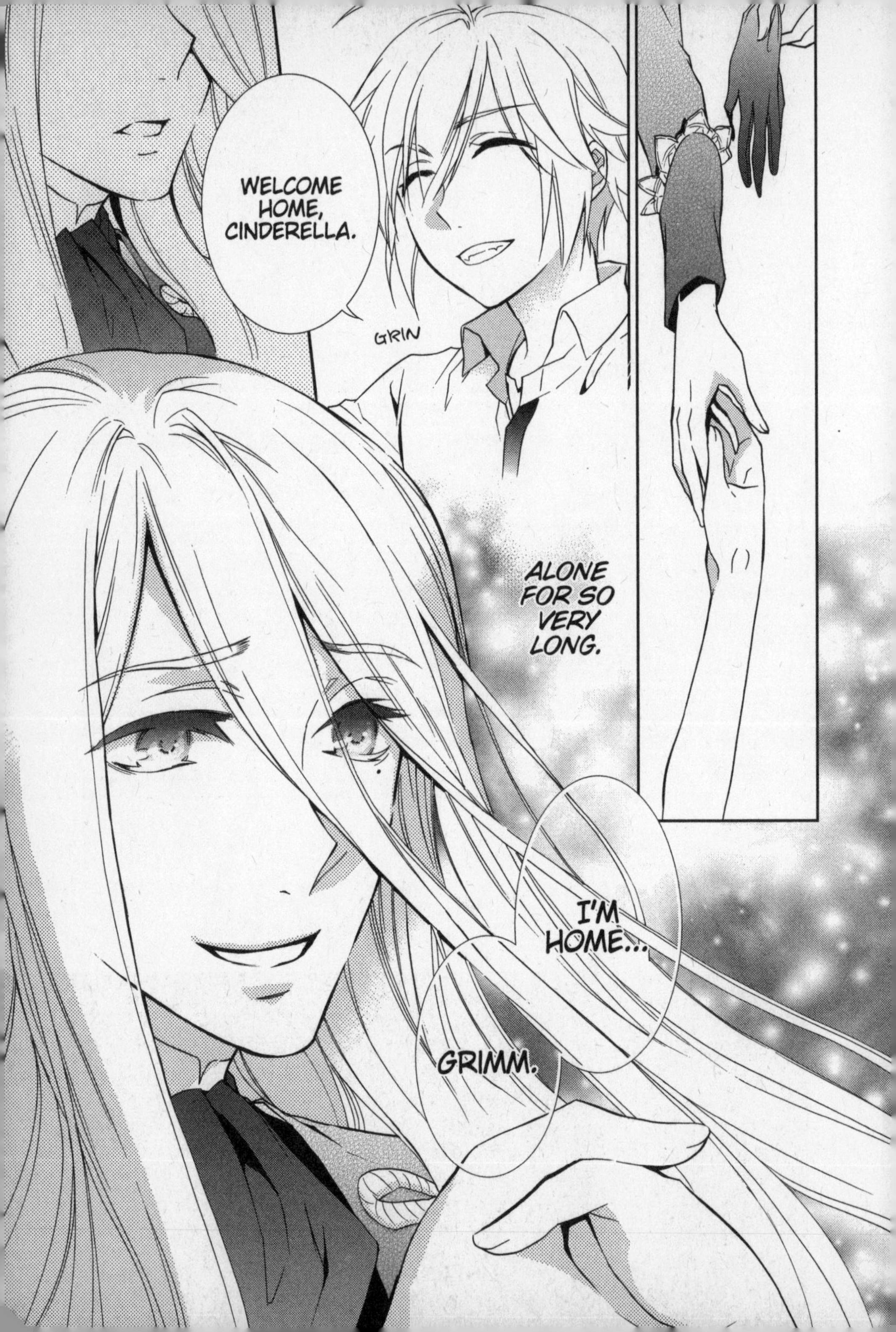
WELCOME HOME, CINDERELLA.
GRIN
ALONE FOR SO VERY LONG.
I'M HOME...
GRIMM.

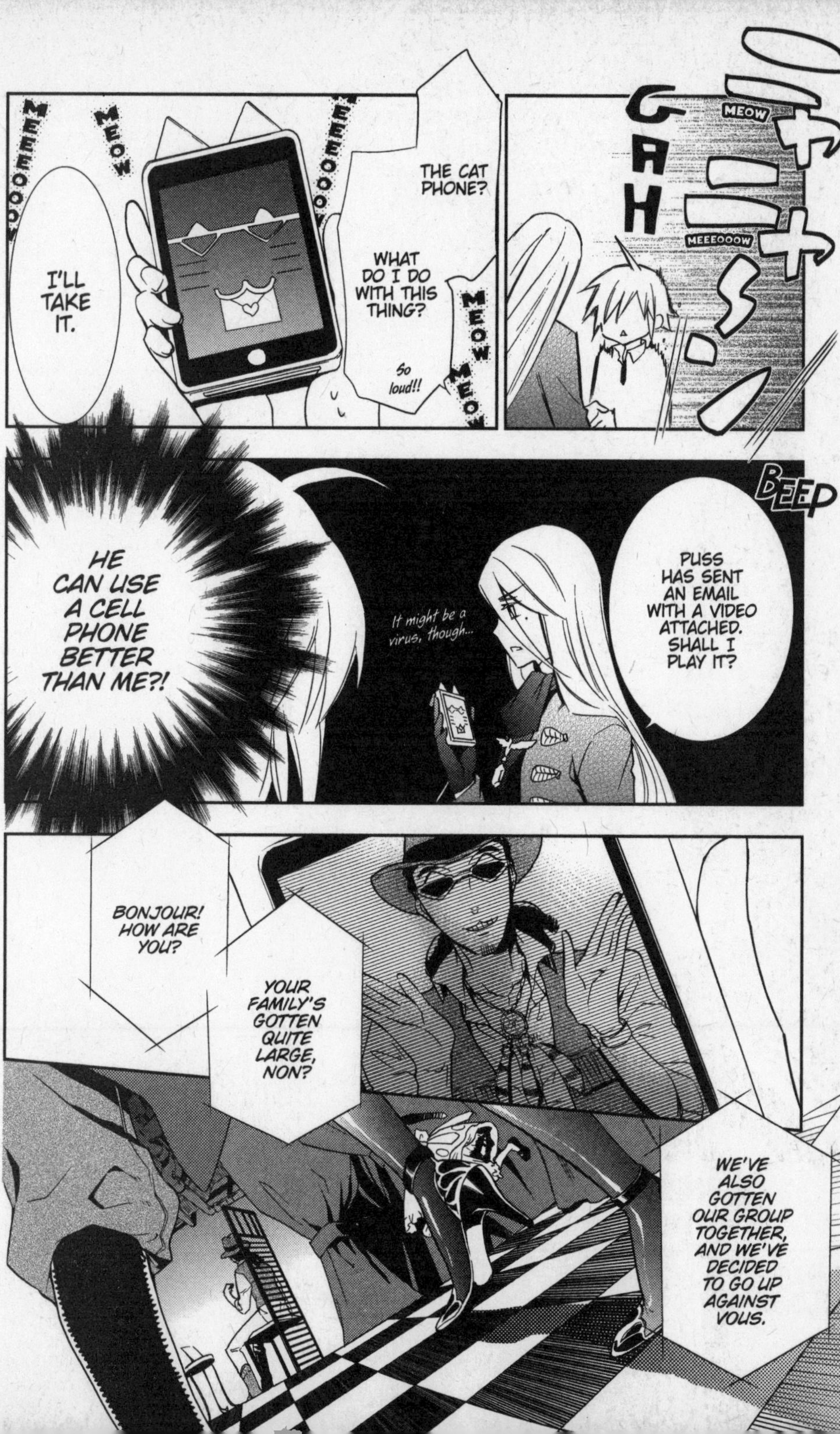
MEOW
GAH
MEEEOOOW
THE CAT PHONE?
WHAT DO I DO WITH THIS THING?
MEOW
MEOW
So loud!!
MEEEOOOW
MEOW
MEEEOOOW
I'LL TAKE IT.
BEEP
PUSS HAS SENT AN EMAIL WITH A VIDEO ATTACHED. SHALL I PLAY IT?
It might be a virus, though...
HE CAN USE A CELL PHONE BETTER THAN ME?!
BONJOUR! HOW ARE YOU?
YOUR FAMILY'S GOTTEN QUITE LARGE, NON?
WE'VE ALSO GOTTEN OUR GROUP TOGETHER, AND WE'VE DECIDED TO GO UP AGAINST VOUS.

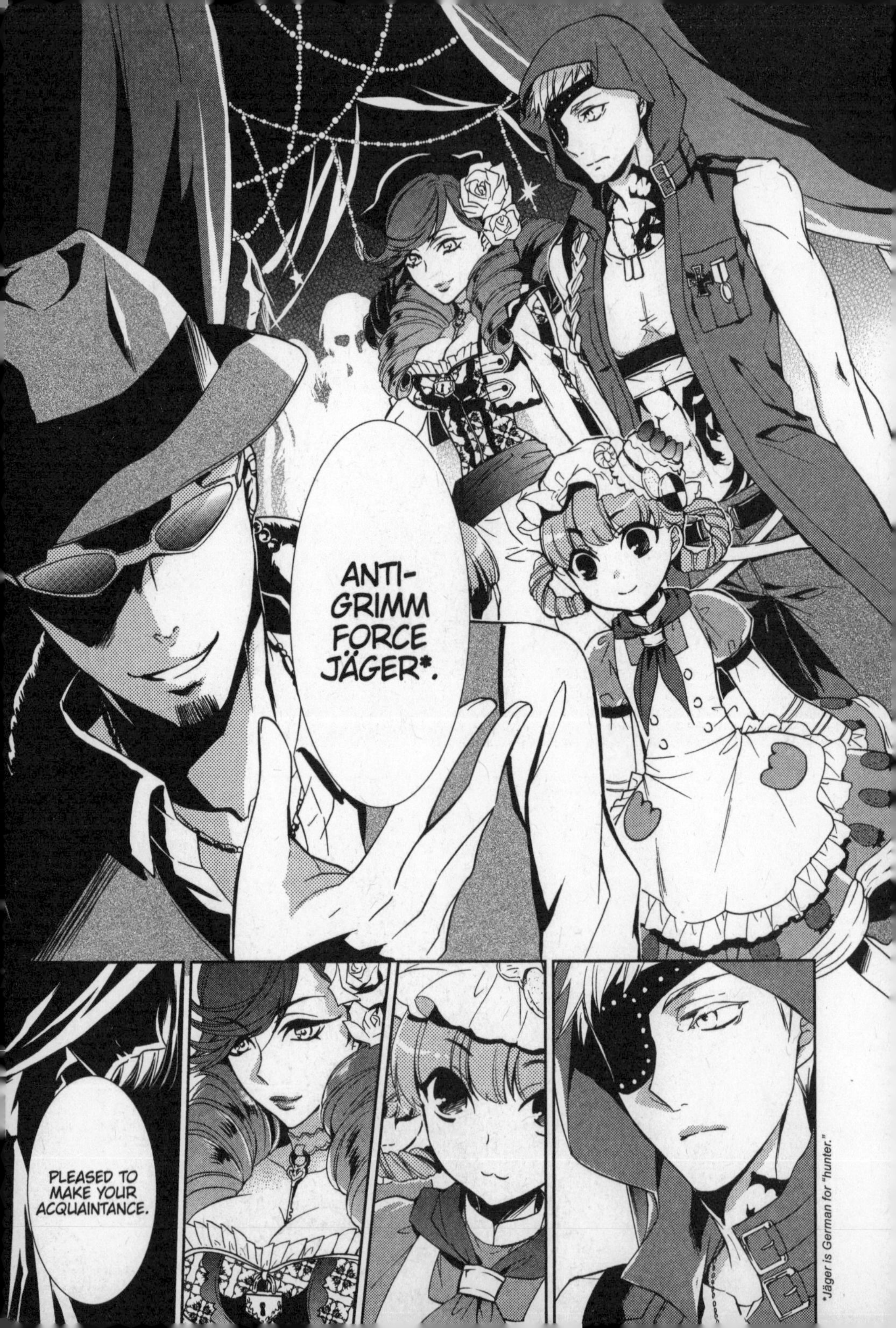
ANTI-GRIMM FORCE JÄGER*.
PLEASED TO MAKE YOUR ACQUAINTANCE.

*Jäger is German for "hunter."

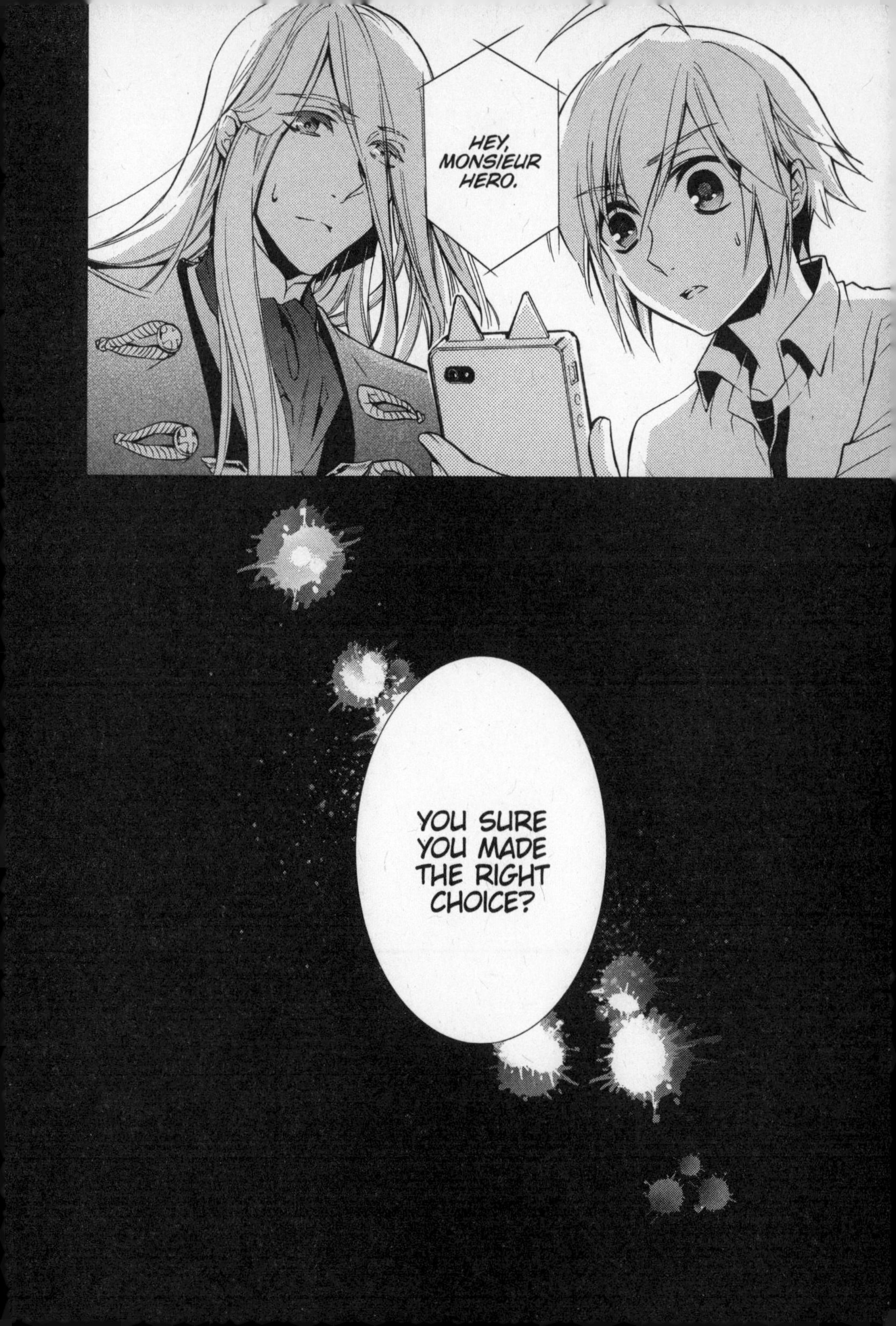
HEY, MONSIEUR HERO.
YOU SURE YOU MADE THE RIGHT CHOICE?

To be continued...

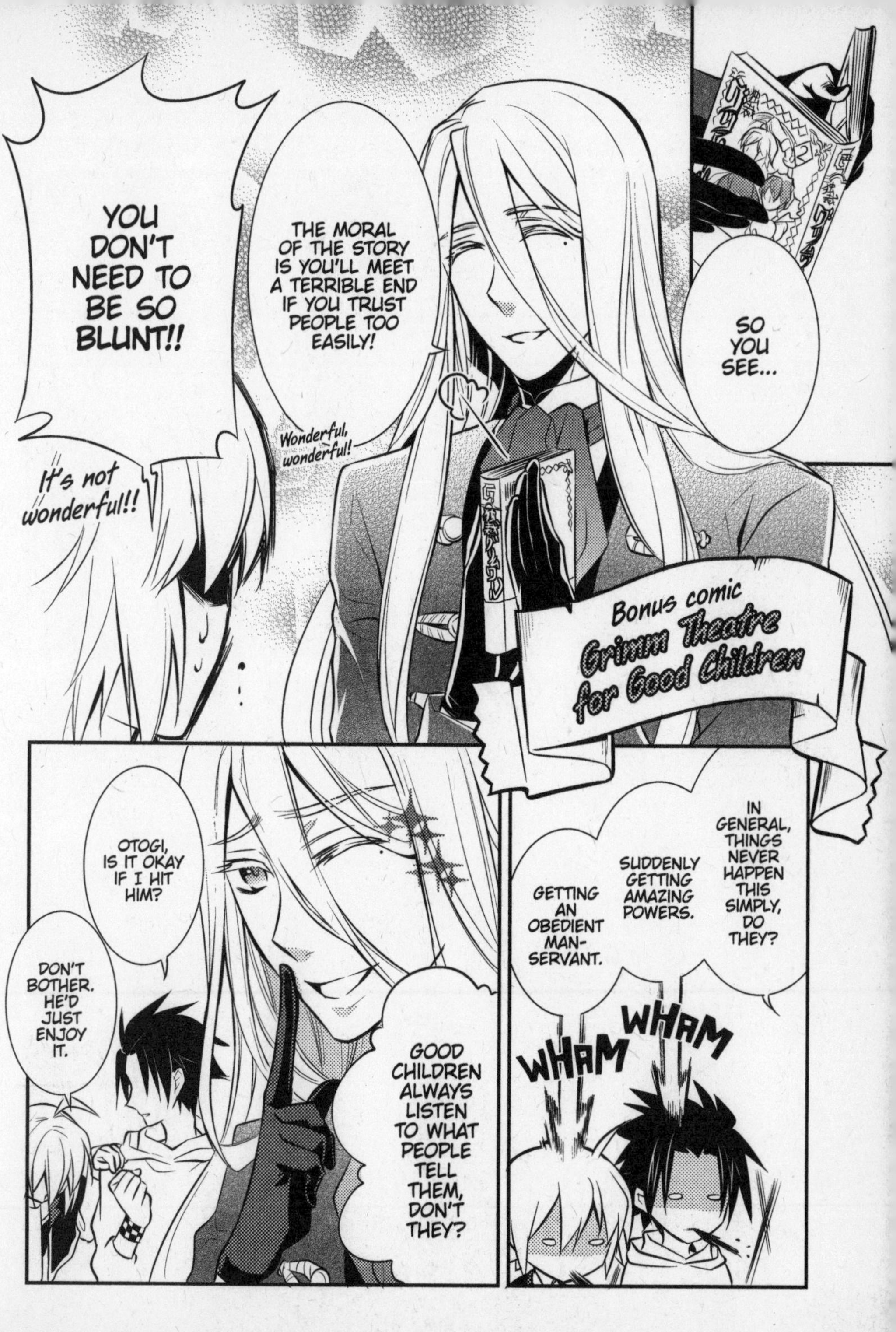
SO YOU SEE...
THE MORAL OF THE STORY IS YOU'LL MEET A TERRIBLE END IF YOU TRUST PEOPLE TOO EASILY!
Wonderful, wonderful!
YOU DON'T NEED TO BE SO BLUNT!!
It's not wonderful!!
Bonus comic
Grimm Theatre for Good Children
IN GENERAL, THINGS NEVER HAPPEN THIS SIMPLY, DO THEY?
SUDDENLY GETTING AMAZING POWERS.
GETTING AN OBEDIENT MAN-SERVANT.
WHAM
WHAM
GOOD CHILDREN ALWAYS LISTEN TO WHAT PEOPLE TELL THEM, DON'T THEY?
OTOGI, IS IT OKAY IF I HIT HIM?
DON'T BOTHER. HE'D JUST ENJOY IT.

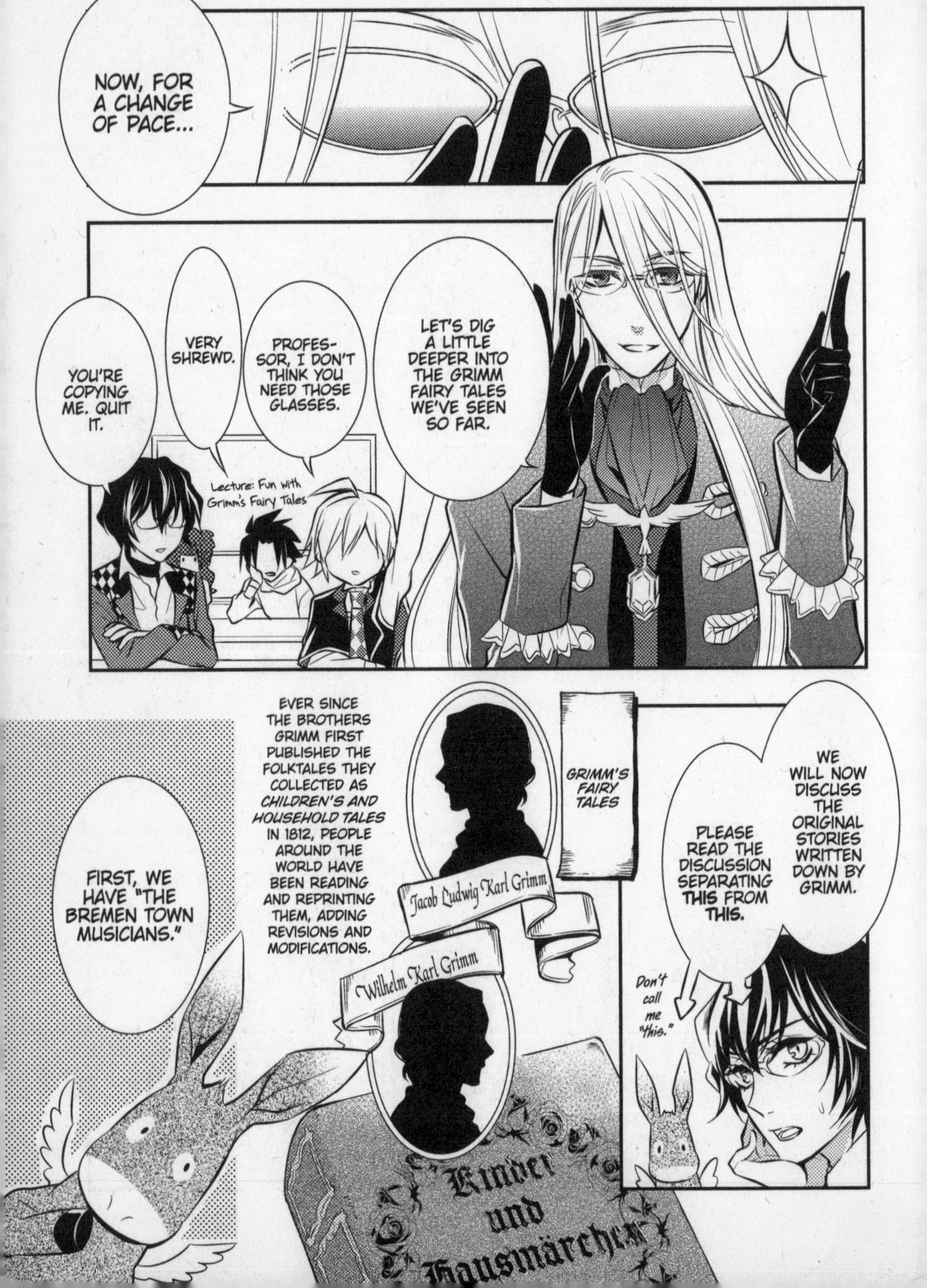
NOW, FOR A CHANGE OF PACE...
LET'S DIG A LITTLE DEEPER INTO THE GRIMM FAIRY TALES WE'VE SEEN SO FAR.
PROFES-SOR, I DON'T THINK YOU NEED THOSE GLASSES.
VERY SHREWD.
YOU'RE COPYING ME. QUIT IT.
Lecture: Fun with Grimm's Fairy Tales
WE WILL NOW DISCUSS THE ORIGINAL STORIES WRITTEN DOWN BY GRIMM.
PLEASE READ THE DISCUSSION SEPARATING THIS FROM THIS.
Don't call me "this."
GRIMM'S FAIRY TALES
EVER SINCE THE BROTHERS GRIMM FIRST PUBLISHED THE FOLKTALES THEY COLLECTED AS *CHILDREN'S AND HOUSEHOLD TALES* IN 1812, PEOPLE AROUND THE WORLD HAVE BEEN READING AND REPRINTING THEM, ADDING REVISIONS AND MODIFICATIONS.
Jacob Ludwig Karl Grimm
Wilhelm Karl Grimm
Kinder und Hausmärchen
FIRST, WE HAVE "THE BREMEN TOWN MUSICIANS."

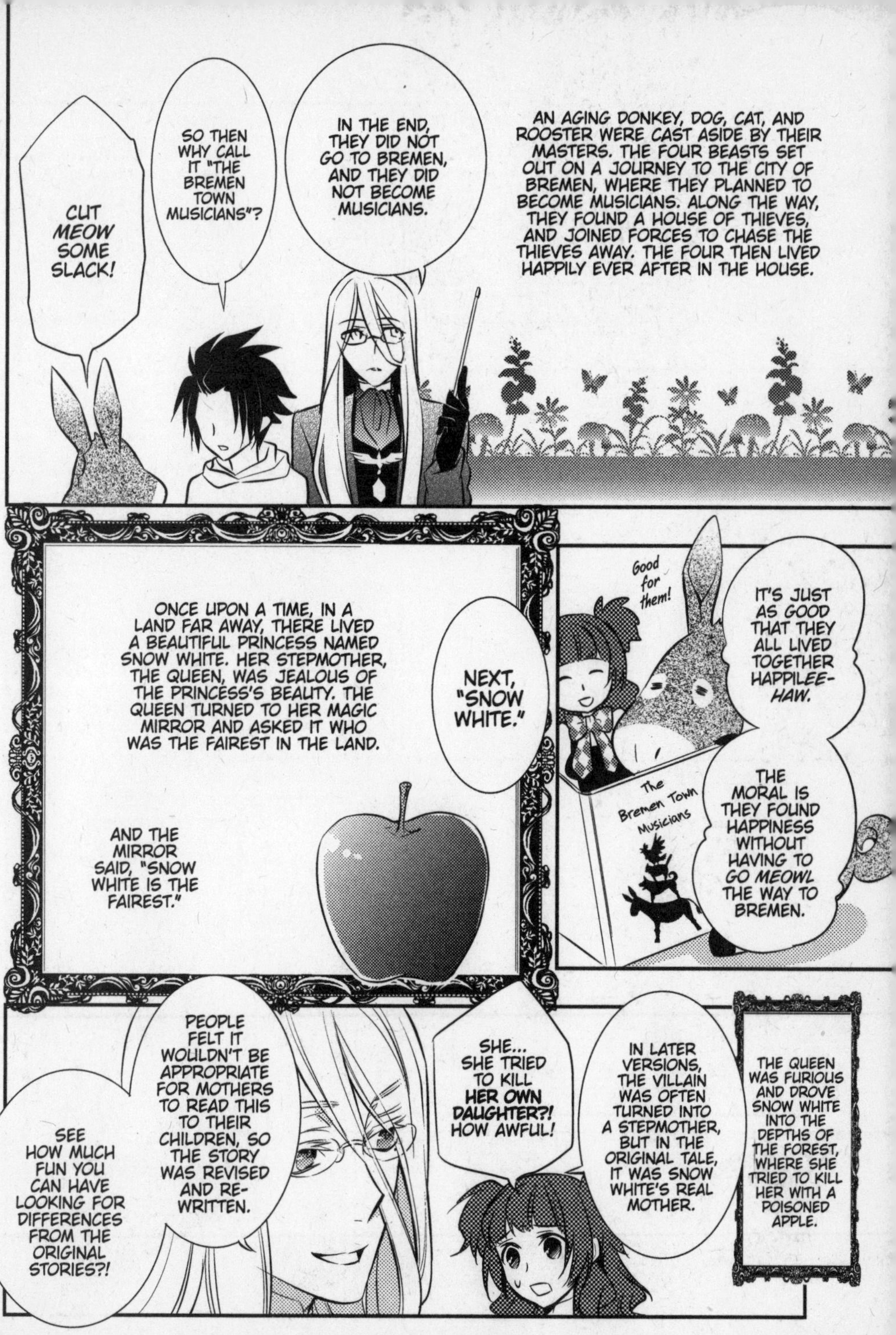
AN AGING DONKEY, DOG, CAT, AND ROOSTER WERE CAST ASIDE BY THEIR MASTERS. THE FOUR BEASTS SET OUT ON A JOURNEY TO THE CITY OF BREMEN, WHERE THEY PLANNED TO BECOME MUSICIANS. ALONG THE WAY, THEY FOUND A HOUSE OF THIEVES, AND JOINED FORCES TO CHASE THE THIEVES AWAY. THE FOUR THEN LIVED HAPPILY EVER AFTER IN THE HOUSE.
IN THE END, THEY DID NOT GO TO BREMEN, AND THEY DID NOT BECOME MUSICIANS.
SO THEN WHY CALL IT "THE BREMEN TOWN MUSICIANS"?
CUT *MEOW* SOME SLACK!
IT'S JUST AS GOOD THAT THEY ALL LIVED TOGETHER HAPPILEE-*HAW.*
Good for them!
THE MORAL IS THEY FOUND HAPPINESS WITHOUT HAVING TO GO *MEOWL* THE WAY TO BREMEN.
The Bremen Town Musicians
NEXT, "SNOW WHITE."
ONCE UPON A TIME, IN A LAND FAR AWAY, THERE LIVED A BEAUTIFUL PRINCESS NAMED SNOW WHITE. HER STEPMOTHER, THE QUEEN, WAS JEALOUS OF THE PRINCESS'S BEAUTY. THE QUEEN TURNED TO HER MAGIC MIRROR AND ASKED IT WHO WAS THE FAIREST IN THE LAND.
AND THE MIRROR SAID, "SNOW WHITE IS THE FAIREST."
THE QUEEN WAS FURIOUS AND DROVE SNOW WHITE INTO THE DEPTHS OF THE FOREST, WHERE SHE TRIED TO KILL HER WITH A POISONED APPLE.
IN LATER VERSIONS, THE VILLAIN WAS OFTEN TURNED INTO A STEPMOTHER, BUT IN THE ORIGINAL TALE, IT WAS SNOW WHITE'S REAL MOTHER.
SHE... SHE TRIED TO KILL **HER OWN DAUGHTER?!** HOW AWFUL!
PEOPLE FELT IT WOULDN'T BE APPROPRIATE FOR MOTHERS TO READ THIS TO THEIR CHILDREN, SO THE STORY WAS REVISED AND RE-WRITTEN.
SEE HOW MUCH FUN YOU CAN HAVE LOOKING FOR DIFFERENCES FROM THE ORIGINAL STORIES?!

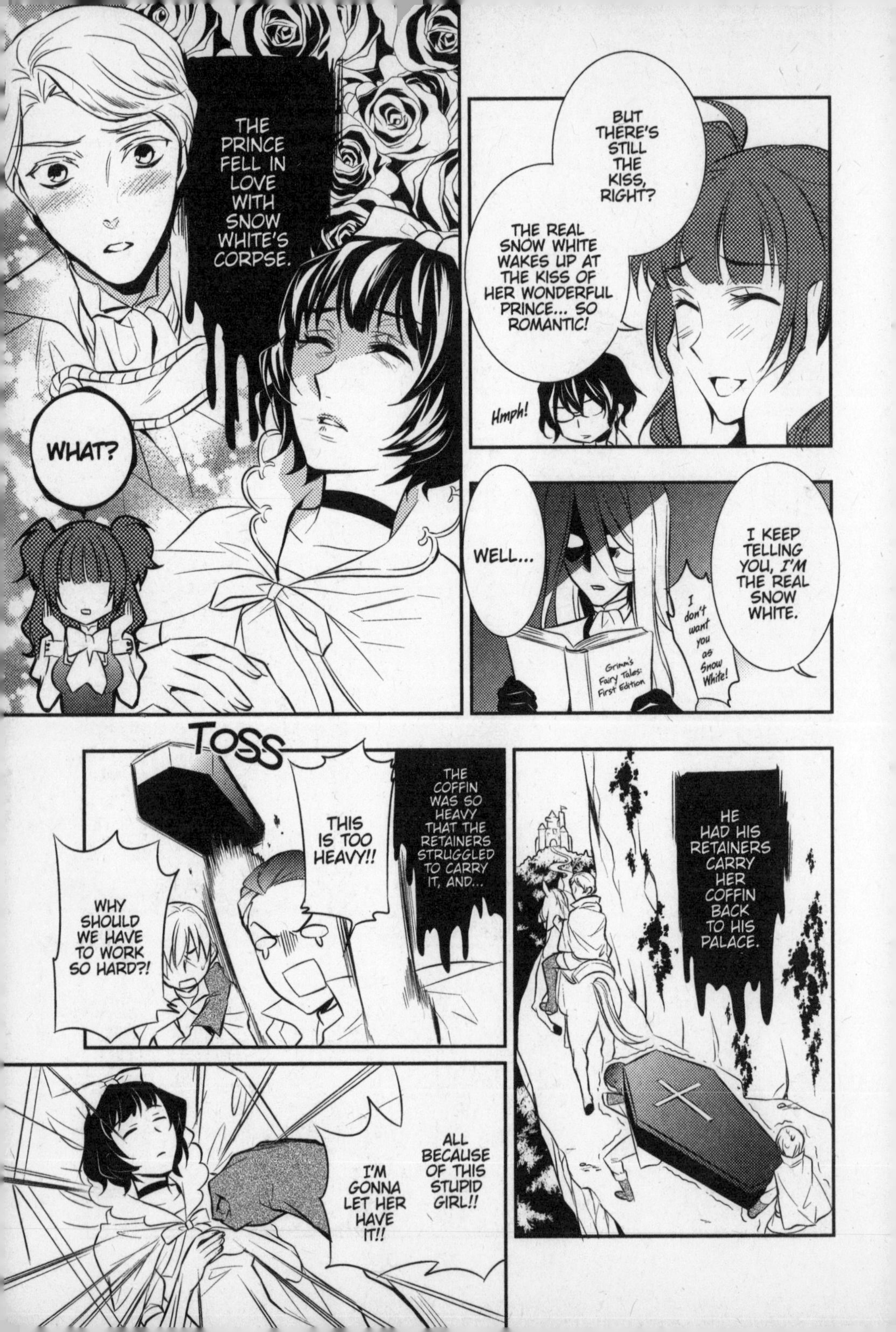

BUT THERE'S STILL THE KISS, RIGHT?
THE REAL SNOW WHITE WAKES UP AT THE KISS OF HER WONDERFUL PRINCE... SO ROMANTIC!
Hmph!
I KEEP TELLING YOU, I'M THE REAL SNOW WHITE.
I don't want you as Snow White!
WELL...
Grimm's Fairy Tales: First Edition
THE PRINCE FELL IN LOVE WITH SNOW WHITE'S CORPSE.
WHAT?
HE HAD HIS RETAINERS CARRY HER COFFIN BACK TO HIS PALACE.
TOSS
THE COFFIN WAS SO HEAVY THAT THE RETAINERS STRUGGLED TO CARRY IT, AND...
THIS IS TOO HEAVY!!
WHY SHOULD WE HAVE TO WORK SO HARD?!
ALL BECAUSE OF THIS STUPID GIRL!!
I'M GONNA LET HER HAVE IT!!

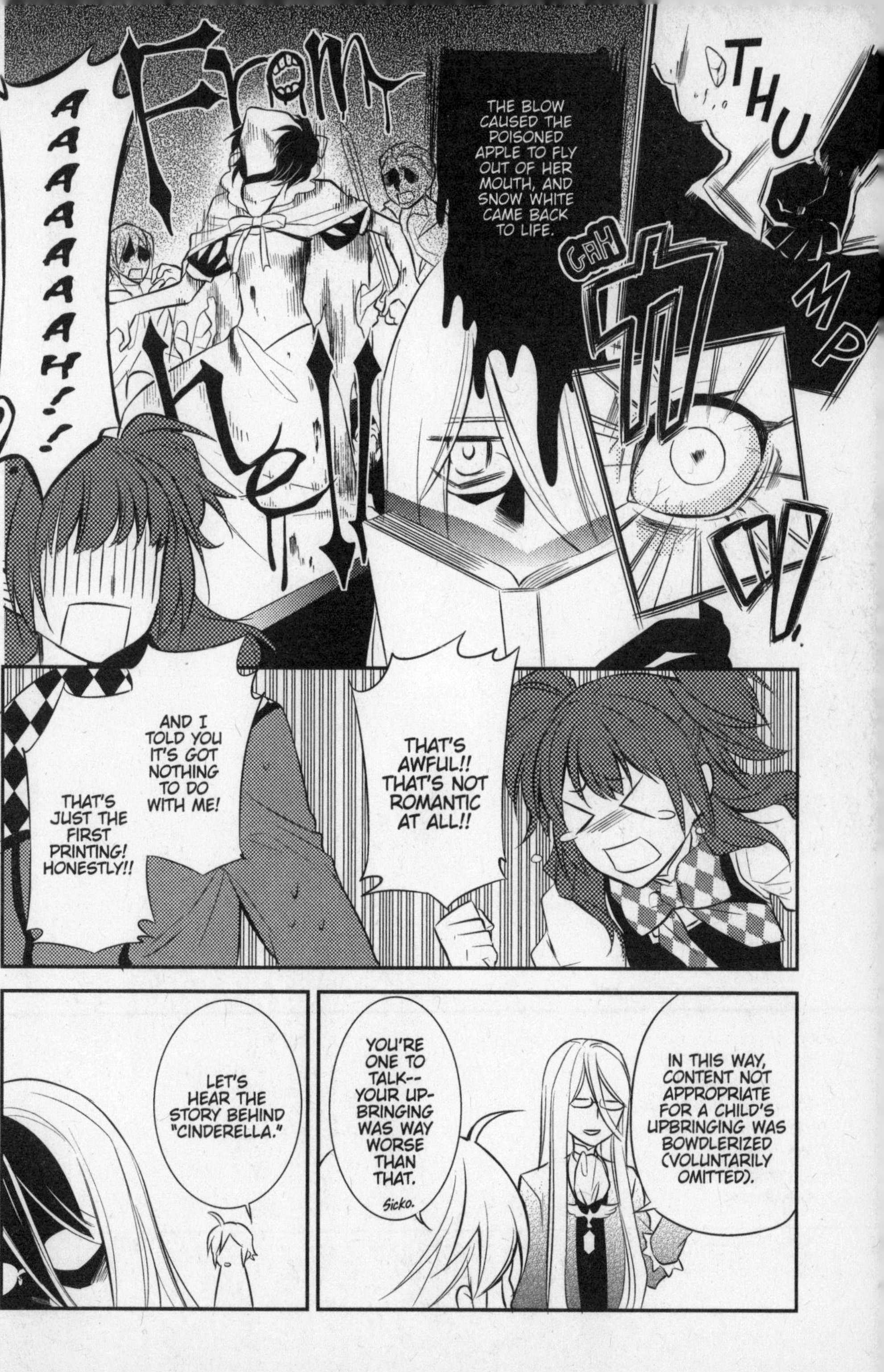
THUMP
THE BLOW CAUSED THE POISONED APPLE TO FLY OUT OF HER MOUTH, AND SNOW WHITE CAME BACK TO LIFE.
GAH
From hell
AAAAAAAAAH!!!
THAT'S AWFUL!! THAT'S NOT ROMANTIC AT ALL!!
AND I TOLD YOU IT'S GOT NOTHING TO DO WITH ME!
THAT'S JUST THE FIRST PRINTING! HONESTLY!!
IN THIS WAY, CONTENT NOT APPROPRIATE FOR A CHILD'S UPBRINGING WAS BOWDLERIZED (VOLUNTARILY OMITTED).
YOU'RE ONE TO TALK-- YOUR UPBRINGING WAS WAY WORSE THAN THAT.
Sicko.
LET'S HEAR THE STORY BEHIND "CINDERELLA."

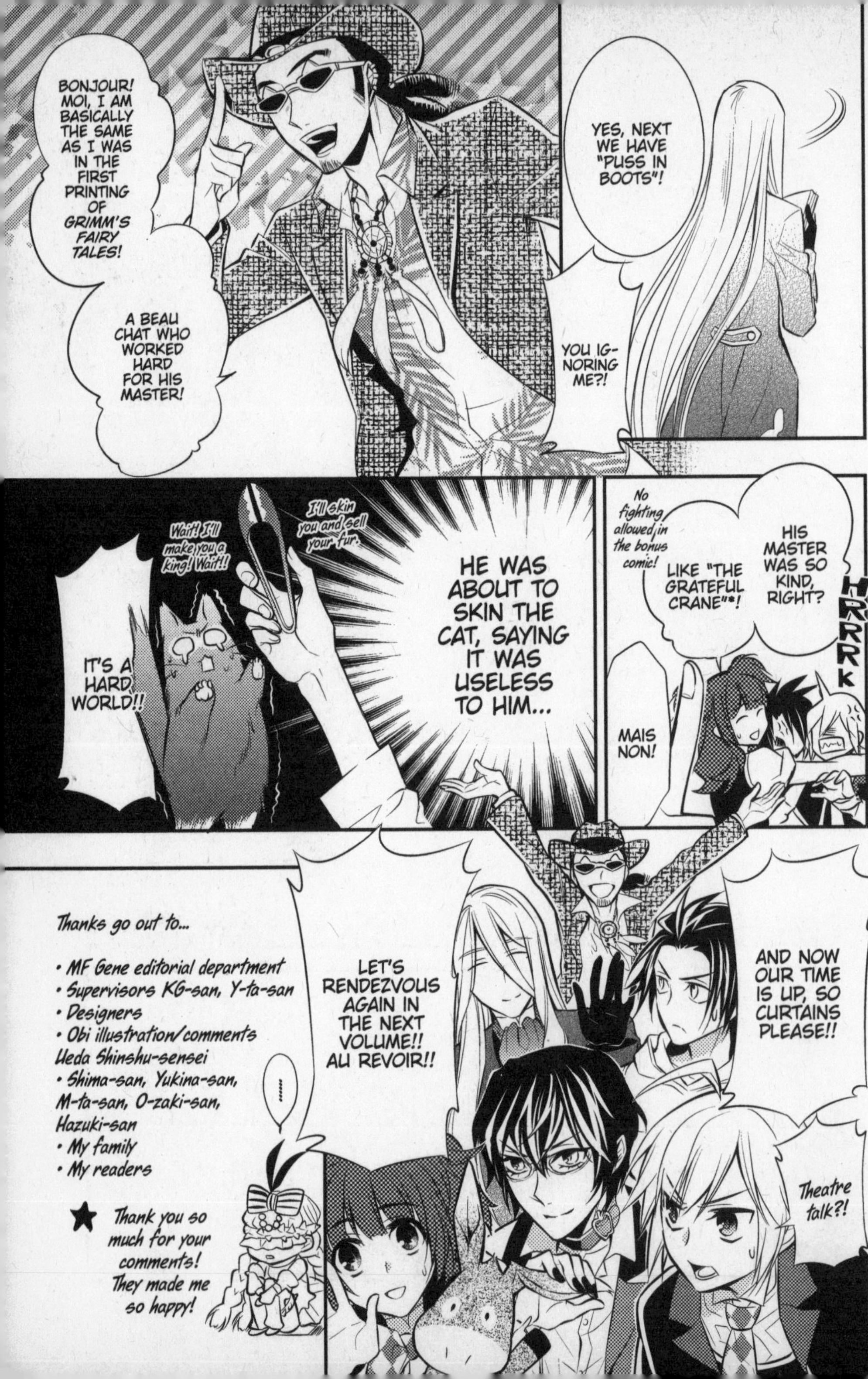

YES, NEXT WE HAVE "PUSS IN BOOTS"!
YOU IG-NORING ME?!
BONJOUR! MOI, I AM BASICALLY THE SAME AS I WAS IN THE FIRST PRINTING OF GRIMM'S FAIRY TALES!
A BEAU CHAT WHO WORKED HARD FOR HIS MASTER!
HIS MASTER WAS SO KIND, RIGHT?
LIKE "THE GRATEFUL CRANE"*!
No fighting allowed in the bonus comic!
HRRRK
MAIS NON!
HE WAS ABOUT TO SKIN THE CAT, SAYING IT WAS USELESS TO HIM...
I'll skin you and sell your fur.
Wait! I'll make you a king! Wait!!
IT'S A HARD WORLD!!
AND NOW OUR TIME IS UP, SO CURTAINS PLEASE!!
LET'S RENDEZVOUS AGAIN IN THE NEXT VOLUME!! AU REVOIR!!
Theatre talk?!
......
Thanks go out to...
• MF Gene editorial department
• Supervisors KG-san, Y-ta-san
• Designers
• Obi illustration/comments Ueda Shinshu-sensei
• Shima-san, Yukina-san, M-ta-san, O-zaki-san, Hazuki-san
• My family
• My readers
★ Thank you so much for your comments! They made me so happy!

*A Japanese folktale which tells the story of a man rescuing a crane from a trap and how that crane repays the favor.

CHARACTERS

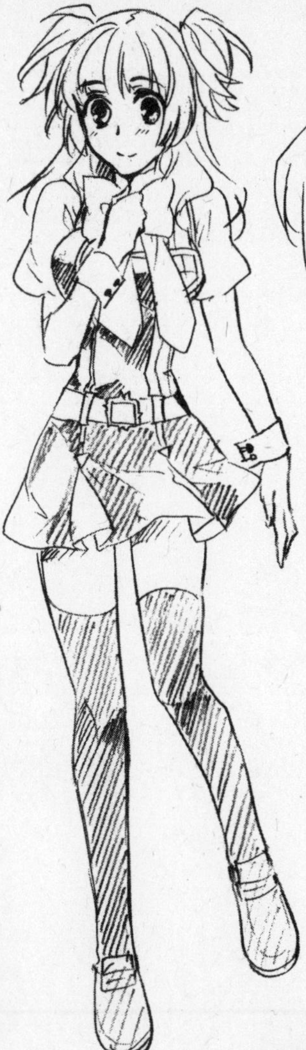

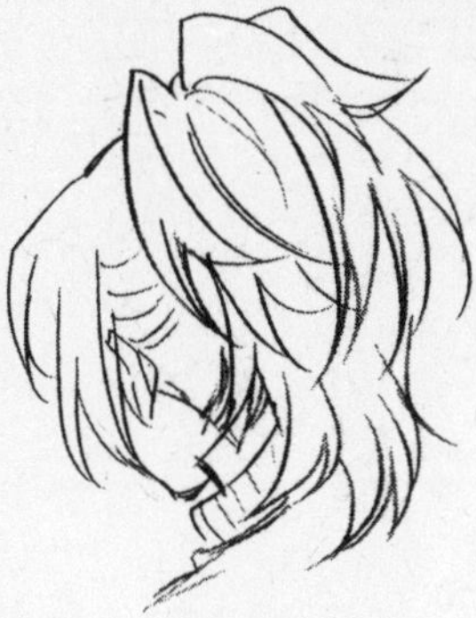

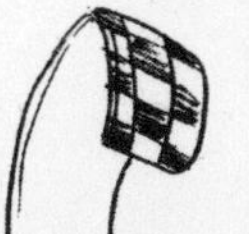

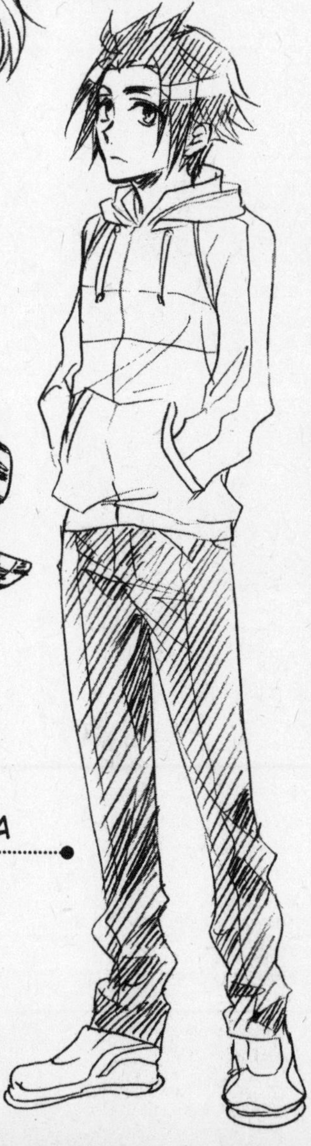

HATSUSHIBA HIYORI

AGE: 14
BIRTHDAY: MAY 13
BLOOD TYPE: O
HEIGHT: 164CM
WEIGHT: NOT TELLING!!
LIKES: STUFFED ANIMALS, CUTE ACCESSORIES
DISLIKES: SCARY STORIES, BUGS, REPTILES
HOBBIES: COLLECTING STUFFED ANIMALS
SPECIAL SKILLS: JUDO

SORIMACHI YUMA

AGE: 13
BIRTHDAY: OCTOBER 25
BLOOD TYPE: AB
HEIGHT: 168CM
WEIGHT: 52KG
LIKES: STUDYING
DISLIKES: PEOPLE WITH NO AMBITION
HOBBIES: READING (RECORDS OF THE THREE KINGDOMS, STRATEGY BOOKS)
SPECIAL SKILLS: SHOGI

SNOW WHITE

AGE: ? (LOOKS TO BE 17)
BIRTHDAY: ??
BLOOD TYPE: ??
HEIGHT: 174CM
WEIGHT: 54KG
LIKES: HIMSELF,
BEAUTIFUL THINGS
DISLIKES: MIRRORS,
UGLY THINGS
HOBBIES: IMPROVING HIMSELF
SPECIAL SKILLS: POISON MAKING

PUSS IN BOOTS

STAGE NAME: NEKOTA YOZO
AGE: ? (LOOKS TO BE 32)
BIRTHDAY: ??
BLOOD TYPE: ??
HEIGHT: 177CM
WEIGHT: 62KG
LIKES: ???
DISLIKES: ???
HOBBIES: LISTENING
TO MUSIC (ANY GENRE)
SPECIAL SKILLS: PRODUCING

RAPUN-ZEL, LET DOWN YOUR HAIR!!

Weird Creature

Man

Man

A girl!

Wow!

SNOW WHITE: "WHAT'S WRONG WITH US?"
CINDERELLA: "GO AHEAD AND ASK HER SEX."

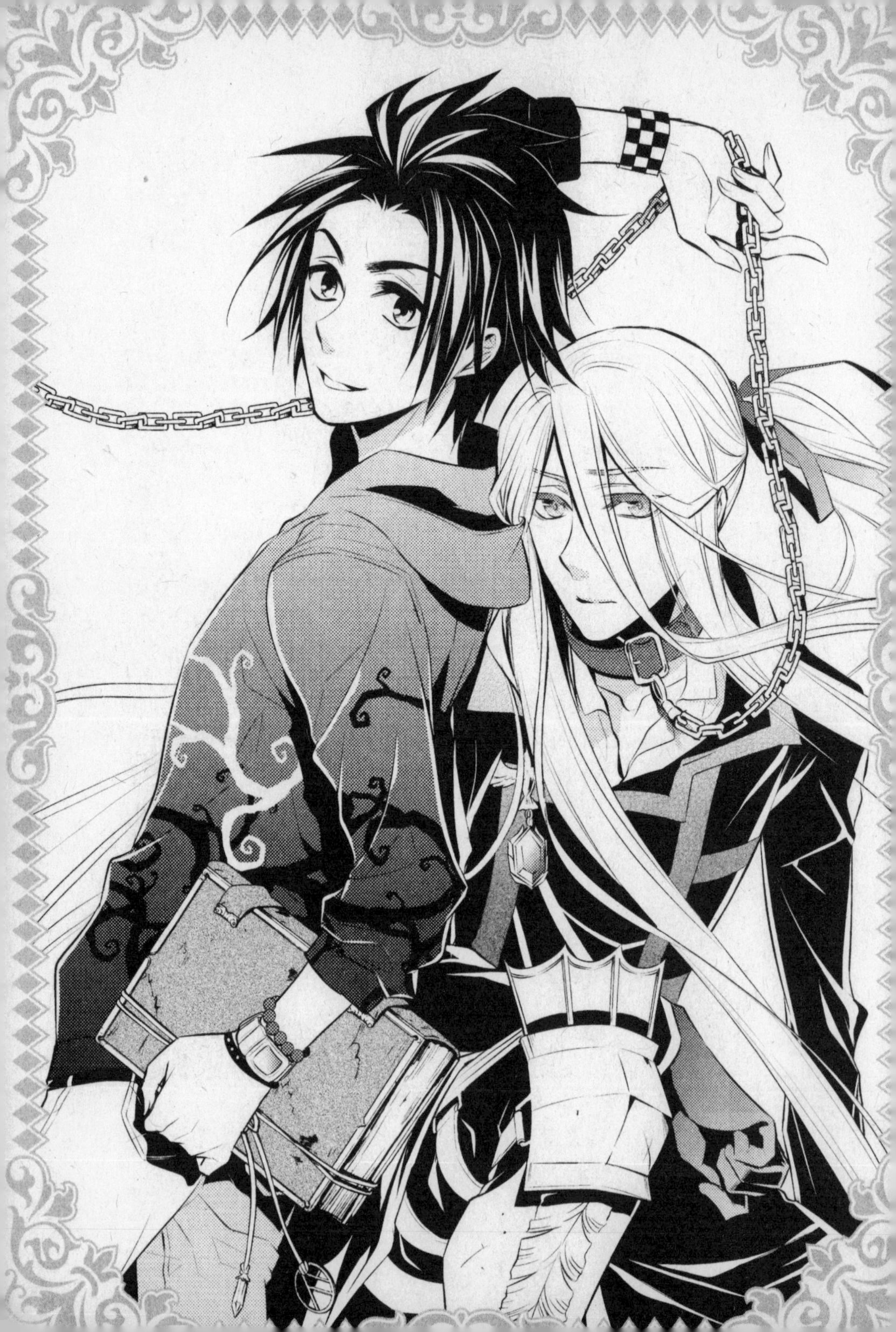

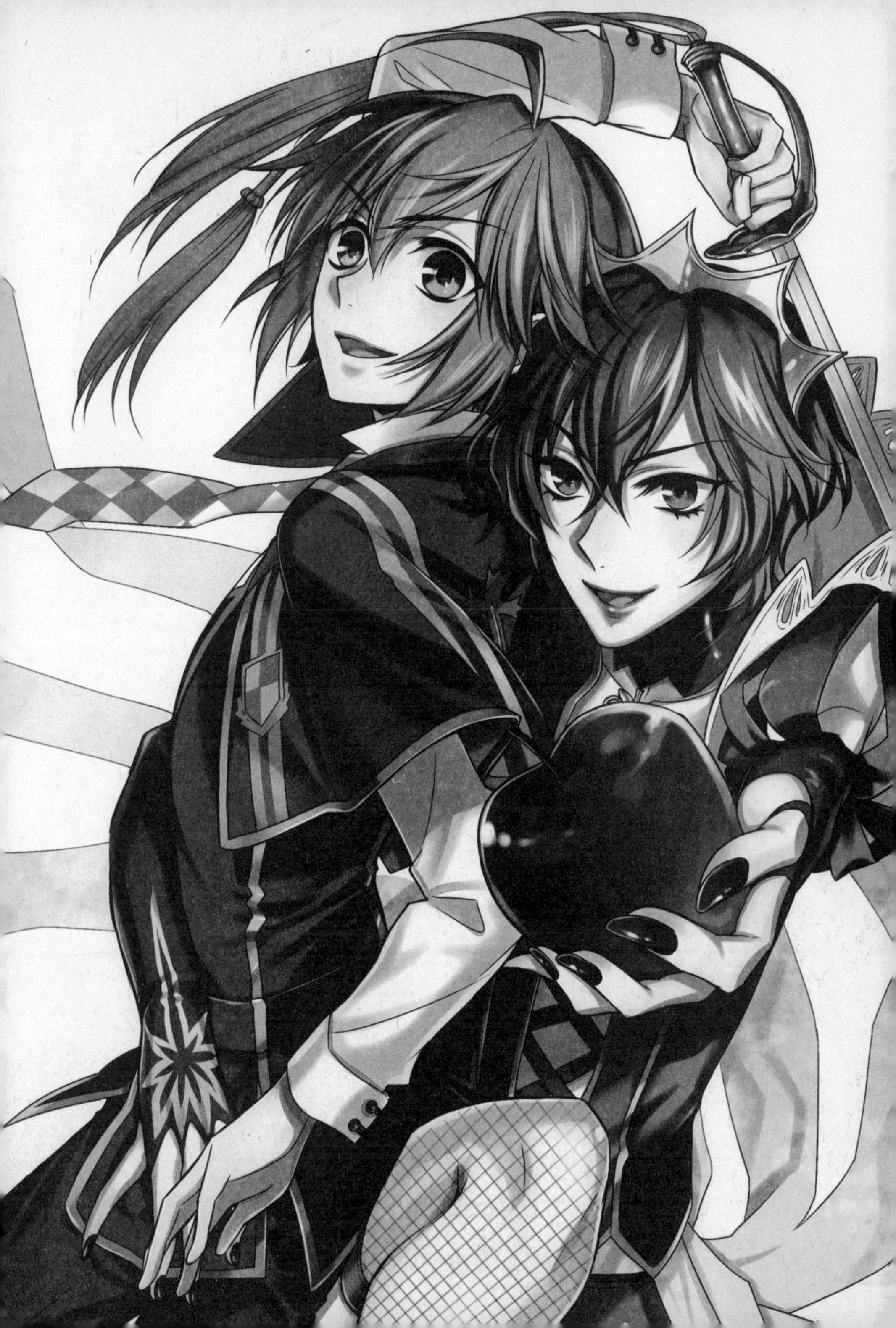

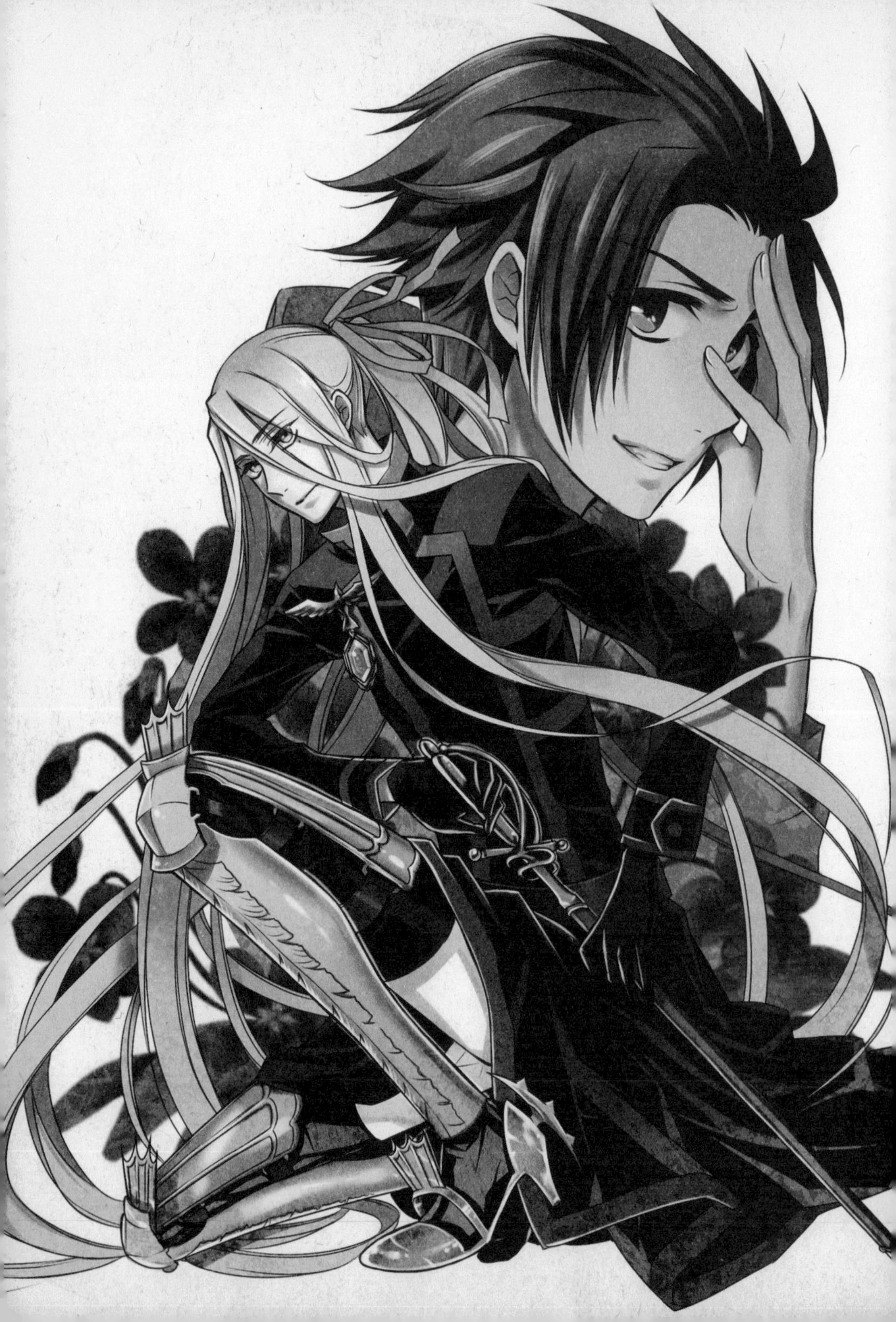

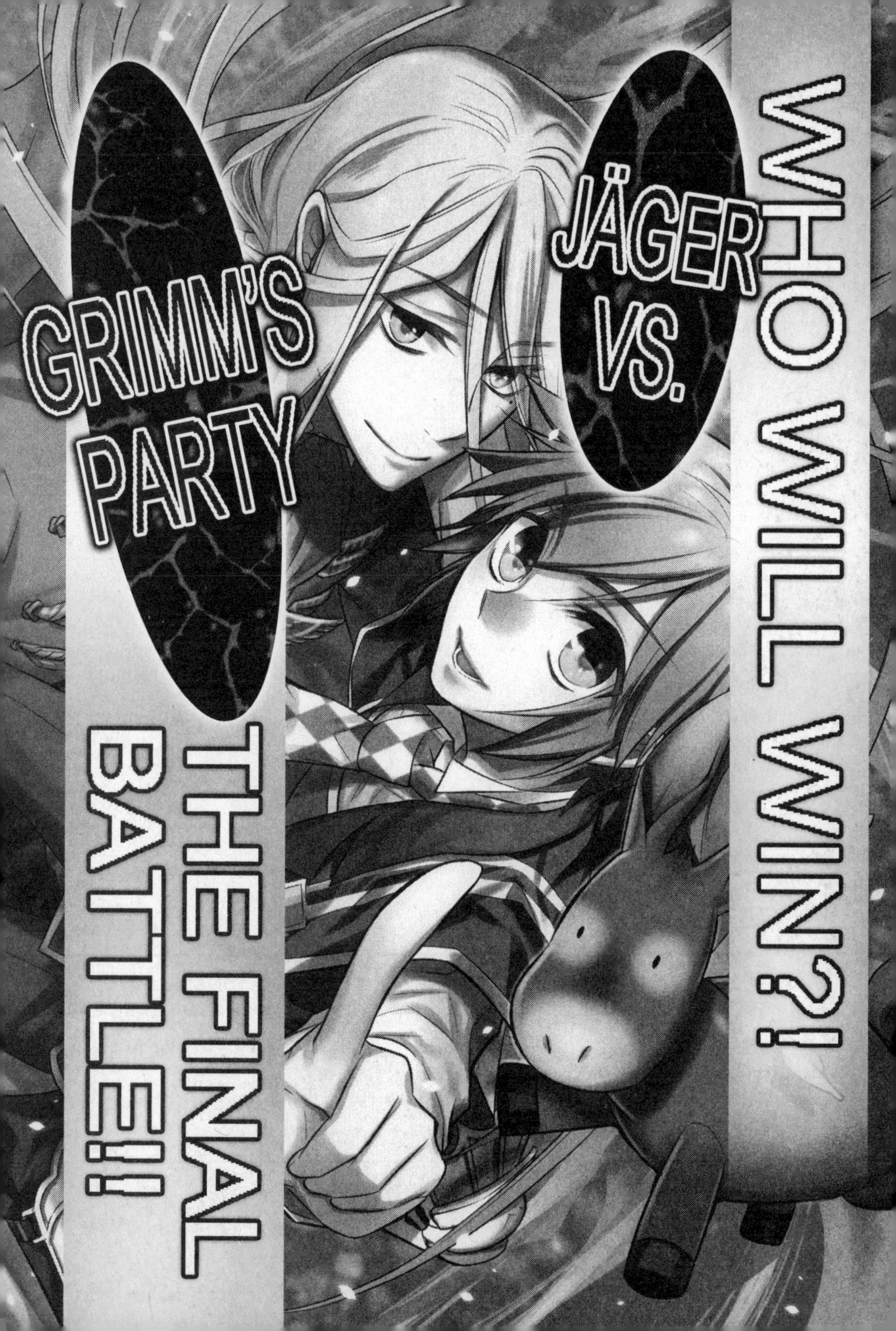
GRIMM'S PARTY
VS.
JÄGER
WHO WILL WIN?!
THE FINAL BATTLE!!